ROMAN ARISTOCRATS IN BARBARIAN GAUL

RALPH
WHITNEY
MATHISEN

ROMAN
ARISTOCRATS IN
BARBARIAN GAUL

STRATEGIES
FOR SURVIVAL
IN AN AGE OF
TRANSITION

UNIVERSITY OF TEXAS PRESS
AUSTIN

Copyright © 1993 by the University of Texas Press
All rights reserved
Printed in the United States of America
First edition, 1993

LIBRARY OF CONGRESS CATALOGING-IN-PUBLICATION DATA

Mathisen, Ralph W., date.
  Roman aristocrats in barbarian Gaul : strategies for survival in
an age of transition / Ralph Whitney Mathisen. — 1st ed.
    p. cm.
  Includes bibliographical references and index.
  ISBN 0-292-77051-0
  1. Gaul—History—58 B.C.–511 A.D.   2. Rome—History—Germanic
invasions, 3rd–6th centuries.   3. Romans—France—Cultural
assimilation.   4. Nobility—Rome.   I. Title.
  DC62.M385 1993
  936.4'02—dc20   92–22725

ISBN 978-0-292-75806-3 (e-book)
ISBN 978-0-292-75807-0 (individual e-book)

TO MY OWN TWO LITTLE BARBARIANS:
KATHERINE WHITNEY AND DAVID ARTHUR

CONTENTS

MAPS

PREFACE

expugnatoris tui ferrum quale producitur ad pugnam,
tale reconditur in vaginam, qualis est ante bellum,
talis est post triumphum . . . itaque inter stupenda circa te
beneficia dei tui gratias tibi referat celeberrimus triumphator,
ut apud arma victricia quieti maneant victi,
et illaesa libertas.

(FAUSTUS OF RIEZ, *SERM.* "IN LITANIIS")[1]

As of the year A.D. 400, several accepted options were open to Gallo-
Roman aristocrats.[2] They could pursue a traditional civil or military career
in the Roman state. Even if they were of limited means, they still could
seek advancement via the Roman educational system. Or they could
choose to lead a life of leisure (*otium*) in the isolated splendor of their
estates.

The fifth century, however, brought great changes to Roman Gaul.
One of the most crucial was the settlement of the barbarians who, in the
early years of the century, began to arrive in Gaul to stay in ever greater
numbers.[3] There has been much debate on just what the significance of
the barbarian settlement in Gaul and elsewhere was.[4] Some have seen the
barbarians as the primary agent of the decline of the western empire; others
have played down their impact.

One social group that was particularly affected by, and concerned with,
the barbarian presence was the resident Roman elite classes.[5] As might
be expected, their perquisites in particular were threatened by the arrival
and settlement of a new privileged group. In some areas of the west, such
as Britain, Africa, and even Italy, the resident aristocrats faced some great
difficulties in coping with the barbarian advent.[6]

But in Gaul, elements of the privileged classes of the Roman population
were remarkably adept at retaining their rank and status, and were particularly noteworthy for their tenacity and durability.[7] Any study of the
late Roman aristocracy of Gaul, therefore, must explain its persistent
survival.

In recent years, one means of doing so has been to minimize the effect
the arrival of the barbarians had upon the resident Gallo-Roman aristocracy.[8] The talk has been either of out-and-out lack of impact, or of
accommodation and integration, and of an essentially peaceful settlement.

The barbarians often are portrayed as having little effect, and the resident Roman aristocrats as continuing a prosperous existence on their estates, if not actually welcoming the barbarian presence.[9] One modern writer has contended, for example, that "Gaul seems to be relatively quiet and peaceful; the roads are open, and travel is not difficult, and . . . landlords enjoy a leisured ease in their country villas amid the vineyards and olive groves."[10] And another supposes that "the property of even rich natives was normally respected," and suggests that there is "no compelling reason to speak of a 'barbarian west.' "[11]

Certainly, few nowadays would contest the view that much of the barbarian occupation of the west was accomplished peacefully and that there was a large degree of continuity. But the following study will suggest that the smoothness of the transition from Roman to barbarian rule and the lack of barbarian impact upon the Gallo-Roman aristocracy have been exaggerated. There also is a significant amount of evidence to contest the assertion that the Gallo-Roman aristocracy survived the barbarian settlement essentially intact and undisturbed.

Gallo-Roman aristocrats faced a very different world in the fifth century, and many of the changes resulted, directly or indirectly, from the barbarian presence. Opportunities to pursue traditional options were reduced. The gradual withdrawal of the Roman imperial administration, for example, meant the disappearance of most of the traditional secular offices. Even if a Gaul sought service with the barbarians, the rudimentary barbarian administrations offered few office-holding opportunities, and even these not until the end of the century.[12] The Germans also appropriated much of the land and social influence. At the same time, the overall level of violence in Gallic society increased dramatically.

The world of the Gallo-Roman aristocrats began to shrink. Contact with their aristocratic brethren in Italy and other foreign parts diminished. Even intra-Gallic relationships became more difficult to maintain. Eventually, even the most influential Roman aristocrats were affected by the barbarians.[13]

This study, therefore, will pay great attention to the arrival and settlement of the barbarians in Gaul. It needs to be stressed, however, that it does not purport to be a history of the barbarians (individually or collectively) or of the barbarian invasions per se. The focus will be, rather, on the overall effect that the barbarian presence had upon the resident Roman population. The social and cultural interactions between Romans and barbarians, and the changes which resulted from them, will be investigated not, as usually is done, from the point of view of the barbarians, but from that of the Romans.[14] Some of these changes, as will be seen, resulted only indirectly from the barbarian presence.

[x]

The fundamental question that this study will ask is, "What kinds of conscious and positive responses did the resident Romans make to the changes in their world?" The changes which occurred in the fifth century will not be interpreted, moreover, in terms of "Roman decline versus barbarian triumph," or "continuity versus change," but from the perspective of "response."[15] And response will not be interpreted adversarially, as being equivalent to "opposition." There will be no insinuation that the Roman response was somehow inadequate because the barbarians "won" (and the Romans, presumably, "lost").

Nor will there be any presumption that the barbarians were the sole cause of the social changes of the fifth century. Some of these changes in fact already were under way before the barbarians arrived. But the barbarians certainly did help the process along, and seem to have imparted a greater focus and sense of urgency to the Gallo-Romans as the latter attempted to redefine their own positions. Indeed the barbarians often served as a catalyst. They wrought extensive changes in the functioning of the Gallo-Roman aristocracy and in the aristocratic mentality without necessarily taking a direct part in them. Sometimes the mere fact of their presence was enough to engender a response.

Previous studies of the late western Roman aristocracy have tended either to concentrate on the fourth-century aristocracy, and to treat the barbarian role only peripherally,[16] or to focus on the subordinate role of Romans in a sixth-century Europe already dominated by the barbarians.[17] Little effort has been made to bridge the gap between the late-fourth-century aristocracy, hostile to the barbarians, and the sixth-century aristocracy, closely affiliated with the barbarians.[18] This investigation will help to do so.

There will be a detailed discussion of how Gallo-Roman aristocrats perceived their own situation. In order to get as close to them as possible, their attitudes often will be cited using their own words. It will be seen that Gallo-Roman aristocrats were very much in touch with their times. They deliberately reevaluated their circumstances. Just how were they to respond to the newcomers? Different individuals adopted different strategies based upon their personal needs.[19] Eventually all Gauls, in one way or another, even the most wealthy and influential, had to make their peace with the barbarians. Some did so sooner, or more effectively, than others.

Even, therefore, if one cannot speak realistically of the barbarians collectively, as if there existed some collective barbarian identity, one can identify collective Roman responses to them. And any differences in response from one part of Gaul to another, it will be seen, probably resulted more from chronological factors (some aristocrats had to deal with the barbarians earlier than others) than from differences in barbarian ethnicity.

The barbarians may not have acted collectively, but the Romans responded to them as if they did.

A decision which many Gauls faced very early on was whether to remain in Gaul or to relocate to more secure parts of the empire. Many chose the latter course. Those who remained faced many other choices. Some remained imperial sympathizers to the bitter end and attempted to continue life in the style to which they had been accustomed before the barbarians arrived, either living a life of ease on their estates or pursuing advancement in the imperial administration, if not both.

For others, however, accepted attitudes about appropriate aristocratic ideals had to change. The criteria for acceptance as an aristocrat evolved in two ways to meet the needs of the times. Some Gauls sought careers in the church and substituted a high ecclesiastical office for a secular one. Aristocrats residing in barbarian Gaul could fulfill virtually all the material and psychological needs, ideals, and trappings of secular nobility even better in the church than they could in secular life. And ecclesiastical office itself was redefined to suit the needs of the times.

Not every aristocrat, however, could become a bishop or a secular official. Aristocrats who had no opportunity for office of any kind, and who had fallen upon hard economic times, benefited from another transformation in the criteria for aristocratic status: a greater emphasis was placed on the pursuit of classical literary culture as the mark of a good Roman aristocrat.

Finally, some Gallo-Romans identified their interests with the barbarians in a more active manner. Some fled to them hoping to find a better way of life. Some looked to them as a new source of patronage. Some gave them assistance, either willing or coerced. And some actually held office in barbarian administrations.

Eventually, the Gallo-Romans developed a coherent set of procedures for dealing with the conditions of the fifth century in general and with the barbarians in particular. There rarely was any sense of panic or despair, or any feeling that things were out of control.[20] By the latter part of the fifth century, Roman attitudes toward the barbarians had changed. Romans had become accustomed to living under Germanic authority and had learned to coexist with Germanic officialdom. Accepted methods for dealing with the barbarians had been developed.

The disappearance of Roman rule seems to have been neither lamented nor even noticed. Subsequent years saw the amalgamation of the Roman and Germanic aristocracies. And two significant Roman legacies—the role of the church and the preservation of classical culture—resulted directly from the fifth-century reevaluation of aristocratic status.

The chronological limits of this survey have been consciously chosen to eliminate, as much as possible, anachronistic material. Gallo-Roman attitudes of the mid to late sixth century, and even the early sixth century, cannot be expected to be representative of the perceptions of the fifth. Too much had changed: Gallic unity had been broken, and the days of true imperial rule had been forgotten. The conversion of the Franks to orthodox Christianity, moreover, resulted in new considerations which had not been present in the fifth century. As much as possible, therefore, only contemporary sources are used.

The decision to focus on Gaul was made for several reasons. There, one has a well-documented continuum, extending from the initial arrival, through the period of transition (during which it was not at all clear what the ultimate result would be), to the eventual replacement of the old ruling order by the new. Furthermore, the settlement reached in Gaul was the most successful and had the greatest long-term effects.

The course of the barbarian settlements of other areas of the western empire, such as Britain, Spain, Africa, and Italy, on the other hand, by no means paralleled that in Gaul.[21] The process of transition showed great diversity in these areas: it occurred at different times, proceeded at different rates, and often had different results. But even if the Gallic model is not exactly paralleled in the other areas, Gaul does provide a "laboratory" for the assessment of the possible responses of aristocrats to the arrival of a new ruling order. In this way, this study of Gaul should help to give some insight not only into the barbarian settlements of other parts of the empire, but also into the effects of the arrival of newly ascendant ruling elements in other places at other times.

It might be useful at this point to interject a few words about personalities and sources. This study covers a critical period during the history of the western European world, a period during which a number of noteworthy individuals appeared, many of whom were the authors of literary works in which they, directly or indirectly, expressed their perceptions of the changes going on around them. Several of them, and their literary circles, seem worthy of being introduced in advance.[22]

There were the monks of Lérins, aristocrats from throughout Gaul who first sought sanctuary in a remote island monastery—and then often left it to assume episcopal sees. These included Honoratus and Hilary of Arles (c. 426–449), Eucherius of Lyons (c. 432–451), Lupus of Troyes (c. 427–472), and Faustus of Riez (c. 455–490), all bishops, not to mention the priest Salvian of Marseilles (c. 420–490).[23] These individuals wrote works ranging from sermons to letters to theological tracts.

There also was Sidonius Apollinaris (c. 430–480), the most blue-blooded aristocrat of Gaul, who served as Prefect of Rome in 468 and then as bishop of Clermont and wrote letters that provide an invaluable firsthand glimpse into Gallic aristocratic life. His acquaintances included all the most important men in Gaul, barbarians as well as Romans. Other writers of large letter collections included Paulinus of Nola (c. 395–431), Ruricius of Limoges (c. 485–508), and Avitus of Vienne (c. 490–518).[24]

Gauls also wrote many biographies of their holy men, such as those of Martin of Tours by Sulpicius Severus, Germanus of Auxerre by Constantius of Lyons, Honoratus and Hilary of Arles by Hilary himself and Honoratus of Marseilles respectively, and Eutropius of Orange by Verus of Orange; of Orientius of Auch, Lupus of Troyes, and Vivianus of Saintes by anonymous authors; and of many others. These works, even some of the later ones, often contain valuable obiter dicta about contemporary reactions to and perceptions of the arrival of the Germans, and the effect it had on the popular imagination.[25] Other sources that survive from this rich period of literary production include law codes, poetry, chronicles, a biographical dictionary, records of church councils, and other religious writings, as well as a large number of inscriptions. A full listing of the manifold source materials can be found in the Primary Bibliography below.

It might be useful to include here a few words about stylistic conventions. Although Latin citations are nearly always translated, translations sometimes are deemed unnecessary for words or phrases whose meaning is obvious either per se (e.g., words like *senator* or *nomen Romanum*) or from the context. The meaning of all Latin terms, whether glossed in the text or not, can be found in the Glossary. Regarding titulature, formal titles of Roman officials are capitalized, hence "Arvandus, Praetorian Prefect of Gaul," "the Patrician and Master of Soldiers Aetius," or "Arbogastes, Count of Trier." Other titles which serve as job descriptions or are not formal job titles are not capitalized, for example, "the master of soldiers Aegidius," "a Gallic prefect," "bishop Hilary of Arles," "the priest Constantius of Lyons," or "the emperor Valentinian III." Finally, the policy of some editors, especially in *MGH*, of preferring nongrammatical to grammatical manuscript readings is avoided; this is reflected in some of the primary source citations.

For the rest, it is my pleasure to extend my thanks to all those who in one way or another helped to make this investigation possible. To the American Council of Learned Societies, the Penrose Fund of the American Philosophical Society, the George A. and Eliza Gardner Howard Foundation, the National Endowment for the Humanities, and the Venture Fund and the Research and Productive Scholarship Fund of the University of South Carolina, all for furnishing financial support. To the University of South Carolina Department of History for occasionally providing released time and a reduced teaching load. To my graduate and undergraduate students for allowing me to work discussions of Romans and barbarians into my lectures—and for coming up with insightful comments about them. To Profs. Tim Barnes, Tom Burns, Mike Clover, John Eadie, Bob Kaster, and Robert Patterson (not to mention an anonymous reader) for providing much helpful criticism. To Frankie Westbrook at the University of Texas Press, who first suggested that it might be possible to make all this into a book. To my wife, Rita, who was dismayed to discover that I had one more book in me after all (we can go to the beach *next* year, honey). And to my own two little barbarians, Katherine and David, who tried often and very successfully to distract me from my work, and to whom this book is dedicated.

ROMAN ARISTOCRATS IN BARBARIAN GAUL

THE BARBARIANS IN GAUL: IN SEARCH OF AN IDENTITY

Even though it is not the intention of this study to discuss the barbarians per se, it nevertheless seems necessary to begin with a brief excursus on the topic of just who the barbarians were. The word *barbarian* itself conjures up several images. In antiquity, as will be seen, the word often conveyed an "us-versus-them" connotation, regardless of whether it was used by the Greeks to describe the Romans, the Romans to describe the Germans, or one group of Germans to describe another.[1] In the modern day, on the other hand, the word often has a romantic coloring, conveying an image of a character dressed in furs with horns on his helmet, bashing on the gates of Rome. For the purposes of this study, the term *barbarian* will be retained as a convenient, nonpejorative generic term encompassing all of the non-Roman immigrants into Gaul.[2]

One repetitious image has been that of "waves" of barbarian invasions. On the last day of 406, groups of Vandals, Suevi, Alans, and Burgundians crossed the Rhine into Gaul. After making their way south, the Vandals, Suevi, and some Alans crossed into Spain in 409. In 411, the Visigoths entered Gaul from Italy, and in 418 they were settled in Aquitania as *foederati* (allies).[3] Soon after, the Franks encroached upon the Rhine and the Alamanni upon the upper Danube; the Burgundians were settled in Sapaudia and the Alans in enclaves throughout Gaul.[4] In 451, Gaul was invaded by the Huns.[5] By the 460s, Saxons were raiding the Atlantic coast and its estuaries, and in the 470s bands of Ostrogoths appeared from the east. Eventually, in this view, Gaul was wholly occupied by these waves of foreign invaders.[6]

It now is clear, however, that it is incorrect to speak of a barbarian collectivity, at least from the point of view of unity of action.[7] It even is doubtful that the individual groups of barbarians had, or retained, a strong sense of ethnic identity.[8] Just what, for example, differentiated a

[1]

Visigoth from a Burgundian, or a Frank from a Vandal? Barbarians did, it is clear, see themselves as being different from the Romans, but how different were they from each other? Sometimes, it will be suggested, only in the sense that one group of barbarians might classify other barbarians as "barbarians," as opposed to, say, Burgundians.[9]

Once barbarian groups entered the empire, any ethnic identity they had often was greatly submerged or diluted. The ethnic composition of each group became increasingly amorphous and indeterminate. The Visigoths, for example, suffered chronic losses, but also benefited from constant infusions of new personnel.[10] The Vandal invaders of Africa, furthermore, were described as "a huge mob of diverse savage enemies, Vandals and Alans, which had with it a mixed company of Goths, and individuals of other diverse backgrounds."[11] And in the Balkans, barbarian groups constantly intermingled with each other.[12] This intermixing has made it difficult to establish the ethnic identity even of some very well known barbarian leaders.[13]

Not only would barbarian groups have had a difficult time maintaining any ethnic identity vis-à-vis other barbarians, it would have been particularly hard to resist the influence of Roman culture.[14] Certainly, none of the barbarian settlers in western Europe were able to do so. Numerous barbarians identified their interests closely with Rome. Many barbarian potentates, of course, too numerous and well known to cite, entered Roman service.[15] The same situation presumably obtained in lower orders of society. A multitude of barbarian retainers, for example, followed Galla Placidia back to Italy after the death of Athaulf.[16]

Unquestionably, some (or many) of the barbarian settlers in Gaul realized early on that the most effective course of action for them would be to reach an accommodation with the Roman population, and not to cling too tightly to their barbarian background. The views of the Gothic king Athaulf on this subject are well known. After initially desiring to substitute *Gothia* for *Romania*, he eventually decided that the wiser course of action would be to use Gothic arms to support the *nomen Romanum*.[17] And he himself practiced what he preached, by marrying the empress Galla Placidia in a Roman ceremony.[18] Other Germanic leaders, such as the Gothic ruler Theoderic II, also seem to have been attracted to *Romania*.[19]

Roman culture influenced the impressionable barbarians in many ways.[20] Barbarian Arianism, of course, had its origins within the Roman world. And barbarian royal administration and ceremonial evolved directly from that of the Roman imperial government. The end of the century saw the transformation of barbarian generals in Roman service into barbarian kings.[21] The barbarian rulers, for example, of the Franks and

MAP 1

GAUL: PROVINCES IN THE FIFTH CENTURY.

● = METROPOLITAN CITY

▓ = OTHER CITY OR SITE

▬▬▬ = BOUNDARY OF PROVINCE

〜〜 = RIVER

MAP 2

GAUL: SELECTED CITIES.

(SEE MAP 3 FOR PROVENCE AND THE RHÔNE VALLEY.)

● = METROPOLITAN CITY

▨ = OTHER CITY OR SITE

━━━ = BOUNDARY OF PROVINCE

〜〜 = RIVER

MAP 3

SELECTED CITIES: PROVENCE AND THE RHÔNE VALLEY.

● = METROPOLITAN CITY

▨ = *CIVITAS*

▪ = OTHER SITE

Burgundians traced their descent from a Romanized "military nobility" of the fifth century.[22] And many of the trappings of Roman officialdom were merely transplanted into barbarian courts.[23] The imperial bureaucracy that had served barbarians in their role of Roman officials continued to serve them in their royal capacity.[24]

This lack of ethnic identity probably goes a long way toward explaining the oft-noticed lack of barbarian impact in many of the areas where they settled. It may be not that the barbarians left no record, but that the record that they left is often indistinguishable from that of those in whose midst they settled. It is hard to tell, therefore, how much true barbarian ethnic identity remained by the end of the fifth century. The following study will approach the problem of the barbarian identity from a different angle; it will examine how the barbarians affected, and were perceived by, the resident Roman population.

PART ONE

SETTING THE STAGE: ROMANS AND BARBARIANS IN CONFLICT

CHAPTER ONE

THE ARISTOCRATIC BACKGROUND OF LATE ROMAN GAUL

qui genus, unde domo?
(VERGIL, *AENEID* 8.114)

qui genus, unde domo?
(SIDONIUS APOLLINARIS, *EPISTULAE* I.II.5)

qui genus, unde patres?
(AVITUS OF VIENNE, *CARMINA* 4.90)

neque te novi, unde sis
(GREGORY OF TOURS, *HISTORIA FRANCORUM* 4.46)

The Roman, and Romanized, aristocracy of Gaul had a long history.[1] After Julius Caesar's conquest of Gaul in the 50s B.C., many Celtic aristocrats enthusiastically embraced the Roman cause. Soon they were virtually indistinguishable—at least on the basis of nomenclature, language, and outlook—from the senators of other parts of the empire.

The Gallic aristocracy of the Principate (ca. 27 B.C.–A.D. 284) is imperfectly known.[2] Gallic senators seem to have concentrated primarily on local interests. Some historians see the late third century as a period of major disruption for the Gallic aristocracy, with the dispersal of some of the large estates, a decline in city life, and an even greater withdrawal to the countryside.[3] A tardy flowering of Gallic participation in imperial life occurred in the late fourth century, exemplified not only by the poet Decimius Magnus Ausonius and his circle but by others as well.[4]

DEFINITION OF ARISTOCRACY

Before embarking on a discussion of the aristocracy of late Roman Gaul, it should prove useful to define who the "aristocrats" were. The word "aristocrat" itself was rarely even used by Latin writers, except occasionally in its Greek form. Words such as *senator, nobilis, optimus,* and so on were used to describe members of the elite class. So just how is a member of "the aristocracy" (or "the elite" or "the upper class") to be defined?

The time period under consideration is an awkward one. It is located at the juncture of antiquity and the Middle Ages, and historians of both periods, as well as subperiods within them, often have their own idiosyncratic criteria for determining the composition of the "aristocracy."[5]

For one thing, controversy continues over just who the *senatores* ("senators") were, and over what, if any, relationship there was between the Roman imperial "senators," on the one hand, and the Gallo-Roman "senators" of the fifth- and sixth-century barbarian kingdoms, on the other.[6]

Another potential problem involves the identification of the *nobiles* ("nobles"). In the Roman Republic they seem to have been an elite group within the senate. But during the Principate, any distinction between "nobles" and other senators seems to have lessened.[7] By the time of the late Roman Empire, the term *nobiles,* even if it still could technically refer to a subgroup within the senatorial order, often was used to refer to the senate as a whole.[8] Many writers, especially ecclesiastics, cannot be expected to have adhered to, or even to have been aware of, fine or anachronistic distinctions in terminology; certainly they did not do so. In Gaul, too, it is clear that any distinction between the words *senator* and *nobilis* were lost by the sixth century if not before.[9]

Historians of Late Antiquity, therefore, have tended to use terms such as "oligarchy," "senatorial order," "imperial aristocracy," and "nobility" synonomously.[10] Terms such as *optimates, senatores,* and *nobiles,* not to mention others of a more medieval flavor (including *maiores, potentates* or *potentiores, primores,* and *proceres*), will be treated in this study essentially as synonyms for each other in the context of the Gallo-Roman privileged class.[11] In general, moreover, the terms "aristocrat" and "aristocracy" will serve as handy generic terms that can be defined, or redefined, by their usage in particular historical contexts. This approach will be particularly worthwhile because, as will be seen, the elite classes of Late Antiquity, in Gaul as elsewhere, were in a state of flux.

THE *BONI* AND *OPTIMI:* THE MEMBERS OF THE ARISTOCRATIC COMMUNITY

By the late fourth century, the term *senator* no longer was limited only to members per se of the senate of either Rome or Constantinople.[12] It now described a bearer of one of the many grades of rank within the senatorial order. These grades included, primarily, *clarissimus* ("most distinguished"), *spectabilis* ("respectable"), and *inlustrissimus* ("most illustrious").[13] A holder of the rank of *clarissimus* would be called a *vir clarissimus,* and so on. All who had held one of these ranks, as well as their sons or even other descendents, had a claim on being identified as senators.[14] As a result, the senatorial order comprised an increasingly large upper class, a true empire-wide aristocracy that was much more representative of all the provinces of the empire than the earlier imperial senate had been.[15]

But only a relatively small number of the senators of Late Antiquity can be identified on the basis of technical titulature. In other cases, indirect means must be used to infer that an individual belonged to the senatorial aristocracy. This primarily involves establishing what can be called the "criteria of aristocracy": what prerequisites was an individual expected to meet in order to be considered an aristocrat-cum-senator?

To the Romans, it always had been clear who aristocrats in general were: they were the ones known to themselves as the *boni* ("good people") or the *optimi* ("best people").[16] In the early fourth century, for example, according to the panegyricist Nazarius, the emperor Constantine (306–337) had admitted to the senate the "best men" (*optimates viri*) of all the provinces.[17] As elsewhere, this usage was common in late Roman Gaul. Circa the 460s, the blue-blooded aristocrat Sidonius Apollinaris could refer to his friend Fulgentius as a "great component of the good men."[18]

Sidonius also listed some of the attributes associated with aristocratic status when he said of the senators of Rome, "There were indeed many in the senate who were adorned with riches and lofty in ancestry, distinguished for maturity and effective in counsel, prominent in rank and well-known by reputation."[19] In general, senators were expected to possess good ancestry, wealth and property, social connections, "good character," and a classical education.[20] All the *boni* would have met all or most of those criteria.

There were two primary routes to membership in the Roman senatorial order: birth and merit.[21] Birth, of course, always was the most important means by which aristocrats could be recognized.[22] The second-century Roman satirist Juvenal, for example, asked, "What good are family ties, what use is there in being esteemed for an extensive family tree?"[23] For him and other Romans, of course, the question was merely rhetorical. They already knew the answer. Family ties were everything. As stressed in the late fourth century by the haughty Roman noble Quintus Aurelius Symmachus, breeding always would tell, "Perhaps by the influence of good blood, which always makes itself known."[24]

In Gaul, Vergil's question of strangers, "What is your background? Where do you come from?", was pointedly applied by Sidonius to a troublesome parvenu.[25] In the early sixth century, bishop Avitus of Vienne was even more specific in his version of the Vergilian tag, asking, "What is your background? What is your parentage?"[26] And at the end of the century, Gregory of Tours had a nobleman superciliously say regarding an ambitious slave, "Nor do I know who you are, or where you came from."[27] The importance of birth in Late Antiquity likewise was underscored by the early-seventh-century Spanish writer Isidore of Seville, who defined a *nobilis* as one who is "not low-born, whose name and family are known."[28]

If an individual was not born into the aristocracy, other means of entry were available. The primary method was by obtaining an office (authentic or honorary) that carried senatorial rank. As a result, the aristocracy of the later Roman empire was infiltrated regularly by *novi homines* ("new men").[29] Such individuals, however, sometimes could have difficulty, at least theoretically, in gaining acceptance.[30] In Italy, Symmachus could say tersely, "The offspring of a family, by whatever extent they are distant from new men, by the same extent they proceed toward the heights of nobility."[31]

Likewise in Gaul. After the appointment of a new man to the post of Vicar of the Seven Provinces circa the late 460s, Sidonius reported, "The trampled-upon gentle birth of our young men grumbled about it."[32] Less privileged individuals, too, could be victimized by these elitist attitudes. Sidonius also complained that a merchant "was advanced farther than the condition of his status allowed on account of either his wealth or his family background."[33]

In many cases, however, the actual practice belied the theory. Some of Symmachus' closest friends were new men.[34] When attempting to advance the career of a low-born protégé, Symmachus simply ignored his origins and stressed his other qualities.[35] Similarly, in a letter to the aforementioned vicar, Sidonius praised him, not for relying on his wealth and family background, but for having achieved advancement "on account of the dowry of his abilities."[36] Sidonius also expressed a grudging admiration for the efforts of the ambitious merchant, who was, in fact, one of his own clients.

What was important was the utterance, rather than the accuracy, of aristocratic sentiments, and the sense of elitism that they imparted to members of the aristocracy, no matter how recent. Simple acceptance into the aristocracy by other aristocrats in and of itself could convey a good deal of a priori "antiquity."[37] Indeed, it is this collective acceptance as an aristocrat by other aristocrats that perhaps was the most important criterion of all of aristocratic status in late Roman Gaul. As bishop Ruricius of Limoges could modestly say of himself in the late fifth century, "One who associates with good men is not totally bad."[38]

Gallic writers repeatedly reassured each other of their personal acceptability. In a letter to his friend Philagrius, Sidonius recalled, "In a group of the greatest men . . . mention was made of you. All the good men felt in common all good things about you."[39] Now, Sidonius himself had never even met Philagrius, so his opinion would have been based solely upon the reports of others. But that was enough. And friends were to be accepted faults and all. Ruricius opined, "So great indeed is the force of unblemished love that nothing is displeasing in a friend."[40]

To make it all the more clear, moreover, just who the *boni* were, they were regularly contrasted with the *multi* ("many") or, for particular emphasis, with the *mali* ("inferior" or even "wicked"). Sidonius, for example, told how a fallen friend, the collaborator Arvandus, had aroused against himself "the enmity of the many rather than the good."[41] This "us" versus "them" mentality contributed even more to the sense of superiority that Gallo-Roman aristocrats wished to engender among themselves, and helped to isolate them from what they considered to be non-elite persons or groups.[42]

Nor were all *optimi* created equal. Far from it. Gallic aristocrats were every bit as status conscious as those elsewhere, and aristocrats of any station were all too aware of the status of their confrères.[43] Sidonius, in an attempt to induce his friend Eutropius to increase his standing through office holding, painted a bleak picture of what could happen if he did not do so: "Would it not be humiliating if you, an ignoble and skulking rustic standing behind juniors who were seated and engaging in the debate at the meeting of the council, were dishonored by the opinion of some glorified pauper, while you observed mournfully that they had taken precedence over you?"[44]

Any slights, real or imagined, were treated very seriously. On several occasions, Sidonius had to apologize to aristocratic friends, both bishops and laymen, who felt their status had not been sufficiently acknowledged.[45] There may have been a community of aristocrats, but within the community, each individual knew his place.

AMICITIA

Once an individual was accepted as one of the *boni*, the most important tie he had with his fellows was friendship (*amicitia*).[46] Gallo-Roman aristocrats had some very firm ideas about how friendship was to be maintained. First of all, it is clear that only the "good people" were worth having as friends (*amici*). Sidonius said of one acquaintance, "He seeks the favor not of all men but of good men, and is not degraded by indiscriminate familiarity."[47]

Aristocratic friendship, and membership in the aristocratic community, was cemented by a clearly understood system of mutual obligations. Friends demonstrated their sincerity (*fides*) by performing favors (*beneficia, munera, officia*) for each other.[48] Sidonius, for example, said of one of his friends, "However often he is joined in friendship to anyone, he obtains favors no more often than he bestows them."[49] The mutual responsibilities among friends were looked upon as being so strong that they were referred to as the "bonds" or "laws" of friendship.[50] One such "law" was the conviction that one could presume upon one's friends. Ruricius of Limoges, for example, sought a favor "on account not of the merit of [his] life but of the privilege of friendship."[51]

Aristocrats placed heavy emphasis on their loyalty and reliability. Even in the case of the traitor Arvandus, Sidonius could assert, "I was a friend to the man over and above what the vanity and fickleness of his character would have required," and he stressed that he had supported him "having preserved reverence for good faith."[52] An aristocrat would bristle if he felt that this reliability was doubted. On an occasion when Sidonius was afraid that he had been estranged from his friend Faustus, he protested, "As God is my witness, not even my enemies can make out that my friendship is undependable."[53]

An aspect of friendship which helped to unify the aristocracy of late Roman Gaul was the idea that friends should "feel, blame, and praise the same thing."[54] Similarly, aristocrats were expected to provide examples of proper behavior to each other. To his friend Potentinus, Sidonius wrote, "I admire in your actions the fact that you do much which is to be imitated by every good man."[55] Shared attitudes were especially important when it came to the choice of friends. Sidonius discussed with his cousin Avitus of Cottion "that which is very powerful and effective in the strengthening of friendships, the fact that in both seeking out or avoiding certain particular persons we competed with a likeness of judgment."[56]

A corollary to this phenomenon was that the friends of one aristocrat were dutifully accepted as the friends of other aristocrats. To an Italian friend who had written to him recommending someone else, Sidonius replied, "I therefore embrace the recognition and friendship of this man not only willingly but also enthusiastically, since I know that our friendship too will become closer through my deference to your wishes."[57]

Shared perceptions not only united contemporaries, they also bound together the generations. Sidonius wrote to his friend Aquilinus of the friendship they had inherited from their fathers and grandfathers, "Whom the likeness of their literary pursuits, offices, perils, and principles united in an admirable intimacy."[58] Noting, "I believe . . . that our friendship is as extensive as our reasons for friendship," he stressed the need to preserve ancestral values: "Let us teach our children in our own turn to desire, to avoid, to eschew, and to pursue the same things."[59] Ruricius of Limoges, in a like vein, wrote to his friend Celsus about their affection: "[It] was left to us by our parents, passed on to us by our teacher, and strengthened by our shared experiences."[60]

The repeated belief that aristocrats should share the same feelings and activities became a virtual topos, and demonstrates once again the degree to which aristocratic *amici* felt they should maintain solidarity. The aristocrats of late Roman Gaul pursued their friendships in ways which were calculated to help to unify themselves as a class. They defined for themselves who they were to be, and they went out of their way to maintain harmony among themselves by discouraging dissent. This is not to say, of course, that dissent and friction did not exist. Far from it.[61] Nevertheless, the aforementioned sentiments represented an ideal that Gallic aristocrats strove consciously and calculatedly to attain.

Perhaps one reason acceptability played such a great role in determining whether an individual was admitted into Gallo-Roman aristocratic circles at this time is that, as will be seen, it was becoming increasingly unclear, based on objective criteria, just who the "aristocrats" were to be. Some of the old definitions were becoming invalid as a result of the uncertainties of the times. If the rationale for the granting of aristocratic status was not immediately apparent on strictly objective grounds, then only by a corporate decision on the part of established aristocrats could individuals be accepted as circumstances changed, and as some aristocrats' eligibility for membership, on the old terms, perhaps became questionable.

In general, the rather subjective criteria for acceptability into aristocratic circles meant, in Gaul at least, that the aristocracy came to comprise a relatively large, and even a motley, group of individuals.[62] It was not limited solely to the members of some elite body, or to those who had held the highest offices. It rather was made up of many individuals who had any of several claims to membership.[63] Even individuals of merely curial or municipal origin were eligible for inclusion.[64] But one thing which all the members of this extended aristocracy shared was their class consciousness, and the resultant desire to maintain their class unity. If aristocrats occasionally alluded to a rarity of close friendships, it only reaffirmed the sense of elitism which true friends shared.[65]

The aristocrats of late Roman Gaul, therefore, were a self-conscious group who defined themselves according to a set of ideals which they collectively determined. One of their most critical concerns was a desire for self-preservation, and the remainder of this study will focus on just how the Gallo-Roman aristocracy perpetuated itself. During the fifth century, Gallo-Romans were faced with extraordinary changes, many of which were caused, or accelerated, by the arrival and settlement of the barbarians. These changes made it difficult for many aristocrats to continue their old aristocratic lifestyle. Some of them found it difficult even to remain aristocrats at all.

CHAPTER TWO

GAUL, ITALY, AND ISOLATIONISM IN THE FIFTH CENTURY

unde igitur ordiar, nisi a tuis, mea Gallia, malis?
(LATINIUS PACATUS DREPANIUS, *PANEGYRICI LATINI* 12/2.24)

GAUL AND THE IMPERIAL GOVERNMENT

Throughout most of the Principate, Gallic aristocrats had been little in-volved in imperial politics and administration.[1] During the troubled times of the mid third century, Gauls even had taken it upon themselves to establish their own "Gallic Empire."[2] The imperial reorganization under Diocletian had brought an expanded imperial presence in Gaul, with an imperial capital at Trier. During the latter part of the fourth century, a number of Gauls had profited from this new imperial attention and had acquired high office in the Roman administration.[3]

Men such as these glorified the benefits bestowed on Gaul by the im-perial government.[4] As the Gallic panegyricist Claudius Mamertinus as-serted to the emperor Julian in 362, "How much more fortunate is our condition? How much more outstanding is our happiness? Not just an ear of grain or common bunches of grapes, but wealth and riches are heaped upon us without any exertion; provinces, prefectures, and con-sulates spontaneously appear . . . Whoever shows himself at any time to be upright and zealous in the administration of the republic is accepted as a partner in the rewards. You choose for the administration of the provinces not someone most familiar to you but someone most upright. All are rewarded by you with money, enriched with wealth, and ennobled with honors."[5]

Even in the fifth century such men continued to glorify Rome and the idea of Rome, and foresaw the restoration of ancient Roman glories.[6] Some of their statements have become virtual commonplaces. Circa 417, for example, the Gaul Rutilius Namatianus asserted, "You created a city where there had been a world."[7] Even in the very last years of Roman Gaul, Sidonius Apollinaris could describe Rome as "the chief place of the world, the fatherland of liberty, in which city, alone in the whole world, only slaves and barbarians are foreigners."[8]

Some of these Gauls retained qualified imperial sentiments until the very end of Roman rule in Gaul. That is to say, they were willing to accept what benefits the empire had to offer as long as the process of obtaining them did not conflict with their ambitions at home. At the same time, however, the old Gallic spirit of isolation and independence never vanished.[9] A number of pre-existing developments concerning the relationships between Gaul, on the one hand, and Italy and the imperial government, on the other, need to be covered even before the arrival and settlement of the barbarians can be discussed.

GALLIC IDENTITY

Several considerations suggest that by the fourth century, at least, Gaul had acquired an idiosyncratic identity within the Roman Empire.[10] One widespread perception, for example, was that the Gauls were apt to revolt whenever they felt their interests were not being served. This impression would have been justified, in part, by the creation of the Gallic Empire in the 260s and 270s. The *Augustan History* (written, it seems, in the late fourth century), for example, referred in several instances to this presumed Gallic predilection. In one place, it spoke of "the Gauls, whose nature it is not to tolerate feeble and luxury-loving emperors who have degenerated from Roman virtue," and in another it mentioned "that custom, whereby the Gauls always are desirous of revolution."[11] In this context, a certain unique "Gallic" identity was assumed, which was shared by all inhabitants of Gaul, and which set them apart from inhabitants of other areas of the empire.

This supposed willingness of Gauls to revolt also would have been a result of a perceived neglect of the region by the imperial government.[12] The anonymous author of *The Description of the Entire World and Its Nations,* for example, speaking of Gaul, noted, "It always has need of an emperor; it makes one of its own."[13] The Gallic panegyricist Latinius Pacatus Drepanius went so far as to blame the imperial neglect of Gaul for the revolt of Magnus Maximus (383–388) when he said to Theodosius I in 389, "Nor, moreover, emperor, should you think that everything I am going to say will be pleasing to your ears. We Gauls—and you may marvel to hear this—are irritated by your victories. While you have been proceeding to the conquest of remote lands, while you have extended the eastern empire beyond its natural borders and markers, while you have hastened toward those natives of the first light, and into that very abode of the sun, if such exists, a tyrant discovered the secret of wickedness . . .

Whence, therefore, should I begin, my Gaul, if not from your misfortunes?"[14]

In spite of such complaints, the imperial government continued a slow withdrawal from Gaul. Valentinian II, the last emperor to reside in Gaul, was assassinated in 392.[15] Probably at the end of the fourth century, the seat of the Praetorian Prefect of Gaul was transferred from Trier to Arles.[16] Soon thereafter, the military garrisons of the Rhine were denuded and withdrawn.[17]

Additional Gallic revolts soon followed, including those of Constantine III (407–411) and Jovinus (411–413).[18] A brief period of repression followed the reassertion of imperial authority, but by circa 416 the Italian government seems to have attempted to be more responsive to Gallic needs.[19] Oppressive tax levies were lightened and an amnesty was granted for "any acts which were done improperly or spitefully."[20] In 418, the Council of the Seven Provinces, a southern Gallic assembly which initially had been established in the early 400s, was revived.[21] The government also instituted a welcome policy of preferring Gauls for service in Gallic office.[22]

But the imperial government also was the agent of the cession of many Gallic regions to the barbarians: parts of the north to the Franks even before the fifth century, and then the southwest to the Visigoths in 418, areas around Valence and Orléans in 441 and 442, Savoy to the Burgundians in 443, and so on.[23] In some instances, at least, Gallo-Roman senators were distressed by this cavalier disposition of their territory.[24] Sidonius Apollinaris, for example, after the cession of the Auvergne to the Visigoths in 475, wrote to bishop Graecus of Marseilles, one of the negotiators, "Our servitude has been made the price for the security of others . . . If we are truly surrendered, it is certain that you cowards engineered the barbarous plan which you recommended."[25]

Even if the Gauls were happy to accept whatever benefits the government offered, the theme of imperial neglect continued.[26] The fifth-century expression of this sentiment was made most eloquently by Sidonius Apollinaris. In his panegyric to the emperor Majorian at Lyons in 458, he maintained, "From the time when Theodosius returned a shared authority to the exiled brother of his sponsor . . . until the present, my Gaul has been ignored by the masters of affairs, and ignored she has served. Because of this, there has been much destruction, because, with the emperor sequestered, whoever he was, it has been customary for the remote parts of the miserable world to be devastated. How can life be satisfactory when the ruler himself is in need of guidance? For so many years our nobility has been held in contempt: the republic's reward to the brave has been resentment."[27] Majorian himself, meanwhile, already had singled out Gaul for a special detrimental measure earlier in the year when he decreed,

"No collector is to refuse a solidus of full weight, except for the Gallic solidus, whose gold is appraised at a lesser value."[28]

The Gallic feeling of rejection surely contributed to the sense of Gallic regional identity that one encounters in the fifth century. It would have been no accident that both the Gallic emperor Eparchius Avitus (455–456) and the count Agrippinus were described by the chronicler Hydatius not as "Romans" but as "citizens of Gaul."[29] The Gallic self-consciousness would have tended not only to unify the Gauls but also to separate them all the more from their aristocratic brethren elsewhere in the empire.

LOCAL INTERESTS AND ISOLATIONISM

The evolution of this Gallic sense of regional identity also was expedited by a development which was affecting not only Gaul but the empire as a whole: the increasing pursuit of local interests and influence.[30] Provincial potentates increasingly dissociated their own interests from those of the imperial government. In 458 the western emperor Majorian complained about one manifestation of this tendency: "This is the method of powerful persons, whose agents in the provinces disregard the payment of taxes, while . . . they arrogantly keep to their estates."[31] Another result was the growing disinclination to hold state office, even among those who had the opportunity to do so.[32] Sidonius, for example, could rhetorically claim that during the reign of Petronius Maximus in 455, one thousand Gauls had refused to hold imperial office.[33]

For some Gauls, however, office holding continued to have an appeal, even if those who did hold office almost invariably did so at home.[34] Sidonius Apollinaris, for example, regularly exhorted his aristocratic confrères to avail themselves of the opportunity to serve in the imperial administration. To his friend Eutropius, he wrote circa 467, "It is no less important for a man with your birthright to see to his rank than to his estate."[35] And Eutropius did in fact go on to serve as Praetorian Prefect of Gaul around 470.[36]

The most aristocratic Gauls viewed imperial office holding as a hereditary right. To another friend, Sidonius spoke grandiloquently of his own ambitions: "Go, now, and enter a charge of ambition against me before the senate because I struggle with ever-vigilant care to obtain my hereditary dignity."[37] One of the attractions of office holding was the status that came along with it. Sidonius, for example, wrote to his wife, Papianilla, about his hopes for the prestige of his family: "Just as we found our families to be of prefectorian rank and by divine favor made them patrician, thus [our children] will make consular that which they received as patrician."[38]

As late as 474, Sidonius could speak glowingly of the advantages that awaited those who supported the imperial government: "Whence, it happens that every best man in turn can and should eagerly exert himself on behalf of the republic, to this end, if he has any power, because he is secure that whatever recompense a prince has promised to the devotion of his supporters, even when the emperor is dead, the emperorship will render."[39] Fewer and fewer Gauls, however, had the opportunity to avail themselves of such opportunities, and even those who did always had the affairs of Gaul as their primary, or even only, concern.

Another common Gallic manifestation of the concentration on local concerns was withdrawal from foreign activities. As the fifth century wore on, Gauls tended to leave Gaul rarely; those who did leave often did so as exiles, and never returned.[40] Extra-Gallic social contacts became infrequent.[41] As Sidonius noted to a friend whom he had invited to accompany him to Rome, "Although you are active at home, your unsophisticated helplessness makes you afraid to undertake a journey, and you fear to set out."[42]

In spite of this innate aversion to foreign travel, Gauls did occasionally leave home during the last three-quarters of the century for reasons of secular or ecclesiastical business. A few Gauls, for example, served in imperial offices of middling rank outside Gaul between circa 425 and 455, and in the 440s the Gaul Constantius was sent off to be Attila's *ab epistulis* (secretary).[43] In 455–456, moreover, a number of Gauls did hold Italian office in the train of the emperor Avitus, but they returned as soon as they could.[44] And in 474, Sidonius' brother-in-law Ecdicius was made Patrician and Master of Soldiers by the emperor Julius Nepos, but his only service in Italy occurred when he was recalled in order to be replaced.[45]

Other Gauls traveled to Italy as part of official delegations. In the mid 440s, bishop Germanus of Auxerre undertook an embassy to Ravenna at the request of the revolting Armoricans.[46] In 467, Sidonius traveled to Rome as the leader of an Arvernian delegation, and in the next year he was made Prefect of Rome by the emperor Anthemius.[47] And the Gallic prosecutors of the collaborator Arvandus journeyed to Rome in 468.[48]

A larger number of Gallic ecclesiastics traveled to Italy on church matters.[49] These visits too, however, always involved business, usually appeals to the bishop of Rome. And as for Italians, they, too, only visited Gaul for business purposes.[50]

Some Gauls, therefore, willingly traveled to Italy on ecclesiastical or secular official business during the fifth century. When they had something to gain from Italian officialdom, they would make the trip. Gauls also were perfectly willing to go to Italy to hold official office. Their failure to do so more often probably resulted not so much from lack of desire as from lack of authentic opportunity. When valid opportunities did arise, as during the reign of Avitus, many Gauls leapt at the chance. But such opportunities were few, and this fact probably only contributed to the Gallic sense of separation.

Socially, too, Gaul became increasingly isolated from Italy. This is seen, for example, in the realm of education. Early in the fifth century, it was still standard policy for well-bred young Gauls to pursue their education in Rome. Germanus of Auxerre's fifth-century biographer noted that "after the Gallic schoolrooms [he] added the knowledge of law in the city of Rome to the fullness of his perfection."[51] Circa 400, the Gaul Nemesius and his unnamed brother were in Rome to study.[52] So was Rusticus, a young man of Marseilles, whose mother, said Jerome, "Sent [him] to Rome, sparing no expense . . . so that Roman solemnity would restrain the extravagance and elegance of Gallic speech."[53] And Rutilius Namatianus' young friend Palladius, to whom he bid farewell in 417, also was a student in Rome.[54]

Subsequent examples of young Gauls pursuing their studies in Rome, however, are difficult, even impossible, to find. That is not to say, however, that studying in Rome did not remain a theoretical ideal. In a letter to his young friend Burgundio of Lyons, Sidonius noted: "You are wholly worthy to have Rome welcome you with applauding hands . . . [and] you doubtless would have achieved this, if we had been at peace and our location had allowed it. There, associating in the companionship of senatorial youth, you would have been educated. . . ."[55] Burgundio, however, was unable to fulfill the tradition, and had to complete his education in Gaul.

Other Gauls, too, eschewed visiting Italy in spite of the attractions of doing so. In 455, for example, Sidonius encouraged his reluctant friend Eutropius to accompany him to Rome in the train of the emperor Avitus. He argued that Rome really was not a foreign place, saying, "If, that is, a man of senatorial birth . . . rightly can say that he has in fact gone abroad if once, even in his youth, he has seen the home of laws, the training ground of literature, the senate of dignitaries, the summit of the world, the homeland of liberty, in which city, alone in the whole world, only barbarians and slaves are foreigners."[56] Eutropius does in fact seem to have gone along, but for the purpose of office holding, not of education or personal satisfaction.[57] Most Gauls, one suspects, would have traveled only vicariously, as did Sidonius' Lyonese friend Heronius, to whom Sidonius wrote two letters about his Italian excursion in 467. He did so, he said, "Because you think it would be pleasant to learn from the more faithful account of those who have been there about the sights which you have only read about."[58]

In spite of the Gallic disinclination to foreign travel, one nevertheless might imagine that some would have satisfied the pious aspiration of going to Rome for devotional reasons.[59] But examples are difficult to find. The accused Gallic traitor Agrippinus supposedly took refuge in the basilica of St. Peter, but only because he had escaped from imprisonment in Rome.[60] In only one known instance, in fact, did Gallic ecclesiastics travel to any place in Italy for reasons of piety. Circa 455, bishop Namatius of Clermont sent priests to Bologna to obtain relics of the saints Agricola and Vitalis.[61]

One seeks in vain, moreover, for any purely social visits by Gauls to Italy in the fifth century. Even in the early part of the century, Gauls declined to do so. Sulpicius Severus, for example, spurned repeated invitations from Paulinus of Nola.[62] This is not to say, however, that the Gauls were averse to travel. Far from it. Gauls undertook many lengthy, arduous, and even dangerous trips for purely social reasons in the fifth century, as attested by their multitudinous correspondence. But all of this travel was restricted to Gaul itself.

The discussion thus far indicates that Gauls did travel outside Gaul, and especially to Italy, in the fifth century.[63] But nearly all of these visits were on official business. The evidence for travel outside Gaul for personal reasons, on the other hand, is much more skimpy, and mostly limited to the beginning of the century.[64] This could lead one to suggest that the social connections between the Gallic and Italian aristocracies were unraveling. But before accepting this conclusion, based upon travel alone, it might be useful to look for any other evidence of continuing close social or family ties between the Gallic and Italian aristocracies.

One might investigate, for example, the extent to which Gauls, even if they did not travel outside Gaul in person, maintained epistolary ties with Italy. Early in the century, at least, they did. Several Gauls corresponded regularly with the expatriate Gaul Meropius Pontius Paulinus of Nola.[65] And even if they did not actually visit each other, at least their couriers made the trip.[66] The constant comings and goings of these messengers presumably demonstrate the kind of regular social intercourse between Gaul and Italy which existed around the turn of the century. Similar epistolary exchanges, too numerous to cite here, occurred among Symmachus, Ambrose, and Ausonius, and their Gallic and Italian correspondents. But this phenomenon did not continue into the fifth century.

Over three hundred letters written by some forty Gauls survive from the years circa 420–500. A fairly good sample, one would imagine. But of all these writers, only one, Sidonius Apollinaris, wrote any extant letters to Italians. His correspondents include Candidianus, an inhabitant of Ravenna; the Prefect of Rome Audax; and the Roman Campanianus.[67] And even these Italian letters seem to have been anomalies, for all three were written in the context of Sidonius' official visit to Rome in 467–468.

One also might note that Ruricius of Limoges, a purported relative of the blue-blooded Italian Anicii, did not think enough of any Roman relatives he might have had to include a single Italian, or even non-Gallic, correspondent in his voluminous collection of eighty-two letters.[68] For him, apparently, his foreign relatives did not count for much in real life. This failure of Gallic aristocrats to include Italians among their correspondents after the early fifth century suggests that by then the Gauls and Italians had few personal ties to each other which they thought were worth cultivating.[69]

SOCIAL RELATIONS

There remains, however, another line of investigation. To what extent did the Gallic visitors to Italy in the fifth century presume upon any friendships or take advantage of any social ties that they had there? In the mid 440s, Germanus of Auxerre did have social interactions with several high-ranking court officials at Ravenna.[70] There is no indication, however, as to whether he had known these individuals before his arrival. And one cannot but note that he had to lodge in a *diversorium*, or inn; apparently he had no friends with whom to stay.

More positive evidence comes from the delegation that Hilary of Arles sent to Rome in the late 440s in an attempt to gain support in his quarrel with bishop Leo of Rome. His representatives sought aid from Hilary's old friend Auxiliaris, a Roman aristocrat of some standing.[71] This case, however, was atypical: Auxiliaris had been Prefect of Gaul in the mid 430s, at a time when Gauls usually held this office. Were it not for this, presumably, there would have been no reason for Gauls to seek him out at a later date.

One might expect to find additional evidence of close Gallo-Italian aristocratic relations, if any existed, in the years 455–456, when the Gaul Avitus actually became emperor in Rome. But one searches in vain for a single Italian appointed to serve in Avitus' administration. Avitus seems to have had no friends or allies in Rome at all.[72] In fact, his actions so alienated the senate in Rome that a conspiracy was formed against him.[73]

The situation was no better in 467, when Sidonius arrived in Rome in an Arvernian delegation. Like Germanus, he had no one with whom to stay and had to take rooms in a *diversorium*.[74] Even the appointments of Sidonius and his brother-in-law Ecdicius to high offices of state at this time—as Prefect of Rome (468) and Master of Soldiers (474), respectively—probably demonstrate not close ties between Gaul and Italy but the need of foreign emperors (the eastern nominees Anthemius and Nepos) to drum up support outside Italy in order to counterbalance the influence of the Italian aristocracy.

The Italians, on the other hand, from the very beginning of the century seem to have been equally disinclined to visit Gaul for any reason. As a result, social connections loosened. Symmachus, for example, in an attempt circa 400 to explain his failure to correspond, told his Gallic friend Protadius, "Bear in mind that, now that the emperor and the highest magistrate are absent, no one of our order travels to the neighborhood of the Rhine."[75] And elsewhere he excused himself, saying, "This defense is available to me, that no departures of travelers were known" whereby letters could be sent.[76]

Symmachus argued that it would be more fitting for Protadius to visit Rome, saying, "First of all, because everyone gathers in the common center of the world, and second, because the various desires and necessities of all men are attendent upon the most clement prince residing in this locale."[77] This chauvinistic Italian attitude probably did not sit well with many equally chauvinistic Gallic aristocrats, and would have contributed to the aforementioned tendency of Gauls to make their own emperors.

There is little evidence, therefore, for the maintenance of any close connections, through either visits, correspondence, or patronage, between the aristocrats of Gaul and Italy during the fifth century.[78] The visits and communications which had been relatively common at the beginning of the century virtually ceased later: The break seems to have been well underway by 418, if not before. It would appear that by the mid fifth century, the social ties between the Gallic and Italian aristocracies had become very remote.

Meanwhile, some of the administrative changes instituted in the early fifth century probably strengthened the Gallic sense of corporate consciousness. The Council of the Seven Provinces, for example, provided an often-used venue for the expression of multi-provincial sentiments, as in 449, when Astyrius entered the consulate in Arles; in 455, when Eparchius Avitus was proclaimed emperor; and in 468, when the prefect Arvandus was indicted for peculation and treason.[79] And the preference for Gauls in high Gallic office, especially the prefecture, gave the most influential Gallic aristocrats an opportunity to satisfy their ambitions for secular public service in a local context, and to assist their non-office-holding confrères in the process.[80]

It is against this backdrop of aristocratic separatism and Gallic self-consciousness that the barbarian settlement of Gaul occurred. The two developments were parallel processes which often interacted with each other; the barbarian settlement, it will be seen, only accelerated the pre-existing Gallic tendencies toward isolationism and the pursuit of local interests.

CHAPTER THREE

THE BARBARIAN SETTLEMENT:
IMPRESSIONS OF HARASSMENT,
INTERFERENCE, AND OPPRESSION

uno fumavit Gallia tota rogo

(ORIENTIUS OF AUCH, *COMMONITORIUM* 2.184)

GAUL IN THE FIFTH CENTURY: CONTEMPORARY THEMES

In the opinion of some contemporary observers, the arrival of the barbarians in Gaul was terrible indeed.[1] The Gallic panegyricists of the fourth century played upon the theme of barbarian destructiveness. Claudius Mamertinus, for example, in his panegyric to the emperor Julian in 362, lamented, "The barbarians seized cities which once had been most flourishing and ancient; the renowned nobility of Gaul either perished by the sword or was condemned to serve cruel masters."[2]

In the early years of the fifth century, some ecclesiastical writers circulated horrific tales regarding the extent of the destruction caused by the barbarian invasions of Gaul.[3] The conventional portrayal of the barbarian settlement in Gaul was notably bleak.[4] Jerome, for example, writing circa 411/412, asserted in a famous passage: "Innumerable and most ferocious nations occupy all Gaul. Whatever is between the Alps and the Pyrenees, that which is bounded by the ocean and the Rhine, the Quadi, the Vandals, the Sarmatians, the Burgundians, the Alans, the Gepids, the Heruls, the Saxons, the Alamanni and, O unfortunate Republic, the Pannonian hordes devastate. And, indeed, Assur comes with them. Mayence, once a noble city, has been taken and overturned, and in the church thousands were slain. Worms has been destroyed by a long siege. Rheims, a strong city, Amiens, Arras, distant Thérouanne, Tournai, Spire, Strasbourg, all carried into Germany. Except for a few cities, the provinces of Aquitania, Novempopulana, Lugdunensis and Narbonensis all have been devastated. Indeed, the same things which the sword destroys outside, hunger destroys inside."[5]

An equally gloomy portrayal was painted circa 415 by the anonymous author of *The Poem on the Providence of God*: "What crime was committed so that so many cities should perish together? So many places, so many peoples, what evil did they deserve? If the entire ocean had poured itself into the fields of Gaul, more would have survived these vast waters . . . By a ten-year siege we are laid low by Vandal and Getic swords. Neither fortresses of rock, nor towns placed on high mountains, nor cities on watery rivers survive the treachery and military might of barbarian furor. They conquer all, we endure the worst . . . Perhaps those older and more worthless, having offended God, get what they deserve, but what of innocent boys? What have young girls done, for whom there has been no time for sin? Why are the temples of God permitted to be burned? Why have the vessels of the sacred ministry been defiled? The honor of devoted virginity does not protect the unwedded, nor does the love of religion preserve the widow."[6]

The priest Salvian of Marseilles, moreover, graphically described the destruction suffered by some of the most illustrious cities of northern Gaul in the first half of the century: Trier, in particular, was sacked some four times, and a neighboring city—perhaps Mainz—also was devastated.[7] Orientius, bishop of Auch in the 430s, rhetorically concluded that "all Gaul smoked in a single funeral pyre."[8] And similar accounts accompanied the invasion of northern Gaul by Attila and the Huns in 451. Prosper of Aquitaine, for example, recounted that "after the crossing of the Rhine, many Gallic cities suffered their most savage assault."[9]

Such reports, however, often were presented in order to further the particular moral or theological agendas of their writers.[10] As a result, they may be more noteworthy for their geographical exhaustiveness than for their literal accuracy.[11] It also might be noted that such portrayals of gloom and doom rapidly declined as the century wore on. Other contemporary sources were more matter-of-fact about the propinquity of the barbarians. The late-fourth-century *Description of the Entire World and Its Nations*, for example, merely stated laconically, "And [Gaul] has next to it the barbarian nation of the Goths."[12]

While there is little doubt that the barbarians caused a good deal of devastation, what there was seems to have been restricted mainly to the north. Even Jerome's list cites specific examples there only. The examples of other writers likewise are primarily northern. And even there, the destruction was not complete. Salvian, for example, admitted, "I myself saw, in fact, men of Trier, of noble houses and exalted in rank . . . for whom, although they had been in fact plundered and pillaged, something yet remained of their wealth."[13]

Away from the north, it now generally is accepted that the barbarian settlement was not as ruinous as once thought. As seen in the Preface, the extent of the destruction frequently has been minimized, and some have gone so far as to characterize the barbarian settlement as generally nonviolent and to suggest that in some areas the barbarians had little impact.

Nevertheless, even in the south, Gallo-Romans had to be concerned about the political and military situation. Gallic cities and regions easily could be caught in the middle of warring factions. Circa 470, for example, Sidonius Apollinaris wrote to his friend Felix of Narbonne, "Thus, we are placed in the midst of rival peoples as their miserable prey; suspected by the Burgundians and neighboring to the Goths, we suffer the rage of those attacking us [the Visigoths] and the jealousy of those defending us [the Burgundians]."[14]

Bit by bit, more and more of Gaul came under barbarian jurisdiction during the fifth century. Regardless of whether this or that area was occupied violently or peacefully, Roman aristocrats found that the barbarian presence affected their lives in a number of ways. On several levels it became difficult, or impossible, to carry on as before. Even Gauls who did not have regular, personal contact with individual barbarians could not ignore some troublesome effects of the barbarian settlement.

OBSTACLES TO TRAVEL AND COMMUNICATION

The dangers caused by barbarian unrest clearly inhibited personal interactions.[15] Travel hazards of the 470s are described in the biography of abbot Eugendus of St. Claude: the population "feared the dire and nearby raids of the Alamanni, who were accustomed to launch attacks upon unsuspecting travelers not by a frontal assault, but in a beastlike and sudden manner."[16] Travelers could be delayed by such difficulties for months at a time.[17]

The frequent personal visits to which aristocrats had become accustomed were hindered. In a letter to Auspicius, bishop of Toul, Sidonius reprised his regretful comments to Felix of Narbonne, saying, "I have less opportunity to enjoy the blessed contemplation of your presence, fearing at one time harm from my neighbors [the Visigoths], and at another resentment from my patrons [the Burgundians]."[18] Sometimes, barbarian rulers even imposed specific restrictions upon specific individuals. In the late 470s, Sidonius wrote, again to Felix of Narbonne, "Should my patron [sc. the Visigothic king Euric] allow it, I will hasten there, so that our friendship, which has languished because of our infrequency of communication, might flourish through deeds."[19]

Aristocrats attempted to make up for the lack of opportunity for personal visits by a regular exchange of letters.[20] But even correspondence could be difficult, at least for the letter-carriers, who could be searched and roughly questioned at watchpoints on the roads.[21] Delicate messages, therefore, were best carried verbally.[22]

ECONOMIC DETERIORATION

In other ways, too, the barbarians had an adverse effect on the ability of aristocrats to pursue the lives they had led before the barbarian arrival. The initial barbarian occupation brought several kinds of economic distress.[23] The author of *The Poem on the Providence of God* catalogued several of them: "One man laments the loss of silver and gold talents; pilfered furnishings, and jewelry divided among Getic daughters-in-law, torment another. A stolen flock, a burned home, guzzled wine, distressed children, and obnoxious servants disturb another . . . You grieve for your untilled fields and deserted halls, your uprooted grounds and your burned villa."[24] For such reasons, Rutilius Namatianus had been forced to return from Italy to Gaul circa 417, saying, "Nor was it proper to ignore the ruin any longer."[25]

Sometimes property was not only devastated, but also occupied by incoming barbarians. Some land grants, it seems, were made directly by the barbarian kings themselves; the source of property is unclear.[26] Distributions of land also were made by the Roman government through the procedure known as "hospitality" (*hospitalitas*).[27] On occasion, as in the case of the Alans settled at Valence in 440, deserted lands were used.[28] At other times, Gauls who participated may have had to hand over one-third or more of their property to barbarian "guests" (*hospites*), although they at least were able to retain the rest.[29]

Gauls who did not take part in such divisions, however, could suffer more dire consequences. Paulinus of Pella, the grandson of the Gallic poet Ausonius, for example, complained that his property was devastated early in the century because he was not protected by a barbarian "guest."[30] It was repeatedly despoiled, and eventually was dispersed, he lamented, "in the midst of barbarian rapine, by right of war."[31] Nor did Paulinus' sons fare any better in Visigothic Aquitania: both soon died after failing in their attempts to recover some of the family property.[32] Paulinus and his family therefore provide an example of a Gallic family which had been prosperous in the fourth century, but was ruined in the fifth.[33] It may have been persons such as these to whom Salvian referred when he mentioned Aquitanian aristocrats who "have lost their homeland and live as paupers in comparison with their former riches."[34]

Some Gallic landowners resisted the distributions of land to the barbarians, but to little avail. One chronicle noted, under the year 442, "The Alans, to whom lands in the further part of Gaul were granted by the patrician Aetius to be divided with the inhabitants, overcome armed resistance and having expelled the owners seize possession of the land by force."[35]

As the century wore on, therefore, by one means or another, more and more of the economic productivity of Gaul came under the control of the barbarians. The end result necessarily was a lessening of the overall economic status of Gallo-Roman aristocrats. Even if the amount of the change cannot be measured quantitatively, there surely was a qualitative decline in the Romans' economic influence. Regardless of whether the barbarian acquisition of land had been accomplished violently or peacefully, the economic result would have been the same, and would have been one more Gallic cause for concern.

LOSS OF SOCIAL STATUS

Another worry of influential Romans would have been the fate of their social influence in barbarian Gaul. Even where Romans and barbarians lived side by side in relative harmony under barbarian authority, barbarians sometimes took advantage of their superior de facto legal status. By the latter part of the century, it would seem that some Burgundians were attempting to transfer their obligations to their Roman neighbors. In the Burgundian Code, for example, it was decreed, "If a man making a journey on private business comes to the house of a Burgundian and seeks hospitality and the latter directs him to the house of a Roman . . . let the Burgundian pay three solidi to him to whose house he directed the traveler."[36] One might wonder whether any affected Romans actually were able to secure the enforcement of such laws.

Gregory of Tours reported an example of barbarian opportunism that occurred in the Visigothic kingdom during the reign of Alaric II (484–507). It seems that the Goth Sichlarius, a favorite of the king, attempted to take advantage of the Roman abbot Ursus, who had built a waterwheel near Tours. According to Gregory, "Sichlarius . . . said to the abbot, 'Give me this mill . . . and I will pay what you wish,' to which the abbot responded, 'We cannot give it up now, lest my brothers die of hunger,' and [Sichlarius replied], 'If you wish to yield it of your own free will, I thank you, but if not, I will take it by force.' "[37] Eventually, says Gregory, the monks' prayers brought about Sichlarius' ruin. Other Gauls in similar straits, however, lacking such divine intervention, would have had to suffer the loss.[38]

LOSS OF OFFICE-HOLDING OPPORTUNITIES

A direct result of the barbarian presence was the decline of Roman imperial authority in Gaul, which went hand in hand with the gradual disappearance of the Roman imperial administration. Even if the administrative structure continued to exist in theory, as in the *Notitia dignitatum* (the official Roman administrative handbook), it would appear that only the very highest ranking officials, such as prefects, vicars, and governors, continued to be appointed and to serve, and these only in the south. There is little evidence for the prolonged widespread use of the more middling positions—office staffs, secretaries, and so on—which had given employment to so many Gauls, especially educated ones, in the past.[39]

The holding of imperial offices had been one of the traditional ways in which a Gallo-Roman aristocrat exercised his standing. With most of these positions gone by mid century, and with few similar opportunities available from the barbarians, other avenues for the expression of aristocratic desires had to be found.[40]

INTERFERENCE IN CHURCH OPERATIONS

The early years of the barbarian occupation of Gaul brought scattered reports of barbarian, primarily Visigothic, interference in the operation of the Gallic church. Jerome, as seen above, had peddled gruesome reports of barbarian massacres in churches circa 407. And the author of *The Poem on the Providence of God* reported that circa 415 some priests were roughly treated and that at least one bishop was driven from his city.[41] Most other such reports, however, concern the Huns and derive from hagiographical sources of rather dubious validity.[42] Otherwise, for the first seven decades of the century, the barbarian treatment of Gallic clerics and the Catholic church appears to have been exceptionally circumspect.[43]

Not until the reign of the Visigoth Euric (466–484) did the situation change.[44] For one thing, he seems regularly to have inhibited the appointment of new bishops: in 474 Sidonius catalogued nine cities where Euric had forbidden ordinations.[45] Euric also exiled pro-Roman bishops of cities which came under his control.[46] Simplicius of Bourges and Sidonius himself were exiled by 475, as was Crocus of Nîmes; they were joined by Faustus of Riez and Marcellus of Die shortly thereafter.[47]

Sidonius even went so far as to accuse Euric of "plotting against Christian regulations."[48] And, at the end of the next century, Gregory of Tours recalled these Visigothic practices as a "grave persecution of the Christians in Gaul."[49] In even later years, the supposed barbarian persecution of the church in the fifth century became a commonplace. *The Deeds of the Bishops of Auxerre*, for example, discussed the difficulties caused "on account, of course, of the savagery of the barbarians who were devastating Gaul."[50]

But the evidence would suggest that, *pace* Sidonius, the Arian Euric was not attacking Catholic orthodoxy per se but the Catholic leadership, and for essentially political rather than religious reasons.[51] In only a single instance before the end of Roman rule are Arian Goths known to have challenged Catholic theology: the celebrated debate, presumably nonviolent, between the Arian bishop Modaharius and the Catholic bishop Basilius of Aix.[52]

Other Gallic references to Gallic (or, more properly, barbarian) Arianism, however, tended to be rather banal and unemotional in nature. The *Gallic Chronicle of 452* referred to "the unspeakable heresy of the Arians, which mingled itself with the barbarian nations."[53] No apparent worry here about any Arian menace to Gallic Catholicism.[54]

Later, in the sixth century, the debates between Catholics and Arians in the Burgundian kingdom were carried out in a genteel, drawing-room atmosphere with little hint of animus on either side.[55] To the south, Caesarius of Arles did not even specify Arianism by name in his *Synopsis against the Heretics*, which was supposedly written against the Arians.[56] He did note, in his *Treatise on the Apocalypse*, that "The heretics indeed have power, and especially the Arians."[57] Given his treatment elsewhere, however, this statement probably reflects not a serious Arian threat, but the negligible concern over any other heterodox beliefs in Gaul; Arianism was the only one which had any appropriateness at all. As such, it always was available as a whipping boy for any bishop wishing to instruct his flock about the need to toe an orthodox line.

In general, Arians and Catholics coexisted side by side rather peacefully. At Bourges, circa 470, the local Arians—perhaps because they lacked any ecclesiastical hierarchy of their own—even concurred in Sidonius' selection of the Catholic bishop.[58] Nor, it seems, did the barbarian Arians make any attempts to proselytize among the Catholic Gallo-Roman population.[59] In the main, it would appear that the Arian beliefs of the Visigoths and Burgundians simply were not a primary cause for concern.[60]

If anything, the true complication for Gallic Catholicism caused by the barbarian occupation lay in the problems it created for Gallic church unity. Before the disappearance of Roman authority, Gallic bishops had been able to assemble their own church councils on their own authority, often uniting the bishops of several different provinces. But as the Germanic kingdoms expanded, attendance at councils became curtailed.[61] After the year 500, only the bishops from a particular kingdom were able to attend councils within that kingdom.[62]

OPPRESSION, IMPRISONMENT, ENSLAVEMENT, AND EXECUTION

The disruption and disorder of the fifth century also resulted in various threats to personal livelihood and security. There was a constant risk of capture and possible enslavement by marauding barbarians, not to mention bandits.[63] The anonymous authors of *The Poem on the Providence of God* and *The Poem of a Husband to His Wife* not only gave commonplace descriptions of the barbarian destructiveness circa 406 and afterward but also told of the personal hardships they had experienced.[64] The former described being carried off as a captive circa 415.[65] And the latter portrayed himself as a landowner "who once tilled the earth with a hundred plows, [but] now yearns to possess a yoke of oxen."[66]

Others faced harsher treatment. The biography of abbot Eugendus of St. Claude mentioned a certain Leunianus, "A native of Pannonia, when barbarism was also spreading into Gaul, who was caught up in the chains of captivity."[67] And Ennodius of Pavia's relative Camilla of Arles also had been carried off as a captive.[68] On many occasions families were separated or disrupted as a consequence.[69] Imperial legislation attempted to mitigate the problem: a law was issued at Ravenna in 408 "so that persons of diverse provinces, of any sex, status, and age, whom the spread of barbarian savagery [had] displaced as a result of captive necessity, would not be held against their will."[70]

Gallo-Romans of high status who had dealings with the barbarian kings ran the risk of captivity or worse. The giving of hostages, for example, seems to have been a practice common to both sides.[71] In 414, Paulinus of Pella, in his attempts to lift the Visigothic siege of Bazas, went to king Athaulf as a negotiator and ended up as a hostage.[72] On the same occasion, the Romans received the Alan queen and prince as hostages of their own.[73] Shortly thereafter, circa 420, the Gallic aristocrat Theodorus, a relative of the future emperor Eparchius Avitus, was held by the Goths as a "noble hostage."[74] In 458, the imperial representative Petrus took hostages from the Burgundians—or possibly even the Romans—after his occupation of Lyons.[75] And shortly after 463, a certain Adovacrius and a band of Saxons "took hostages from Angers and other places."[76] These last unfortunates perhaps were no more than captives, held for ransom.

Presumably, service as a true hostage usually was not particularly dangerous or onerous.[77] But in later years, at least, there were certain risks. In the early sixth century, the sons of Gallo-Roman senators were used as hostages to ensure a treaty between Clovis' sons Theoderic and Childebert. When the peace broke down, the hostages were enslaved.[78]

Other Gallo-Roman aristocrats were imprisoned for various reasons. In the third quarter of the century, the *vir spectabilis* Simplicius of Bourges was confined by the Goths in a "barbarian prison."[79] At about the same time, the nobles of Saintes supposedly were imprisoned in an attempt to confiscate their wealth; they were released only after the intervention of their bishop.[80]

Imprisonment led to an even worse fate for a friend of Sidonius, the *vir inlustris* Eucherius of Bourges, who had been unsuccessful in a bid to become bishop of the city circa 470. At the end of the decade, he ran into difficulties with the Visigothic-appointed duke Victorius. According to Gregory of Tours, Victorius "poured malicious accusations down upon the senator Eucherius, whom one night he ordered to be dragged from the prison in which he had been placed, and having tied him next to an ancient wall, he ordered this very wall to be pulled down on top of him."[81] Eucherius did not survive.

It is unclear what the nature of the accusations against Eucherius was, but he is known to have been a supporter of the imperial government right up to the end.[82] This may have given Victorius the chance to pursue some personal grievance against him without fear of Visigothic reprisal. Certainly, any restraints upon such activities and any means of legal recourse which had existed under the imperial government were largely removed under the barbarians.[83]

The arrival of the barbarians had a great effect upon the Gallo-Roman aristocratic lifestyle. During the fifth century, it was not simply business as usual. No, this was a period Sidonius Apollinaris could describe as a time "when the population of barbarian allies not only uncouthly administered Roman resources but even fundamentally undermined them."[84] As seen in this chapter, from the point of view of Roman aristocrats this "undermining" of the Roman world by the barbarians brought with it many disagreeable changes. In order to cope with the detrimental aspects of the barbarian settlement and to preserve their status—and on occasion even their lives—Gallo-Roman aristocrats had to devise new strategies intended to respond to the changing times.

PART TWO

IMMEDIATE RESPONSES:
THE DISRUPTION OF
OLD INSTITUTIONS

CHAPTER FOUR

THE INTELLECTUAL RESPONSE: CONFLICTING PERCEPTIONS OF THE BARBARIANS

ubi namque sunt antiquae romanorum opes ac dignitates?
fortissimi quondam Romani erant, nunc sine viribus;
timebantur Romani veteres, nos timemus
(SALVIAN, *DE GUBERNATIONE DEI* 6.18)

One response to the barbarian presence was an intellectual one. This entailed the development of what might be dubbed a "barbarian ideology."[1] Such an ideology involved giving the barbarians an appropriate and acceptable intellectual and literary context in the Roman world. This was done by defining the mutually exclusive spheres of *Romania* and *barbaria* (or *barbaricum*).[2] Presumably, doing so assisted in defusing any threat the barbarians posed to aristocratic self-assurance. The barbarians, even if apparently preeminent in matters political and military, could by this means be "put in their place."

This is not to say, however, that Gallic writers of the fifth century gave any indication at all that they were excessively concerned about barbarians. Indeed, given the great volume of literary work which survives, it is remarkable how little impact the barbarians had on the Gallic mentality. References to barbarians, and opinions about them, appear in surprisingly few places.[3] Those that do appear indicate that attitudes expressed about barbarians could result not only from one's personal experiences with them but also from the particular rhetorical effect one was attempting to create. For, as will be seen, the barbarians regularly provided literary fodder for Roman writers.

THE ENCYCLOPEDIC TRADITION

One concern was simply that of identification. Who were "barbarians," anyway? On the simplest level, the question was easily answered. They were the peoples who always had been barbarians. Every author worth his salt could trot out standard lists of barbarians on demand.[4] Ausonius, for example, wrote:

hostibus edomitis, qua Francia mixta Suebis
certat ad obsequium, Latiis ut militet armis,
qua vaga Sauromates sibi iunxerat agmina Chuni,
quaque Getes sociis Histrum adsultabat Alanis . . .[5]

In his list of the invaders of Gaul in 406, Jerome uncritically cited "Quadus, Vandalus, Sarmata, Alani, Gepides, Heruli, Saxones, Burgundiones, Alemanni, et . . . [so as not to leave anyone out] hostes Pannonii."[6] His knowledge of barbarian ethnography presumably was roughly equivalent to that of Ausonius.[7]

In the fifth century, after the barbarian settlements in Gaul, one might expect that literary references to barbarians would have become more precise. Not so. Sidonius Apollinaris, in what he must have considered a literary tour de force, pulled out all the stops in his list of the barbarians who invaded Gaul with Attila, proclaiming (*Carm.* 7.321–325),

. . . pugnacem Rugum comitante Gelono,
Gepida trux sequitur, Scirum Burgundio cogit,
Chunus, Bellonotus, Neurus, Bastarna, Toringus,
Bructerus, ulvosa vel quem Nicer alluit unda
prorumpit Francus . . .

He did so again when he catalogued the barbarians who had been recruited into Majorian's army, asserting (*Carm.* 5.474–477)

hoc totum tua signa pavet; Bastarna, Suebus,
Pannonius, Neurus, Chunus, Geta, Dacus, Halanus,
Bellonotus, Rugus, Burgundio, Vesus, Alites,
Bisalta, Ostrogothus, Procrustes, Sarmata, Moschus . . .

An impressive array indeed.[8] And this encyclopedic tradition was continued in the early sixth century by Avitus of Vienne, who, in his list of barbarians who had been converted to Christianity, cited "Alemannus, Saxo, Toringus, Pannonius, Rugus, Sclavus, Nara, Sarmata, Datus, Ostrogotus, Francus, Burgundio, Dacus, Alanus . . . Suevus."[9]

At this level of interpretation, barbarian groups were mere names and had no individuality. Such lists give no indication at all of any ethnic or cultural differences among the various groups. Their names simply were to be plugged in as needed, or where the poetic meter required, in order to achieve a particular rhetorical purpose. This practice is exemplified by the early-fourth-century panegyricist Nazarius. After rattling off a list of barbarian groups—"Bructeros . . . Chamavos . . . Cheruscos, Vangionas,

Alamannos, Tubantes"—he opined, "The names blare out a call to arms, and the savagery of barbarity evokes dread through their very names."[10] Clearly no concern here, for example, with how the Alamanni differed from the Cherusci. On another level the Roman practice of citing names may reflect an old commonplace of folk magic: to know something's name is to be able to control it.[11] Roman writers at least knew the names.

TRADITIONAL VIEWS OF THE BARBARIANS

Even if the Romans were almost completely unconcerned about the ethnicity or ethnogenesis of particular barbarian groups, on some occasions they did indicate how they felt about barbarians in general.[12] For the chauvinistic or insecure late Roman it often sufficed to describe barbarians generically as obviously subordinate creatures.[13] Doing so was only consistent with the "us-versus-them" mentality, already described above, which Roman aristocrats used to differentiate themselves from non-elite groups in general.[14]

Some concrete methods were employed by the Romans to preserve their sense of identity vis-à-vis the barbarians. One was an effort to discourage miscegenation. The senatorial attitude toward such unions was clear. The mid-fourth-century historian Aurelius Victor, for example, said of the supposed marriage of the emperor Gallienus (253–268) to the Germanic princess Pipa, "For this reason, even more serious civil unrest arose."[15] Later, the *Augustan History* could joke about the marriage of the usurper Bonosus to a certain Hunila, described as "a woman of noteworthy example and of a noble family, but of the Gothic race."[16]

Officially, too, mixed marriages were clearly frowned upon. A law of the early 370s prohibited inhabitants of the provinces "of any rank or place" from marrying barbarians, "Because in these [marriages] something suspect or noxious is encountered."[17] And this is one imperial directive which, as far as can be seen, seems to have been followed, at least as regards the elite elements of society.[18]

The rare violations of this prohibition seem to have been for political reasons. One occurred at Narbonne in 414, with the marriage of the empress Galla Placidia to the Gothic ruler Athaulf. The anonymous, but presumably aristocratic, author of *The Description of the Emperors of the House of Valentinian and Theodosius* took a decidedly dim view of this union, commenting, "The sister of the emperor, the augusta Placidia, disgraced the condition of the times first as a captive, then as the wife of a king, but indeed a barbarian one."[19] Another such marriage was that of the Roman generalissimo Aetius to an unnamed barbarian princess, whom some have identified as Pelagia, the Arian earlier wife of another generalissimo, Aetius' deceased rival Boniface. In his panegyric to Majorian, Sidonius portrayed her as a spiteful shrew, jealous of the future emperor's promise.[20]

Publicly and officially, Romans eschewed not only barbarian wives, but barbarian ways as well. High-ranking individuals who adopted barbarian garb, for example, always were portrayed in a negative light—and often came to a bad end. Consider the anonymous report about the emperor Gratian, who was murdered in 383: "While he neglected the army and preferred a few Alans to the old Roman soldiery, he was so taken by barbarian comradeship, if not even friendship, that sometimes he traveled in barbarian costume [and] roused the hatred of the soldiers against himself."[21] Likewise, the poet Claudian lampooned a praetorian prefect's supposed fondness for barbarians: "[Rufinus] himself in public, lest he omit any aspect of barbarity, pulled forward onto his breast tawny skins . . . He was not ashamed to assume the degrading manners and dress of the Goths, and to abandon the distinguished dress of the Latin toga. The captive laws grieved under a skin-clad judge."[22] He was murdered in 395. In 397, the imperial government even decreed (Codex Theodosianus 14.10.2) punishments of exile and confiscation of property for the heinous crime of wearing barbarian breeches!

In general these antibarbarian sentiments were manifested, in Gaul and elsewhere, by a long tradition of barbarian bashing. In 362, for example, the emperor Julian declined to make a preemptive attack on the "deceitful and perfidious Goths. . . . He said they could be dealt with by Galatian merchants, by whom they were sold everywhere without account for their status."[23]

The Gallic panegyricists of the late third and the fourth centuries regularly referred to barbarian rebelliousness, rapacity, cruelty, and destructiveness.[24] The poet Claudian, just after 400, spoke sarcastically of the "hairy fathers, the skin-clad senate of the Goths."[25] The Spaniard Prudentius was even more disparaging, and opined in a famous passage, "But the Roman is as distant from the barbarian as the quadruped is separate from the biped or the mute from the speaking, as far indeed as those who properly obey the precepts of God are distant from stupid beliefs and their errors . . ."[26] Some Romans actually may have believed such opinions; others perhaps simply found it convenient, or reassuring, to do so. Meanwhile, in Gaul, circa 417, Rutilius Namatianus expressed an optimistic view of the ultimate fate of the barbarians, exhorting, "Take heart, then: the sacrifice of the sacrilegious nation finally will drop, the trembling Goths will submit their perfidious necks, the pacified lands will provide rich income, the barbaric plunder will fill the imperial lap."[27]

Later in the fifth century, traditionalists found similar non-violent methods for demonstrating their superiority to, and conventional distaste for, the barbarian occupiers of Gaul. Barbarians were routinely described in aristocratic circles as skin-clad, smelly, uncultured, and unreliable.[28] Sidonius reprised the opinion of Claudian. After referring contemptuously in 456 to a "Scythicus senatus," he described "a gathering of the Gothic elders" noting, "their vestment is unkempt . . . their skins are worn high."[29]

Even when they were clearly under the barbarian thumb, Gallo-Roman littérateurs did not desist from lampooning barbarians at every opportunity. Speaking of his life in Burgundian-occupied Lyons, for example, Sidonius described his "seven-foot patrons," and the reek of garlic and onions in his nose from ten breakfasting Burgundians.[30] Even when discussing his imprisonment at the fortress of Livia in 475, Sidonius seemed to delight in recounting his experiences with "two Gothic old women next to the skylight of my room: nothing will ever be more quarrelsome, drunken, and vomiting than they."[31]

In general, finally, educated Romans seem to have used the term *barbarian* generically to refer not only to foreigners, but also to undesirable natives resident within the empire. Salvian, for example, lumped together "Goths, Bacaudae, and other barbarians."[32] The Goths, in the past, had come from beyond the Danube; the Bacaudae, it seems, were native Romans. But they were equally disreputable, and both therefore were equally classed as barbarians. In a different context, the anonymous mid-fifth-century author of the *Praedestinatus* ("Predestined One") referred to heretics as "secret enemies [of the church], new barbarians who deceive with a peaceful mien."[33] In such cases, it was not their geographical origin but nonconforming habits that made individuals into barbarians. Small wonder, then, that Roman traditionalists like Sidonius could shudder at the thought of coming under barbarian jurisdiction and being compelled to "be barbarians."[34]

PERCEPTIONS OF ROMAN DECLINE

At other times, however, Gallic writers found it difficult to dismiss the barbarians as literary foils or subordinate creatures. The signs of Roman decline were all around them, and to many, as seen in the previous chapter, the barbarians were the agents of this decline. How was the Roman population, intellectually, to respond to this state of affairs? The barbarian invasions sometimes were seen as representing more than just immediate death and destruction; they also symbolized a more pervasive deterioration of the Roman world.[35]

Visions of impending doom, over and above the conventional accounts of the barbarian invasions, crept into Gallic literature. One manifestion was a disillusionment with the state of the secular world in general. This attitude was summed up by Eucherius of Lyons in 432 in his treatise *On the Contempt of the World and Secular Philosophy:* "There now is a certain tale among us of recent and renowned kingdoms: all those things which were great here now are nonexistent. Nothing, I think, or rather I certainly know, from those powers, honors, kingdoms did they take with them, unless, if there was any in them, the substance of faith and piety . . ."[36] Gauls with such attitudes often sought solace in religion.

On a broader scale, several fifth-century Gallic writers, both secular and ecclesiastical, saw the entire world in decline. Sidonius, paraphrasing Cyprian of Carthage's view ("now the world has grown old"), referred to "the world's present old age."[37] Various writers reported on numerous prodigies, and saw in them a sign of worsening times. Sidonius, for example, told of earthquakes, fires, and even deer invading the marketplace at Vienne.[38] And the chronicle of the Spanish bishop Hydatius is replete with portents, including even some from Gaul.[39]

These points of view were expressed at greater length in the early 430s, once again by Eucherius in the same work, where he noted, "The final age of the world is full of evils just as old age is full of death. These things have been seen for a long time and continue to be seen in this white-haired age: famine, pestilence, destruction, wars, terrors. They demonstrate the malaise of the final years. As a result, celestial portents often are observed, and movements of the earth, and changeable fortunes in the times, and monstrous births of animals. All these things, moreover, are prodigies of a progressing time, but of one which now is in decline."[40]

As the century wore on, even some Roman traditionalists were not always sanguine about the prospects of the empire in Gaul. On occasion, Sidonius indicated his awareness that all was not well. In 455, he made his famous lament about the rule of Valentinian III: "For us, it was death to have lived among these disasters and entombments of the world."[41] Not long after, he suggested that Gallo-Roman loyalists often did not receive their just rewards. He consoled his disenchanted friend Eucherius, "If the Roman Republic has sunk to these extremes of miseries, so that it never rewards its supporters . . . inasmuch as it is patently obvious that the Republic is delaying the rewards which you deserve, it is no wonder that it is not so much the deeds of noble and military men which are lacking as their rewards."[42] He also commiserated with the prefect Polemius in the early 470s because, as a result of Roman adversity, Polemius no longer had the means to do any favors for his friends.[43] Elsewhere, in an obvious reference to barbarian successes, he could refer to the "shipwreck of Latin arms."[44]

At the last, in 475, after the Auvergne had been surrendered to the Visigoths, Sidonius questioned the very future of the aristocratic classes of Gaul. In a letter to Graecus of Marseilles, he prophesied, "No longer will our ancestors even glory in this appellation [of ancestor], because they now begin to lose their descendents."[45] For Sidonius, the cause of this unfortunate eventuality was the continued success of the barbarians.

RATIONALIZATIONS OF BARBARIAN SUPERIORITY

Indeed, Gallic writers marveled at the apparent barbarian supremacy and wondered why it had occurred. Salvian of Marseilles, for example, asked, "Where are the ancient Roman resources and honors? Once the Romans were the most powerful, now they lack strength. The ancient Romans were feared, we are afraid. The barbarian peoples used to pay them tribute; we are dependent upon the barbarians . . . How unfortunate we are! How far we have declined! And for this we give thanks to the barbarians, from whom we purchase ourselves at a price. What can be more abject or more miserable?"[46]

Roman intellectuals developed several methods for rationalizing, justifying, or explaining away this barbarian political and military superiority. On strictly political and military grounds, the barbarians could be viewed merely as Roman federates, or allies, in the service of the Roman government.[47] They may have been more difficult to manage at some times than at others—Sidonius could call the Goths a "treaty-breaking race"—but that in no way affected their subordinate position.[48] If they abused their authority, they would be rebuked, at least verbally and in private; Sidonius once described the residents of the Burgundian kingdom in the 460s as "tyrant-governed citizens."[49]

Ecclesiastics could rationalize the barbarian superiority as the fulfillment of biblical prediction. Just before the barbarians arrived, the Gaul Sulpicius Severus—better known as the biographer of St. Martin of Tours—composed a chronicle in which he dealt with some Old Testament portents.[50] In his analysis of Daniel 2.31, which describes a great statue, Severus interpreted the golden head as the Chaldean Empire, the chest and arms of silver as the Persian Empire, the bronze belly as the Empire of Alexander—and the iron legs as the Roman Empire. This left the feet of clay and iron, which Severus saw as referring to his own day. "These," he

opined, "portend that the Roman Empire is to be divided . . . which likewise has been fulfilled, as when the Roman state is administered not by
a single emperor, but indeed by several, always disagreeing among themselves either philosophically or militarily."[51]

"Finally," Severus concluded, "by the mixture of pottery and iron,
materials which never form a cohesive bond, the mixtures of the human
race, which one after another are going to separate from each other, are
signified, inasmuch as it is well known that Roman soil has been occupied
by foreign or rebellious peoples or has been surrendered to those who
have surrendered themselves through the fiction of peace, and we see
barbarian nations, and especially the Jews, which have been mixed into
our armies, cities, and provinces, living among us but not assimilating
our customs."[52]

At this point, of course, the barbarian invasions of Gaul had not yet
begun. One can only imagine what Severus' interpretation would have
been had he written but a few years later. It might have paralleled that
of the early fifth-century Byzantine chronicler Philostorgius, who used
the same passage to interpret the marriage between Athaulf and Galla
Placidia as a union of iron and clay, "which [could] only end in the kingdom of God."[53]

The Spaniard Hydatius, on the other hand, used the marriage to gloss
a different passage of the same book, "In which the prophecy of Daniel
is thought to have been fulfilled, who said that the daughter of the king
of the south would be allied to the king of the north, nor would any of
his offspring from her survive."[54] And Orosius rationalized the marriage
in another way, suggesting that "through her alliance with the powerful
barbarian king, Placidia did much to benefit the state."[55]

Even more reassuring were the barbarians' own admissions of the superiority of the Roman system. Tales of barbarian adoption of Roman
customs were fashionable. Sidonius, for example, gleefully told—perhaps
with tongue in cheek—how the future emperor Avitus had instructed the
Visigothic king Theoderic I (418–451) in Vergil.[56] And he had Theoderic
II (453–466) profess soothingly to the future emperor Avitus, "For a long
time, through you, the Romulean laws have been pleasing to me . . . with
you as leader, I am a friend of Rome, with you as emperor, I am a soldier
[of Rome]."[57] Rather later, Sidonius also purported to welcome count
Arbogastes of Trier into the circle of the Gallo-Roman literary elite.[58]

But the most telling exposition of this theme comes from Orosius, who
repeated a Gallic tale, which he had overheard at Bethlehem. He stated
that the Gothic king Athaulf, after initially desiring to substitute *Gothia*
for *Romania*, had eventually decided upon a wiser course of action.[59]

Athaulf, expressing sentiments that worried Romans wanted to hear, asserted that "much experience had demonstrated, on the one hand, that the Goths in no way were suited to obeying laws on account of their unrestrained barbarism, and, on the other, that the laws of the Republic ought not to be obliterated, without which a republic is not a republic . . ." Athaulf, therefore, set out "to restore to its former glory and even to augment the Roman name by means of the strength of the Goths."[60]

This concept of Goths working in the service of the empire not only was consistent with the conventional idea of Goths as loyal federates, but also epitomized the attitude that Romans liked barbarian chieftans to have.[61] Regardless of whether this incident happened just as Orosius reported, one can be sure that many Romans were willing to believe that it had, for it touched them in a very sensitive spot.

AMBIVALENT ATTITUDES

Other Romans, too, if pressed, could indicate that barbarians were not all bad. This can be seen, for example, even in Sidonius' expression of the conventional wisdom on barbarians in a letter to his friend Philagrius: "You avoid barbarians because they are considered bad; I do so even if they are good."[62] Even this damning sentiment had a certain ambivalence to it, for Sidonius did admit that barbarians potentially could be good. As will be seen, even Gauls like Sidonius, who glibly mouthed the conventional antibarbarian diatribes as the need arose, could deal personally with the barbarians perfectly well, also as the need arose.

Still other Gauls exemplified in other literary genres an ambivalent view of barbarians.[63] Ecclesiastics in particular sometimes saw positive elements in the barbarian presence and exhibited a certain admiration for the barbarians, even if only to obtain a particular rhetorical effect.[64] An early fifth-century Gaul, for example, preaching against luxury, admonished, "Consider the Scythian leaders and Getic kings, who, having disdained the purple wool of the east, glory more grandly to appear frightful in the skins of wild beasts."[65]

And Salvian could associate particular barbarian groups not only with particular vices but with particular virtues as well. He maintained, "The Gothic nation is lying, but chaste; the Alans are unchaste, but they lie less. The Franks lie, but they are generous. The Saxons are savage in cruelty, but admirable in chastity. In short, all peoples have their own particular bad habits, just as they have certain good habits."[66] One might wonder, however, whether these supposed ethnic characteristics might have been more rhetorical than real.[67] And elsewhere Salvian saw the Germans as possessing a certain moral superiority over the decadent Romans, who could not, like the barbarians, be excused for their misdeeds on the grounds of ignorance of proper behavior.[68]

Those who professed admiration for the barbarians also had their own explanation for the barbarian successes. They viewed the Germans as the means used by God to teach the Romans a lesson for their sinfulness—a lesson the Romans had not learned.[69] In Africa, Augustine could assert, "You have not repressed your wantonness even after being subdued by the enemy; the benefit of the calamity has been lost upon you, and you have become most miserable and you remain most wretched."[70] And Salvian opined, "I think it lighter for a Christian to bear captivity of the body rather than of the soul."[71]

One reason, perhaps, for the lack of ecclesiastical animus toward barbarians may have been the aforementioned disinclination of the Arian Germans to mount any concerted attacks upon Catholic orthodox beliefs.[72] Barbarian Arianism was not perceived by the Catholic Romans as a serious menace. Indeed, Arian barbarians even could be praised for their Christian piety and devotion. Augustine, for example, repeatedly referred to the Visigoths' respect for Christ and Christian churches without once mentioning that they were Arians.[73]

Nor do Gallo-Roman aristocrats give any indication that they felt at all threatened by Germanic Arianism. On the contrary, they often seem remarkably restrained. In his characterization of the Visigothic king Theoderic II (453–466), for example, Sidonius reported on the king's daily predawn attendance at Arian mass. Without even mentioning that Theoderic was an Arian, he spoke approvingly of his "great sedulity" of worship, although he also purported to confide that "his reverence was a result more of habit than of reasoned belief."[74] If anything, Arianism often may have been viewed by both Romans and barbarians as a useful segregating and distancing element. This is not to say, however, that barbarians were wholly beyond the pale. As one Gallic Christian poet could assert, "Man, woman, slave, free, Jew, Greek, Scythian, barbarian, we are all one in Christ."[75]

Others, too, could hope for an eventual rapprochement between Romans and barbarians. As early as 417, Orosius optimistically asserted, "The barbarians [in Spain], having forsworn their swords, have turned to the plow, and nurture the surviving Romans as allies, now, and friends."[76] And in 455, Sidonius referred rhetorically to a peaceful Goth who was loathe to beat his pruning hook back into a sword, and was happy to be able to go back to his plow.[77] Barbarians like these surely were no cause for alarm.

All these differing perceptions of the barbarians' presence, and their significance, resulted in one way or another from the arrival of the barbarians in Gaul. In general, the intellectual responses to the barbarians served as a distancing element, a means of keeping the barbarians at arm's length. They also helped the Romans to rationalize the barbarians' presence, and to give the barbarians a formal conceptual position in the Roman world. But such rationalizations did not always accurately reflect the real world, and were not always applicable to real-life situations. If a true modus vivendi with the Germans was to come about, more tangible ways of coping with them would have to be found.

CHAPTER FIVE

GALLIC TRADITIONALISTS AND THE CONTINUED PURSUIT OF THE ROMAN IDEAL

facito ut sim privatus et potens
(*QUEROLUS* I.2)

Some of the most powerful and influential Gallic senators, even as their ties to Italy and the imperial government were weakening, nevertheless continued to pursue the same ideals, goals, and ambitions as senators throughout the empire. One of the cornerstones of their lifestyle was the cultivation of local interests and the quest for local influence.[1]

PATRONAGE AND *POTENTIA*

By retiring to the security of their estates, senators could hope to isolate themselves from the vagaries of politics, imperial as well as barbarian. This pursuit of local interests first and foremost led to a desire by Gallic aristocrats to possess as much power, influence, and authority (*potentia* or *potestas*) as possible.[2] Local potentates exulted in their status. Paulinus of Pella, describing his circumstances in the early part of the fifth century, stated, "The glory of my status flourished in no small way, furnished with submission and supported by a crowd of clients."[3] Such individuals not only possessed the greatest power and influence in status-conscious Gallic communities; they also exercised it in ways that would ensure everyone knew they possessed it.

Faustus of Riez, for example, described how things worked in the real world of late Roman social relations, and revealed graphically why *potentia* was a desirable commodity, when he sermonized circa the 460s, "Finally, if some powerful person [*potens*] does us an injury, even if he insults us to our face, we do not dare to make any harsh response, nor, I might say, to respond in kind. Why not? Lest we suffer as a result a greater injury from that powerful person than we bore initially . . . If, therefore, a powerful person rages against us, we are silent and dare to say nothing, but if an equal or, perchance, an inferior person abuses us . . . we arise and we either avenge our injury immediately or we certainly prepare our spirit for rendering a greater response. Why is it, that when a powerful individual inflicts injury upon us, we bear it patiently, but when one inferior in rank does so, we are aroused with excessive fury?"[4]

The supreme ambition of these powerful potentates was parodied by Querolus ("the Complainer"), the protagonist of an anonymous early-fifth-century Gallic comedy. When asked to what he aspired, he responded, "Make it so that I might be a powerful civilian [*privatus et potens*]." He went on to say, "Let me be able to despoil those who owe me nothing, to slaughter those I do not know, even to despoil and slaughter my neighbors." His questioner responded to these wishes, "You desire banditry, not authority."[5] Querolus then was advised to go and live beside the Loire River if he wanted that kind of life.[6]

Other Gauls were more earnest in their condemnations of the conduct and practices of Gallic potentates. The theme that the rich and powerful were necessarily wicked as well was a commonplace in some ecclesiastical circles.[7] The anonymous author of *The Poem on the Providence of God*, for example, asserted, "The greatest status in the world is found among the unjust; good men, however, have almost no share in it. Whoever is violent, cruel, crafty, and greedy, whose heart lacks faith and whose voice lacks modesty, such a one is admired, loved, revered, and honored by all; upon him wealth and the highest offices are bestowed . . . Falsity prevails in judgments and the truth falters; punishment attends the innocent, and salvation the guilty."[8]

In one of his many vilifications of the Gallic aristocracy, Salvian of Marseilles asked, "Who indeed is the rich man or noble who . . . keeps his hands free from crime of all sorts? . . . The socially great wish to have . . . the privilege of committing the lesser crimes as of their right."[9] He suggested that even landowners of middling rank in out-of-the-way places were guilty: "What cities are there, and even towns and villages, where there are not as many tyrants as there are decurions? Although perhaps they glory in this designation, because it seems to be powerful and honored."[10]

Even if one might question the motivations for such abuse, it is clear that other writers, with different perspectives, recognized the validity of these perceptions. The presumably aristocratic author of the *Querolus*, for example, put into the mouth of a slave the words "It is in fact common knowledge and manifestly clear that all lords are wicked."[11] Such perceptions presumably arose, in part, as a result of the great gulf which lay between the Gallic "haves" and "have-nots." And what allowed the privileged class to preserve its perquisites was its possession and exercise of *potentia*.

The benefits which accrued to the possessors of power were well known, as noted by the author of *The Poem on the Providence of God:* "It is customary to call those most blessed whom delightful authority [*potestas*] has raised up to the highest pinnacles of haughty offices, whom great wealth enriches, and for whom property scattered throughout the entire world heaps up an ample profit. Their expensive clothing and beautiful furnishings, and magnificent mansions, innumerable slaves, and attentive clients are praised."[12] The similarity between these perquisites and those which graced aristocrats in general is, of course, no coincidence. For without *potentia*, no one could hope to attain or maintain aristocratic status.

One of the primary means for strengthening one's local *potentia* was by concentrating upon the expansion and consolidation of one's land-holdings.[13] Salvian of Marseilles, for example, suggested that those who sought the "magnanimity of the powerful" and the "patronage of the privileged" ended up by losing their property.[14] In the middle of the century, bishop Valerianus of Cimiez could preach, "Behold, the neighborhood frequently is armed for conflict; why is this, unless because one perhaps plans to cross his boundaries and to occupy ground belonging to another?"[15] This was no time for the retiring or the faint of heart. Individuals such as Paulinus of Pella, whose primary concern was the pursuit of a life of ease, did not always fare well.[16] Paulinus complained that his estates were despoiled not only by barbarians, but also by ambitious Romans.[17]

To be a powerful local potentate, it also was necessary to have as many clients as possible, and another concurrent trend helped to accomplish just this.[18] It was not at all uncommon for *impotentes*, individuals without influence or authority, to place themselves under the protection of a powerful senator, even if this meant falling to the status of a quasi-free peasant, or *colonus*.[19]

Aristocrats acquired and retained clients by maintaining, and expanding, their role as patrons (*patroni*) and the providers of patronage (*patrocinium*).[20] A local *potens* asserted, demonstrated, and maintained his reputation and status (*dignitas, honor, status*) as the local "big man" by bestowing favors and services (*beneficia, officia, munera*).[21] His membership in a circle of other such potentates meant that he could exercise influence (*suffragium, gratia*) with them on behalf of himself or his clients.[22]

IMPERIAL OFFICE HOLDING

Most Gauls performed these activities in the local arena. As seen above, the Gallic desire to pursue strictly local ambitions resulted in part from a widespread lack of inclination, ability, or opportunity to hold imperial office; to be a *potens* in private life had become an honorable if limited pursuit in and of itself. Nevertheless, the most influential and ambitious Gallic potentates still found the holding of some form of public office in Gaul to be a useful adjunct to landholding in the pursuit of local authority.[23] They also regarded it as a hereditary right.[24]

Indeed, for an aristocrat who was truly interested in exercising the most extensive patronage, office holding still was the best way to do it. On several occasions, Gauls, as clients, referred to their governor as *suus patronus* ("their own patron").[25] Of course, Gauls who were in office at any particular time would be expected to assist those of their aristocratic cousins who were not.[26] When his friend Polemius became Praetorian Prefect of Gaul in the early 470s, Sidonius matter-of-factly wrote to him, "You will remember of course that at the time when you hold a public office you always ought to be mindful of private favors."[27] In general, then, small-scale, local patrons could hope to share in the benefits of the office holding of their more influential confrères.

SERVICES

The role of senators as local *patroni* was, of course, nothing new, but in the later empire not only were the services performed often more extensive, not to mention more mundane, but the patrons also were local residents.[28] On a day-to-day level, local potentates provided many kinds of services for their clients, such as help in lawsuits, reconciliations between quarreling relatives, letters of introduction, and intercession with other potentates.[29] These activities often effectively bypassed the machinery of the Roman government.[30]

Some potentates also provided services which more usually were associated with ecclesiastics. Eparchius Avitus' son Ecdicius, for example, circa 470 provided extensive famine relief at his own expense.[31] The aristocrat Eugenia of Marseilles fed the hungry, and the nobles Firminus and Gregoria of Arles were said to have expended their wealth on the poor.[32] Influential *saeculares* (laypersons) also participated in the redemption of captives, as did the noblewomen Syagria of Lyons, in the 490s, and the aforementioned Eugenia.[33]

Secular patronage often extended to the church. A number of aristocrats were involved in the construction of churches or monasteries; others contributed money or property.[34] The aforementioned Syagria, for example, was referred to as "the mother of churches and monasteries through her almsgiving."[35] And the basilica in Arles may even have been renamed the Basilica Constantia in honor of the patrician Constantius, emperor in 421, presumably on account of favors received or favors anticipated.[36] A canon of the Council of Orange in 441 that attempted to restrict the construction of churches by *saeculares* may have been a recognition of the influence that could accrue to a layman from association with a particular saint.[37] The Gallic emperor Avitus' devotion to St. Julian, for example, apparently led to his burial in the tomb of the saint at Brioude, and a resultant magnification of the memory of both.[38]

MEDIATION

Another way in which influential Gauls, in and out of office, could fulfill their role as patrons was by serving as mediators. In the most conspicuous instances, these mediators represented their local areas in any interactions with external authority, whether the imperial government or the barbarian newcomers. Doing so also allowed them to attempt to steer a middle course between the Roman and Germanic authorities.

The Arvernian senator Eparchius Avitus, for example, in his youth obtained tax relief circa 420 from the Roman patrician Constantius.[39] Subsequently, according to his son-in-law Sidonius, he undertook several missions to the Visigothic court and was responsible for many "treaties with kings."[40] In 451, moreover, "while still in private life," he helped to obtain the aid of the Visigoths against Attila.[41] Not wishing to overdo Avitus' Gothic attachments, however, Sidonius also was careful to stress patriotically that Avitus "refused to act more as a friend than as a Roman."[42]

Others performed similar services. Tonantius Ferreolus, Praetorian Prefect of Gaul in 451, was able to induce the Visigoths—supposedly by means of a banquet—to lift a siege of Arles.[43] Sidonius himself obtained tax relief for Lyons from the emperor Majorian in 458 and a decade later led an Arvernian embassy to Rome.[44] In the mid 470s, another Avitus, from Cottion, served as mediator between the Romans and Visigoths.[45] And the *vir spectabilis* Simplicius of Bourges "on behalf of [his] city stood before either skin-clad kings or purple-clad princes."[46]

Such activities, however, were not without their risks. Circa 414, when

Bazas was being besieged by an army of Visigoths and Alans, Paulinus of Pella attempted to appeal to his erstwhile friend, the Gothic king Athaulf. But the king himself had to admit, Paulinus said, that "the Goths again were making dire threats against [him]."[47] Only by striking a deal with the Alans was Paulinus able to escape further peril.

When mediation failed, Gallo-Roman potentates had other means of dealing with troubling situations, and of offering protection and security to their dependents. For one thing, the estates of the Gallic magnates either were fortified themselves or had fortlets located nearby.[48] In the late fourth century, Ausonius had spoken of such places on the Moselle, describing the "villas perched on a summit bristling with rocks."[49] And in the fifth century, Sidonius Apollinaris described several of these fortified villas, such as the "fort, protected by the Alpine cliffs," of his friend Elaphius.[50] He also asked his friend Aper, "Do you, perhaps, enjoy a mountain residence in the midst of fortresses, and do you experience some difficulty in the choice of a residential refuge on account of the multitude of fortifications?"[51]

Even within barbarian kingdoms, aristocrats such as Pontius Leontius of Bordeaux and his family continued to maintain themselves in the isolated splendor of such fortified estates. Sidonius described in detail the fortifications of Leontius' villa, named "Burgus."[52] Sidonius even prophesied, "No siege-engine, nor battering ram, no tall structure nor nearby mound, no catapult which launches whizzing boulders, nor even a tortoise, nor mantlet, nor rolling wheel with ladders in place, ever will have the strength to overcome these walls."[53]

The function of such *castella* (forts) was suggested by Salvian, in his reference to those "who, compelled by fear of the enemies, betake themselves to fortlets."[54] These private forts provided a particularly appropriate kind of service: physical protection for one's clients from the dangers of the times, whether from barbarians, Bacaudae and local brigands, or imperial tax collectors.[55]

One estate which served such a purpose was that known as Theopolis ("City of God"), built circa 410 in the Alps between Digne and Sisteron by the former Gallic prefect Claudius Postumus Dardanus, his wife, Naevia Galla, and his brother, a previous governor of Germania Prima, Claudius Lepidus.[56] Their dedicatory inscription proclaimed, "In the place which has the name Theopolis they provided the use of roads, with the sides of the mountains pierced on both sides; they furnished walls and gates, which, established on their own estate, they wished to serve as a common refuge for everyone."[57] Such places of refuge came to be known as *perfugia, refugia, castella,* and *castra.*[58] As will be seen below, they also were provided by ecclesiastical potentates.[59]

RESISTANCE AND INDEPENDENCE

There remains, finally, the problem of the extent to which Gallic traditionalists actively offered military resistance to the barbarians. Some contemporary observers questioned whether it was worthwhile for anyone, even the imperial government, to resist the barbarian invaders at all. The easterner Themistius, for example, in 368 asserted, "Even if we succeeded in doing so, the only ones to notice would be the Syrians, Thracians, and Gauls, and the victory in each case would belong only to the neighboring territory."[60]

In the fifth century, the Roman general Aetius in particular did campaign extensively against the Gallic barbarians, but—except in the case of the Huns—in no instance was any apparent effort made actually to expel the barbarian settlers from Gaul.[61] Many now see the barbarian settlements of the west as a conscious aspect of western imperial policy.[62] And the Gauls too, if their perceptions of the barbarians described above are any indication, seem to have accepted the permanence (if not the acceptability) of the barbarian presence. Trying to expel them, they might have felt, would have made as much sense as trying to expel, say, the Gallic *coloni*.

Indeed, this sentiment may be one reason behind the common assumption that there was little organized popular resistance against the barbarians by the provincials either.[63] And if one defines resistance as large-scale, organized resistance to all barbarian settlements in western Europe, this conjecture would be justified. On the other hand, however, an enumeration of specific examples of resistance suggests that there certainly was occasional opposition to the Germans, but it was of a sort that was consistent with the nature of the times: isolated examples of ad hoc local resistance against particular groups of barbarians for particular reasons.[64]

Any opposition, therefore, seems to have been not against the idea of barbarian settlement per se, but a manifestation of the pursuit of local concerns. If any Gallic localities, cities, or potentates felt that the barbarian settlement was fundamentally inconsistent with local interests, they very often were quite ready to challenge the barbarian presence, just as they likewise would have confronted bandits or brigands. Some Gallo-Roman potentates therefore were more active in the defense of their perquisites; they took their dealings one step beyond serving as intermediaries or providing places of refuge, and actively attempted to oppose barbarian undertakings.[65]

After all, unlike their more timid cousins to the south, the aristocrats of Gaul always had affected something of a military bearing.[66] *The Description of the Entire World and Its Nations*, for example, noted that "the entire area [of Gaul] has men who are courageous and noble in warfare."[67] This warlike spirit may have influenced some of the aforementioned dispossessed landowners at Orléans to resist the settlement of the Alans in the early 440s.[68] In a number of instances, Gallic cities actively resisted barbarian encroachments. In 451, Orléans closed its gates against Attila, and on several occasions the cities of Arles and Narbonne held off the Visigoths.[69] And according to one account, the city of Verdun undertook to revolt against Clovis.[70]

In some cases of resistance, the role of Gallic potentates is more specifically attested. Circa 439, for example, Eparchius Avitus drove off on his own authority a band of Hunnic marauders who may even have been in imperial service at the time.[71] In the early 470s, his son Ecdicius raised a force of cavalry to drive Visigothic raiders away from Clermont. Sidonius wrote to him, "You collected a kind of a public army with private resources, assisted by small contributions from outside potentates."[72] At about the same time, a relative of Sidonius was involved in a scheme to detach Vaison from the Burgundians.[73] And in the early sixth century, a certain Hillidius drove off raiding Burgundians with his personal retainers.[74]

In the north, moreover, some quasi-Roman officials were able to maintain a great deal of independence of action, free from control either by the barbarians or by the imperial government.[75] The master of soldiers Aegidius effectively resisted the barbarian generalissimo Ricimer and his puppet emperor Severus in the early 460s.[76] After his death in 464, his role was assumed by his son, the "rex Romanorum" Syagrius, and he and a certain count Paul, an ally of the Franks who died circa 469, defended areas of Belgica in the neighborhood of Soissons and Angers against sundry barbarians until the defeat of Syagrius by Clovis in 486.[77] Meanwhile, a romanized count Arbogastes administered Trier circa 470.[78] His position vis-à-vis the Roman state and the Franks is unclear, but he did have friendly ties with some of the most influential Gallo-Roman aristocrats.[79]

Some of the most powerful Gallic *potentes*, therefore, used several methods for attempting to continue their traditional lifestyles despite the presence of the barbarians. But as the years went by, it became increasingly difficult for them to do so. In one way or another, even the most influential Gauls had to respond to the ultimate decline and disappearance of Roman imperial authority. They had to come to grips with the fact that the barbarians not only were there to stay but had the upper hand as well. As will be seen, there were several ways in which this could be done.

CHAPTER SIX

FLIGHT AND DISLOCATION, EMIGRANTS AND EXILES

parate exulibus terram, capiendis redemptionem,
viaticum peregrinaturis
(SIDONIUS APOLLINARIS, *EPISTULAE* 7.7.6)

For many Gauls, the barbarian arrival was so traumatic that their method of dealing with it was not to deal with it at all, and to flee.[1] Indeed, the idea of withdrawal from the troubles of the times came to be something of a commonplace, especially in religous circles. Often, merely metaphorical flight—withdrawing from worldly cares and seeking sanctuary in religion—was envisioned.[2] This kind of spiritual escape was recommended by Faustus of Riez, who preached, "I therefore urge each of you men of our time to flee eagerly from these whirlwinds of the world to the house of God."[3] Vincentius of Lérins wrote in 434 of his own personal retreat from the world: "Avoiding the turmoil and crowds of cities, I inhabit a little dwelling on a remote farmstead and within it the retreat of a monastery."[4]

This concept, as expressed in two Gallic poems written during the initial barbarian settlement, offered a psychological escape from the physical sufferings which could result from the barbarian invasions. The anonymous author of *The Poem of a Husband to His Wife*, for example, sought solace in religion, saying, "If I am shut up in a dark prison, and bound in chains, I will turn to God, freed through the release of my spirit. If the executioner prepares to cleave my neck with his sword, he will find me fearless: death is quick, punishment is brief. I do not fear exile; the world as a whole is a home for everyone."[5] And the author of *The Poem on the Providence of God* suggested that the just man "lives as an exile in all parts of the world."[6] For such individuals, "exile" was just a state of mind.

Others, however, favored more dynamic and corporeal forms of exile. This was the course recommended by the Spanish priest Orosius who, in a discussion of the barbarian devastation in Spain, repeated the biblical injunction, "When you are persecuted in one city, flee to another."[7] By this time, moreover, he already had followed his own advice and moved to North Africa.[8] And in the face of what must have been viewed as impending ruin, many other well-to-do individuals also chose to depart, especially from previously peaceful areas unaccustomed to a barbarian presence.[9] Aristocratic flight is attested in the early fifth century, for example, from Spain, Italy, Africa, Britain, and Illyricum.[10]

FLIGHT FROM NORTHERN GAUL

In Gaul, too, it generally has been accepted that there was an accelerated withdrawal by the aristocracy from the Rhine frontier after the transfer of the Praetorian Prefect of Gaul from Trier to Arles circa 395 and the barbarian invasion of 406.[11] The abandonment of the north already has been seen in Symmachus' comment of circa 402, when he asserted, "No one of our order travels to and from the neighborhood of the Rhine."[12] One example of this Italian withdrawal perhaps was Fabius Maianus, the body of whose wife, Valeria Vincentia, was transported from Trier to Pavia for burial at about this time.[13]

Several Gauls also chose to relocate to Italy at the same time, perhaps as a result of the threat or the appearance of the barbarians. The brothers Minervius, Protadius, and Florentinus of Trier, where they probably had been in imperial service before the withdrawal of the prefecture, moved to Italy at the end of the fourth century and held office at Rome.[14] In 407, Eventius, a former governor of Viennensis, died in Rome after moving there, accompanied by his wife Faustina, in hopes of obtaining higher office.[15] And in 442, the Gauls Remus and Arcontia, aged eighteen and fifteen, were buried in Rome; they may have come from northwestern Gaul.[16]

Other aristocrats departed from the north, but remained in central or southern Gaul. Aelianus of Rheims, the son of Paulus, a former provincial governor, was buried at Lyons in the early fifth century.[17] If Paulus too was a native of Rheims, he may be identified with the Paulus of Rheims who became bishop of St.-Paul-Trois-Châteaux at this time.[18] At the end of the fourth century, the Armorican (or Briton) Tolosanus, the son of a proconsul, was buried at Arles.[19] Geminus, a Christian native of Cologne who had served as *rationalis quinque provinciarum* ("Auditor of the Five Provinces"), also was buried there.[20] And a three-year-old Mauricius, probably of Trier, died at Vienne.[21]

Some southern clerics also had a northern origin. During the reign of Magnus Maximus (383–388), Artemius, Maximus' envoy to Spain, stopped and remained at Clermont, where he eventually became bishop.[22] In a like case, bishop Leontius of Trier reportedly sent his deacon Julianus to Benarnum in Novempopulana, where the latter became bishop.[23] At about the same time, bishop Severinus of Cologne was said to have departed to Bordeaux and to have served as bishop there until his death in 402.[24]

The best example of this phenomenon is provided by the monks of Lérins, a monastery founded circa 410 off the coast of southern Gaul.[25] Some of the monks, such as Honoratus, Hilary, Lupus, and Vincentius, had their origin in eastern Lugdunensis.[26] Others, such as Salvian and, it seems, an unnamed relative of his, came from Trier or Cologne, farther to the north.[27] It has been suggested, moreover, that the monastery served as an aristocratic refuge from the barbarian invasions in the north.[28] If so, the perceived threat in some places may have been short-lived, for several of these individuals, such as Lupus of Troyes and Eucherius of Lyons, eventually did return to the north.[29] And Honoratus, the monastery's founder, returned home to visit circa 425, when "he then acknowledged his original homeland, which he once believed had to be shunned."[30] Those who remained in the south—such as the Briton (or Breton) Faustus, eventually bishop of Riez, and Salvian, later a presbyter of Marseille—seem to have come from more outlying areas, and may have had less to go home to.[31]

FLIGHT FROM AQUITANIA

Nor was the north the only area that was vacated. The arrival of the Visigoths in southeastern Gaul in 412 coincided with a large number of departures from that area as well.[32] Even though all such departures, which usually are unexplained, need not have been out-and-out flight from the Goths, they did occur at a time when Gauls in general were tending to avoid foreign travel.[33] It may be, therefore, that the departees had pressing reasons to leave.

Some of the best evidence for departures caused by the arrival of the Visigoths in Aquitania is presented in the poem *De reditu suo (On His Return)* of Rutilius Claudius Namatianus, a Gallic aristocrat who wrote of his journey from Rome to Gaul circa 417. He mentioned, for example, that he left behind at Rome his young relative Palladius, who had come to the city to study law. Palladius was the son of Exsuperantius, a native of Poitiers and Praetorian Prefect of Gaul in 424, and on the grounds of nomenclature he sometimes has been identified with the *vir inlustris* Palladius Rutilius Taurus Aemilianus, the author of an extant *De re rustica (On Rustic Concerns)* who had estates in Italy and Sardinia.[34] If this identification is correct, it may be significant that no mention is made of Gallic estates, perhaps implying that they had been lost and suggesting that the author never returned home.

More conclusive evidence for emigration is provided by Victorinus, a native of Toulouse and a former vicar of Britain, whom Rutilius stopped to visit as he traveled up the Etruscan coast. Rutilius referred to him as "a wanderer, whom the capture of Toulouse compelled to settle in the Tuscan lands and worship foreign gods."[35] And further up the coast, Rutilius stopped to see the aforementioned Protadius. Of him, Rutilius said, "He exchanged his paternal inheritance for middling estates in Umbria: his virtue has made each an equivalent fortune; his unconquered spirit oversees small things in place of great."[36] Protadius, therefore, not only had departed from Gaul but also had accepted a lowered standard of living in order to do so.[37] It is probably no coincidence that both areas where he had Gallic ties, Trier and Aquitania, were the first to be affected by the barbarian settlement.

Later in the century, Sidonius Apollinaris mentioned an unnamed Aquitanian, a poet and native of Cahors, who, circa 430, knew Sidonius' father, became a follower of the imperial generals Boniface and Sebastian, and ultimately surfaced at Athens: "The young man shrank from his Cadurcan birthplace, loving Pandionian Athens more."[38] The youth's education and circle of associates suggest an aristocratic background, and even though Sidonius does not tie his departure to the Visigothic occupation directly, one might suppose that he found the environment of Athens more agreeable than that at home.

The question of emigration was of particular concern to several members of one of the more prominent Aquitanian families, albeit one of rather recent origin, that of the poet, and consul of 379, Decimius Magnus Ausonius.[39] His indecisive grandson, Paulinus of Pella, after being economically ruined, considered leaving the country to escape the barbarians. He declared, "[Their] many repeated hostilities which I, delaying, had often endured convinced me that I must leave my homeland as quickly as possible—to have done so before would have been more useful for me—and that I should seek with an eager step those shores where even now a great part of my maternal inheritance remained intact, scattered about through many cities in Greece, and Old and New Epirus."[40]

Paulinus, then, even though he eventually chose to remain (he blamed his wife's refusal to leave), at least did have other property outside Gaul which gave him the opportunity to depart.[41] And his regret at not having done so was justified by his subsequent fate: he entered what he called "perpetual exile," and referred to himself as a "poverty-stricken exile."[42]

After a stay at Marseilles he finally returned to Bordeaux, where in exchange for relinquishing any claim to his former property he was supported by his relatives.[43] Only Paulinus' daughter was able to escape: "Departing her homeland, she avoided the common ruin."[44]

Evidence for the flight of another family member may be sought in a letter written by Jerome just before 410 to a certain Julianus and carried by Julianus' brother Ausonius, who then was serving in some official capacity, perhaps as a *tribunus et notarius* (Tribune and Notary).[45] Given Ausonius' name, one might suggest that he is to be identified with Censorius Magnus Ausonius, the brother of Paulinus of Pella and the son of Decimius Magnus Ausonius' daughter and the senator Thalassius.[46] Such a suggestion, however, would be the sheerest speculation were it not for an argument of nomenclature: both brothers, Ausonius and Julianus, then would have been named after their and Paulinus' paternal grandfather, Severus Censor Julianus, the father of Thalassius.[47] Either Julianus or Ausonius, moreover, might have been the unnamed brother from whom Paulinus was estranged because of a dispute over property.[48]

Julianus, like Paulinus, had suffered during the barbarian invasions; Jerome wrote to him, "The loss of your family property followed, the devastation of the entire province by a barbarian enemy, and in the midst of the general destruction the personal ruin of your possessions."[49] Now, Jerome also described Julianus as building monasteries and supporting monks on the islands off the coast of Dalmatia, even though he had not entered the religious life himself.[50] Nevertheless, for several reasons Julianus sometimes is assumed to have been a Gaul: the invasions mentioned seem to fit the Gallic ones, particular stress is placed on the example of the Aquitanian Paulinus of Nola, and other letters in this section of Jerome's corpus are addressed to Gauls.[51]

If Julianus was in fact a Gaul, his identification as the brother of Censorius Magnus Ausonius and Paulinus of Pella becomes all the more reasonable, and he would have been yet another Aquitanian aristocrat who fled the devastation in Gaul to foreign estates. Indeed, his activities in Dalmatia—the very area where Paulinus of Pella attests his family had property—not only support the suggestion that the two were related, but also indicate that Julianus accomplished the flight that Paulinus had only contemplated. And if the Ausonius mentioned by Jerome is identified correctly as Censorius Magnus Ausonius, it would indicate that he found his own method for leaving Gaul: by entering the imperial civil service.[52]

A number of other individuals with Aquitanian ties also left Gaul after 406, often for the sake, or on the pretext, of religion. Several went to the Holy Land. The Aquitanian Artemia went to Palestine, as did the Aquitanian cleric Apodemius and an unnamed Narbonese *vir inlustris*.[53] Such

Palestinian pilgrimages may have been encouraged by the new barbarian presence. This certainly was the case with two Spanish clerics—the aforementioned Orosius, and Avitus of Braga—who went to the Holy Land at the same time. Avitus wrote of his inability to return home: "But my desire is impeded by the enemy now dispersed throughout all of Spain."[54]

Other Aquitanians went elsewhere. Vigilantius, a priest of Comminges, chose to go to Spain.[55] Prosper of Aquitaine, after appearing in Marseilles in the late 420s, ultimately settled into a position in the Roman curia by the early 440s.[56] And another Aquitanian who went to Rome was the *calculator* (mathematician) Victorius, who circa 457 was requested by the archdeacon, later bishop, of Rome, Hilarus, to compose a *Paschal Cursus* (a table of the dates for Easter).[57]

It would appear, therefore, that for many Aquitanian aristocrats it was not simply business as usual after the Visigothic arrival and occupation. Many faced some difficult prospects and decisions. A good number of them chose to take foreign employment or to depart for the comparative safety of foreign estates, presuming that they had them—even though, as in the case of Protadius, they might be of inferior quality.

A few other Gallic clerics, from various parts of Gaul, also eventually surfaced in Italy. Some noble Gauls even became Italian bishops. Meropius Pontius Paulinus of Bordeaux (who perhaps does not quite qualify as a "refugee") became bishop of Nola soon after 395.[58] In the mid fifth century, Justinianus, a deposed bishop of Tours, died in exile at Vercelli.[59] In the 460s, the Gaul Bonosus, said to have been "as noble for his sanctity as for his blood," served as a priest at Pavia.[60] And in the 470s, Magnus Felix Ennodius, whose family came from the area of Arles, departed for Italy and circa 514 became a bishop, also at Pavia.[61]

Of course, as with some of the aforementioned refugees, none of these individuals is said to have departed specifically because of the barbarians. Nevertheless, one can suggest that they found the situation in Italy more congenial than that in Gaul. It is at least worthy of note that there are no known examples of Italians making similar moves to Gaul at this time.[62]

In general, however, after the withdrawal from the Rhine, one does not find the evidence for immediate flight from other parts of Gaul to nearly the extent that it is found in Aquitania. It may be that the Aquitanian aristocrats were the first in Gaul to experience life under barbarian rule on a large scale, and they had to learn by trial and error. Some clearly did so better than others. If the Visigothic occupation of Aquitania did not destroy the resident Roman aristocracy, therefore, it nonetheless certainly did give Gallo-Romans a wholly new situation to cope with which occasioned a wholly new set of responses. And if the Aquitanians were not totally successful in dealing with the changed conditions of the fifth century, the lesson they provided was not lost on their aristocratic cousins in central and southern Gaul.

SECONDARY DISLOCATION

The final disappearance of Roman authority from Gaul as of the 460s resulted in a second spate of dislocations of the Roman population. By this time, moreover, it seems that any aristocrats who had the desire and means to depart Gaul altogether already had done so. The relocations which now occurred, therefore, were almost exclusively within Gaul. They sometimes resulted from conflicts among the barbarians, and the resultant adjustments in the territories controlled by each group. In such instances, even if Gauls could not escape the barbarians altogether, they at least could indicate a preference for one group over another.

Two of Sidonius Apollinaris' relatives, the brothers Simplicius and Apollinaris, chose in the 460s to move from their estates near Nîmes to Vaison, and another brother, Thaumastus, moved from his near Narbonne to Vienne. They all apparently preferred the Burgundians to the Visigoths.[63] In 475, Sidonius' brother-in-law Ecdicius, a native of Clermont and the Patrician and Master of Soldiers of Julius Nepos, was recalled to Rome, and some evidence suggests that he and his sons may have remained there, perhaps believing it imprudent to return to an area of Gaul now controlled by the Visigoths.[64] In a case similar to Ecdicius', another Gallic military leader, the count Titus, decided to take his band of *bucellarii* (mercenaries) to serve in Constantinople in the early 460s.[65]

In 475, the Auvergne was ceded to the Goths. Just before the occupation Sidonius, one of the leaders of the resistance, wrote to the bishop of Marseilles, Graecus, about what he thought was the only strategy left and what should be done as a result: "Prepare land for the exiles, redemption for those soon to be taken captive, provisions for those about to travel."[66] Nor were Sidonius' predictions of dislocation as a result of the Visigothic occupation just rhetorical exaggeration, for several of the predicted refugees did appear. Sidonius himself, and a number of bishops, went into exile, not by choice, but on the order of the Visigothic king Euric.[67] An individual who may have departed of his own volition was Injuriosus, a parishioner of Sidonius who during the 470s moved to Langres, which was under Burgundian control.[68]

Another who left Visigothic Aquitania was the count and duke Victorius, who in 479, supposedly fearing for his life because he had been "excessively carnal in his love of women" at Clermont, fled to Rome accompanied by Sidonius' son Apollinaris.[69] Unlike earlier departing aristocrats, these two had no Italian estates. But they did have a more pressing reason for immediate departure: their personal safety. Their stay, however, was not pleasant. After arriving at Rome, Victorius was assassinated, and Apollinaris was first imprisoned and then exiled to Milan, whence he eventually escaped and returned home.[70] Their inauspicious example may have dissuaded others from adopting a similar course.

Northern dislocation, especially of clerics, also continued later in the century, a result of the expansion of the Franks under Childeric and Clovis beginning in the 460s and of the eventual abandonment of their federate status. Not only did bishop Polichronius of Verdun choose to go into exile, perhaps in the 460s or 470s, but so did four of his clerics, the presbyters Francus, Paulus, and Valerianus, and the deacon Sisinnus, who sought refuge with a bishop Castor, apparently of Chartres. In a subsequent letter to Polichronius, who was in exile in a different, unnamed place, they wrote, "We have been compelled by grave necessity to leave our homeland, and the misfortune which has made you an exile from our homeland also has compelled us to go into exile."[71] Polichronius himself ultimately may have become bishop of Chartres: Castor's successor twice removed was another Polychronius.[72]

The Frankish expansion also seems to have brought a new spate of departures from Trier. The aforementioned count Arbogastes of Trier may have sought refuge in the church, curiously enough, also at Chartres, for Castor's successor thrice removed, and the immediate successor of Polychronius of Chartres, was an Arbogastes.[73] All of this might suggest that Chartres remained something of a center for Roman sympathies in the north. As for Iamblichus, bishop of Trier when Arbogastes was count, he too may have withdrawn, for at Chalon-sur-Saône was found a fifth- or sixth-century epitaph of an otherwise unknown bishop Iamlychus.[74]

The aforementioned persons presumably were able to move in some comfort. But others, apparently of more modest means, also made the decision to relocate.[75] One such was the monk Marianus, who is said in a late source to have fled after 450 from Bourges to Auxerre to escape the Goths: "Evading their pollution, he migrated from his home."[76] Another was the deacon who circa 470 abandoned his property in the Visigothic kingdom, became a wanderer (peregrinus), and fled to Auxerre, "avoiding the whirlwind of the Gothic depredation."[77] And Ruricius of Limoges wrote to Aeonius of Arles circa 500 on behalf of the presbyter Possessor and reported, "In order that he not lose his life through a most cruel death, he himself has been made an exile from his homeland."[78]

Individuals like these also could become wanderers as a result of the disruption of their families. Sidonius wrote to Lupus of Troyes circa 470 in support of several travelers seeking a kinswoman who had been kid-naped and sold some years previously by local bandits known as the "Vargi."[79] Shortly thereafter, another such individual, seeking to free his wife, "was tossed about in exile through diverse areas."[80] And Faustus of Riez wrote to Ruricius of Limoges on behalf of the priest Florentinus, who, he wrote, "wanders seeking freedom for his sister."[81] Faustus also wrote, again to Ruricius, in support of his letter-carrier. Of him he said, "He suffered captivity in Lugdunensis . . . and, at least having been set free himself, he is held captive because of the servitude of his wife and children."[82]

As for those of even lesser means, Salvian of Marseilles had his own explanation for why they did not seek refuge elsewhere: "And, indeed, I can only marvel that all dependent and impoverished paupers do not do this together, unless there is only one reason why they do not do so, because they are unable to transfer thence their possessions and little habitations and families."[83] Even the imperial government in 416 rec-ognized officially that some, even if they had the desire, would not have had the opportunity to flee.[84]

In many instances, therefore, Gallo-Romans of diverse social and eco-nomic backgrounds were compelled to uproot themselves because of the barbarian presence. On some occasions they were able to do so more or less at their leisure and in relative security; at other times circumstances were more pressing. In either case, the refugees who remained in Gaul, even after they had settled down once again, still had to reevaluate their circumstances and eventually reach some kind of modus vivendi with the local barbarians.

CHAPTER SEVEN

BETWEEN *ROMANIA* AND *BARBARIA:*
THE BARBARIAN ALTERNATIVE

barbaris paene in conspectu omnium sitis nullus erat metus
hominum, non custodia civitatum
(SALVIAN, *DE GUBERNATIONE DEI* 6.14)

Those Gauls who chose, or were compelled, to remain in Gaul sooner
or later had to reach some kind of accommodation with *barbaria.* The
arrival of the Germans placed some Gauls in a difficult predicament. The
aforementioned law of 416 dealing with the imperial restoration in Gaul
stated, "If, during the barbarian invasion, any acts were done improperly
or spitefully, either because of flight or because of the congregation of
accursed peoples, let them not be summoned before the spitefulness of
an avenging law by the crafty charges of litigants. Let them have impunity
from all accusations . . . Let those who had no opportunity to flee have
impunity from all accusations . . . nor let anything be called a crime which
was done under threat of death."[1] Even the imperial government, then,
recognized that many individuals would have had little choice but to
cooperate with the Germans on whatever terms were available.[2]

Some Gauls, moreover, seem to have done so quite willingly. They
saw in the barbarians not a problem but an opportunity, for they believed
that the barbarians could offer options which the Roman Empire did not.
All the barbarian invaders of Gaul found Gallo-Romans who were willing
to work with them in some manner. In many instances, Gallo-Romans
cooperated with them on an individual or ad hoc basis, and attempted
in various ways to make their own personal peace with the newcomers,
or to gain some personal advantage from them.

Even in the fourth century, some Gauls had found promise in life under
barbarian rule. In 362, the Gallic panegyricist Mamertinus, after lamenting
the destruction caused by the barbarian invasions, went on to say, "Furthermore, other cities, which are some distance away from the barbarian
devastation, fall under the control of nefarious bandits, who claim to be
magistrates. The bodies of the freeborn suffer unworthy tortures; no one
is free from injury, no one is safe from ill treatment, except for those

who mitigate the cruelty of the bandit at a price. The result is that these people now long for the barbarians, and the lot of a captive is preferred to their miseries."[3] This was the state of affairs, Mamertinus suggested, before the emperor Julian (361–363) came to the rescue; the defeat of the Germans was easy, but reform of the administration "was a task full of danger."

In the fifth century, too, it appears that some Gauls, for one reason or another, preferred life with barbarians. Circa 470, for example, Faustus of Riez presented a hypothetical case: "If some legate or bishop, acting as an intercessor for his captured city, pays a great ransom and frees from the grip of captivity his entire people, who were being held by right of conquest, and if all condition and necessity of servitude is altogether removed, and, in the midst of this, if perhaps either the delight of intimacy or a flattering marauder wickedly solicits someone, the slave of his [or her] desire, to refuse the gratuitous favor [of release], does the contempt of the ungrateful one not lessen the favor of the ransom?"[4] Some individuals, therefore, may have sought opportunities with their captors that they had not had before.[5]

The preacher and moralist Salvian of Marseilles, moreover, tendentiously suggested that Romans dissatisfied with Roman rule pursued several means of allying themselves with the barbarians. The poor could adopt an attitude similar to that reported by Mamertinus and Faustus: "Therefore, there is one desire among all the Romans there [in areas under barbarian control]: that there never be any need for them to pass under Roman authority. And there is one common prayer of the Roman plebs there, that they be permitted to lead the life which they live with the barbarians. And should we marvel if the Goths are not defeated by our side, when Romans prefer to live among them rather than among us? Therefore, not only do our brothers positively refuse to flee from them to us, they also leave us in order to flee to them."[6]

This last course of action, Salvian claimed, also was utilized by Gauls who were rather better off. The situation was so bad "that many [Gauls], even those of not obscure birth and liberally educated, flee to the enemy, lest they die by the affliction of public persecution, seeking Roman humanity among the barbarians because they cannot bear the barbarous inhumanity among the Romans . . . They prefer to suffer a worship unlike their own among the barbarians rather than savage injustice among the Romans . . . Therefore, here and there they flee to the Goths or to the Bacaudae or to other barbarians who rule everywhere, nor are they ashamed at their migration; they indeed prefer to live free under the guise of captivity rather than to be captives under the guise of liberty."[7]

And regarding the most elite classes, Salvian asserted, "Many, well-born and noble, to whom Roman status ought to be of the greatest splendor and dignity, are compelled by Roman iniquity and cruelty to wish not to be Roman. And as a result even these who do not flee to the barbarians are compelled nonetheless to be barbarians."[8] It remains to be seen just what Salvian meant by this apparent repudiation of *Romanitas* and adoption of a "barbaric" manner of life. It also remains to be seen just to what extent his testimony can be believed.

In the case of the "plebs," one cannot doubt Salvian's assertions. As seen already, the poor would have had little opportunity to flee anyway, so they perforce would have had to make the best of things.[9] As for flight to the barbarians by the more well-to-do, it would be easy to downplay Salvian's assertions as a preacher's hyperbole were there not at least a few examples which could be analogous to the kind of flight he was discussing.[10] Several instances of generalized flight by city-dwellers are attested, although no indication is given of their destinations. A law of the emperor Majorian issued in 458 discussed the flight of the inhabitants of cities throughout the provinces, "who, because of injuries caused by the tax collectors, seek rural solitudes and habitations."[11] And Sidonius referred to the "departure of the leaders and masses" from Vienne in the 460s.[12]

Specific examples of flight to the barbarians, however, are rare. The Gallic physician Eudoxius, after being implicated in an uprising of the Bacaudae, did flee to the Huns in 448.[13] He, perhaps, would qualify as one of those described by Salvian as being "of not obscure birth and liberally educated."

Meanwhile, the case of another Roman, albeit not a Gaul but a Greek from Viminacum in Moesia, who fled to the Huns also is instructive. His explanation, given to the historian Priscus in 448, for why he had done so has similarities to Salvian's account of the situation in Gaul: "The Romans . . . are in the first place very liable to perish in war . . . But the condition of the subjects in time of peace is far more grievous than the evils of war, for the exaction of taxes is very severe, and unprincipled men inflict injuries on others, because the laws are not imposed equally upon all classes. A transgressor who belongs to the wealthy classes is not punished for his injustice, while a poor man, who does not understand business, undergoes the legal penalty . . . The climax of the misery is to have to pay in order to obtain justice."[14]

As for the aristocrats themselves, even Salvian did not claim that they actually fled to the barbarians. The Moesian's explanation for his own actions perhaps helps to explain why this was the case: the well-to-do often were the cause of any injustices leading to flight, not the recipients of them. There certainly is no extant example of any Gallic aristocrat actually taking refuge with a barbarian group resident in Gaul.[15] In Spain, however, the usurper Maximus (409–411) did take refuge among the barbarians after his defeat.[16]

SOCIAL INTERCOURSE AND FAVOR SEEKING

Gallo-Roman aristocrats did, however, move freely in barbarian circles. In 414, at Narbonne, the deposed emperor Priscus Attalus, as well as the Romans Rusticius and Phoebadius, delivered the *epithalamium* (marriage poem) for the marriage of the Visigothic king Athaulf and the imperial princess Galla Placidia, which took place in the house of the Roman Ingenius.[17] The marriage had occurred "through the enthusiasm and advice" of an otherwise unknown Candidianus, and was carried out "to the great joy of both the barbarians and Romans who were present."[18] At the same time, an anonymous former official of the emperor Theodosius I and confidant of Athaulf spoke with Jerome at Bethlehem circa 414, telling him of Athaulf's aforementioned desire to unify *Gothia* and *Romania*.[19]

Very often, this kind of social interaction involved Gauls who were attendant upon the barbarian kings in pursuit of some favor or other. Such persons probably led to a complaint by Paulinus of Pella: "I observe that many are flourishing through the favor of the Goths."[20] And examples of those who did so abound. In the late 460s, the aristocrat Evodius, having been summoned to Toulouse "at the order of the king," attempted to influence the Visigothic king Euric by presenting an engraved silver bowl to queen Ragnahilda: he was described by Sidonius as her "client."[21] Another Gallo-Roman who found favor with Euric was the rhetor Lampridius, who in the mid 470s was able to recover his lost estates.[22]

Some Gauls were very adept at playing both sides of the fence. Sidonius Apollinaris, for example, although he could readily repeat the conventional derogations of barbarians, also could praise them and work with them as the need arose. In the 460s he frequented the court of Theoderic II (453–466), and he went so far as to write a lengthy letter to his brother-in-law Agricola praising the personal habits of the king.[23] Elsewhere, he described Theoderic as the "support and security of the Roman people."[24] Sidonius also described his method for obtaining from Theoderic any requests he may have had: "When I wish to obtain some favor, I achieve a favorable result when I lose at the dice table in order to win my case."[25] Sidonius likewise fulsomely praised the next king Euric when he desired another favor—in this case the lifting of his own sentence of exile.[26]

As for the Burgundians, Sidonius could praise their king as well when it suited his purpose. On one occasion, he compared king Chilperic and his wife to Germanicus and Agrippina.[27] The king himself likewise complimented Roman potentates: bishop Eucherius of Lyons reportedly was praised "by Chilperic for his feasts and by his wife for his fasts."[28]

Of course, those who sought favors from the Germans were not always successful. Not only did the aforementioned Paulinus of Pella suffer misfortune at the hands of the Goths, but his son, who sought the favor of the Visigothic king in the 450s, was equally unsuccessful: "Finally, even he himself, who remained as our solace, having experienced at the same time, through unfortunate action and result, both the friendship and anger of the king, lost nearly all my property in a like fate."[29]

BARBARIAN PATRONAGE AND PERSONAL PROFIT

Aristocrats who played their cards right were able to survive the storm, or even to profit, during the barbarian occupation. As already seen, some landowners were able to preserve part of their holdings by sharing the rest with the barbarians.[30] These distributions usually were carried out on a large scale, at the instigation of the Roman government. But in some instances, Gallic landowners appear to have done so on their own initiative.[31] Circa 414, for example, Paulinus of Pella detached the Alans from the Visigoths besieging Bazas, apparently by promising them grants of land.[32] And in 456, the Burgundians were said to have "occupied part of Gaul and divided the lands with the Gallic senators."[33]

Nor was the opportunity to retain part of one's property the only potential benefit from such an arrangement. A late source, for example, suggested that the Romans undertook the aforementioned division with the Burgundians "so they could renounce their imperial taxes."[34] And some Gallo-Romans even seem to have used disruptions caused by the barbarian occupation as a cover for expanding their landholdings. Paulinus of Pella, for example, complained that the dispersal of his inherited property was a result not only of barbarian rapine, but also "of the mistreatment of Romans, who, contrary to all legality, in the midst of barbarian rapine by right of war, boldly plotted at my loss on different occasions."[35] These Roman opportunists, to add insult to injury, even included some of Paulinus' own relatives.

The law code of Euric, dating to the 470s, described another sharp practice used by some Romans. It seems that Roman landowners were turning over to Goths property which currently was in litigation, presumably in lieu of turning over their own property. Such property was to be restored to the original claimant, and the Roman was to provide property to which he had a clear title.[36]

Romans also could obtain personal security from the barbarians. Another of Paulinus' complaints, of circa 414, concerned Goths who shared Gallic estates: "For we know that certain of the Goths strove with the greatest humanity to do good for the hosts whom they were protecting."[37] The source of Paulinus' discontent, apparently, lay not in the practice itself, but in his own failure to benefit from it. And in Spain, at the same time, Orosius spoke of travelers who "used barbarians as servants, attendants, and defenders."[38]

From the very beginning of the barbarian occupation of Gaul, therefore, some Romans profited from barbarian patronage.[39] Indeed, this practice became so endemic that it eventually had to be forbidden more than once in barbarian law codes. A section of the Burgundian Code, for example, entitled "Of the Abolition of the Assistance (patrocinium) of Barbarians in Lawsuits Involving Romans" and dating to the early sixth century at the latest, stated, "Whenever a Roman hands over a case which he has with another Roman to be transacted by a Burgundian as advocate, let him lose the case."[40]

Such prohibitions, however, apparently had little effect. Another section of the same law code mandated, "Inasmuch as it has been established under certain penalty that no barbarian should dare to involve himself in a suit which a Roman has brought against another Roman, we advocate a stricter handling of these cases, and command that the law remain just as we established it in earlier times."[41] All of this indicates that the law still was not being either obeyed or enforced, and that some Romans continued to find it to their advantage to seek barbarian patronage in the pursuit of their lawsuits.

The same law also indicated what some of these lawsuits concerned, for it went on to say, "As often as cases arise between two Romans concerning the boundaries of fields which are possessed by barbarians through the law of hospitality, let the guests of the contestants not be involved in the quarrel . . . and the guest of the victor shall have a share of the property obtained as a result of his success." With so much to gain, one might doubt whether the guests of the Romans concerned would stand idly by while the case was being adjudicated.

The unfortunate Paulinus would have been a ready target for Roman opportunists such as these, and it may be they whom Salvian had in mind when he spoke of noble Romans who chose to "be barbarians." In these times of transition, it would seem, many faced a sink-or-swim situation, and it was the incapable, the unimaginative, and the lethargic who often bore the brunt of the economic loss.

Barbarian patronage also could be sought on a wider scale. In several instances, the disgruntled losers in episcopal elections appealed for help not to the Roman authorities, but to the barbarians.[42] In one instance, pope Hilarus wrote to Leontius of Arles on 3 November 462 about the supposedly irregular ordination of Hermes, the bishop of Narbonne.[43] Hilarus had only learned of the incident, he said, "From the deacon John, who was recommended to us by our son, the magnificent man Fridericus, in his letter."[44] Now, this Fridericus, the so-called "son" of Hilarus of Rome, can be none other than the Arian brother of the Visigothic king Theoderic II.[45] Such unprecedented Germanic intervention would have followed immediately upon the cession of the city to the Visigoths in that very year.[46] The Gothic presence offered the losers in the Narbonese disputes a new stratagem: now they could appeal not only to Rome, but also to the barbarians.

Nor would Fridericus have been loathe to lend his support, for Hermes, it seems, was involved with the established Gallo-Roman, and anti-German, aristocracy of Narbonne.[47] In his description of the literary circle of Narbonne, Sidonius included Hermes along with such aristocrats as Magnus, who had been the emperor Avitus' Master of Offices and Majorian's Gallic prefect, and Avitus' *cura palatii* (Caretaker of the Palace) Consentius.[48] Hermes hardly could escape being labeled a Roman sympathizer. This could have made him persona non grata with the Visigoths. In this instance, however, neither Fridericus nor Hilarus could take any effective action. Fridericus soon was dead, and Hilarus, lacking influential Gallo-Roman support, could do nothing more than accept the fait accompli.[49]

A similar appeal to the barbarians occurred in a case involving ecclesiastical jurisdiction in Viennensis. In a letter dated 10 October 463 and addressed, again, to Leontius of Arles, Hilarus complained about the ordination by Mamertus of Vienne of a new bishop, Marcellus, for the city of Die. The source of the complaint was from a rather unorthodox quarter: "Indeed, it has been pointed out by the report of my son, the illustrious master of soldiers Gundioc, how the aforementioned bishop [sc. Mamertus], against the will of the inhabitants of Die . . . occupying the city, so it is said, in a hostile manner, presumed to ordain the bishop."[50]

Once again, the bishop of Rome's involvement had been motivated by the report of a barbarian potentate. Die, like Narbonne, had but recently fallen to the Germans.[51] Unlike the Visigoth Fridericus at Narbonne, however, the new Burgundian ruler of Die was not only a barbarian king, but also a legitimate Roman official, a master of soldiers.[52] His ambiguous position could have made the local networks of loyalty, patronage, and authority even more confused at Die than they had been at Narbonne.

After their candidate lost to Marcellus, disaffected locals at Die may have found in this situation an opportunity for an appeal, and Gundioc, like Fridericus, would have been happy to lend them his support.[53] Barbarians, therefore, now had come to serve the same role as Gallo-Roman potentates: they provided a source of patronage, to which appeals could be made by disaffected Gauls.

INFORMERS

Some Gauls went even further in their pursuit of barbarian patronage. They sought to gain favors or influence by denouncing their compatriots to the Germans.[54] Of course, these informers, or *delatores*, were nothing new, and long had struck fear into the hearts of Roman aristocrats.[55] The fifth century was no exception. In 438, for example, after the Theodosian Code had been received at Rome, the senate addressed fervent appeals to the emperors as "the eradicators of informers, the eradicators of false accusations."[56]

The emperor Majorian was especially attentive to such concerns. In 457, immediately after his accession, he made the reassuring, albeit conventional, pledge, "Let no one fear denunciations."[57] Shortly thereafter, in 461, Sidonius Apollinaris encountered such an accusation, when he was anonymously accused of having authored some scurrilous satire. When questioned about it by Majorian himself, Sidonius responded, "Whoever that [informer] is, lord emperor, let him make his charge publicly."[58] And true to his inaugural promise, Majorian let the matter drop when Sidonius' accuser, his nemesis Paeonius, declined to speak out publicly.[59]

On other occasions too, Gallo-Roman aristocrats were sensitive to the possible presence of informers. Sidonius, for example, in his account of a gathering of nobles in Burgundian Lyons circa 468, told why it was particularly pleasant: "Because there blessedly was no mention of officials or taxes, nothing said which could be betrayed and no individual who would betray."[60] At about the same time, Sidonius condemned *delatores* in a set piece, addressed to his son, on the kinds of persons to avoid. He described such a one as "a maelstrom created from the inventors of rumors, from the creators of accusations, and from the repeaters of unpleasant opinions," and as a "supporter in good times and a betrayer in bad."[61] Indeed, in Sidonius' opinion even the barbarians were preferable to the despicable informers, about whom he declared, "They are certainly the ones . . . whom Gaul grieves she has long endured amid the more compassionate barbarians."[62]

These general perceptions are confirmed by specific examples of *delatores* who sought the favor of the Germans. According to one tradition, the bishop Orientius of Auch interceded with the Visigoths circa 439 when "a most nobly born individual, from Spain and rich in property, incurred the envy of a most wicked accuser."[63] In this instance, the saint was able to preserve the Spaniard's life only at the cost of the confiscation of his property. Circa 468, the abbot Lupicinus of St. Claude was accused before the Burgundian king Chilperic, perhaps by a Gallo-Roman, of having made false predictions of doom.[64] And Sidonius not only condemned the false accusations supposedly made by Seronatus, a Gallo-Roman collaborator with the Visigoths circa 470, he also suggested that such accusations made Seronatus little more than a barbarian: "He accuses falsely, just like a barbarian."[65]

Meanwhile, Sidonius' own wariness of informers would have been compounded by another case involving his family. In 475, he wrote to his cousin Apollinaris that he was worried "lest military knavery or a barbarian uproar concoct any false accusations against [him]."[66] Apollinaris' brother Thaumastus, he said, "confirms that [accusations were] whispered secretly to . . . the most victorious Chilperic in the poisoned tale of certain villains."[67] Sidonius rhetorically described these villains as "those . . . whom Gaul grieves that it suffers in the midst of the more merciful barbarians . . . They are those whom even those who are feared fear, they are those whom this kind of activity in particular occupies: to level false accusations, to betray individuals, to apply threats, and to snatch property."[68]

Sidonius promised to intercede on his cousin's behalf, and later reported that Apollinaris had been spared through the intercession of Chilperic's wife, who "enlightened the ears of her husband, which had been stuffed with the slimy filth of whisperings."[69] He also confided, "We finally have tracked down those who made the accusation . . . if in fact the circuitous trail of the informers has not misled the reliability of our comrades."[70] In this instance, Sidonius, not surprisingly, condemned the activities of the informers, at least some of whom presumably were of aristocratic origin. This is not to say, of course, that Sidonius and his own comrades did not circulate whisperings of their own, and make their own attempts to secure the favor of barbarian kings.

Overall, then, the relations between the Roman and barbarian populations were not always adversarial, and could even be positively amicable. Some Romans saw in the barbarians little to fear. As Salvian noted in another context, "With the barbarians situated nearly within sight of all, there was neither fear by the population nor defense of the cities."[71]

At the very time that some influential aristocrats were attempting to preserve as much of their old lifestyle as they could, many of these same individuals also were gradually—if reluctantly—coming to grips with the reality of the barbarian occupation. Still other Gauls embraced the barbarians more enthusiastically. Accommodations would have to be made. Some Gauls did so more easily than others.

CHAPTER EIGHT

CONFLICTING LOYALTIES: COLLABORATORS, TRAITORS, AND THE BETRAYAL OF TERRITORY

multis ficta fides, multis periuria, multis
causa fuit mortis civica proditio
(ORIENTIUS, *COMMONITORIUM* 2.173–174)

Sometimes cooperation with the barbarians went beyond currying favor and informing. The changing political situation of fifth-century Gaul caused additional difficulties for many Gallo-Romans. As the authority of one barbarian group or another, or that of the imperial government as well, ebbed and flowed back and forth over Gaul, it often became necessary for influential Gauls to choose sides. Some Gallic officials, whether local, imperial, or ecclesiastical, chose to collaborate with the barbarians in military and political matters. A wrong choice of sides could put one in a very precarious position.

RENDERING AID AND ASSISTANCE: THE BETRAYAL OF CITIES

Throughout the empire, collaboration with the barbarians sometimes involved the provision of direct assistance to them in some form or other. In Spain, for example, the actions of Roman *proditores* (betrayers) led to the destruction of the emperor Majorian's fleet in 460.[1] In Gaul, too, Romans often became involved in schemes detrimental to the best interests of the Roman state. Many such cases of collaboration involved the political control of Gallic cities.

On a number of occasions, cities were betrayed to one barbarian group or another. A rather garbled incident reported by Fredegarius involves the betrayal of Trier to the Franks. In the context of the years circa 410, he reported that "the city of Trier was captured and burned [through the efforts] of the faction of one of the senators, Lucius by name."[2] The pretext for this betrayal supposedly had been the seduction of Lucius' wife by the emperor Avitus (455–456), although Fredegarius' chronology suggests that he may have confused Avitus with the Gallic usurper Jovinus (411–413).

An equally muddled account describes an abortive betrayal of the city of Angoulème to the besieging Vandals, perhaps circa 407/408.[3] In this case, the bishop Ausonius, after the siege supposedly had continued for seven and a half years, was said to have been directed by an angel of the Lord to send to the Vandal king several of his clerics, "who were to announce that the city would be betrayed to him." Ausonius then reportedly met the barbarians at the gate and was killed, whereupon the Vandals then fell upon each other. This curious report may in fact have been intended to whitewash the bishop's role in some kind of dealings with the besiegers. Both of these incidents, even if their details remain in doubt, illustrate the powerful effect that such betrayals had upon the popular imagination.

Other such incidents are more securely attested. In 451, the city of Orléans resisted the attacks of the Huns. But fear that the city would be betrayed, in this instance by barbarian federates, arose, "For Sangibanus, the king of the Alans, terrified by fear of the future, promised to surrender himself to Attila and to betray into his power the Gallic city of Orléans, where he then was stationed."[4] He was prevented from doing so only by the timely arrival of the Roman general Aetius and his allies.[5]

Barbarian attacks on cities also could serve as a cover for, or be related to, other kinds of disreputable activity. Paulinus of Pella related how, circa 414, Bazas was beset both by barbarian attack and by "a servile faction mixed with the insane fury of a few young, and even freeborn, men, which was armed in particular for the slaughter of the nobility."[6] Paulinus himself barely escaped assassination.[7] And Sidonius Apollinaris told of the civic dissension which arose in Clermont in the early 470s when the city was being besieged by the Visigoths; apparently, some of the citizens were not as commited to the resistance as he was.[8] Different loyalties and allegiances could result in friends being on opposing sides in such campaigns. The Aquitanian Calminius, for example, served in the Visigothic army besieging Clermont; Sidonius purported to believe that his friend had been compelled to do so.[9]

In at least one case, moreover, a Gallic city, Bordeaux, did open its gates willingly to the barbarians. Paulinus of Pella noted that circa 414, Athaulf and the Goths, "who had been admitted in peace," burned the city when they left it, acting "in no other manner toward us than toward those defeated by right of conquest."[10] This treatment may have encouraged many other Gallic cities—Arles, Orléans, Lyons, Narbonne, and

Clermont, to name a few—to close their gates to the Germans later in the century.

The betrayal of cities to the Germans tended to be frowned upon by the Gallo-Roman population. Circa 416, Orientius of Auch lamented, "Fictive faith, perjury, and civic betrayal were the cause of death for many."[11] And the problems at Orléans and elsewhere may have helped lead to a decree, in 453 by a church council held at Angers, that stated, "If anyone is apprehended having been involved in the betrayal or capture of cities, let him not only be excluded from communion, let him also be excluded from dinner parties."[12] A weighty sentence indeed.

Not all such cases involved the betrayal of Roman cities to the Germans. In at least one instance, the opposite was the case. The aforementioned denunciation of Sidonius' relative Apollinaris in 475 involved the charge, according to Sidonius, "That through [his] scheming in particular the city of Vaison was being attached to the side of the new emperor [Julius Nepos]."[13] Sidonius' account of this incident illustrates the intrigue that went on in Gaul as the Germans, intermittently and in no organized fashion, gradually expanded their influence at the expense of the imperial government. Roman aristocrats must have been hard-pressed to decide where they should place their loyalties. For many, the ultimate decline of Roman authority was by no means a foregone conclusion. In the case of Apollinaris, there can be little doubt that he did in fact plot to turn Vaison back over to the imperial government, and that he was caught in the act. Only Sidonius' intervention on his behalf saved him from retribution.

Nor did such plotting only pit the barbarians against the empire. In many cases, especially later in the century, Gauls, and in particular bishops, became involved in schemes to transfer a city from the authority of one barbarian group to another. They too faced reprisals. One such case, in the late 470s, concerned Aprunculus, bishop of Langres. Gregory of Tours reported that "when the fear of the Franks was resounding in this region, and all were wishing them to rule with longing desire, the blessed Aprunculus, bishop of the city of Langres, began to be held suspect by the Burgundians, and as this hatred grew from day to day, it was ordered that he secretly be cut down."[14] Aprunculus saved himself by slipping out of Dijon at night and making his way to Clermont, where he eventually succeeded Sidonius as bishop.

Similar accusations confronted Gallo-Roman bishops in the Visigothic kingdom. Volusianus, bishop of Tours, ran into trouble circa 498, as also reported by Gregory of Tours: "Having been considered suspect by the Goths because he wished to subject himself to the rule of the Franks and having been condemned to exile in the city of Toulouse, he died there."[15] Volusianus' successor Verus suffered the same fate: "And he, because of his enthusiasm for the same cause, was considered suspect by the Goths, and having been carried off into exile, he died."[16]

At the same time, Quintianus, bishop of Rodez, already exiled from Africa, was faced with both civic dissension and accusations of treachery. Of this case, Gregory reported that "after a quarrel had arisen between the citizens and the bishop, a suspicion came to the Goths who then were stationed in [Rodez] that the bishop wished to subject himself to the rule of the Franks, and having considered the matter, they decided to run him through with a sword."[17] But Quintianus, apprised of this plot, emulated Aprunculus and fled the city at night. He, too, was received at Clermont and ultimately became bishop of the city. In this case, it would appear that Quintianus' rivals at Rodez had informed on him to the Goths, on real or trumped-up charges, and thus secured the removal of their opponent.

In the south, accusations of similar treachery involving Caesarius of Arles were made to the Visigoths circa 505 by Licinianus, one of his own notaries, whom Caesarius' biographers compared to Judas. According to their report, "Fortified by the venom of a most savage accusation, [Licinianus] suggested to King Alaric through members of the court that the most blessed Caesarius, because he was a native of Gaul, desired with all his might to subjugate the territory and city of Arles to the authority of the Burgundians."[18] As a result, Caesarius was summoned to Bordeaux, "as if he had been sent into exile." Subsequently, Caesarius seems to have cooperated with the Visigothic king.[19]

Nor was that the end of Caesarius' difficulties. After the defeat of the Visigoths by the Franks at Vouillé in 507, Arles fell into the hands of the Ostrogoths of Italy. In 508, the city was besieged by an army of Franks and Burgundians. Once again, Caesarius was implicated in a plot to betray the city. On this occasion, "One of the clerics, a fellow-townsman and relative of [Caesarius], terrified by his fear of captivity and influenced by juvenile frivolity, let himself down from the wall by a cord at night, and most wickedly offered [to turn the city over] to the besieging enemies on the next day."[20] Caesarius, consequently, was briefly imprisoned in the city. Regardless of his biographers' attempts to downplay Caesarius' role in this failed betrayal—they also tried to affix blame on the Jews—there can be little doubt that Caesarius was involved in the plot.

Around 513, moreover, after Caesarius had been implicated in yet another plot, or, as his biographers said, "When another accusation had been concocted," he was taken under guard to Ravenna to explain himself to the Ostrogothic king Theoderic.[21] He eventually was allowed to return to Arles, where he seems studiously to have avoided such activities in the future.

It would appear, therefore, that bishops, as the leading figures in most Gallic localities, were particularly susceptible to involvement in the continuing jockeying for the possession of territory.[22] The kingdoms may have been different, but the undertakings were the same. In some instances, if the sources can be believed, bishops came very close to assassination, although there is no attested case of one actually being killed. In many instances they also were remarkably adept at landing on their feet. Some were able to refute or otherwise neutralize even multiple accusations. Others, after being expelled from one see, succeeded in obtaining another. These would appear to have been individuals who were very much in touch with their times.

THE ROLE OF ROMAN OFFICIALS

Similar uncertainties over where their true loyalties lay must have been felt by Roman imperial officials in Gaul, whose dual roles as imperial officials and local magnates must have caused conflicts of interest. It would have become increasingly difficult for them to carry out their duties without running afoul of either the imperial government or the local barbarian king. Nor would this have been a trivial problem, for there are indications that the Roman administrative structure continued to exist well into the fifth century, even in areas supposedly controlled by the barbarians. The law which reestablished the yearly meetings of the "Council of the Seven Provinces" in 418 presumed that Roman officials would continue to serve in the territory occupied by the Visigoths, noting, "So that with regard to Novempopulana and Aquitania Secunda, which provinces are located further away, if a fixed duty occupies their governors, let them know that legates must be sent according to custom."[23] Thus, even if the Roman government continued to claim some kind of administrative authority in these areas, the realization existed that there might be difficulties when it came to these officials actually attending the meetings of the council.[24] Nor is there any evidence that any of them ever did.

There is additional evidence, however, that the Roman administrative structure persisted quite late in far-flung areas of Gaul, some of them under barbarian control.[25] In the north, Salvian indicated that municipal administration continued at Trier.[26] And in the 420s, or later, a *princeps praesidalis* is attested as collecting taxes in Lugdunensis Quarta; he was the senior bureaucrat attached to the staff of the *praeses* (governor) of the province.[27]

Even later, several suggestive church canons were issued in western Lugdunensis. In 453, the Council of Angers legislated against clerics who, "having left the clergy, return to secular service and to the laity."[28] Apparently, however, the decree did not have sufficient effect, for eight years later the Council of Tours decreed that clerics, who, "having abandoned their rank of office, wish to live the life of a layman or to turn themselves over to state service," were to be excommunicated.[29] Presumably, there not only must have been state offices available for these erstwhile clerics, but there also must have been a good number of clerics who were filling them. The continued functioning of state institutions in this area also is suggested by Sidonius' report circa 470 that the relatives of a kidnaped woman were preparing a "criminal proceeding" at Troyes against those involved.[30] The appropriate legal machinery must still have existed.

As late as 469 there also seems still to have been a *praeses* of Aquitania Prima, Evantius, who was responsible for maintaining the road between Toulouse, the Visigothic capital, and Clermont.[31] To whom, one might ask, did he report? It also has been seen above that even in the 470s there was a resident Count of Trier, although it also is unclear to whom, if anyone, he was responsible.[32] The Frank Clovis, too, may have retained the Roman provincial organization in the Belgic provinces which he conquered in the mid 480s.[33]

The position of Roman officials in territory under the de facto, or de jure, control of the barbarians would have been precarious. Presumably, any Roman officials stationed in such areas would have worked under the eye, and even with the approval, of the local barbarian kings. This situation very easily could have caused conflicts of interest. Sidonius, for example, in 475 praised the Quaestor of the Sacred Palace, Licinianus, because he was not one of those "who, offering for sale the secrets of the emperors who sent them, solicit good treatment from the barbarians."[34]

In several instances, Roman officials, legitimate or otherwise, attempted to use barbarian support against the interests of the Roman state. In 411, the defeated proponents of the usurper Constantine III joined the Gallic aristocrat Jovinus in making common cause with the Burgundians of Gundahar and the Alans of Goar on the Rhine river.[35] Subsequently, Jovinus failed to gain the support of the Visigoths and was defeated and executed.[36]

Conversely, Visigoths on occasion collaborated with influential Romans in attempts to establish quasi-Roman governments. In 414, the Gothic chieftan Athaulf married the imperial princess Galla Placidia at Narbonne. His puppet, Priscus Attalus, then again was proclaimed emperor and it even seems that a *comitatus* (court) based on the Roman model was established; Paulinus of Pella, for example, was made Attalus-cum-Athaulf's *comes privatarum largitionum* ("Count of the Private Largesses").[37] Attalus soon was deposed, and this experiment came to nought.

Another Gallic aristocrat, the Arvernian Eparchius Avitus, was more successful in working with the Goths. In 455, he was appointed master of soldiers, and in this capacity he became a participant in another Gothic effort at emperor making. With their support, as well as that of the Burgundians and even the Franks, he was able to have himself declared Roman emperor.[38] Sidonius, for example, had Avitus say, "I once was accustomed to manage the affairs of the Goths."[39] Sidonius also gave his own version of the secret of empire, saying that Avitus realized "that he could not conceal from the Gauls the fact that with him as emperor, the Goths would submit."[40]

This attempt at a Romano-Gothic rapprochement was rather more effective than that of Attalus. Its success, based on the comforting perception of the barbarians as Roman supporters, may demonstrate a new stage of Gothic acceptability and legitimacy in the minds of at least some Gallo-Romans.[41] Avitus, meanwhile, quickly advanced into Italy, was recognized at Rome, and, like any new emperor, assumed the consulate there, on 1 January 456. His grasp at power, however, was short-lived, and in October of 456 he was defeated by the imperial generals Ricimer and Majorian and forcibly consecrated bishop of Piacenza.[42]

TRAITORS, PATRIOTS, OR OPPORTUNISTS?

Other Roman officials, whose purview included territory in barbarian control, had difficulty navigating the perilous waters between the barbarians and the Roman state, and were accused of attempting to betray Roman territory to the barbarians. In the late 450s, for example, the Gallic count Agrippinus was accused by the Gallic general Aegidius, who asserted "that [Agrippinus], jealous of Roman rule, undoubtedly favored the barbarians and was attempting with clandestine plotting to detach provinces from Roman rule."[43] The barbarians, in this case, would seem to have been the Burgundians.[44]

Similar charges were leveled against other imperial officials. In 468, the Gallic prefect Arvandus was apprehended in treasonous dealings with the Visigothic king: "[Arvandus'] letters seemed to have been sent to the king of the Goths, advising him against peace with the Greek emperor [sc. Anthemius] . . . [and] suggesting that Gaul ought to be divided with the Burgundians according to the law of nations, and additional insanities approximately in this vein."[45] And in yet another case, in the early 470s,

Seronatus, who may have been Vicar of the Seven Provinces, was accused of "offering provinces to the barbarians."[46]

In the first two of these cases, at least, the charges seem to have caused some soul-searching among influential friends of the suspects back in Gaul. The accused were not universally condemned. With regard to Agrippinus, some Gauls disagreed with Aegidius; the abbot Lupicinus of St. Claude, for example, agreed to act as *fideiussor* (surety) for him.[47] Then, after Agrippinus had been imprisoned in Italy, Lupicinus supposedly appeared to him in a vision, counseled him to have faith, and showed him a way out of his cell. Nor did the accusation against Agrippinus bear fruit. He eventually was found innocent, and allowed to return "loaded with honors" to Gaul, where he later served as a partisan of Ricimer: in 462, he was the agent of the Italian administration for the cession of Narbonne to the Visigoths.[48]

The case of Arvandus was even more controversial. The aforementioned letters clearly proved his guilt. Even so, however, some of his Gallic friends, including Sidonius and the Arvernian Auxanius, stood by him. According to Sidonius, "We thought that it would be perfidious, barbarous, and shameful to abandon our friendship with Arvandus, regardless of how we had strayed into it, while he was in the midst of difficulties."[49] Sidonius even advised Arvandus on how to conduct his defense.[50] Even after he was convicted and sentenced to death, his friends continued to work on his behalf. Eventually, it seems, their efforts were rewarded, for his sentence was commuted to exile.[51]

An evaluation of Arvandus' case is complicated, moreover, by an additional report that he also was accused of desiring to usurp the throne.[52] If so, he may have been attempting to resurrect, à la Attalus and Avitus, the concept of imperial authority supported by a Romano-Gothic power base. Unlike Avitus, however, he was unsuccessful, and went down in history as a traitor rather than as a short-lived emperor.[53]

Seronatus, however, was a different story. There is no evidence that his case aroused any sympathy at all. Sidonius was especially vitriolic in his condemnation, referring to him as "the very Catiline of our age."[54] Elsewhere, Sidonius described his maladministration in great detail: his mistreatment of prisoners, his excessive taxation, his false accusations, and his general venality.[55] Seronatus not only was sentenced to death but was actually executed, even if, as Sidonius claims, the state barely had the courage to carry out the sentence.[56]

Examples such as these indicate that during the transition from Roman to barbarian rule, Gallo-Romans, and imperial officials in particular, could be placed in the difficult position of having to serve two masters. Those who identified their interests too closely with the Germans could run risks ranging from social ostracism to execution. Even if the imperial government predictably condemned such dealings, the perceptions of the Gauls themselves were mixed. In many cases, it would appear that Gallic responses were determined not by policy but by personality. Aegidius' accusation against Agrippinus seems to have been motivated by personal animus as much as anything else. And Sidonius nowhere condemned Arvandus for his treason, if it was in fact that, but only for the naïveté of his defense. Conversely, Sidonius' primary grievance against Seronatus concerned the latter's treatment of the Gallo-Roman population and his bad habits, not his relations with the Visigoths. All of this could lead one to suspect that by the 460s dealings of this nature with the Germans were not unusual. The most important considerations for aristocrats who engaged in such activities were to be reasonably circumspect, not to get caught, and to have the right friends if they were.

The preceding chapters have indicated that Gallo-Roman aristocrats often found themselves in difficult circumstances during the fifth century. Their economic condition often was reduced. There were fewer opportunities for conventional imperial office holding. There was occasional interference in church operations. Normal aristocratic social intercourse was hindered. Gallo-Romans often were dragged into the conflicts between the Roman state and the barbarians, or between one barbarian group and another. Often, Gallo-Romans could not even trust each other. What strategies could these aristocrats adopt to preserve as much of their status and authority as possible?

PART THREE

COMING TO TERMS
WITH THE BARBARIANS:
THE RESTRUCTURING OF THE
GALLO-ROMAN ARISTOCRACY

CHAPTER NINE

THE ACQUISITION OF CHURCH OFFICE AND THE RISE OF AN ECCLESIASTICAL ARISTOCRACY

absque conflictatione praestantior secundum bonorum
sententiam computatur honorato maximo minimus religiosus
(SIDONIUS APOLLINARIS, *EPISTULAE* 7.12.4)

In the early 470s, as he gloomily despaired of the imperial fortunes, Sidonius Apollinaris described to his brother-in-law Ecdicius two strategies for dealing with the difficulties of the times: "If there is no strength in the republic, no assistance, and if, as the rumor goes, the emperor Anthemius has no power, our nobility has decided, with you as our leader, to give up either its homeland or its hair."[1] One of these alternatives, flight from the threatened area, was discussed in an earlier chapter. The other involved another kind of flight: the possibility of receiving the tonsure and seeking refuge in church office.[2]

If entering ecclesiastical office now could be presented as the only alternative to leaving the country, one can imagine the importance it must have assumed as an aristocratic occupation, and the desirability it must have had. Just why, one might ask, was Sidonius so specific about church office as a viable option?

THE REEVALUATION OF ARISTOCRATIC STATUS IN LATE ROMAN GAUL

The changed conditions of the fifth century forced a response from Gallo-Roman aristocrats at a very rudimentary level. Those who remained found themselves compelled to reevaluate the very criteria upon which their aristocratic status was to be based. Earlier aristocratic attributes, such as wealth, property, and imperial office were no longer available to all individuals who otherwise would qualify as aristocrats on the basis of other criteria, such as noble birth. Substitutes had to be found.

Some aristocrats, for example, may have placed an even increased stress on wealth as an aristocratic attribute at the same time that they down-played the significance of imperial office holding and concentrated on local interests.[3] The great importance of wealth as a criterion of aristocracy was certainly recognized by Salvian of Marseilles. According to him, "Either the nobles and the rich are the same people, or if there are any rich aside from the nobles, they themselves nevertheless act like nobles . . . with the result that no one is considered to be more noble than the one who is excessively rich."[4] The rich, however, always had had an air of nobility. Other factors indicate more clearly how the criteria of ar-istocracy were undergoing change in fifth-century Gaul.

THE "VERA ET INTEGRA NOBILITAS"

One way in which aristocratic status now came to be reassessed was through the increasing value assigned by aristocrats to the adoption of the religious life. Of course, ever since the time of Constantine, high-ranking ecclesiastics had been appropriating the perquisites of aristocratic status throughout the empire.[5] Religious, clerical, and especially episcopal status came to be endowed with a nobility, and authority, all its own.[6]

Among aristocratic Gallic churchmen it soon became a commonplace that *vera et integra nobilitas* ("true and unblemished nobility"), in the words of Avitus of Vienne, lay in ecclesiastical rather than secular office.[7] As Sidonius Apollinaris claimed, "Without doubt, in the opinion of all good men, the least ecclesiastic ranks higher than the greatest secular official."[8] Here Sidonius skillfully attributed this sentiment to the *boni* in general, and made clear that ecclesiastics were every bit as much a part of the aristocracy as purely secular aristocrats.

The same attitude was reflected in the hagiographical topos that noble churchmen were even further ennobled by their calling, as expressed in the standard claim that a cleric was "noble by birth, more noble by re-ligion."[9] And in the case of the rare bishop who was not noble to begin with, his office could endow him with noble status. Few would have agreed with Salvian's pessimistic assessment, "If any noble begins to be converted to God, he immediately loses his rank among the nobility."[10]

In many ways, secular and ecclesiastical attitudes about status coa-lesced. The contrast made by Gallic secular aristocrats between the *boni* ("good people") and the *mali* ("inferior people") was paralleled by the ecclesiastical opposition of "the upright" (*boni*) to "the wicked" (*mali*).[11] In this context, churchmen considered such questions as why, in this world, "The *mali* sometimes acquire good things and the *boni* are afflicted with evils."[12] They took it for granted that "the *boni* always suffer the persecution of the *mali*," although they also piously asserted that "we should pray for the *boni*, so that they always might ascend to better things, and for the *mali*, so they might flee quickly to an emendation of their life . . ."[13] If they did not, Eucherius of Lyons presumed, they would suffer in the afterlife, "where there is the greatest and incontrovertible distinction between the *boni* and the *mali*."[14]

It would be but a small step to equate "good men" in a theological sense with "good men" in a social sense. After all, a good Gallic aristocrat would assume, both groups of *boni* were comprised of the same people. And just as secular aristocrats expected the *boni* to provide examples of upright behavior, so did ecclesiastics, as disclosed by Eucherius: "Every best man transforms his earthly honors and earthly riches into celestial honors and celestial riches."[15]

This parallel between secular and ecclesiastical *boni* presumably underlay a theological point made in a sermon attributed to Faustus of Riez, which noted: "One who has goods [*bona*], you shall be a good man [*bonus*]: wealth is good, gold is good, silver also is good, family ties are good, possessions are good. All such things are good, but whence do you do good?"[16] Here, secular aristocratic ideology regarding the *boni* dovetailed seamlessly with ecclesiastical sentiment.

THE ACQUISITION OF CHURCH OFFICE

The acceptability of the religious life helped to fuel a great demand for high church offices. Indeed, Gallic nobles regularly had been appropriating episcopal office ever since the end of the fourth century.[17] Episcopal office and aristocratic status came to be so interrelated that in some ecclesiastical circles secular aristocratic status could be viewed as a prerequisite for episcopal office.[18] At one election of circa 470, Sidonius noted that some episcopal candidates advertised their "ancient precedence of birth," and at another he supported his candidate by saying, "His forebears presided over both episcopal sees and secular tribunals."[19] A century later, Gregory of Tours could write that the fourth-century bishop Simplicius of Autun had been elected "on account of his secular rank."[20]

Ecclesiastical office, like secular office, came to be seen as an hereditary right.[21] Officially, of course, this was not supposed to happen. At the Council of Rome of 19 November 465, for example, the bishop of Rome, Hilarus, complained, "Some bishops think that the episcopate is not a divine gift but a hereditary interest, and they believe that, like transitory and mortal things, they can dispense it as if by legal and testamentary right."[22]

But this is exactly what was happening in Gaul.[23] A saint's life said of Marcellus, who succeeded his brother Petronius as bishop of Die circa 450, "He doubtless nourished you as his successor, and his bishopric, as a private possession, came to you by fitting right through the fraternal propinquity of your brother, nor did it pass to anyone else."[24] By the late sixth century, the epitaph of bishop Chronopius of Périgueux could say openly that "the episcopal rank was transmitted to him from both parents; the pontifical crown came to its heir."[25] Such practices led to the formation of episcopal dynasties, where some sees remained in the hands of certain families for generations.[26] With these families monopolizing episcopal office in any given area, such office would be all the more difficult, well nigh impossible, for any outsider to attain.

At the same time, the religious life became an increasingly appropriate activity for noble laymen, regardless of whether they actually became clerics.[27] Sidonius, for example, could say, "I admire a priestly man more than a priest."[28] He praised aristocrats for their adherence to the ascetic ideal.[29] In many instances Sidonius encouraged his aristocratic confrères to take up the religious life. In a letter to the former prefect Tonantius Ferreolus, he said that he hoped "that your greeting would be more fittingly associated with the names of bishops rather than of senators," and that he "thought that it would be more just if you were numbered among the perfected in Christ than the prefects of Valentinian."[30] And many of his friends, like himself, did in fact enter ecclesiastical orders, not only as bishops, but in lower-ranking offices as well.[31]

As a result of this aristocratic appropriation of religious life and office, an ecclesiastical aristocracy now arose in Gaul in which secular and ecclesiastical office both had equal places in an aristocratic cursus.[32] Gallo-Romans often saw in church office the chance to pursue careers which no longer were available to them in the secular world.[33] In the 460s, for example, Sidonius Apollinaris told how one Arvernian family had come to seek its future with the church rather than the state: "Their service has been carried out in clerical rather than Palatine company."[34] Rather later, an ambitious young noble could consider whether "he should seek ecclesiastical or lay employment."[35]

In general, the aristocratic assumption of ecclesiastical office seems to have accelerated soon after the fall of the Gallic emperor Eparchius Avitus (455–456).[36] Avitus himself, of course, had been forcibly made bishop of Piacenza. His son-in-law Sidonius likewise became a bishop circa 469. Furthermore, the Eparchius whom Sidonius succeeded at Clermont surely was a relative, perhaps even a brother, of the emperor.[37] It may be that the failure of Avitus' imperial initiative, and the resultant increased alienation between Gaul and Italy, finally convinced many Gallic aristocrats of the futility of a continued commitment to a secular career in the service of what had become an Italian-oriented government. Other considerations also made ecclesiastical careers attractive.

Aside from genuine religious motivation, perhaps the most important single reason why ecclesiastical office became so important as an aristocratic option in late Roman Gaul is that it was so admirably suited to the needs of the time. It offered Gallo-Roman aristocrats the very kinds of things they had been seeking in their secular lives. Along with its role as an ersatz for state office, a church career was consistent with many other attributes of the aristocratic lifestyle.

For one thing, ecclesiastics, like secular nobles, placed great stock in education and literary activities.[38] Monks like those of Lérins and Marseilles, priests like Mamertus Claudianus of Vienne, Salvian and Gennadius of Marseilles, and Julianus Pomerius of Arles, and bishops like Hilary of Arles, Eucherius of Lyons, Faustus of Riez, Sidonius Apollinaris of Clermont, Ruricius of Limoges, and Avitus of Vienne, all indulged in their literary inclinations.[39] Cultural and literary achievements which no longer received many, or any, rewards from the state now could lead to advancement in the church.[40]

PATRONAGE AND *POTENTIA*

More significantly, perhaps, church office gave aristocrats an opportunity to fulfill local interests and responsibilities, to solidify their local authority, and to act as patrons in the context of an influential local office.[41] In many ways, the holding of episcopal office allowed an aristocrat to carry out the same kind of activities, provide the same kind of services, and acquire the same kind of clients that he had been accustomed to in secular life. And there was one item of authority, of inestimable value, which bishops had, but which no laymen, no matter how powerful, had: control over the sacred and religious life of the community.[42]

Bishops could exercise virtually monarchical authority in their cities. Their authority, and the kinds of patronage they provided, in many cases vastly exceeded anything they could have done as *saeculares*. A bishop, and especially one belonging to an episcopal dynasty, could consolidate property and influence to an extent that no layman could. He had not just individuals, but an entire *civitas* (city), as his client.[43]

A bishop's local authority and clients extended to all levels of society, a point repeatedly made in contemporary sources. Germanus of Auxerre, in the course of his many travels, was regularly greeted by crowds of people representing all ages, ranks, and sexes. On a trip to Arles, for example, the inhabitants of "all the villages, municipalities, and cities, however many he encountered in the course of his journey, rushed to meet him with their wives and children, and an accompanying and great column clung to him, as those who met him were joined to those following."[44] Eutropius of Orange likewise was accosted by a "multitude of ages, with a mixture of sexes."[45] And Sidonius, in his description of Constantius of Lyons' visit to Clermont in the early 470s, exclaimed, "How you were most encompassed by every rank, sex, and age."[46] Conversely, secular patrons could be described similarly: Sidonius reported that his brother-in-law Ecdicius was greeted by "every age, rank, and sex" after his defeat of the Visigoths in the early 470s.[47]

It therefore should be no surprise that the same terminology of patronage and authority which had been applied to secular potentates also was applied to bishops. Germanus of Auxerre, in the fifth century, was called the "special patron" of all Gaul.[48] And in the sixth, Pantagathus of Vienne and Viventiolus and Priscus of Lyons all were described as *potentes*.[49]

Ultimately, Gallo-Roman bishops became so powerful in the local sphere that they often have been seen as the logical successors to the Roman imperial officials.[50] Indeed, the very survival of a city in these troubled times could depend on the presence of a strong and effective bishop.[51] Eventually, in the mid sixth century, the Frankish king Chilperic could make his often-quoted lament, "No one at all rules except for the bishops alone; our dignity has perished and been transferred to the bishops of the cities."[52]

The local devotion accorded to a favorite bishop, moreover, customarily exceeded even that given in the past to a secular patron, for a bishop influenced not only the material life but also the spiritual life of his clients. He was the defender of Catholic orthodoxy and the instructor of his flock in proper belief. He oversaw the reception of new members into the church at baptism, their expulsion through excommunication, and their return to the fold through the appropriate penitence. The many church festivals only augmented the glory of the city, the church, and the bishop. His spiritual authority endowed his person and character with an aura of influence and invulnerability which no secular potentate possessed, and which served as a local unifying element.

Furthermore, a bishop, after his death, often would gain the status of a saint, and as such could continue his role as an even more powerful patron.[53] Eutropius, bishop of Orange in the 460s, often told his flock, "Pray that I might find my own little place with the Lord: for, with the help of God, I will not cease my prayers for my Orangites."[54] Influential fourth- and, in particular, fifth-century Gallic ecclesiastics such as Martin of Tours, Germanus of Auxerre, Hilary of Arles, Anianus of Orléans, Lupus of Troyes, and even Sidonius of Clermont received greater devotion after their deaths than they had while alive as their reputations were increased by popular tales of their deeds and sanctity. But all such cults were carefully administered by the local bishops. Unlike the east, where independent "holy men" proliferated, free-lancing was frowned upon in Gaul.[55] Only rarely were autonomous holy men, or women, such as St. Genevieve, able to establish themselves.[56]

Of course, it also was felt that if a local saint had a glorious reputation, this would reflect glory on the city as a whole. In some instances, as in the case of Tours, a local saint's cult could become a primary raison d'être for an entire city.[57] Indeed, as of the fifth century, there were occasions when the locals of different areas engaged in conflict over the possession of the body, or relics, of a favored local hero-saint.[58]

The great authority of episcopal office, however, also created problems. As a result of the increasing desirability of episcopal office, partisan conflicts often arose over elections.[59] There were but a small number of episcopal sees, and only limited numbers of aristocrats were able to gain them. Not all of those who sought refuge in the church or church office were successful. Paulinus of Pella, after failing to get out of Gaul, likewise failed in an attempt to become a monk.[60] And the viri inlustres Pannychius and Eucherius failed in their bids to become bishops of Bourges circa 470.[61]

Several Gallic writers questioned the motivations of some who sought office. Ambition in office seeking in general was condemned by Eucherius of Lyons because it allowed wicked men to prevail over good. He complained, "Truly, what dignity can one think there is in the honors of this world, when along with good men, wicked men promiscuously ascend to them through ambition."[62]

There was particular condemnation of the ambition of those who sought, and obtained, episcopal office. Circa 400, for example, Sulpicius Severus wrote, "Now episcopates are sought through depraved ambitions."[63] And the anonymous fifth-century Gallic author of On the Seven Orders of the Church complained about bishops who were excessively concerned with secular affairs and influence: "There are many who, pursuing the favor of the people, do not observe the discipline of the church ... they sinfully cultivate the nobility rather than upright behavior . . ."[64]

A number of specific instances attest the prevalence of this kind of behavior. Circa 460, the bishop-elect Eutropius was rebuked for his initial reluctance to accept the unprestigious see of Orange because he was not "received by a church overflowing with wealth, decorated with its ministers, puffed up with its privilege, restless with its retinue of nobles . . ."[65]

Eutropius may have had his eye on the see of Marseilles, where he had been a deacon. But that see was taken, so he eventually had to be satisfied with the less illustrious post.

Ambition was condemned in the lower orders of the clergy as well. The early-sixth-century life of Romanus of St. Claude denounced monks who gained precedence over their elders by taking clerical orders: "When they have attained clerical office through rabid ambition, at once, inflated by the majesty of their pride, these youngsters are borne, anointed and elegant, not only over more worthy coevals, but even over the elderly and the seniors, nor have they been imbued first of all even with the primary and simple teachings; they strive to preside over episcopal sees and the episcopate, persons who at that point, because of their juvenile pride and vanity, have need of being chastised by the juvenile rod."[66] Here, as is often the case in such denunciations, one perhaps can detect a bit of personal animus on the part of the author: was he himself one of the *seniores* who resented the advancement of more aggressive juniors?

Ecclesiastical authorities repeatedly, and in vain, attempted to place a curb on such practices. In 418, pope Zosimus complained about the ambitions of those who sought high church office, saying, "This is brought about by the excessive negligence of our fellow bishops, who seek out the acclaim of the multitude, for they believe that from such a crowd they can acquire some kind of glory for themselves. Thence, here and there, the numerous supporters of such individuals are even found in those places where there is solitude, when they wish their parishes to be extended, or they bestow holy orders upon those whom they are not able to justify."[67]

This kind of episcopal assertiveness, reflected in bishops' desires to extend their jurisdiction, merely paralleled the aspirations of secular nobles, discussed above, to expand their estates. A number of quarrels between bishops involved the control of this or that parish.[68] In the late fifth century, Ruricius of Limoges, who was involved in such a quarrel with Chronopius of Périgueux, wrote that bishops should exercise "concern for guardianship, not contention over expansion, lest they be stigmatized as hired thugs."[69] Meanwhile, in a letter headed "To the Bishops of Gaul," the bishop of Rome Symmachus in A.D. 513 reiterated earlier prohibitions against ambitious bishops: "Let them neither through secular patronage, nor through a grant of any kind of exception, with illicit presumption exceed the boundaries of their allowed jurisdiction."[70]

These activities were so endemic that they even attracted imperial attention and condemnation. In 473, the emperor Glycerius, in an edict against simony issued to the Praetorian Prefect of Italy, and soon thereafter reissued to the Praetorian Prefect of Gaul, complained, "The reverence for bishops is considered more to be a secular power, and those called bishops prefer themselves to be tyrants of cities, and, neglecting religion and trusting to the patronage of men, they care more for public than divine affairs."[71] No amount of legislation, it seems, could inhibit the pursuit of episcopal ambitions, which continued apace as bishops strove to enlarge their influence.

SERVICES

Like secular potentates, ecclesiastics also enhanced their status by the performance of services. As early as the 360s, Hilary of Poitiers, speaking of the afterlife, had discussed ecclesiastical office using the conventional terminology applied to the fulfillment of the traditional aristocratic responsibilities and ambitions: "In a state of leisure which is aware of its security, the happy spirit relaxes in its anticipation . . . it likewise speaks out to others through the service of an imposed priesthood, expending its favors in its responsibility for public salvation."[72] This concept of the performance of duty through Christian service also was reflected in the commonplaces of *militia Christi* ("service for Christ"), *militia spiritualis* ("spiritual service"), or *militia caelestis* ("celestial service"), in contrast to the conventional *militia saecularis* ("secular service").[73]

Bishops had many local responsibilities, as revealed by a tale that immediately after his ordination in 526, bishop Nicetius of Trier felt a great weight on his shoulders; eventually "he also understood that this was the burden of the sacerdotal dignity itself."[74] Some of these responsibilities had been delegated by the imperial government.[75] *Episcopalis audientia* ("the bishop's tribunal"), for example, was available to those parties who would agree to have their cases tried before the bishop; indeed, clerics were expected to seek ecclesiastical rather than secular judgment.[76] Bishops were granted the right to manumit slaves.[77] A church was a recognized place of sanctuary.[78] Bishops even were given imperial authority for the suppression of heretics.[79] In 425, Valentinian III gave Patroclus of Arles authority to suppress Pelagianism, and Hilary of Arles apparently exercised this right in both 429 and the mid 440s.[80]

Bishops also assumed responsibility for the care of prison inmates.[81] In some cases bishops even were responsible for the release of those imprisoned.[82] Martin of Tours, for example, while visiting the emperor Magnus Maximus in Trier, saw to it that Maximus "set the incarcerated free from prison, restored those who had been exiled, and returned property which had been confiscated."[83] And circa 450 Anianus of Orléans prevailed upon the master of soldiers Agrippinus to "order all those who were held in jail to be released without any delay."[84]

Many other local services were performed by bishops simply on their own authority. Circa 470, for example, Patiens of Lyons and Eutropius of Orange both provided relief for a wide-spread famine.[85] As seen above, secular patrons sometimes furnished the same services; Ecdicius, the son of the emperor Eparchius Avitus, also assisted in the relief of this famine.[86] As will be seen, bishops also exercised patronage of another sort, in the literary arena.[87]

Another episcopal service, a legacy of local secular potentates of the past, involved building activity. During the earlier empire, wealthy individuals had sponsored the construction of public works such as aqueducts, baths, porticoes, and pagan temples. Bishops, however, generally concentrated on churches. New churches were constructed, and old ones remodeled, throughout Gaul under the sponsorship, if not always at the expense, of the local bishop.[88] Such activity came to be expected of any bishop worth his salt, and is attested at Marseilles, Arles, Narbonne, Fréjus, Riez, Orange, Clermont, Lyons, Dijon, Orléans, Tours, and elsewhere.[89]

MEDIATION

One particularly common way a bishop exercised his local authority was by serving as a mediator. This role was an important part of the episcopal ideal. One good bishop, for example, was described as an "extinguisher of quarrels," and it was said of another that he "was constantly occupied in mediation."[90] This mediation often involved very mundane affairs, such as patching up quarrels over slaves or lost pigs, smoothing disputes between relatives, interceding for those accused of crimes, or securing loans.[91]

A bishop's services as a mediator became even more valuable when he mediated between the local population and external state authority, whether Roman or barbarian. In the former case, one might note Germanus of Auxerre, who obtained tax relief for his city from the Roman prefect at Arles, and Hilary of Arles, of whom it was said, "He very often secretly advised a prefect of that time to refrain from unjust judgments," and who then threw the prefect out of the *basilica constantia* (Constantian basilica) when he failed to do so.[92] In 456, moreover, Eusebius of Milan was said to have interceded with the rebellious generals Ricimer and Majorian on behalf of the defeated Gallic emperor Avitus.[93]

Bishops also provided a buffer between the local Roman population and the barbarians. As the fifth century wore on, this became an increasingly significant responsibility. Sometimes a bishop would be all that stood between Romans and barbarians, as in the early 440s when Germanus of Auxerre served as an intermediary between the revolting Armoricans and the Alans who had been sent by Aetius to deal with them; he restrained the Alan king Goar by physically seizing the reins of his horse.[94] In 451, Lupus of Troyes supposedly intervened with Attila the Hun.[95] At the same time, Anianus of Orléans was said to have sought the aid of Aetius when the city was besieged by Attila.[96] And in the 460s, Vivianus of Saintes interceded with the Visigothic king Theoderic for a reduction of the exactions upon his townsmen.[97]

Episcopal mediation became so extensive that eventually, like secular potentates, bishops became involved in treaty making, and were used as intermediaries both by the imperial government and by the barbarian kings.[98] In 439, for example, the Visigoths were said to have used bishops, including Orientius of Auch, as ambassadors to the Roman general Aetius.[99] And according to a late source, in 451 Aetius sent Anianus of Orléans to the Visigoth Theoderic "in legationem" ("on an embassy").[100]

The most famous example of episcopal mediation occurred in 474 in the negotiations between the emperor Julius Nepos and the Visigothic king Euric. Nepos first of all, it seems, chose Epiphanius of Pavia as his emissary.[101] Now, Epiphanius had a wide reputation as a mediator; during the disputes between Odovacar and the Ostrogoth Theoderic, he supposedly was "the only one who, in the midst of these quarreling princes, enjoyed good relations with them both."[102] After his mission, four Gallic bishops then were sent to complete the negotiations; to one of them, Sidonius wrote, "Through you, the evils of treaties are expedited, through you, the agreements and conditions of both kingdoms are channeled."[103] And the bishops did indeed finalize the treaty, even if to the detriment of the Auvergne.

REFUGES AND DEFENSE

In instances where mediation failed in dealing with the barbarians, bishops could offer other kinds of protection. Another phenomenon shared by both secular and ecclesiastical potentates was the use of the refuges known variously as *castella, perfugia, refugia,* and *castra*. In 451, when Troyes was being threatened by Attila, the bishop Lupus reportedly transferred the population "to the mountain refuge [called] Latisco" because Troyes was "exposed in open fields and was not protected by fortifications or walls."[104] And circa 463, a monastery at the fort of Chinon (*castrum*

Cainonense) was used as a refuge by the people of Tours when the city was attacked by the Roman general Aegidius.[105]

The fort of Dijon (*castrum Divionense*) established by the emperor Aurelian (270–275) later served as a stronghold for fifth- and sixth-century Gallic bishops of Langres such as Aprunculus and Gregorius Attalus.[106] In his short biography of the latter, Gregory of Tours stressed the significance of this fortress: "I thought it proper to insert in this account a description of the site of Dijon, where he usually resided. It is a fortress built with the most stalwart walls in the middle of a very suitable plain . . . On the south is the river Oscara [whose] gentle waves flow about the entire site of the fortification . . . Four gates are positioned at the four orientations of the world, and thirty-three turrets adorn the entire building; its wall, indeed, is known to be constructed of squared stones to a height of twenty feet, [and] of small stones from above, with a total height of thirty feet and a width of fifteen feet. Why it does not have the status of a city [*civitas*], I do not know."[107] A formidable residence indeed for a bishop![108] Other sixth-century bishops also enjoyed such fortified residences.[109]

Some interesting reports of the use of fortifications and refuges by ecclesiastics also appear in saints' lives of rather later date and lesser repute, and attest the contemporary wisdom on how to resist barbarian assaults. The life of Antidius of Besançon asserts that in the early fifth century, "When the city was besieged by the Vandals, he retreated into the fort which long ago the emperor Theodosius Junior had given to him as a gift . . . There he found many of the faithful who were fleeing the savagery of the barbarians."[110] Another vita noted that "the ferocious enemy . . . devastated all the locations [of Provence] with the enthusiasm of aggressors, and they seized captives, and they madly hastened to asault the fortress of Toronna, which the blessed bishop Paul had fortified [and] where the population then had retreated."[111] Accounts such as these attest to the popular image of the bishop as a provider of physical protection in times of trouble.

Bishops also could assist in the defense against the barbarians by taking a more active role. In Britain, for example, the Roman inhabitants were led to victory against the Saxon invaders in 429 by the Gallic bishop Germanus of Auxerre, who, it should be noted, in secular life had been a *dux* (general), and thus was no stranger to military affairs.[112] Anianus of Orléans helped to defend his city against the Huns in 451 and Vivianus of Saintes did the same against the Saxons in the 460s.[113] Early in the next decade, Sidonius Apollinaris, as bishop of Clermont, was instrumental in the resistance of the Auvergne against the Visigoths.[114]

REDEMPTION OF CAPTIVES[115]

Some Gauls, however, were not lucky enough to find refuge or security during barbarian raids, and, as noted above, were taken captive. Here, too, bishops provided useful services. Indeed, one of their most visible roles after circa 400 was in obtaining the release or ransom of captives and hostages held by the barbarians.[116] Patrick of Ireland, for example, in his own effort in the mid fifth century to free those taken captive by the "tyrant" Coroticus, noted, "This is the custom of the Christian Gallo-Romans . . . They send trustworthy blessed men to the Franks and other peoples with many thousands of solidi for the purpose of redeeming baptized captives."[117]

Specific examples of such redemptions abound. Martin of Tours, for example, as early as the 390s, allocated a hundred pounds of silver, donated by the former vicar Lycontius, for the redemption of captives.[118] Hilary of Arles (429–449) was said to have used the silver of all his basilicas for the same purpose.[119] And the abbot Lupicinus of St. Claude in the 460s interceded with the Burgundian king Chilperic on behalf of some paupers who he claimed had been wrongfully enslaved.[120]

Caesarius of Arles was especially active in the ransoming process. In 508, after the Ostrogoths had defeated an attack of the Burgundians and Franks, "When the Goths had returned to Arles with a multitude of captives, the sacred basilicas were filled, even the house of the church was filled, with a crowd of infidels . . . until [Caesarius] could free them one by one . . . using all the silver which his venerable predecessor Aeonius had left for the church table."[121] Soon after, in 513, Caesarius redeemed "captives from beyond the Durance, and especially from the town of Orange."[122] At about the same time, "When . . . captives from all over were displayed at Arles to be redeemed . . . a great multitude of those who had been redeemed, freeborn and many nobles, were fed daily at Arles by [bishop Caesarius] himself."[123] Part of the supplies were contributed by the Burgundian kings Gundobad and his son Sigismund. Gundobad already had negotiated in the 490s with Epiphanius of Pavia for the release of hostages and captives held by the Burgundians; on that occasion contributions came not only from bishop Avitus of Vienne, but also from the noblewoman Syagria of Lyons.[124] As during imperial times, bishops also assisted in the release of inmates from other kinds of barbarian incarceration.[125]

Bishops could encounter some pitiable situations during these attempts to redeem captives. A bishop Victorinus, apparently of Fréjus, wrote to Ruricius of Limoges circa 500 on behalf of a presbyter who had sought to free his wife from captivity, only to have her die immediately after being redeemed. The priest then had to go through the same process trying to free his daughter.[126] Ruricius himself wrote a letter on behalf of the presbyter Possessor. Not only had the latter lost his property "because what he had he had expended for the redemption of his brother," but he also fell into debt while doing so: "In order to render his brother free of the enemy, he preferred that he himself be a captive of his creditors."[127]

Their role as redeemers of captives gave bishops a particularly visible way of exhibiting their authority, of exercising their local patronage, and, along the way, of broadening their base of clients. It also has been suggested that this was one way in which bishops could take control of the church purse strings.[128]

In general, the very important episcopal role in mediation, both at the local level and with distant authorities, makes it all the more clear why a city would have wished to seek out as bishop one whose word would carry some weight. Such an individual, of course, often would be a powerful secular *potens* who, as has been seen, may already have been exercising some of these same responsibilities while he was a layman.

CHURCH OFFICE AS A UNIFYING ELEMENT

Another function of episcopal office was to provide a high-level unifying element for the often separated Gallic aristocrats. The aristocratic bishops all had a corporate interest in consolidating, maintaining, and expanding their own pseudo-monarchical powers. They did this most effectively at church councils which they summoned on their own authority. Between 439 and 452, no less than ten councils were called in southern Gaul.[129] In the 460s, several councils united bishops from throughout Lugdunensis.[130] And as late as 470, a council could bring together bishops from cities ranging from Arles to Lyons and Autun.[131] These meetings, the largest of which served as a virtual ecclesiastical equivalent to the "Council of the Seven Provinces," also gave bishops the opportunity to meet with each other and renew their acquaintance, often on "neutral territory." Such personal encounters gave them an additional opportunity to find common ground and to settle disputes among themselves.[132]

The great attention given to ecclesiastical affairs by Gallo-Roman aristocrats in the fifth century also gave them another means of dealing with the barbarians: the Gauls could ignore them and carry out their church activities with nearly total disregard for the newcomers. Prior to the 470s, when the Visigoths finally did begin to interfere in the operations of the

Catholic church, the Gauls were able to pursue their church affairs essentially free of barbarian interference. Church records contain little evidence of Germanic involvement in church affairs.[133] Even in 451/452, when the Gallic bishops excused themselves for not having responded earlier to pope Leo's request for assistance, they drew attention to the distances between them and to the bad weather—but failed to mention such an eminently reasonable excuse as the invasion of Attila and the Huns.[134]

The Gauls also had the freedom to choose their own bishops, and in the fifth century, episcopal office was limited, exclusively it would seem, to those of Roman origin. Barbarians, most of whom were either Arian or pagan, were not yet competing for episcopal office. Likewise, monastic institutions during the fifth century were largely coopted by Gallo-Roman aristocrats, unlike other areas of the empire where lower-ranking elements of society often were represented in monastic orders.[135] As noted above, many of these Gallic monks then went on to become bishops.

BISHOPS AND THE BARBARIANS

Finally, episcopal office also had another inestimable attraction. It provided a certain amount of personal security.[136] Even the barbarians had a reputation for usually respecting the persons of clerics.[137] *The Poem on the Providence of God* does mention priests being mistreated (but not killed) during the initial attacks of the Vandals and Goths, but this example was not emulated.[138] Only in a few hagiographical instances were bishops killed, and even here the guilty barbarians—Huns and Vandals—were not among the permanent settlers in Gaul.[139]

But if the victors in episcopal elections obtained a form of life insurance, the losers sometimes were not so fortunate: the aforementioned Eucherius failed circa 470 in a bid to become bishop of Bourges and shortly thereafter lost his life.[140] Others, however, such as the pro-Roman Simplicius of Bourges and Sidonius of Clermont, were able to find security in episcopal office as the imperial presence in Gaul came to an end in the 470s. As a result, they experienced exile, and perhaps confiscation of their property, rather than execution when the Gothic occupation ultimately came.[141] One might conclude that, if anything, the Gothic regard for religion introduced an element of restraint into their response, rather than serving as a pretext for persecution.

During the fifth century, then, the Gallic church was still a Roman and largely aristocratic preserve. It offered Gallic aristocrats the opportunity to pursue local interests, to maintain their class consciousness and collegiality, and to satisfy their desire for public office. At the same time, it gave the Gallo-Romans an institution which they could use to preserve their own *Romanitas* in the face of the ever more conspicuous barbarian presence.[142]

Indeed, in some ways it was the arrival of the barbarians itself which expanded the opportunities available for Gallo-Roman aristocrats in church office. The decline, and eventual disappearance, of imperial authority meant that local jurisdiction tended to devolve into the hands of the most influential local potentate. And this person usually was the bishop, who assumed the important roles of mediator, protector, and local factotum.

The acquisition of high church office, along with its other functions, thus solved for some Gallo-Roman aristocrats one of the problems caused by the barbarian occupation: the eventual disappearance of all the secular offices of the Roman state. They now could acquire episcopal office instead. But the availability of this option was limited by the relatively small number of episcopal sees. As seen above, other aristocrats also availed themselves of the opportunity for lesser ecclesiastical office, such as that of priest or abbot. Still others had to find other kinds of careers under the barbarians.

CHAPTER TEN

THE PURSUIT OF LITERARY STUDIES:
A UNIFYING ELEMENT

solum erit posthac nobilitatem indicium litteras nosse
(SIDONIUS APOLLINARIS, *EPISTULAE* 8.2.2)

As seen in the previous chapter, the Gallo-Roman aristocracy went through a crisis at a very fundamental level during the fifth century. Aristocrats were compelled to reconsider the criteria upon which their acceptability in Gallo-Roman aristocratic circles was to be based, and to look for new ways in which aristocratic unity could be manifested. Some aristocrats compensated for the dearth of secular offices by seeking a high ecclesiastical office, but there were only a few episcopal sees available, so only a relatively small number of aristocrats could avail themselves of this opportunity. What were other aristocrats to do?

It appears that at the same time, aristocratic status became even more dependent on the sense of unity and elitism which came from an appreciation of classical literary culture which Gallo-Roman aristocrats shared with each other. Of course, literary interests always had been part of the aristocratic ideal, and especially so in Gaul.[1] They were even more noticeable when they were lacking. One recalls the historian Ammianus' famous description of the Roman prefect Orfitus as "imbued with the splendor of liberal teaching less than was fitting for a nobleman."[2] In a like vein, Sidonius described the collaborator Seronatus as "not even sufficiently instructed in the ABCs."[3] During the barbarian occupation of the Roman west, such pursuits seem to have attained an even greater importance. This phenomenon was particularly true in Gaul.

THE THEME OF LITERARY DECLINE[4]

Modern views of the literature of late Roman Gaul, however, rarely have been flattering. Nearly every modern writer on the subject takes it for granted, in fact, that there occurred a pervasive literary decline.[5] Nor is it difficult to understand how this impression has arisen; much of the evidence for it seems to come from the works of the Gauls themselves, who repeatedly decried the cultural decline of their age. Sidonius Apollinaris did so on several occasions. Around 470 he wrote to his young friend Hesperius, for example, "Consider this, that the multitude of the slothful has grown to such an extent that unless some very few indeed rescue the undiluted purity of the Latin language from the blight of base barbarisms, in a short time we shall be mourning its decay and death: thus, all the purple garb of the discourse of the nobility will be discolored by the carelessness of the mob."[6]

To his friend Namatius he wrote circa 470, "Who, nowadays, stimulated to match the deeds of our ancestors, would not prove to be most lacking in energy, or who also, striving to match their words, would not be most infantile? For the ruler of the ages implanted more in past times the virtues of arts such as these, which nowadays, like worn out seeds, have lost their vigor in the world's present old age and demonstrate only rarely in anyone, and this in the few, anything marvelous or memorable."[7]

Soon thereafter, in a letter to the rhetor Sapaudus of Vienne, Sidonius wrote, "Thus, if anyone, emulating you, has a liking for Latin learning, he desires to be included in your circle . . . But nowadays, few have a care for such studies."[8] And in a letter to the same individual, the Viennese priest and philosopher Claudianus Mamertus wrote, "There has occurred ever since the times of our ancestors a discarding of the good arts, and a rejecting of the cultivation of the intellect, by which alone humanity outshines the beasts . . . I see, in fact, that for the Romans, Roman speech is a matter not only of neglect but even of disgrace . . . But such things give cause to admire you . . . for you, one and alone in our Gaul, are equal to your occupation."[9]

Such reports of the imminent demise of Gallic culture continue into the sixth century. Avitus of Vienne described one of his poems as a work "which sings by preserving the length of the syllables, which few understand."[10] And at the end of the century, Gregory of Tours noted in the preface to his *History of the Franks*, "With the study of liberal learning disappearing or rather dying in the Gallic cities . . . many often lament, saying, 'Woe to our times, for the study of literature is lost to us.' "[11]

These Gallic assertions of a dying culture have been taken at face value to mean that the Gauls believed that their own literary culture was in rapid decline. But there are several potential problems with this interpretation. One must take into account, for example, the conventional *pudor* (modesty) of any writer at any time. When Sidonius questions whether he is "a writer equal to [those of] the times of our ancestors," is this necessarily an acknowledgment of decline?[12] The decline also took an awfully long time: even though the sources suggest it was well underway by the mid fifth century, it was still going strong circa 600. Furthermore, in the very period when Gauls were lamenting the decay of their literary culture, they were producing more literary works than at any time in their entire history.[13]

Finally, one can only note the Gauls' own inconsistency in their descriptions of the decline. If at some times they could wonder whether they measured up to the standards of the past, at others they could compare their literary efforts to those of their ancestors. Sidonius, for example, could say of a long-dead Gallic writer, "The talents of his descendents, especially in regard to literature, have degenerated not even in the least from his."[14]

At the same time that they spoke of cultural decline, the Gauls also saw themselves as the preservers of classical literary culture. Sidonius himself was described by Claudianus Mamertus as the "restorer of the old eloquence."[15] The only good Gallic writers were those who followed established classical norms. Claudianus elsewhere suggested that "whoever in recent times [had] written anything worthy of memory" had used as his models such writers as Naevius, Plautus, Cato, Varro, Gracchus, Chrysippus, Fronto, and Cicero.[16]

Nor did the Gauls use each other's works as specific examples of the literary decadence of which they so often spoke. Even if an individual author such as Sidonius could be appropriately circumspect when describing his own literary efforts, he would enthusiastically eulogize the works of his friends. Gallic writers customarily were likened to the greatest classical authors. A friend of Hilary of Arles exclaimed to him, "If Augustine had come after you, he would have been judged inferior."[17] To his friend Tonantius, Sidonius wrote, "I confess, indeed, that your opinion of my verses is . . . so laudatory that you believe me to be comparable to some of the most select poets, and even preferable to many."[18] The Gauls compared each other to Homer, Pindar, Varro, Vergil, Horace, Pliny, Tacitus, Fronto, and Apuleius.[19]

But if the literary circles of late Roman Gaul were in fact flourishing, and if the Gauls trumpeted the excellence of each other's literary works, how then are their claims of literary decline to be interpreted? One possible answer is to be found by reading these assertions more closely. To Hesperius, Sidonius wrote of "the very few indeed" who were to rescue the Latin language. To Namatius, he opined that only "very few" in the modern day wrote anything memorable. To Sapaudus, he wrote that "the few" who had a fondness for literature desired to be included among his friends. And who were these "very few"? Why, Sidonius and his friends, of course.

All the descriptions of cultural decline have one thing in common: at the same time that they discuss literary decline, they also stress the sense of superiority shared by the select few who continued to partake in classical culture. This perception surfaces repeatedly. To this same Sapaudus, Claudianus Mamertus wrote, "I would have entombed a kind of death of these studies with a tearful, as it were, epitaph, if you yourself had not revived them."[20] He asked what could be the cause if "any noble aspired not only to the renewing but even to the learning of any discipline without you alone."[21]

In a similar vein, Sidonius wrote to Faustus of Riez, "In these times [intellectual activity can be pursued] only under the supervision of your knowledge or through the virtue of your learning. For who could follow your lead with an equal step—you, to whom alone has been granted the ability to speak better than you learned?"[22] And to Arbogastes, Count of Trier, he could write, "Thus, the glory of Roman speech, if it exists now anywhere at all . . . resides in you . . . I greatly rejoice that at least in your illustrious breast vestiges of our vanishing culture remain . . . You will learn that the learned surpass the rustics to the same extent that men surpass the beasts."[23]

In general, the Gallic emphasis seems to have been not on any qualitative decline of their own literary efforts, but on a perceived quantitative decline in the number of those who participated in classical culture. Such a numerical decline would be attested by the Gallic littérateurs' own claims of how few they were. It also could explain Claudianus' assessment of the "decline": "In our age it is not the talent [for literature] which is lacking but the study [of it]."[24] The decrease would have resulted, in part, from the contemporary retrenchment in the Gallic educational system. There simply were not as many schools or teachers as there had been in the fourth century.[25] Nor, perhaps, were there as many aristocrats left with the leisure or wherewithal to pursue literary interests.

To be interpreted properly, the repeated Gallic claims of cultural decline must be examined in their fuller social and historical context. One must take into account the extent to which literary pursuits shored up the sagging morale of Gallo-Roman aristocrats who were faced on all sides by the decline of Roman imperial authority and the rise of Germanic power. Educated Gauls placed increasing emphasis on the sense of superiority they derived from the appreciation of classical literary culture which they shared with their fellow aristocrats.

The pursuit of literary interests, of course, always had been one mark of good Roman aristocrats, and helped to occupy their senatorial *otium* (leisure).[26] In an earlier age, literary activities also had been the means by which a new man like Ausonius could become a member of the aristocracy; in fifth-century Gaul, however, such endeavors became a means by which someone born an aristocrat could remain one.[27] They provided an arena in which all could continue to participate on equal terms.[28] In such a context, Sidonius could write to his otherwise undistinguished friend Philagrius, "You delight in the company of the learned; I call any crowd, however large, which is lacking in literary learning the greatest solitude."[29]

The increased importance of culture as a determinant of aristocratic status can be seen, for example, in Sidonius' letter to Hesperius, cited above, in which he equated educated speech with the purple raiment of emperors and high officials. And in his letter to Philagrius, Sidonius asserted, "For by universal judgment, the dignity, virtue, and preeminence of knowledge are acclaimed, and through its ranks one ascends to the highest peak of accomplishment."[30]

Later in the century, a classical education could be seen as a means by which a young aristocrat might reaffirm his aristocratic status.[31] Around 485, Ruricius, bishop of Limoges, wrote to Sidonius' friend Hesperius, who had become the rhetor responsible for educating Ruricius' sons, "Surely, in the midst of such great confusion in the world, they would lose their nobility if they did not have you as an example."[32] And in the early sixth century, Magnus Felix Ennodius could write to the teacher of one of his young Gallic relatives, "It is allowed to you alone to grant or to restore the nobility of our ancestors."[33]

But the strongest evidence for the expanded role of literary interests in late Roman Gaul comes, again, from Sidonius, in a letter to his friend Johannes, in which he predicted, "Because the imperial ranks and offices now have been swept away, through which it was possible to distinguish each best man from the worst, from now on to know literature will be the only indication of nobility."[34] This sentiment was conveyed implicitly in a letter of Sidonius to his friend Syagrius, in which he referred to one of the latter's ancestors as a man "to whom his literary ability would have granted recognition, if his imperial offices had not done so."[35] This individual had had the opportunity for secular advancement; most of Sidonius' friends did not, and had to seek solace in their literary activities as a substitute.[36]

It would appear, then, that in late Roman Gaul participation in literary pursuits came to play an even larger role than before as a determinant of aristocratic status. The importance of this criterion of aristocracy was reinforced by assertions that the supposed decline in literary culture was being forestalled by the select few who preserved and appreciated it. Literary accomplishments and acceptance in a literary circle now could give enduring recognition to an aristocrat otherwise stricken by adversity. As Sidonius wrote to the Spaniard Fortunalis, whom he consoled on his misfortunes, "Nor indeed is your familiarity with literature so slight that you do not deserve to have something of yourself survive, through this very letter, after you are gone. The glory of your name shall live on."[37]

The Gauls' descriptions of cultural decay, therefore, should not be used as evidence that they believed their own voluminous works were lacking in quality. The real significance of the topos of decline is made clear instead by Sidonius in his letter to Hesperius: "Apply yourself, therefore, and the ignorant mob will not lessen the value of literary inclinations for you, for it has been ordained by nature that in all the arts the glory of learning is more valuable by however much it is more rare."[38]

ARISTOCRATIC UNITY

Far from being an amusement, the pursuit of literary interests in late Roman Gaul had become a serious business. Literary interests became a lowest common denominator which bound Gallic aristocrats together and gave them an arena in which all could relate equally.[39] They allowed educated Gallo-Roman aristocrats to demonstrate their acceptability in aristocratic circles. As Sidonius wrote to one friend, "I love in you the fact that you love literature."[40]

Another way in which literary pursuits helped to unify the Gallo-Roman aristocracy was by giving them a cultural rallying point against the barbarians: the perceived need to resist the encroachments of barbarism seems already to have been expressed by Hilary of Arles circa 430, when he rhetorically asked about his predecessor Honoratus, "To what extent did he not alleviate barbarism?"[41] Barbarians were viewed as being unsuited for literary pursuits. Sidonius, for example, suggested that a discussion of "literature among barbarians" was the height of absurdity.[42] The idea that culture and education allowed Gallo-Romans to segregate themselves from the barbarians persisted even into the sixth century. Avitus of Vienne described Ceretius, the son of the *vir inlustris* Heraclius, as "having secured from his mother's wisdom the aptitude for avoiding barbarians gladly, and from his father's integrity the ability not to turn his back on literature."[43]

For educated Gallo-Roman aristocrats, then, a magnification of their classical literary culture served as a means not only of asserting their *Romanitas*, but also of setting themselves apart from, and above, their new Germanic overlords in a nonviolent way—in just the same way that religious incompatibilities also provided a useful segregating element. It is no accident that of the hundreds of extant personal letters written by Gallo-Roman literati, only a very few were written to possible barbarians.[44]

The role of literature as a unifying element became so great that it was seen as second only to a blood tie. In a letter to a cousin, Sidonius noted that their most important tie was that of blood, but that "the second bond of our spirits comes from the similarity of our studies."[45] And in other ways too the pursuit of literary studies helped to foster aristocratic unity and collegiality.

LITERARY CIRCLES

Literary composition and analysis in late Roman Gaul was very much a public and group activity. Every Gallic city of note had its own literary circle, in which both secular and ecclesiastical aristocrats participated equally, and where the works of local authors were on display. New works were composed on the spot.[46] The compositions of local, or distant, littérateurs were read and discussed. Nor were there any restrictions on literary subject matter: topics ranging from poetry to theology all were grist for the Gallic mill.[47]

Local literary circles are attested, for example, in Arles, Marseilles, Narbonne, Bordeaux, and Lyons.[48] These literary circles gave Gallic aristocrats additional opportunities to socialize and to demonstrate their unity of spirit. Sidonius said of a meeting of one such circle: "O the feasts, stories and books, the laughter, seriousness and jests, the gatherings and comradeship, one and the same . . ."[49] It should come as no surprise, therefore, that barbarians did not participate in any of the attested literary circles or literary activities.[50]

The operation of these literary circles was marked by the use of certain conventions which were intended to foster aristocratic collegiality. For one thing, there seems to have been a kind of enforced literary uniformity. It was not enough just to share literary interests; it helped to share the same opinions about literature. Sidonius noted in a letter to a relative that the bond between them was strong because "in literature we feel, we blame, and we praise the same thing, and any sort of discourse pleases or displeases us equally."[51] This desire for literary uniformity, along with the afore-mentioned literary elitism, may have been what led the Gauls to affect an obscure literary style which even they themselves sometimes had a hard time understanding. Ruricius of Limoge could write to Sidonius' son Apollinaris, "Just as [Sidonius'] writing restores my past affection for him, it likewise does not encourage my own talents because of the obscurity of his statements."[52] In the modern day, this convoluted Gallic style has been viewed as a sign of cultural decadence, but it may be that it was yet another unifying element: only the initiated were able to enjoy and appreciate it.[53]

A repeated theme in literary circles was the encouragement to write. After all, the act of composition perhaps was the most important way in which literary interests were manifested. Gallo-Roman aristocrats continually exhorted each other to compose some work or other.[54] Sidonius, for example, wrote to his friend Lupus of Troyes, "For whom would you yourself not arouse to the rashness of composition? You who encourage the talents of all littérateurs, not to mention myself, even if they seek to remain concealed . . ."[55]

And the Gauls did rise to the challenge. As noted above, they were engaged in the most productive period, in a literary sense, of their entire history. These works then were copied and widely circulated.[56] Avitus of Vienne, for example, sent a composition to Euphrasius of Clermont and tactfully suggested that he pass it on to Sidonius' son: "I hope that you will deign, if you see fit, to . . . pass on this same little work, such as it is, neither edited at my leisure nor fully emended, to that sublime and most pious individual, our brother Apollinaris . . ."[57]

The publication process, moreover, clearly was a collegiate undertaking. The greatest responsibility fell upon those who had encouraged the publication in the first place, who assumed the role, consistent with conventional aristocratic ideology, of literary "patrons." Paulinus of Périgueux, for example, in a dedicatory letter described bishop Perpetuus of Tours as "an intimate patron in the presence of God," and Faustus of Riez, in a similar letter to Leontius of Arles, purported to be acting "just like an obsequious attendant, [who] clings tightly to his patron or master."[58]

Literary sponsors shouldered a heavy burden. Not only were they in charge of publicity, but they had editorial duties as well. To an editor of his own letters, Sidonius wrote, "But of course I have obeyed you, and I have entrusted these letters to your examination not only for revision, for this alone is not enough, but also for purification and polishing, knowing that you are an unbounded supporter not only of literature but also of littérateurs."[59] Likewise, Agroecius, later bishop of Sens, wrote to Eucherius of Lyons, the dedicatee of his *On Orthography*, "To you, therefore, is this little work sent, in which you will labor mightily, you, for whom it is necessary to emend the very one who presumed to emend anything."[60]

It further was understood that if anything was published, it became the responsiblity of the sponsor as well. Claudianus Mamertus of Vienne, for example, circa 469 wrote to Sidonius, the dedicatee of his *On the Nature of the Soul*, "Now see to it that you remember that you share the responsibility for the production of the work which you order to be published . . . Accordingly, protect and defend your position, for if I run any risk by being the author of this work, you do so by being the editor."[61]

And after the rhetor Hesperius had published some otherwise unknown "little pages" of Ruricius of Limoges, the latter modestly suggested, "Therefore, if you will take my advice, if you have both our best interests at heart, if you desire me to gain renown as an orator in your judgment and yourself to gain a reputation as an upright critic, bury this volume which is unworthy of memory and most deserving of oblivion."[62] One might doubt, however, whether such advice was really meant to be taken seriously.

If Sulpicius Severus can be believed, some literary sponsors went to great lengths to find publishable material. At the beginning of the fifth century, he scolded his mother-in-law, Bassula, complaining, "You have left me at home not a single page, not a single booklet, not a single letter."[63] And Sidonius protested on a number of occasions to friends, who had requested that his collection of letters be expanded, about his difficulties in finding suitable letters to include, although, in truth, he always was able to do so.[64]

For those aristocrats who actually published anything, the most important concern was how their works were received by other aristocrats. The sponsor also was responsible for promoting the work, and for reporting on the result.[65] Sidonius declared to Firminus of Arles, the dedicatee of his ninth book of letters, "It is fitting that you, in a sort of guard-tower for the protection of my reputation, clarify for the curious my reasons for doing this and disclose to me in a report, as quickly as possible, what all the best people think about it."[66] Elsewhere, he confided to a friend, "It would suffice for me that my writing be pleasing to my friends."[67] In both instances, it should come as no surprise that only the opinions of the boni were of any value.[68]

There was really, however, no need to worry. Once their works had been published, Gallic authors could be certain of receiving effusive praise from their fellows. This expectation was expressed by Sidonius in the context of conventional aristocratic terminology when he noted to an apprehensive young writer, "But as to anyone who is so depraved (malus) that he does not praise that which he knows is written well, good men (boni) are wise to him, and do not praise him."[69]

Specific examples of such praise abound, the more extravagant the better. A friend of bishop Hilary of Arles, for example, effused, "He has acquired not learning, not eloquence, but something indefinable beyond the reach of men."[70] Later, Sidonius wrote to one friend about another friend, Nicetius: "[He] extolls with immense praise, as I have learned, the volumes of my current work."[71] And to his friend Petronius he wrote, "I hear that you devote an enjoyable forbearance to the reading of my letters."[72] In both instances, Sidonius had heard the praise secondhand, as if this endowed it with extra luster; presumably, a respondent would speak more honestly when the author was not within hearing.

Favorable responses such as these to their literary efforts served to reassure Gallic writers of their continued personal acceptability in literary and aristocratic circles. Of course, such responses were no more than the Gauls expected. As Sidonius noted, in order to relieve the insecurities of a young author of declamations, "All who hear will approve, all will encourage."[73] Small matter that the Gauls at times candidly admitted that they might not be the most impartial judges of each other's works. To a friend who had praised his own works, Sidonius responded, "But I realize full well that, as is your custom, it is not the effect of the work itself which creates this enjoyment for you but affection for the author; therefore, I am all the more in your debt, because the point of honor that you deny to my composition you grant to friendship."[74] And the rhetor Paulinus of Périgueux, circa 480, went so far as to write to bishop Perpetuus of Tours, "You believe to be good what you choose to be good, and you admit into Your Devotion's fraternity even those poorer writers whom you read."[75]

Another manifestation of the Gauls' quest for literary collegiality is seen in their efforts not to show one another up. Sidonius told of a gathering at Lyons in 458 where the guests amused themselves by composing extemporaneous poems on the same topic but in different meters, "Lest any one of us, who wrote more feebly than the others, be stricken first with shame and then with envy."[76] Similarly, Ruricius of Limoges could comment to Sidonius, "It is customary to support, not to envy, the learned."[77]

The Gauls also were scrupulously modest in their evaluation of their own works. As Sidonius wrote to Ruricius, "While you strive to praise me in no small measure, you especially forbid praise for yourself."[78] Sidonius could even go so far as to deprecate his own writing in order to raise the self-esteem of a friend. He wrote to Heronius, "Certainly I advise you . . . never to compare this rubbish [of mine] to your hexameters. Indeed, set beside yours, my poems deservedly would be compared . . . to the wailings of the composers of epitaphs."[79] It would appear, therefore, that a conscious effort was made to maintain amity within the group by reducing competition. At a time when the aristocratic status of some Gauls would have depended heavily upon their literary inclinations, it may have been felt that any challenge to their abilities, and thus to the very basis of their perhaps marginal aristocratic status, should be avoided.

In general, one might suspect that it was not one's literary endeavors themselves that were important, whatever objective merit they might have, but the purpose that these endeavors served: to give Gallic aristocrats an arena in which all could relate on common ground. Therefore, if an individual with literary inclinations was personally acceptable to other aristocrats, his literary efforts perforce would be acceptable as well, and would receive fulsome and extravagant praise.

EPISTOLOGRAPHY

One genre of literary studies was particularly useful in unifying the Gallic aristocracy: epistolography.[80] In the fifth century, there was little geographical unity among Gallo-Roman aristocrats, who usually lived apart from each other throughout central and southern Gaul. They were relatively few in number, and often had little or no opportunity to meet.[81] Letter writing allowed them to maintain friendly relationships. Ruricius of Limoges, for example, wrote circa 500 to Aeonius of Arles of "the shared affection, which is always initiated and fostered by epistolary speech, between those who are separated and have not met."[82] He expressed similar sentiments to his correspondent Censurius of Auxerre: "Nor does it matter whether [our correspondence] occurs from necessity or from personal preference, as long as those who esteem one another communicate reciprocally among themselves and as long as a true conversation of their minds and senses links those whom spatial distances separate in body."[83] And Sedatus of Nîmes wrote to Ruricius, "I assert with God as my witness that, aside from your presence, nothing is more sweet to me than to deserve discourse of the most desired piety even through the dispensation of your letters."[84]

Sidonius Apollinaris even argued that it was educated men (*instituti*) who lived apart who had the most affection for each other; he went on to say, "With the assistance of a pen, [friends] can communicate their thoughts to those absent in remote provinces, and through it a degree of affection is formed among those who are separated, at least among the educated, that cannot be produced by corporeal contact."[85]

During the troubled times of the fifth century, epistolography also served a more practical purpose, as a means of counteracting the difficulties in communication specifically caused by barbarian unrest.[86] Sidonius, for example, noted to Auspicius of Toul, "But because the storm of conflicting kingdoms totally disrupts our desire for fraternal serenity, at least the custom of literary speech is rightly retained among solitary and separated individuals, for, introduced rightly long ago for the purpose of friendship, it is endorsed by ancient precedents."[87]

Epistolography also was looked upon as a literary genre which was particularly appropriate for clerics, an important consideration now that many aristocrats were entering that occupation. Sidonius, for example, in discussing why he abandoned writing secular poetry after he became bishop, noted, "Horrified by it, I transferred every kind of care to the cultivation of letter writing, lest, guilty of impudence in verse, I should be guilty of such in deed."[88]

Even more, letter writing was viewed by many as a duty, as noted by Hilary of Arles in the life of his predecessor, Honoratus: "His dutiful letters were carried everywhere."[89] Sidonius referred to letter writing as a "duty of friendship" and took care "to cultivate friendships with dutiful words."[90] And Ruricius of Limoges wrote to a bishop Clarus, "I bestow through my letters the appropriate duty of greetings."[91] He also could lament a friendship which had fallen into desuetude because he and a friend failed to cultivate each other "through mutual favors and correspondence."[92]

Because of the preeminent role of epistolography in maintaining friendships, the Gauls missed no opportunity to correspond with each other. They continually bombarded each other with demands for letters.[93] Failure to correspond could result in peevish complaints and accusations of favoritism, as when Claudianus Mamertus of Vienne wrote to Sidonius, "Very often others, who do not seek it or perhaps do not deserve it any more than I, have your letters bestowed upon them, and I do not think that such a deed can be perpetrated with impunity against the laws of friendship."[94] Being left out of a published collection also could lead to complaints. In his final book of letters, Sidonius apologized for not being able to include all his friends, saying, "The same limit which can be placed upon one's pages cannot be placed upon one's friendships."[95] Given the great importance of epistolography, it is therefore no accident that so many letters written by and to so many different individuals survive from this period; for the century circa 420–520, some 475 letters written by some 45 Gauls are extant.[96]

FAMILY TIES

Literary interests, finally, also seem to have assisted in fostering another kind of unity: family ties. In several cases, literary inclinations were said to have been inherited, and to have resulted from blood ties rather than from formal instruction. Claudianus Mamertus wrote to the rhetor Sapaudus, "See to it that you remember that the hereditary gift of teaching [was passed] to you from your great-grandfathers and [will be passed on] in turn . . . A manifold learning, having arisen among your ancestors, has coalesced in you."[97] And to his friend Leo of Narbonne, Sidonius wrote, "That renowned river of oratory, which is yours by both family and domestic right, . . . is poured into your breast through succeeding generations from your ancestor Fronto."[98] Fronto, of course, was the famous second-century rhetor, of Numidian descent, who flourished under Marcus Aurelius.

Soon thereafter, Ruricius of Limoges described Sidonius' son Apollinaris as the "interpreter of the paternal eloquence," and said to him, "That you are his son you demonstrate not only by the nobility of your ancestry, but also by the flower of your eloquence and by every kind of virtue, for this good is inculcated in you not so much by teaching as by nature."[99] Likewise, in the early sixth century, Avitus of Vienne complimented Apollinaris on a letter that the latter had sent to Avitus, saying, "I recognized there that in which I was sufficiently delighted, your hand, that in which I was more delighted, a paternal declamation, and that in which I was most delighted, a hereditary kindness . . ."[100]

These references to inherited inclinations attain a special significance because many of these Gallic literati were interrelated. Avitus of Vienne, Ruricius of Limoges, and Ennodius, for example, all were related to Sidonius.[101] And Sidonius even claimed that in one case a marriage which united two illustrious families was consummated because the father of the bride was so taken by the bridegroom's oratory—although Sidonius admitted that the young man's "family and wealth, youth, good looks, and modesty" also assisted his suit.[102]

These considerations would seem to suggest that the extended literary circle of late Roman Gaul not only was a closed corporation but also was relatively small: the same names keep occurring over and over again.[103] Their very lack of numbers probably added to the need of Gallo-Roman aristocrats to find some rallying point for their aristocratic sentiment, and their shared interest in classical literary culture filled this need.

The pursuit of literary interests in late Roman Gaul, therefore, was one more way in which Gallo-Romans responded to the needs of their times. Many aristocrats had to seek out new ways to maintain their status. As seen above, some adopted the religious life in order to do so. Others resorted to an increased reliance on literary pursuits. Nor were these approaches mutually exclusive. Some canny Gallic families used both methods; Sidonius described the Palladii of Bourges as individuals "who, to the delight of their class, held either chairs of literature or episcopal thrones."[104]

In sum, the bishop Eucherius of Lyons in 434 tied the old and new criteria of aristocracy together in his discussion of the attractions of the religious life: "For what nobility of the world, what honors, what rank, what wisdom, what eloquence, what literary skills, do not already associate themselves with this service of the celestial kingdom?"[105] In this view, there were no inconsistencies. Aristocratic status was as neatly defined for the senator-cum-churchman Eucherius in the fifth century as it had been, on different grounds, for the poet and consul Ausonius in the fourth.

CHAPTER ELEVEN

COMING TO TERMS WITH
THE BARBARIANS

romano ad te animo venit, qui barbarus putabatur,
et ex omni parte conclusa romana barbaries
(FAUSTUS OF RIEZ, *SERMO* "IN LITANIIS")

By the 460s, it was increasingly clear that the barbarians were in Gaul to stay. The year 461 saw the fall of the emperor Majorian and the last strong imperial presence, or even interest, in Gaul. In the next year, 462, the Italian government cavalierly ceded Narbonne to the Visigoths. At the same time the Gallo-Roman potentate Aegidius openly flouted Italian authority.[1]

Furthermore, by this time the generation of Hilary of Arles, Germanus of Auxerre, and Salvian of Marseilles, which had known a world free of barbarians, was gone. The post-430 generation of Sidonius and his confrères had never known a world without barbarians. By now, barbarians had become an accepted part of the Gallic landscape. As Gallic ties to the rest of the empire unraveled, the Roman inhabitants of Gaul seem to have reevaluated their relationships with the barbarians, and to have recognized the necessity of reaching some kind of permanent accord with them.

CHANGING PERCEPTIONS OF THE BARBARIANS

Several late-fifth-century sources indicate how Roman perceptions of barbarians had evolved, and how the barbarians no longer were perceived as rapacious outsiders. In the ecclesiastical sphere, for example, portrayals of the barbarian occupation underwent a subtle change, and a new ideology for dealing with the barbarians appeared. The theme of resignation and refuge in prayer remained, but this time with a new twist: the barbarian bite now had lost its sting.

The sermon "In litaniis" ("In Supplication"), delivered perhaps by Faustus of Riez circa 477 when Riez was occupied by the Visigoths, presents clearly the new ecclesiastical rationalization of the barbarian presence.

The author rebuked his flock for their overly pessimistic view of their circumstances. Things were not as bad either as they seemed, he argued, or as they could be.

He began with the conventional argument that his people, because of their sins, were responsible for any misfortunes which they had suffered at the hands of the barbarians:

> Much remains to him whose life . . . is preserved. One who, residing in his homeland, speaks with the grief of a captive is excessively ungrateful to his liberator; you therefore say, 'What does it profit us to pray, and to labor with total contrition of the spirit?' . . . Thus, when we dare to say such things against God with a haughty spirit, we demonstrate that we suffer worthy [retribution]. Let us ask our consciences whether God found anyone perfect among us after the castigation of the first hostility.[2]

He then went on to present a reinterpretation of the barbarian presence. The situation could have been much worse. In fact, it had turned out rather well. It all depended, he stressed, upon one's point of view:

> Let us consider, moreover, what the offerings of common prayers and the aid beseeched from the saints have granted to us in the present hostilities. Whence, let us display before our eyes, as it were, this present time: Behold, the whole world trembles before the clamor of this most potent race, and nevertheless he, who is considered to be a barbarian, comes to you with a Roman spirit, and on every side a Roman barbarism is encompassed . . . In the midst of all this you express amazement because you are punished for your unredeemed sins; why are you not amazed, rather, at the sword which does no harm and at the forbearance of the armed soldier? The same sword of your attacker which is drawn for battle is resheathed in the scabbard; it is the same after the triumph as it was before the battle. And thus the most brave army of so great a ruler knows how to conquer, but knows not how to be an enemy. Therefore, among the stupendous favors of your God on your behalf, the most renowned victor renders service to you, so that in the midst of victorious arms the conquered might remain at peace and liberty might remain unharmed: for your sake a bloodless triumph is given to the victor.[3]

Fundamentally, the writer argued, things were not so bad. The barbarians were no longer as threatening as they once had been. In their own way, they even had become Roman. The city, it seems, had been occupied peacefully. There had been no bloodshed. Life went on as before. The writer, of course, piously attributed this turn of events to the mercy of God. But whatever the cause, the result was the same.

This sermon suggests that there had been a decided change in the ecclesiastical portrayal of the barbarians. The barbarians had become more than merely the enforcement arm of the punishment of God. Their secular authority now had the ecclesiastical stamp of approval. The bishop, rather than lamenting their presence, justified their rule and sought to secure for them the good will of his flock. This remained true even when the barbarians behaved badly, which, after all, was a common occurrence. Ennodius of Pavia, for example, could have a number of persons enslaved by the Burgundians in 494 plaintively protest, "Are you not our Burgundians?"[4]

Gallo-Roman aristocrats of a more traditional bent also changed their tune, and made the best of the barbarian predominance. Athaulf's earlier perception of the Goths as the defenders of *Romania* now was echoed by bishop Sidonius of Clermont, who in the mid 470s appealed to his erstwhile opponent, the Visigothic king: "Your forces are called for, Euric, so that the gallant Garonne, through its martial settlers, might defend the feeble Tiber."[5]

In northern Gaul, other bishops pointedly accepted the transition from Roman to Germanic rule. Remigius of Rheims, in a famous letter written during the 480s, not only portrayed Clovis in the guise of a Roman administrator but also presumed to advise him on how to conduct himself in that capacity: "The important news has come to us that you have undertaken the administration of Belgica Secunda . . . You ought to choose advisers who will be able to augment your reputation . . . and you ought to defer to your bishops and often to have recourse to their advice, because if there is harmony between you and them, your province will be more effectively administered . . . Whatever paternal wealth you possess you furthermore should use to free captives and to liberate them from the yoke of servitude . . . Joke with the young men and deliberate with the elders if you wish to be judged a noble ruler."[6] It seems noteworthy that all of these perceptions of the barbarians, and especially of the Franks, occurred before their conversion to orthodox Christianity, an event which would remove one of the important segregating elements.[7]

LIFE UNDER BARBARIAN JURISDICTION

This acceptance of the barbarian presence brought Gallo-Roman aristocrats of all types into closer contact with the Germans, and made it even more incumbent upon them to have cordial relations with the Germans. Gallo-Roman aristocrats who in the past might have openly disparaged the barbarians now moved to reach accommodations with them. In matters involving politics, Gauls sometimes had to be even more circumspect about what they said than they had been in imperial times. After all, the emperor usually had not been resident in Gaul, but the local barbarian king might be living just down the road. Sidonius, for example, circa 475 declined to write a history of his own times because to do so would require that "either falsehood be spoken with disgrace or the truth with peril."[8] And Ruricius of Limoges, in his corpus of eighty-two letters, prudently limited himself to discussions of local and personal affairs; the word *barbarus* and its variants appear nowhere at all.[9]

The new spirit of prudence also was manifested in the ecclesiastical world. Religious incompatibilities between barbarians and Romans which in the past had had the potential for disruption, dissension, or confrontation now were played down or ignored. The results of this new policy are demonstrated by two remarkably analogous incidents. At an earlier time, during the reign of the Visigothic king Theoderic II (453–466), bishop Vivianus of Saintes was invited to sup with the king at Toulouse. He accepted, but was put in an awkward position when he was offered a cup which had been shared by the Arian bishops in attendance. He had no choice but to refuse, and as a result was imprisoned for this insult to the king.[10] Somewhat later, in 474, bishop Epiphanius of Pavia also was invited to dinner with the Visigothic king, on this occasion Euric, at Toulouse. He, however, was more discreet. Rather than openly confronting the Arian bishops he knew would be there, he dissembled, saying that "he was not accustomed to eating out and wanted to get an early start two days hence."[11]

The new ideology for dealing with barbarians appears regularly in late-fifth- and sixth-century hagiography. The barbarian rulers might be quick-tempered and bellicose (what else could one expect from barbarians?), but the fact of the matter was that they could be dealt with. They were clearly subordinate to a strong-willed Gallic holy man. What Gallo-Roman reader, for example, would not have swelled with pride when reading about how Germanus of Auxerre halted the advance of the Alan warlord Goar by seizing his horse's bridle?[12]

This kind of ability to deal with, and face down, barbarian potentates also appears in accounts of Gallo-Romans pursuing their legal cases before barbarian judges. A revealing incident occurred circa 468, when the abbot Lupicinus of St. Claude was involved in a hearing before the Burgundian king Chilperic. Lupicinus was there on behalf of some Romans he asserted had been wrongly enslaved by a member of the Burgundian court.[13] The affair has several revealing aspects.

The incident occurred, the author said, "when the servant of God [sc. Lupicinus] struggled with a most pious defense to speak out in the presence of that illustrious individual, then the patrician of Gaul, Chilperic (for the public law at that time was administered under royal jurisdiction), on behalf of the anguish of some paupers, whom a certain individual, bloated by the honor of his courtly dignity, had placed under the yoke of servitude by the force of an illegal assault . . ."[14]

The proceedings began with an accusation against Lupicinus, when "that nefarious oppressor, aroused by the fury of rage and full of rage, belching forth a kind of froth of words detrimental to the most blessed man, said, 'Are you not that recent trickster of ours who, around ten years ago, while you were insolently denigrating the policies of the Roman government, asserted that even then ruin threatened this region and our families? I ask you, therefore, false prophet, to explain why the terrible portents of your prediction are confirmed by no evidence of woeful occurrence.' "[15]

The incident to which Lupicinus' accuser referred would have occurred circa 457/458, in the troubled times immediately after the fall of Avitus, when the Burgundians were extending their control into the area of Lupicinus' own monastery. Presumably, Lupicinus had been speaking out on the failure of Roman policies, and his predictions of gloom and doom may have involved a catastrophe which he felt was sure to follow the Burgundian takeover.[16] The accuser, however, adopted a rationale similar to that of Faustus above, suggesting that, in spite of Roman fears, the barbarian occupation had not, in fact, brought ruin and disaster.[17]

Lupicinus, for his part, responded to this charge by adopting the pose of an Old Testament prophet: "Extending his hand to the aforementioned Chilperic, a man singular for his talent and special goodness, he boldly said, 'Behold, you perfidious and depraved man! Give heed to the wrath which I used to preach to you and those like you. Do you not see, degenerate and unfortunate one, that law and right have been disrupted, on account of the repeated attacks of you and yours upon the innocent, [and] that the purple fasces have been transformed under a skin-clad judge? Finally, come to your senses for a time and consider whether a new guest might not appropriate and seize for himself your fields and acres by means of an unexpected application of the law. Moreover, just as I do not dispute that you know or perceive these matters, I likewise do not deny that you have decided to sully my little person by the mark of the stigma of a two-pronged dilemma—either to be made timid by the king or to be made fearful of the outcome.' "[18] Here, one again sees how perceptions changed between the 460s and the 520s: the author carefully separated his own view of Chilperic ("singularly good") from that attributed to his protagonist ("perfidious, depraved, and degenerate").

The abbot, meanwhile, argued that it was his very outspokenness which would prevent the disasters he had predicted from coming to pass. Were he to keep silent, for fear of the king, he then would have to be equally fearful that his predictions would come true. He also suggested that the only way to achieve law and order would be by an even-handed application of the laws. If the Burgundians failed to do so, they would risk the loss of the lands which they themselves had legally obtained.

The supposed result of the confrontation was predictable: "What more? The aforementioned patrician was so enchanted by the audacity of truth that, by divine judgment, with his courtiers standing near, he confirmed, with many examples and a long discussion, that it had happened thus. Indeed, soon afterward, when his decree had been published with royal vigor, he restored those who were free to liberty, and he allowed the servant of Christ to return honorably to his monastery, with gifts provided for the needs of the monks and the monastery."[19]

This kind of scene, of confrontation and resolution, was played out repeatedly—at least in the Gallo-Roman literary sources.[20] Even if one might wonder whether such accounts were actual verbatim reports, there are so many of them that there can be little doubt that such encounters did in fact occur. One presumably could apply to any number of incidents the concluding words of Ennodius in his description of a similar confrontation between Epiphanius of Pavia and the Burgundian king Gundobad in 494: "Behold, then, we see that the warriors' vigor is overcome by sanctity, and that the king yielded to the pleas of the chosen one . . . Let the reader learn from this the extent to which weapons of words are more piercing than those of iron: words overcame one who relied on the sword."[21] The underlying message always was the same: justice could be obtained from the barbarians.

On a more pedestrian level, one can see this principle in action. There is the law-abiding Visigoth who, of his own accord, in the 450s sent Paulinus of Pella payment for a property which Paulinus had deemed totally lost.[22] And the newfound respectability of the Germans led Syagrius, a descendent of an old noble family, to adopt his own method for dealing with legal matters under the Germans in Lyons. He learned Burgundian, and was described by Sidonius as an *arbiter* (mediator), a *disceptator* (judge), and "the new Solon of the Burgundians."[23] This is not to say however, that he served in any official capacity; he seems rather to have been reorienting his legal practice in response to the needs of the times.[24]

Such an activity suggests a realization by Syagrius that the Germans were there to stay as the adminstrators of Gaul. He found his own kind of permanent solution to the problem of pursuing a legal career in their domain. Such episodes all suggest something of a return to normality.

Even during periods of warfare, there were certain standard procedures which seem to have been understood on both sides. The Gallo-Roman population in the sixth century, for example, continued to trust to fortified refuges for security. Gregory of Tours mentioned several of them. The *castrum Iovolotrum* ("Fort Jovolotrum") in the Auvergne, for example, was said to have fallen in the mid 530s only because of the carelessness of the defenders, if it was not betrayed by a slave.[25] The defenders of the even more impregnable *castrum Meroliacense* ("Fort Meroliacum") made the mistake of attempting a sally in which fifty of their number were taken captive. This problem, however, was resolved by the paying of a ransom—after the Franks had gone through the charade of preparing the captives for execution.[26] There eventually developed under the barbarians, therefore, standard practices and procedures for the redress of grievances, which some might have argued were even more effective than before.

GALLO-ROMANS IN BARBARIAN SERVICE[27]

Eventually, some Romans made their peace with the barbarians in a more substantive way, and actively sought employment in barbarian administrations. There were practical reasons why they would have been compelled to do so. As seen above, the old Roman administrative positions were vanishing rapidly—they were gone by the 470s—and there were only a relatively few episcopates available for those with ecclesiastical inclinations. By the late fifth century, many Gauls who wished to satisfy their desires for public service and personal advancement would have had to look for other outlets for their office-holding inclinations. Many increasingly took the opportunity to hold office in barbarian administrations. Their willingness to do so probably was enhanced by their readiness to believe, like Remigius, that the Germans had simply appropriated the Roman administrative machinery.[28]

The question therefore now arises of exactly when Gallo-Romans openly advertised their collaboration by holding official positions in barbarian administrations. Certainly, individual Romans often worked with the barbarians in an ad hoc way, and occasionally were employed by them as particular circumstances dictated. In 439, for example, the bishop Orientius of Auch was used by the Gothic king Theoderic I (418–451) as an ambassador to the Roman master of soldiers Aetius.[29] But such incidents do not demonstrate actual office holding. At what time, one might ask, were the official positions of Gallo-Romans in Germanic administrations regularized? When did Gallo-Romans receive the official titles of *consiliarii* ("counselors"), *comites* ("counts"), *duces* ("dukes"), or whatever?

ROMANS IN VISIGOTHIC SERVICE

The best early evidence for Gauls in office under the barbarians comes from the Visigothic kingdom, so it will be considered first.[30] Now, as early as 414/415 the Gaul Paulinus of Pella had been named *comes privatarum largitionum* ("Count of the Private Largesses") in the administration of the usurper and Visigothic puppet emperor Priscus Attalus.[31] The whole thing, however, was a sham; even Paulinus called it an "empty honorary title."[32] This, therefore, hardly could be called an office in a Gothic royal administration.

Better examples come in the early 460s, under king Theoderic II. The fifth-century Spanish chronographer Hydatius, for example, noted that in 461, the master of soldiers Nepotianus "accepted Arborius as his successor at the behest of Theoderic."[33] In this instance, it would appear that the Gothic king simply appropriated the right of appointing an official of the old Roman administration, who then presumably reported to him rather than to the emperor. No other certain examples of Gallo-Romans in the service of Theoderic, however, survive.[34]

The next Visigothic king, Euric (466–484), made more extensive use of Gallo-Roman officials.[35] At the same time, he began to tailor the Visigothic administrative system to suit his own particular needs. The Gallo-Roman Victorius was appointed as *dux super septem civitates* ("Duke of the Seven Cities") in Aquitania Prima; he also was referred to as a *comes* ("Count"), so perhaps his full title was *comes et dux Aquitaniae Primae* ("Count and Duke of First Aquitaine").[36] Such an office had no clear Roman antecedent. Shortly thereafter, in 473, the *dux Hispaniarum* ("Duke of Spain") Vincentius commanded Visigothic armies in Spain.[37] This, too, was a newly created position. The equivalent Roman officer would have been the *comes Hispaniarum* ("Count of Spain").[38]

In the same year, Vincentius was sent "like a master of soldiers" (*quasi magister militum*) by Euric to invade Italy.[39] Now, it usually is assumed that in this capacity Vincentius was just another master of soldiers, the successor to the aforementioned Arborius.[40] But the insertion of the qualifier *quasi* indicates that this was not the case: the writer apparently believed that Vincentius fulfilled the function of a master of soldiers, but that he was not the genuine article.[41] In this instance, the Roman writer was at a loss as to exactly what kind of official titulature to use. And once again, the developing Visigothic administration is seen to be diverging from its Roman model.[42] Furthermore, it is interesting that it is to a Vincentius, probably this very individual, that Sidonius sent his letter (*Epist.* 1.7) detailing the disgrace of the unfortunate collaborator Arvandus in 468. One might conclude that Vincentius, as one Visigothic collaborator, may have had a very personal interest in the circumstances leading up to the disgrace and conviction of another one.

Another Gallo-Roman in Visigothic military service, in the late 470s, was the "admiral" Namatius of Saintes, who commanded naval forces defending the Atlantic coast against the raids of the Saxons. Sidonius wrote to him, "Recently you sounded the bugle in the fleet and performing the duties first of a sailor, then of a soldier, you wandered about the sinuous shores of the ocean in opposition to the serpentine pirate ships of the Saxons . . . You accompany the standards of a victorious people [sc. the Visigoths]."[43]

Although Sidonius detailed Namatius' military duties in the service of the king, his official title was not cited. His multifarious responsibilities, however, would have been similar to those of the Roman *dux tractus armoricani ac nervicani* ("Duke of the Armorican and Nervian Region"). Although this *dux* commanded troops stationed only in Lugdunensis Secunda and Tertia, his duties "extended . . . through five provinces, through Aquitania Prima and Secunda, Senonia [sc. Lugdunensis Quarta], and Lugdunensis Secunda and Tertia."[44] Under Euric, of course, Namatius' geographic responsibilities would have been not nearly so extensive, but here, again, the old Roman office apparently had been adapted to suit the needs of the Visigoths.

In the 470s, Gallo-Romans also served the Visigoths in civil capacities. Sidonius suggested, for example, that his friend Potentinus was a *iudex*, that is, a provincial governor, and at this time such a function presumably would have been performed under the Visigoths.[45] At the same time, or shortly thereafter, a Rusticus, who may have lived near Bordeaux, also seems to have been in office.[46]

A more instructive example is provided by the jurist Leo of Narbonne, who by circa 474 was serving as a *consiliaris* ("Counselor") of Euric.[47] In 474/475 he received the embassy of bishop Epiphanius of Pavia, sent by the emperor Julius Nepos, at Toulouse. Ennodius described him as "the moderator and arbiter of the counselors of the king."[48] And Sidonius said of him, circa 476/477, "Today, solicitous of the whole world, you oversee in the councils of the most powerful king contracts and laws, war and peace, localities, regions, and rewards."[49] Leo preserved his position of *consiliaris* under Alaric II (484–507).[50] So Leo would have been an influential person indeed.

The remaining years of the fifth century and the first years of the sixth saw an even larger number of Gallo-Romans in Visigothic service. Several of them, for example, were involved in the compilation in 506 of the *breviarium* of Alaric II, a law code based on the Theodosian Code.[51] Such individuals, too numerous to discuss individually, all undertook careers in a Visigothic administration.[52]

ROMANS IN BURGUNDIAN SERVICE

Meanwhile, in the other barbarian kingdoms of Gaul, certain examples of Gallo-Romans in barbarian offices prior to the post-Roman periods are less easy to find. In the Burgundian kingdom, the aforementioned accuser of St. Lupicinus, "a certain person made arrogant by the honor of his court office," sometimes has been identified as a Gallo-Roman.[53] The example of Syagrius, too, has been mentioned. One also might note Gregorius Attalus, who was appointed in 468 as *comes civitatis Augustodunensis* (Count of Autun). He well may have held this office under the Burgundians.[54]

An indisputable example of a Gallo-Roman serving in office in the Burgundian kingdom does not occur until 494, when Laconius, a counselor of king Gundobad (473–516), oversaw the release of some Italian prisoners. Ennodius described him as the one "to whom the authority of deeds and words was safely entrusted by the king . . . with whom he often conferred."[55]

In the early sixth century many other Gallo-Romans followed his example. Circa 500, the *vir inlustrissimus* Heraclius held some unspecified office under Gundobad.[56] Soon after, a *vir inlustris* Laurentius seems to have gone to Constantinople as a Burgundian envoy; circa 515 he was followed by his son.[57] Shortly thereafter, in 516, an educated *consiliaris*, presumably a Gallo-Roman, of the Burgundian king Sigismund (516–523) also was sent to Constantinople.[58] At about the same time, the *officialis* Stephanus was described as "[the one] from the administration of king Sigismund . . . who had authority over all the control of the royal fisc."[59]

The Burgundian Code, moreover, in a section probably issued under king Sigismund, lists a number of officials of the Burgundian administration, including *comites* (1.2), *administrantes* and *iudices* (1.3), *consiliarii, domestici, maiores domus, cancellarii, comites civitatis* ¿vel villulae?, "Burgundian as well as Roman," *iudices*, and *iudices militantes*

(1.5), and *notarii* of the judges. It is unclear why it is stressed that both Burgundians and Romans could be counts of cities; does this imply that Romans usually did not hold the other positions as of this time, or only that Roman areas had Roman counts and Burgundian areas Burgundian?[60]

ROMANS IN FRANKISH SERVICE

Evidence for Gallo-Romans in the service of the Franks at an early date is especially difficult to find. The status of the aforementioned Arbogastes, Count of Trier, circa 470, is unclear.[61] Was he a local generalissimo, à la Aegidius, or was he a Frankish appointee?[62] The first known Gaul in formal service with the Franks seems to be the Aurelianus who is described as a *consiliaris* and *legatus* of Clovis (481/482–511) in the first years of the sixth century.[63] Many others soon followed his example.[64]

A curious report in Gregory of Tours, moreover, may reflect another of the experiments which occurred during this time of transition as a result of the uncertainties about just what the boundaries between Romans and barbarians were to be. Some aristocrats were remarkably resourceful in seeking resolutions with the barbarians. Perhaps the most unusual case occurred circa 456. According to Gregory and others, the master of soldiers Aegidius found a novel way of dealing with the local Franks: "Finally the Franks, having expelled Childeric, unanimously appointed as their king Aegidius, who ... ruled over them for eight years."[65] This experiment, however, was but a stopgap, and ended with Aegidius' death in 464.

GALLO-ROMAN ATTITUDES

These observations about Gallo-Romans in barbarian service lead to several conclusions. They indicate that there was no sharp break between the Roman and Germanic administrations. There seem, rather, to have been phases in the transition. As seen in an earlier chapter, by mid century several Roman officials were cooperating more or less openly with the Germans. Not long afterward, the Germans, most notably the Visigoths, began to take a more active role in the appointment of these same Roman officials. Finally, by the 470s, the Visigoths, at least, were altering the structure of the Roman administration to suit their own needs. This developmental pattern gives a little more specificity to the existing general belief that the Roman administrative system survived in some manner in the barbarian kingdoms.[66]

It would appear, therefore, that it was not until the final disappearance of the Roman administration from Gaul that the barbarian kings actually began to accept the responsibility for establishing an administrative system which met their own needs. A number of the offices in these barbarian administrations were held by Gallo-Romans, but it does not appear that such office holding began in earnest, or even at all, until the very last days of Roman authority in Gaul. Of course, one reason for this may have been the developmental pattern just described: before circa 470, the rudimentary barbarian administrations simply did not have such offices available.

Another possibility, however, may involve the perceptions of the Romans themselves. As seen above, some of the most influential Gallo-Roman aristocrats retained their imperial sympathies until the very end. Even circa 470, Sidonius expressed the forlorn hope that his or Ecdicius' sons still could hope to hold a consulate. But even if it was considered improper in Sidonius' circle for a good Roman aristocrat to be too closely affiliated with the Germans, all Gallo-Romans apparently did not agree. For in Sidonius' discussion of those who informed to the barbarians, he indicated just who some of these individuals were: a growing class of new men.[67]

Sidonius disclosed their recent emergence when he described them as "jealous of the lineage of the nobility," and as those "who, inebriated with their new wealth . . . through their intemperance in using it betray their inexperience in possessing it."[68] Even worse, Sidonius continued, such men had the ear of the Burgundian king Chilperic: "With such character traits they overwhelm a man outstanding no less for his goodness than for his power. But what can one man do when he is everywhere surrounded by venomous advisers?"[69] It may be, therefore, that Sidonius' grievance was not only with *delatores* per se, but also with Gallo-Romans who had allied their fortunes not with the declining Roman state, as had Sidonius and his confrères, but with the rising star of the barbarians.

As to who these new men were, only a handful of them can be identified with any certainty, although even this might have seemed like a great many to old-line aristocrats. One was Sidonius' nemesis, Paeonius, who had taken advantage of the chaos after the fall of the Gallic emperor Avitus in 456 to usurp the prefecture.[70] Sidonius' disparaging reference to him as "town bred" (as opposed to being "of noble birth") suggests that men of previously merely local prominence now were aspiring to higher status.[71] Other new men included Arvandus (Praetorian Prefect of Gaul circa 464–468), whom Sidonius described as "of plebeian family," and Gaudentius (Vicar of the Seven Provinces circa the late 460s).[72] Of these, Arvandus, at least, clearly did ally himself with the barbarians. Furthermore, some Gallo-Roman families, undistinguished during the Roman period, do in fact seem to have prospered under the barbarians. The family of the aforementioned Gregorius Attalus, which later included Gregory of Tours, provides perhaps the most spectacular example.[73]

Even if individuals such as these were the first to affiliate themselves openly with the barbarian kings, it was not until the 460s that they did so on a regular basis. It would appear that, until the last, most Gallo-Roman aristocrats remained too closely tied to the Roman past to take the portentous step of holding a formal office under a barbarian king. But with the final disappearance of Roman authority, attitudes changed, and service in barbarian administrations, such as it was, began in earnest.

CHAPTER TWELVE

THE FINAL RESOLUTION:
ARISTOCRATIC OPTIONS IN
POST-ROMAN GAUL

non ideo, quia clericus factus sum, et ultor iniuriarum
mearum non ero

(GREGORY OF TOURS, *HISTORIA FRANCORUM* 8.39)

By the 480s, Gaul had been partitioned among Franks in the north, Visigoths in the southwest, Burgundians in the Rhone Valley, and smaller enclaves of Alamanni, Alans, Armoricans, and others. The entire Gallo-Roman population now had to deal with the reality of life in barbarian Gaul. One seeks in vain, however, for any indication in the sources of this period that Gallo-Roman aristocrats in any way lamented the final disappearance of Roman authority. No, they had long since learned to order their own local affairs in the manner which suited them, and to come to terms with the resident barbarians.

The withdrawal of the largely ineffective Roman administrators and generals and the disappearance of a legitimate Roman government in Italy had no visible impact. There are no extant sentimental yearnings for any "good old days" under Roman rule. On the contrary, the Gauls, if they desired any imperial connection at all, preferred a distant one. Soon after 476, they rejected any nominal claims of the Italian government of the barbarian *rex* Odovacar, and opened up negotiations of their own with the emperor Zeno in Constantinople.[1]

The Roman attitude toward the barbarians, which had begun to change in the late fifth century, reached its logical culmination in the sixth. Writers such as Gregory of Tours not only accepted the barbarian presence, but even reevaluated the past relations between Romans and barbarians.[2] Even fifth-century barbarians no longer were seen in a pejorative light. Gregory, for example, in his discussion of the defeat of the Huns, glorified the Franks at the expense of not only the Visigoths but even the Roman generalissimo Aetius.[3]

BARBARIAN LAW CODES

Perhaps one reason for the general lack of widespread, open dissatisfaction with barbarian rule was the lengths to which the barbarian rulers went to protect the interests of their Roman subjects.[4] This policy is especially clear in the legal arena. Gregory of Tours, for example, said of king Gundobad, "He instituted more humane laws for the Burgundians, so they would not oppress the Romans."[5] The legal difficulties which could have arisen as a result of the transfer of jurisdiction from Roman to barbarian rule would have made it clear that some kind of resolution and clarification was necessary. As a result, the technical definitions and requirements of the relations between barbarians and Romans began to be formulated as early as the 460s in several barbarian-sponsored law codes.[6]

The earliest such code seems to be the Visigothic, which was initiated by Theoderic II (453–466). Sidonius, for example, mentioned "laws of Theoderic."[7] And the law code of Theoderic's son Euric, which may have been issued circa 476, confirmed a law originally issued by his father, and also noted, "Moreover, we do not permit to be contested any longer any of the cases which were prosecuted, either for good or ill, during the reign of our father of blessed memory."[8]

Both Theoderic and Euric attempted to preserve the relationship between Romans and Goths which had existed at the time of the original settlement and shortly thereafter.[9] On the one hand, Euric, in particular, seems in doing so also to have been concerned with preserving the identity of the Goths.[10] But on the other, many institutions dear to the hearts of Roman aristocrats were preserved. Several laws concerned landholding.[11] A decree of Euric stated, "Ancient boundaries are to stand, just as our father of blessed memory prescribed in another law"; it would have reassured Gallo-Roman landowners in the Visigothic kingdom that their interests would be protected.[12] One such property owner would have been Sidonius' friend Lampridius, who after having his property rights restored by Euric was described by Sidonius as a *civis* ("citizen") of the Gothic kingdom.[13]

An updated Visigothic code that was even more Roman in nature, the *Breviarium Alarici*, was issued in 506 by Euric's son Alaric.[14] Alaric, it seems, faced with pressure from the Franks, felt that this was one way to conciliate his Catholic subjects.[15] The code was distributed by two Gallo-Romans, the *vir spectabilis* count Timotheus and the *vir spectabilis* Anianus. Its prologue proclaimed that it had been issued "So that all the obscurity of Roman laws and ancient jurisprudence, led into the light of a better intelligence with the assistance of bishops and the nobility, might be made clear and so that nothing might remain in doubt," and it asserted

[133]

that "the assent of the venerable bishops and chosen provincials has strengthened" it.[16] Here again, one sees the union of interest and action of the Gallo-Roman secular and ecclesiastical aristocratic establishments.

In the Burgundian kingdom, the compilation of the Burgundian Code, the *Liber constitutionum sive lex Gundobada*, began in the 480s, perhaps with the assistance of the Roman specialist on Burgundian law, Syagrius of Lyons.[17] The preface, probably written under king Sigismund (516–523), noted, "We command that Romans be judged by the Roman laws, just as has been established by our predecessors."[18] Unlike the Visigoths, the Burgundians dated their legal jurisdiction from the Battle of the Campus Mauriacus against Attila in 451.[19]

Some Burgundian laws, clearly of great concern to Roman estate owners, paralleled the Visigothic laws dealing with property and landholding. One stated, "If any one of our people has invited a person belonging to a barbarian nation to live with him, and if he has voluntarily given him land to dwell upon, and he . . . has held it for fifteen years without prohibition, let it remain in his possession."[20] The subsequent sections added that land taken by force could be recovered before thirty years had passed.[21]

In instances where Burgundians were allowed to sell their land—and they were permitted to do so only if they had other land elsewhere—their Roman host was given preference in the sale, suggesting that some Romans must have been prospering.[22] A later restriction added, "We ordain this with respect to Romans, that nothing more may be required by Burgundians who have come among them than that which is prescribed at present."[23] Meanwhile, the Franks too eventually published law codes of their own.[24]

SOCIAL RELATIONS

Several barbarian laws clarified the social relationships between Romans and barbarians. Both the Burgundians and Visigoths attempted to reprise the earlier Roman restrictions on intermarriage. A Burgundian law stated, "If indeed a Roman girl, without the consent or knowledge of her parents, unites in marriage with a Burgundian, let her know she will have none of the property of her parents."[25] The *Breviarium* of Alaric II, on the other hand, repeated the 370s-era prohibition of the Theodosian Code, merely substituting the words *Romani* and *barbari* (non-Romans) for *provinciales* and *gentiles* ("non-Romans").[26] And there also is Sidonius' intriguing aside that the Gothic wife of Aetius had been "excluded from Gothic royalty," although whether this was a direct result of her marriage is unclear.[27] Meanwhile, the Gauls, too, apparently continued to advise against such unions: a possible canon of the Council of Agde in 506 decreed, "It is not proper to mix marriages with any heretics, and to give them sons or daughters, but [it is proper] to accept them, if they promise that they are going to become Catholic Christians."[28] Presumably, the repeated prohibitions against intermarriages only indicate how prevalent the practice must have been.

Such laws perhaps represent half-hearted barbarian attempts to maintain, if not ethnic identity (little evidence for doing so otherwise survives), at least political and social identity. But the increasing evidence for intermarriage indicates how unsuccessful they were.[29] Admittedly, specific instances of Romans marrying Germans are rare. The cases of Athaulf and Galla Placidia, and Aetius and his Visigothic wife, already have been discussed.[30] But the next attested examples do not occur until the sixth century. Especially instructive is Gregory of Tours' account of how Theodebert, the son of the Frankish king Theoderic, after having been affianced to the barbarian Visegard, eventually fell in love with and married the Gallo-Roman Deoteria. Only the resultant uproar among the Franks eventually induced him to abandon her and their son Theodobald and to fulfill his obligation to Visegard.[31]

The evidence of nomenclature, as attested by the appearance of Roman and Germanic names in the same immediate family, also could be taken to indicate intermarriage.[32] An inscription, perhaps of the fifth century, names Agricius and Mellita as the parents of an Inusaigulfus at Tours.[33] Gregory of Tours cites several similar examples, such as Eustochius and his relative (cognatus) Baudulfus, who were involved in a quarrel at Tours c. 556/573.[34] Indeed, Gregory himself probably had barbarian blood in his family: his unnamed maternal grandfather was the brother of Nicetius, bishop of Lyons, and the dux Gundulphus, who in turn were the offspring of the aristocrats Florentius and Artemia of Geneva.[35]

Hagiographical sources, moreover, which also cite barbarian and Roman names in the same immediate family, attest at least to the acceptability of the practice, even if the specifics might remain in some doubt. Supposed fifth-century examples include Senator and Gisliarda, the parents of bishop Urbanus of Langres and a Leodegaria; and Latinus and Syagria, parents of a Gondobadus.[36] And no discussion of this nature would be complete without mention of the Domus carolingicae genealogia (Genealogy of the Carolingian House), which has Ferreolus and Industria of Narbonne as the parents of Ansbertus and Firminus, bishop of Uzes circa 540, and thus as the ancestors of the Carolingians.[37] For Ansbertus married the Merovingian Blitilda—and they, in turn, were the parents of Ferreolus, a bishop of Uzes who died in 581.

The law codes also demonstrate how Roman definitions of "barbarians" came to be adopted by the barbarians themselves. In the Burgundian Code, for example, "Romans" and "Burgundians" have roughly equal status— but both are contrasted to the more ignoble "barbarians."[38] This use of the term "barbarian" reprises the preceding Roman "us-versus-them" mentality, except that now both the Romans and the Burgundians are included in the "us" category; "barbarians," however, continue to be social outsiders. This change of attitude is seen in the tale of how the Roman senator Aridius counseled the Burgundian king Gundobad when the latter was assailed by the Frank Clovis in A.D. 500. Gundobad lamented, "I do not know what to do, because these barbarians have attacked us." Aridius, a good Roman opportunist, volunteered to pretend to desert to Clovis and then "to soothe the savagery of this man [sc. Clovis]."[39] And the plan succeeded—an apparent victory of civilization over "barbarism."

ARISTOCRATIC OPTIONS

The brief foregoing discussion would suggest that Roman aristocrats living under barbarian rule had some reason to believe that their interests were being protected. This is not to say, however, that life under the barbarians continued as it had under the Romans. No; several aspects of aristocratic life were quite different, either in degree or in kind. By now, several options of the fifth century no longer were available. Those Gauls who had the means and the desire to leave Gaul altogether had long since done so. Those who would have wished to pursue careers in imperial service no longer could, although they could seek service in the rudimentary barbarian administrations. Furthermore, the freedom of action which had been available in the fifth century, when Gallo-Roman bishops could summon church councils uniting bishops from throughout central and southern Gaul, was lacking in the sixth. So just what options and opportunities, one might ask, were available to Gallo-Romans in the sixth century?

For one thing, cultural and literary interests continued to be an important part of the aristocratic ideal in the sixth century.[40] Even if literary pursuits did not offer the same degree of career mobility as they had under the Romans, opportunities still remained. Gregory of Tours discussed one such case: "Asteriolus and Secundinus had great influence with the king; both were wise and educated in rhetorical studies."[41]

In the sixth century, Gallo-Roman aristocrats likewise followed the pattern which had been established in the fifth of pursuing careers and ambitions in the church. An ecclesiastical career had become an aristocratic standard. Even here, however, Gallo-Romans had to be very attentive to the Germanic authorities, much more so than they ever had been to the

Romans. In some cases they were able to prevail over the Germans on this or that issue; in other instances they themselves were overawed. At all times they had to be circumspect.

Another result of the barbarian victory was that church councils assumed a much more restrictive tenor.[42] The days when bishops could meet in private on their own authority were gone. Now the summoning authority of the king was required, and church councils were limited to the residents of a particular kingdom. At the same time, however, there also arose a degree of close cooperation between the bishops and the kings which had not existed before.

This dependence upon the goodwill of the local king inspired a new spirit of servility in Gallic bishops wishing to assemble. In the Visigothic kingdom, when the Gallic bishops met at the Council of Agde, held in 506, they began their canons with the statement, "When in the name of the Lord, with the permission of Our Lord the Most Glorious, Magnificent, and Pious King [Alaric], the blessed synod had gathered, and there with our knees bent to the ground we prayed for his kingdom and for his long life, so that the Lord might expand the realm of him who had permitted to us the opportunity to meet . . ."[43]

These sentiments are a far cry from the adversarial relationship which had existed between the Roman bishops and Alaric's father, Euric. It would appear that the Gallic bishops and the Visigothic kings, in spite of the latters' Arian faith, had made their peace with each other.[44] Both parties would have seen advantages in their new relationship. The Gauls, in spite of their apparent obsequiousness, were very cognizant of the importance of councils as a unifying element.[45] And Alaric would have been only too aware of the impending threat of the Franks in the north, and of the resultant need to mollify the resident Gallo-Roman aristocracy. If he had not come to this conclusion himself, one can be sure that Caesarius of Arles would have instructed him during his enforced stay at Bordeaux only very shortly before.[46]

In the kingdom of the Franks, the relations between bishops and the king were similar.[47] The canons of the council of Orléans, held in 511, were addressed as follows: "All the bishops whom you commanded to come to the council to Their Lord Clovis, Son of the Catholic Church, Most Glorious King . . . ," and began, "When, under the authority of God, at the command of the Most Glorious King Clovis, the council of the bishops had gathered . . ."[48] Now, the victory of the Franks over the Visigoths at Vouillé in 507 had made the Franks the predominant barbarian authority in Gaul. Furthermore, the Franks were by now at least nominally not only Christian, but Catholic to boot.[49] There was no religious incompatibility here such as existed between Romans and Visigoths. It would have been especially important, therefore, for the Gallo-Roman bishops to remain on good terms with the Frankish authorities.

Another phenomenon of the sixth century was the presence of laymen at church councils.[50] In 517, for example, Avitus of Vienne in his invitations to the Council of Epao noted, "We permit laymen to attend," although he did stress that the resultant canons were "to be ratified by the bishops alone."[51] The Council of Orange, sponsored by Caesarius of Arles in 529, took matters one step further. There, Caesarius assembled no less than eight *viri inlustres* in support of his theological agenda; like the bishops, they subscribed to canons dealing with the most serious matters of church doctrine.[52] And again in 533, the Council of Marseilles occurred "in a meeting of bishops and laymen, who happened to be present."[53] By such practices, one might suppose, Gallo-Roman aristocrats-cum-bishops attempted to preserve as much of their class unity and authority as they could.

Church councils, however, met only infrequently. On a daily basis, the usual intermediaries between Gallo-Romans and barbarian kings were the Gallo-Roman bishops.[54] Bishops under the authority of the Franks attempted to portray themselves as the representatives of the Roman population. As seen already, Remigius of Rheims presumed to offer advice to Clovis in a letter written after the latter's victory over the Roman generalissimo Syagrius circa 486.[55] And after Clovis' conversion to Christianity in the late 490s, Avitus of Vienne could write to him, "Your faith is our victory."[56] The Gallo-Roman bishops, therefore, did their best to make common cause and seek common interests with the barbarian kings.

The Christianity of Frankish and Burgundian kings provided the Gallo-Roman bishops with a new strategy for dealing with them: by playing upon, and if possible taking advantage of, their Christian piety. Circa 520, for example, at the Council of Lyons, the bishops indicated a method they could use to exercise influence over the Burgundian king: "But if the most excellent king, moreover, suspends himself from the communion of the church or the bishops, let the blessed bishops, giving him the opportunity of returning to the lap of the blessed mother [church], betake themselves to monasteries without any delay, until the king . . . thinks it fitting to restore full communion, so that not a single one will depart from the monastery until communion has been promised or returned to all the brothers in common."[57] In instances like this, the bishops continued to draw strength from their unity. Nor should it be surprising, moreover, that the Burgundian kings allowed themselves to be manipulated in such a way, for they were squeezed between the Ostrogothic and Frankish kingdoms, and needed all the support from their Gallo-Roman subjects that they could get.

The kings, on the other hand, had their own ways of manipulating the bishops. Episcopal appointments now required at least the consent of the king, and many were preordained by him.[58] The Council of Orléans of 517, for example, even decreed, "No layman can aspire to clerical office without either an order from the king or by the will of the governor."[59] And not only that, but eventually—once most of Gaul was in the hands of the newly converted Franks—Gallo-Romans often had to compete with Germans for high ecclesiastical office.[60] Church property, too, often was threatened by barbarian and especially royal appropriations, and Gallo-Roman bishops constantly had to be on their guard.[61]

FROM VITRIOL TO VIOLENCE

In the fifth century, the administration of justice, with regard to the lower elements of society, had had its rough-and-ready aspects. Sidonius' heavy-handed treatment of those he apprehended desecrating his grandfather's grave is well known.[62] Aristocratic interactions, however, had tended to be genteel in nature. Certainly, there had been occasional exchanges of insults, and, as seen above, the fear of *delatores* had been omnipresent. But, except in the most extreme cases, one's personal security had not been threatened. These pleasant circumstances disappeared under barbarian authority.

In the sixth century, many Gallo-Romans enthusiastically embraced the Germanic legal concept of "self-help" when it came to seeking redress for real or imagined wrongs perpetrated against them.[63] The disappearance of much of the traditional legal and other machinery for the settling of disputes seems to have resulted in a new level of violence in Gallo-Roman society.

Any number of cases can be adduced in which Gallo-Romans took the law into their own hands and physically assaulted each other. The fate of Sidonius' friend Eucherius, who was buried alive under a wall in the 470s, presumably at the instigation of the *dux* Victorius, set a precedent for many similar deeds later, most of them without even the vestiges of legal justification that Victorius had.[64]

There are many examples of such violence. Some involved individuals of relatively modest social standing, others involved those of the highest rank. In some instances, Germans seem to have been involved as well. Several cases arose from family disputes. At some time before 548, for example, Parthenius, the nephew of Magnus Felix Ennodius, murdered both his wife, Papianilla, the granddaughter of Eparchius Avitus, and her lover, Auxanius. He himself later was murdered by a mob of Franks at

Trier.[65] At Tours in 581, the tables were turned, when the lover of the wife of a certain Ambrose slaughtered both Ambrose and his brother Lupus. The two then fled the city.[66]

Shortly thereafter, in the early 580s, a cleric of Le Mans, "a lover of women and feasting and fornication and given to every kind of vice," disguised his lover as a man and the two fled to Lisieux. The woman's relatives, however, apprehended them, burned the woman, and accepted twenty solidi as recompense from the cleric.[67] Gregory attributed their willingness to accept such payment to their "hunger for gold," but it is in fact merely consistent with Germanic legal practice.

A particularly tangled set of circumstances arose at Clermont in the early 570s. It all began when a certain Eulalius, who later became Count of Clermont, was suspected of having strangled his mother with her own hair shirt. Eulalius then married a Tetradia, but after he became involved with several maidservants, she undertook to elope with his nephew Verus. Verus, however, fearing the enmity of his uncle, sent her and the family property to his patron, the dux Desiderius, for safekeeping. Eulalius, learning of the deception, murdered Verus, and Desiderius married Tetradia himself. Eulalius then married a girl he had kidnaped from a convent in Lyons, and killed her cousin Aemerius. He also murdered the brother of his half-sister along the way. Not only did he suffer no punishment, but a church synod ordered Tetradia to reimburse him fourfold for what she had taken.[68]

The avenging of injuries done to one's family seems to have been particularly popular. Circa 550, Syagrius of Verdun, the son of the bishop Desideratus, repaid a certain Syrivaldus, who had denounced Desideratus to the king, by raiding Syrivaldus' villa. After initially murdering the wrong man, Syagrius and his band of retainers later returned, tore down a wall, and likewise murdered Syrivaldus.[69]

Shortly after 572, Gregory of Tours' own brother Peter was lanced to death by the son of the bishop Silvester of Langres, who believed that Peter had magically caused the death of his father. After fleeing, the murderer killed another man on the road, whose relatives responded by hacking him limb from limb.[70] And circa 585, Nanthinus, the Count of Angoulême, set out to avenge the death of his uncle Maracharius, a former count and bishop of the city. After killing a presbyter and several laymen, he himself died of the plague.[71]

Rioting after the death of Nicetius of Lyons in 591 led to additional violence. While "swords and axes were flying around," one man was killed. A few days later, the murdered man's brother cornered and killed the perpetrator. The guilty man then sought sanctuary at the tomb of Nicetius, and was permitted by the secular authorities to return home.[72] Once again, self-help had triumphed.

Some cycles of violence were even more senseless. Gregory tells of an incident at Tours which began as an example of Romano-Germanic concord. In 585, a Sicharius, the son of Johannes and presumably of Roman extraction, was celebrating Christmas outside of town with a certain Austreghysilus, who apparently had a Germanic background. A local presbyter sent his slave to invite some friends of Austreghysilus, but one of them, for no clear reason, killed the slave. Sicharius, who was a friend of the presbyter, decided to take it out on Austreghysilus. A conflict ensued in which four of Sicharius' supporters were killed.

Sicharius then, with an armed band, killed not only Austreghysilus, but also his brother Eberulgus and son Auno. Auno's son Chramnesindus responded by plundering Sicharius' house and killing some of his slaves. The quarrel then supposedly was patched up, and Sicharius and Chramnesindus became fast friends. But one night, Sicharius, in his cups, recalled to Chramnesindus how he had killed the latter's relatives, and Chramnesindus thought to himself, "Unless I avenge the death of my relatives, I deserve to lose the name of a man and to be called a helpless woman." He therefore killed Sicharius, for which he then was pardoned.[73]

Some of this new violence erupted as a result of quarrels over more tangible items, such as office holding and royal preferment. Circa 539, the royal favorites Asteriolus and Secundinus quarreled: "It proceeded to the extent that, having forgotten their verbal complaints, they took to pummeling each other with their own hands." Eventually, the king dismissed Asteriolus, who then was protected by the queen, but after her death, Secundinus killed him. Nor was that the end of the matter, for Asteriolus' son, after he grew up, resolved to avenge the death of his father. He pursued and trapped Secundinus, who poisoned himself, "Lest he fall into the hands of his enemy."[74]

Another example of the enmity that could arise over office holding occurred in 573/574 when Jovinus, the governor of Provence, was replaced by Albinus. It flared up again when Albinus attempted to become bishop of Uzès in 581. Jovinus, however, obtained royal permission to do so, but before he arrived the populace ordained a certain Marcellus. Jovinus responded by besieging the city, and Marcellus had no recourse but to buy him off.[75] Such shenanigans were unheard of in the fifth century.

Additional violence resulted from quarrels over money and property. In the early part of the sixth century, the mother of Stratidius, a relative of Germanus, later bishop of Paris, attempted to poison Germanus in order to get his property; her son drank the poison instead.[76] In 584, at

Tours, the Jew Armentarius was killed and dumped into a well by the former vicar Injuriosus and the tribune Medardus when he tried to collect money owed to him by Injuriosus and the former count Eunomius.[77] The influential murderers went unpunished.

In 585, Domnula, daughter of the bishop of Rennes, became involved in a quarrel over some vineyards with the *referendarius* (chancellor) Bobolenus. He responded by recruiting an armed band and killing her and her retainers, "the women as well as the men."[78] Not until 587 was Bobolenus punished, by having his property confiscated, and even this seems to have been for political reasons.[79]

Bishops, too, although sometimes more circumspect, used their office to avenge personal injuries. According to Gregory of Tours, for example, bishop Badygesilus of Le Mans used to brag, "I will not therefore, just because I have been made a cleric, cease to be an avenger of my injuries."[80] Gregory also rhetorically described the enmity between two families of Lyons circa 571. He claimed that Priscus, who had succeeded Gregory's uncle Nicetius as bishop, "began to persecute and kill many of those whom the man of God had held dear," and that he exulted, "I give thanks to you, Jesus Christ, that after the death of the most vile Nicetius I have succeeded in trampling upon his house."[81] Gregory himself was not averse to using his authority as bishop in his own quarrels. In one instance he asserted, not very convincingly, "I suspended him from communion, not as an avenger of my injuries, but so that I might render him more easily cleansed from his insanity."[82]

These kinds of quarrels and the violence which often accompanied their settlement are, of course, characteristic of the sixth century, not the fifth. But one cannot but contrast them with the more peaceful methods which almost invariably resolved such disputes in the fifth century. The letters of Sidonius, for example, are replete with examples of how standard procedures involving patronage, arbitration, and legal processes were used to settle disputes over land and property.[83]

This is not to say, of course, that these old Roman methods of solving disputes disappeared. If one desired, one still could have recourse to the old methods. But, once again, the arrival of the Germans had introduced a new possibility into Gallo-Roman society. The old machinery still remained, but it now was an option, not a necessity. And one of the results seems to have been the breakdown of much of the Roman aristocratic solidarity which had existed in the fifth century.

An example of the failure of the old institutions can be seen in an incident that occurred at Clermont circa 525/530, when the senator Hortensius imprisoned Honoratus, a relative of the bishop Quintianus. Quintianus initially suggested, "through his friends," that Honoratus be freed, but Hortensius refused. Quintianus then went in person, but the soldiers refused to release their prisoner. Quintianus' final recourse was to go to Hortensius' house, blow dust upon it, and ritually curse the site: "Cursed be this house, and cursed be its inhabitants unto eternity, and let it be deserted, and let there be no one to live within it."[84] This may have given Quintianus some satisfaction, but the grievance was left unresolved.

For many Gauls, the Germanic system of self-help was preferable. If one had a weak case, if one had a ready band of roughnecks, if one's opponent could be caught by surprise, all the more reason to take matters into one's own hands. Of course, even in the Germanic system such actions carried a price: the wergelds which accompanied various violent deeds and which were formalized in the Germanic law codes.[85] An example of this practice can be seen in the case of the libidinous cleric cited above. Many Gauls, apparently, felt that their violent actions were cheap at the price.

Aristocrats now could pursue their quarrels using the same kinds of self-help and rough-and-ready justice as their Germanic rulers. Under the Romans, the most a Gallo-Roman aristocrat usually had to fear was the loss of reputation, property, and domicile; under the Germans he now had to fear for his life, which could be taken just as easily by his peers as by his new rulers.[86] Such considerations would have made factionalism and quarreling even more bitter than it had been before.

What perhaps is most striking, finally, about these accounts of endemic and senseless violence is the matter-of-fact way in which they were reported.[87] No indication is ever given that the assaults, lootings, kidnapings, and murders were anything unexpected or out of the ordinary. They seem rather, by the end of the sixth century, simply to have been accepted practice. All of this is a far cry from the conventional social practices of the fifth century, and indicates that the aristocrats now had adopted a new ideology in the pursuit of their ambitions and the settlement of their disputes.

EPILOGUE

The aristocrats of Roman Gaul faced a very different world after the arrival and settlement of the barbarians, and they responded accordingly. Indeed, they showed themselves to be a very adaptable breed. When the criteria of the old Roman aristocratic order proved unsatisfactory, they restructured them to suit their own purposes. Literary interests and pursuits, for example, assumed a magnified importance as a determinant of aristocratic status.

More significant, perhaps, was the expanded role assumed by ecclesiastical office, not only as an ersatz for secular office in an aristocratic career, but also as a means for pursuing a general aristocratic ideology. Virtually all of the material and psychological needs of secular aristocracy were available in the church. The secular noble might consider flight to safer areas of the Mediterranean; the churchman attained metaphorical exile in the church. The secular noble who remained in Gaul sought personal security in his fortified stronghold; the bishop found it in the church: even barbarian kings eschewed harming a ranking ecclesiastic.

The secular noble hoped to be accepted as one of the "good people" of this world; the bishop was assuredly also one of the "good people" of the next. The secular noble sought landed estates; the bishop administered more of them than most nobles could hope to possess. The secular noble strove to provide services in the role of a patron and thus to acquire influence; the bishop did all these things on a greatly expanded scale. The Gallo-Roman aristocrats had redefined ecclesiastical office in response to the needs of their times.

Nor was this all. Gallo-Roman aristocrats also learned to coexist with barbarian officialdom. They developed standard, accepted, and understood methods for dealing with the barbarians. Captives could be ransomed. The imprisoned could be freed. The accused could be cleared. The exiled could be recalled. The dispossessed could have their property restored. In all such instances, both the resident Roman aristocrats and the newly arrived barbarians knew what the rules were. The Romans also eventually made effective use of certain barbarian practices: the use of violence as a method of self-help became particularly endemic in Gallic society in the sixth century. As for the barbarians, their integration was hastened by their issuance of law codes designed to normalize relations with the Roman population.

THE LEGACY OF THE GALLO-ROMAN ARISTOCRACY

The post-Roman period saw the fusion of the old Roman and new Germanic nobilities.[1] By the eighth century, earlier ethnic distinctions had lost their significance: in the north, Franks called themselves "Romans" and Roman aristocrats became "senators of the Franks"; inhabitants of southeastern Gaul became "Burgundians" (supposedly because the Roman population had been exterminated); Romans of Septimania could be called "Goths"; southwestern Gauls became "Aquitanians" or "Gascons."[2] Not only did Germans adopt Roman names, but Romans used Germanic names.[3]

Some later writers had a hard time explaining the "disappearance" of the Romans, and came up with some fanciful explanations for these changes. The dearth of "Romans" in Burgundia supposedly had resulted from the slaughter of any Romans who had not fled.[4] And as for the Franks, one version had it that "Clovis exterminated all the Romans who then lived in Gaul, so that scarcely one could be found. And the Franks at this time are seen to have learned the Roman language, which they still use, from those Romans who lived there."[5] But the Romans, of course, had not disappeared without a trace. They had merely "gone barbarian" at the same time that the barbarians had "gone Roman."[6]

This surviving Roman element in barbarian Europe left important legacies to posterity.[7] It is no accident that two of the most significant of them resulted directly from the Roman redefinition of aristocratic status in the fifth century, and the increased significance which was accorded to ecclesiastical service and literary inclinations. The church, in particular, became the special preserve of the descendents of Gallo-Roman senators, even if during the sixth century they began to face competition from barbarians. In later years, however, the integration of the Roman and barbarian aristocracies made any distinction moot.

At the same time, there was a broader significance to the Gallic pursuit of literary culture. In addition to its importance in its own day, the compulsive Gallic pursuit of literary interests also had a far-reaching effect on the direction of later medieval culture, for it was these aristocrats who were responsible for the appreciation, preservation, and dissemination of classical culture. Gallic aristocratic families conscientiously preserved the literary efforts of family members. Sidonius' son Apollinaris, for example, saw to the continued circulation and copying of the letters of his father.[8] And the source of the ninth-century *codex Sangallensis* (Codex of St. Gall) contained not only letters of Sidonius, but also the collected letters of Sidonius' relative Ruricius of Limoges, thirteen letters addressed to Ruricius, and two books of letters of another possible relative, the early-seventh-century bishop Desiderius of Cahors.[9] Someone, perhaps a family member, made a conscious effort to collect and preserve the work of this familial-literary circle.

Educated Romans also eventually encouraged the barbarian appreciation of classical literature and culture.[10] Germans, even kings, became littérateurs in their own right. The Frankish king Chilperic, for example, not only wrote hymns and "several books of verse in the manner of Sedulius," he even attempted to add additional letters to the alphabet.[11] Had it not been for these Roman littérateurs, the history of the classical tradition in the Middle Ages might have been a very short one indeed.[12]

The amalgamation of the Roman and Germanic administrative systems also was directly responsible for the preservation of Roman law and legal institutions. The survival of the Theodosian Code itself in Gaul, as well as the elements of Roman law which were integrated into the barbarian law codes, affected the direction of medieval law and education.[13] In all such cases, even if the Roman aristocracy, as separate from the barbarians, eventually disappeared, the precedents and policies that it established in the fifth century continued as strong and influential as ever.

ROMAN ARISTOCRATS IN BARBARIAN EUROPE

There now remains the question of the extent to which the Roman populations of other areas of the western Roman Empire dealt with the barbarian arrivals. Were their responses similar to or different from those of the Romans in Gaul? And did they have the same degree of success?

One might begin a survey of these questions by looking first at Roman North Africa. Although the evidence is not as extensive as it is for Gaul, there are some good indications of what Roman perceptions were.[14] The Vandal occupiers had some policies which were decidedly different from those of the barbarian inhabitants of Gaul, and relations between the

Vandal and Roman populations were decidedly more inimical.[15] The situation in Africa also was complicated by the presence of a third element, the native Moors of the North African uplands, who often opposed the Vandals actively.

The Roman aristocrats of North Africa faced some of the same difficulties and choices as those of Gaul.[16] Some landowners simply went into exile, such as the senator Gordianus in 442.[17] Unlike their Gallic brethren, however, many of these insistently lobbied with the eastern emperor for imperial intervention.[18] Those who remained presumably often suffered the effects of the *sortes Vandalorum*, the distribution of tax-free, inalienable land allotments to Vandal warriors.

Africans in secular life could continue to pursue literary careers, and even hope to find favor with the Vandal kings as a result.[19] Like Sidonius, the poet Dracontius used his literary skills to try to obtain his release from prison.[20] In the late fifth and sixth centuries, a number of African writers continued their literary pursuits.[21] Other African Romans not only placed great stress on literary accomplishments but also sought advancement in the church.[22] Here, however, the similarity ended: of all the Arian settlers in the west, the Vandals were the most notorious and ferocious persecutors of orthodox Christians.[23]

Ultimately, of course, the Vandal kingdom fell, and what was left of Roman society was resorbed into the Roman state. Eventually, North Africa would even give birth to another Roman emperor, Heraclius (A.D. 610–641). In this sense, then, any efforts at a rapprochement between the Roman and Vandal populations came to nought. The Roman population itself, meanwhile, soon was submerged by the arrival of the Muslims in the mid seventh century.

At the other geographical extreme of the western Roman Empire lay Britain, which to all intents and purposes had dropped out of the Roman world as of the first decade of the fifth century. The role of the Roman aristocracy there vis-à-vis the Anglo-Saxon invaders in the fifth century can largely only be speculated upon; what evidence there is suggests that relations initially were adversarial in nature.[24] Nevertheless, classical culture did survive, and by the seventh century what remained of the Roman heritage would appear to have been assimilated into barbarian society.[25]

Closer to Gaul lay Spain, and there one finds similarities, albeit less well documented ones, to the situation in Gaul.[26] This may have resulted, in part, from the eventual occupation (after 456) of Spain by one of the same peoples who had occupied Gaul: the Visigoths. The chronicle of Hydatius, which concludes circa 468, details many of the interactions between Romans and barbarians, including accounts not only of oppression, especially by the Suevi, but also of collaboration. In general, the picture is one of accommodation between the Roman and barbarian populations.

Like their Gallic brethren, Hispano-Roman aristocrats seem to have survived by seeking refuge in the church.[27] As for literary culture, after a lusterless period in the fifth and sixth centuries, there was a great revival of the Latin cultural heritage in the seventh century.[28] As in Gaul, barbarians soon were integrated into the Roman cultural heritage. The Visigothic king Sisebut (612–620) wrote biography and poetry, and his successors Chintila (636–640), Reccesvinth (649–672), and Wamba (672–680) also wrote poetry.[29] By the time of the Moorish invasion of 711, it would appear that the integration of Romans and barbarians in Spain had been successfully effected.

The response of Italo-Roman aristocrats to the arrival of the barbarians is especially well documented, and provides some significant contrasts to the situation in Gaul.[30] It would appear that in Italy, many diehard senators made little effort to reach a true rapprochement with the barbarians, whether followers of Odovacar, Ostrogoths, or Lombards; they tried to ignore them, even if this meant withdrawing from society.[31] And they did so in spite of Germanic efforts to facilitate cooperation.[32] The Ostrogothic king Theoderic (491–526), for example, was described in 512 as the "guardian of liberty and the propagator of the Roman name."[33]

Other Italian aristocrats, however, were more flexible, and were more successful in dealing with the newcomers in particular and the changed conditions of the fifth and sixth centuries in general.[34] Cyprianus, for example, a senator who secured advancement under the Ostrogoths, was praised by Theoderic for learning Gothic.[35] The end result of these divergent perceptions was a failure of the Italians to develop a coherent response to the barbarian presence. As a result, the Italian aristocracy became fragmented and disunified.[36] And this situation was exacerbated by an apparent lack of common cause between the great urban senatorial families and the Italian provincial aristocrats.[37]

The schizophrenic Italian approach to life in barbarian Europe is seen in the role played by the church. There was no agreement on the role church office was to play. Many senators continued to seek advancement in secular careers, in both Roman and, after 476, barbarian administrations.[38] Some senators do seem to have made a relatively half-hearted effort to shift their interests and emphasis to ecclesiastical affairs.[39] But even the office of bishop does not seem to have had the attraction for Italians that it did for Gauls.[40] As a result, the papacy itself often fell under the control of foreigners, and could serve as a cause for contention rather than cooperation between the ecclesiastical and secular aristocracies.[41]

[148]

In the field of literature, a classical education in Italy continued to be a road to secular advancement for some.[42] Others, rather than using literary interests as a rallying point, as in Gaul, simply withdrew from society.[43] Of course, as before, Italian writers did continue to produce a vast amount of literary output—but the function of literary pursuits does not seem to have been reevaluated to meet the needs of the times as it was in Gaul.[44] In general, all these factors indicate the inadequacy of the Italian response to the barbarian settlement, and the end result was the demise of the Italo-Roman aristocracy in the latter half of the sixth century.[45]

This brief survey would suggest that aristocrats in different areas of the Roman west responded in different ways to the repercussions of the barbarian settlement. Some were more successful than others. But no aristocrats, it would seem, were quite as successful as those in Gaul, where the development of a unified response to the barbarian presence contributed greatly to their success and survival. In Italy, in particular, the failure of the Italian senatorial order to develop a coherent response to the conditions of barbarian Europe was an important cause of its decline. In Spain and Africa, on the other hand, the situation was complicated by the eventual arrival of the Muslims. But in Gaul the Franks went on to become the most successful, and long-lived, of the barbarian invaders of western Europe. And one cannot but wonder whether much of their success was due to the Romano-barbarian amalgamation which resulted from the strategies for survival formulated by the Gallo-Roman aristocrats of the fifth century.

ROMAN EMPERORS

WEST

Valentinian I (364–375)
Gratian (367–383)
Valentinian II (375–392)
Magnus Maximus (383–388) (usurper in Britain, Gaul, and Spain)
Theodosius I (379–395) (east and west)
Honorius (395–423)
Marcus and Gratian (406) (usurpers in Britain)
Constantine III (407–411) (usurper in Britain and Gaul)
Priscus Attalus (409–410, 414–415) (usurper in Italy and Gaul)
Maximus (409–411) (usurper in Spain)
Jovinus (411–413) (usurper in Gaul)
Maximus (420–422) (usurper in Spain)
Constantius III (421)
Johannes (423–425) (usurper in Italy)
Valentinian III (425–455)
Petronius Maximus (455)
Eparchius Avitus (455–456)
Majorian (457–461)
Libius Severus (461–465)
Anthemius (467–472)
Olybrius (472)
Glycerius (473–474)
Julius Nepos (474–480)
Romulus (475–476) (usurper in Italy)

EAST

Valens (364–378)
Procopius (365–366)
Theodosius I (379–395) (east and west)
Arcadius (383–408)
Theodosius II (402–450)
Marcian (450–457)
Leo I (457–474)
Zeno (474–491)
Basiliscus (475–476)
Anastasius (491–518)

(Legitimate emperors in bold face type)

BARBARIAN RULERS

BURGUNDIANS (IN GAUL)

Gundahar (c. 411–437)
Gundioc (–455–c. 473)
Chilperic I (–455–)
Chilperic II (–458–c. 480)
Godegisel (c. 473–500)
Gundobad I (c. 473–516)
Sigismund (516–523)

FRANKS (IN GAUL)

Faramund (?–c. 436)
Chlogio (c. 436–456)
Childeric (c. 456–482)
Clovis (482–511)
Chlodomer (511–524)
Theoderic I (511–533)
Childebert (511–558)
Chlothacar (511–561)

ITALY

Odovacar (476–491)

OSTROGOTHS (IN ITALY)

Theoderic I (491–526)

VANDALS (IN SPAIN AND NORTH AFRICA)

Godigisel (406)
Gunderic (406–428)
Gaiseric (428–477)
Huneric (477–484)
Gunthamund (484–496)
Thrasamund (496–523)

VISIGOTHS (IN GAUL AND SPAIN)

Alaric (c. 391–410)
Athaulf (410–415)
Segeric (415)
Wallia (415–418)
Theoderic I (418–451)
Thorismund (451–453)
Theoderic II (453–466)
Euric (466–484)
Alaric II (484–507)

GLOSSARY

Agens in rebus. Imperial agent.
Amicitia. Friendship
Augustus. Emperor.
Auricularius. Royal official.
Caesar. Junior emperor.
Clarissima femina (*c.f.*). "Most Distinguished Woman."
Comes. "Count," usually a high-ranking military officer.
Comes civitatis. "Count of the City," a city administrator.
Comes domesticorum. "Count of the Domestics," commander of the imperial bodyguards.
Comes rei privatae. "Count of the Private Purse, " an imperial finance minister.
Comes sacrarum largitionum. "Count of the Sacred Largesses," an imperial finance minister.
Consiliarius. Royal counselor.
Consul. Two "ordinary consuls," who gave their names to the year, were chosen each year.
Consularis. "Consular," provincial governor of intermediate rank.
Corrector. Governor of a province in Italy.
Cura palatii. "Caretaker of the Palace," an imperial official.
Curialis. Member of a local senate, a town counselor.
Decurion. Member of a local senate, a town counselor.
Delator. "Betrayer": an informer.
Diocese. Administrative unit made up of several provinces.
Domesticus. Member of the imperial bodyguard or of a royal court.
Dux. "Duke," a general.
Foederati. Barbarian allies of the Romans.
Honoratus. A person with any claim to rank or status.

Iudex. "Judge," usually a provincial governor.

Legatus. An imperial or royal representative or ambassador.

Magister equitum. "Master of Horse," an imperial generalissimo.

Magister militum. "Master of Soldiers," an imperial generalissimo.

Magister officium. "Master of Offices," akin to a Prime Minister.

Magister peditum. "Master of Foot," an imperial generalissimo.

Magister utriusque militiae. "Master of Both Services," an imperial generalissimo.

Maior domus. "Mayor of the Palace," a royal court official.

Maiores. "Very important persons."

Militans. A secular or military official.

Nobilis. An aristocrat.

Notarius. An imperial factotum.

Novus homo. "New man," a man newly come to high rank.

Officialis. A secular official.

Optimus, Optimates. "The best man or men."

Otium. "Leisure" (usually that of an aristocrat).

Palatinus. An imperial court official.

Patricius. Patrician, the highest non-imperial rank.

Potentates. "Very powerful persons."

Potentiores. "Very powerful persons."

Praefectus praetorio. "Praetorian Prefect," overseer of several dioceses.

Praefectus urbi. "Prefect of the City," the administrator of Rome.

Praepositus. An overseer.

Praepositus sacri cubiculi. "Overseer of the Sacred Bedchamber," a eunuch.

Praeses. Lowest-ranking governor, of a minor province.

Prefecture. Administrative unit of two or more dioceses.

Primicerius notariorum. "Chief of the Notaries," an imperial official.

Primores. "Men of the first rank."

Procer, proceres. "Leading man or men."

Proconsul. Highest-ranking provincial governor.

Protector. Member of the imperial bodyguard.

Protector et domesticus. Member of the imperial bodyguard.

Province. Smallest imperial administrative unit.

Quaestor sacri palatii. "Quaestor of the Sacred Palace," akin to an Attorney General.

Rationalis. Accountant.

Referendarius. Royal court official.

Saecularis. Secular official.

Scholasticus. Scribe.

Senator. General term for a Roman aristocrat.

Tribunus (et notarius). Imperial factotum.

Vicarius. "Vicar," administrator in charge of a diocese.

Vir clarissimus (v.c.). "Most Distinguished Man," the lowest senatorial rank.

Vir egregius. Member of the equestrian class.

Vir gloriosissimus. High-ranking *vir inlustris.*

Vir inlustris, vir inlustrissimus (v.i.). "Most Illustrious Man," a high senatorial rank.

Vir magnificentissimus. High-ranking *vir inlustris.*

Vir spectabilis (v.s.). "Respectable Man," an intermediate senatorial rank.

ABBREVIATIONS

AASS	*Acta sanctorum*
Bury, *LRE*	Bury, J. B., *History of the Later Roman Empire* (2d ed.) (London, 1923)
CIL 12	O. Hirschfeld ed., *Corpus inscriptionum latinarum*, vol. 12: *Inscriptiones Galliae Narbonensis latinae* (Berlin, 1888)
CIL 13	O. Hirschfeld, C. Zangemeister, A. von Domaszewski, O. Bohn, and E. Stein eds., *Corpus inscriptionum latinarum* 13: *Inscriptiones Trium Galliarum et Germaniarum latinae* (Berlin, 1899–1943)
CJ	*Codex iustinianus*
Clavis	E. Dekkers and A. Gaar eds., *Clavis patrum latinorum* (2d ed.) (Turnhout, 1961)
Corp.chr.lat.	*Corpus christianorum, series latina*
CSEL	*Corpus scriptorum ecclesiasticorum latinorum*
C.Th.	*Codex theodosianus*
FHG	C. Müller ed., *Fragmenta historicorum graecorum* (Paris, 1874–1885)
Haenel, *Corp.leg.*	G. Haenel, *Corpus legum ab imperatoribus romanis ante Justinianum latarum* (Leipzig, 1857)
ILCV	E. Diehl ed., *Inscriptiones latinae christianae veteres* (Berlin, 1925–1931)
ILS	H. Dessau, *Inscriptiones latinae selectae* (5 vols.) (Berlin, 1954)
Jaffé	P. Jaffé, *Regesta pontificum romanorum* (2d ed.) (Leipzig, 1885)
Jones, *LRE*	A. H. M. Jones, *The Later Roman Empire*

MGH AA	Monumenta Germaniae historica, Auctores antiquissimi
MGH Epist.	Monumenta Germaniae historica, Epistulae
MGH Leg.	Monumenta Germaniae historica, Leges
MGH Poet.	Monumenta Germaniae historica, Poetae latini
MGH SRM	Monumenta Germaniae historica, Scriptores rerum merovingicarum
MGH SS	Monumenta Germaniae historica, Scriptores
PG	J.-P. Migne ed., Patrologia graeca
PIR	Prosopographia imperii romani, saec. I–III
PL	J.-P. Migne ed., Patrologia latina
PLRE I	A. H. M. Jones, J. R. Martindale, and J. Morris eds., The Prosopography of the Later Roman Empire, Volume I, A.D. 260–395 (Cambridge, 1971)
PLRE II	J. R. Martindale ed., The Prosopography of the Later Roman Empire, Volume II, A.D. 395–527 (Cambridge, 1980)
PLS	Patrologia latina, supplementum
RE	Paully-Wissowa-Kroll, Real-Encyclopädie der klassischen Altertumswissenschaft
SC	Sources chrétiennes
Thiel, Epist.	Andreas Thiel, Epistolae romanorum pontificum (Brunsburg, 1867)

For other abbreviations, and full source citations, see Primary Bibliography.

NOTES

1. See Chapter 11.

2. For the Gallic aristocracy of Late Antiquity, see Dill, *Gaul;* Gilliard, "Senators"; Heinzelmann, *Bischofsherrschaft;* Held, "Aristokratie"; Jullian, *Gaule* 8.126–136; Kurth, "Sénateurs"; Mathisen, *Ecclesiastical Aristocracy;* Matthews, *Aristocracies;* and Stroheker, *Adel* and "Die Senatoren."

3. For general historical outlines of the barbarian settlements, see the Introduction.

4. See Baynes, "Decline"; Blasquez, "Niederlassungen"; Bloch, "Observations"; Bury, *Invasion;* Chrysos, "Concepts"; Demandt, *Fall;* Drew, "Origins"; Goffart, "Rome" and "Invasions"; Latouche, *Invasions;* Lot, *Invasions;* MacMullen, *Corruption;* Musset, *Invasions;* Prevost, "Invasions"; Rémondon, *Crise;* Riché, *Invasions;* Saunders, "Debate"; and Thompson, *Romans.* The fascination with the topic of the relations between barbarians and Romans is attested by the many books with that title; note Barrett and Fitzpatrick, *Barbarians and Romans;* Goffart, *Barbarians and Romans;* Cunliffe, *Greeks, Romans and Barbarians;* Randers-Pehrson, *Barbarians and Romans;* and Thompson, *Romans and Barbarians.*

5. For a discussion of who these "elite classes" were, see Chapter 1; see also Wormald, "Decline."

6. See Epilogue.

7. See Stroheker, *Adel,* p. 3.

8. See, for example, Matthews, *Aristocracies,* pp. 343–344; Oost, *Placidia,* p. 126 n. 49; and Wallace-Hadrill, "Gothia," p. 220ff.

9. See Dill, *Gaul,* pp. 25, 159; Goffart, *Barbarians,* pp. 124–125; Matthews, *Aristocracies,* p. 342; Rouche, *Aquitaine,* p. 24; Stroheker, *Adel,* p. 20; Thompson, *Romans* pp. 23–27; and Wallace-Hadrill, "Gothia," p. 222.

10. Saunders, "Debate," p. 16; for similar, see Goffart, "Rome," p. 294.

11. Goffart, "Rome," p. 295.

12. Although Barnish, "Transformation," p. 142, suggests that some aristocrats favored the barbarians because they "promised many senators a hope of less expensive advancement."

13. See Momigliano, "Caduta," pp. 11–12.

14. For Roman influences on the barbarians, see Introduction.

15. For "continuity and change," see Classen, "Kaiserreskript"; Clover and Humphreys, *Tradition;* Drinkwater, "Attitudes" and *Gallic Empire;* Genicot, "Nobility"; and Heinzelmann, *Bischofsherrschaft.* For Gallic response in an earlier period, see Drinkwater, "Attitudes," p. 152. Compare Stroheker, *Adel,* p. 67, who suggests that "how they responded . . . does not appear much in the thoughts of the aristocracy."

16. See Arnheim, *Aristocracy;* Matthews, *Aristocracies;* and McGeachy, *Symmachus.*

17. See Dill, *Gaul,* p. 25; Grahn-Hoek, *Oberschicht;* Irsigler, "Character"; Martindale, "Aristocracy"; and Zöllner, *Geschichte.*

18. For the problem of the relation between the late Roman aristocracy of Gaul and that of the sixth century, see Gilliard, "Senators."

19. Loyen, "Résistants," p. 437, saw only two options: collaboration or resistance.

20. Compare Goffart, "Invasions," p. 95, on the fourth-century authors: "They had no sense of a mounting peril."

21. For a brief discussion of these areas, see Epilogue.

22. For a detailed discussion of Gallic literary activities, see Chapter 10.

23. See Cristiani, *Lérins;* and Pricoco, *Isola.*

24. See Engelbrecht, "Beiträge."

25. See Delehaye, *Passions.*

INTRODUCTION. THE BARBARIANS IN GAUL:
IN SEARCH OF AN IDENTITY

1. See Chapter 4.

2. For "barbarian" in its ancient sense of "non-Roman," see Goffart, "Theme," p. 96.

3. See Loyen, "Débuts"; Oost, *Placidia,* p. 153ff; and Thompson, "Visigoths."

4. Franks: Schmidt, "Anfängen" and "Ende." Burgundians: Byvanck, "Burgondes"; Grégoire, "Burgondes"; Perrenot, "Etablissement"; Perrin, *Burgondes;* and Perroud, "Savoie."

5. See Altheim, *Attila;* Demougeot, "Attila"; Täckholm, "Aetius"; and Thompson, *Attila.*

6. In general, see Bury, *LRE,* vol. 1; Seeck, *Untergangs,* vol. 6; Stein, *Geschichte,* vol. 1; and Stroheker, *Adel.* For the imperial policies of the settlement of the Germans in Gaul, see Bachrach, "Another Look"; Goffart, *Barbarians;* and Thompson, "Settlement." Even before 406 there had been settlements of barbarian *laeti* on the left bank of the Rhine: see Demougeot, "Restrictions," pp. 381–388; and MacMullen, *Corruption,* p. 178.

7. A view expressed, for example, by Goffart, "Rome," who objects (p. 277) to the use of the term *barbarian* at all, because it "tends to transform the neighbors of the Roman Empire into a collectivity."

8. For Mediterranean Germanic as a "welter of tongues, little more than a lingua franca ... a conglomerate of dialects," see Markey, "Germanic," pp. 57,62. Just what language, one might wonder, was spoken by the interpreter when Germanus of Auxerre accosted the Alan Goar in the 440s (VGermani 28: "medioque interprete").

9. See Chapter 12.

10. For admixtures of Huns, Alans, Ostrogoths, and other assorted barbarians, refugees, and brigands, see Zos. Hist. Nov. 5.34–37; Philostorg. HE 12.3; Jord. Get. 283–284; and Paul.Pell. Euch. 377–398. See also Thompson, Romans, p. 234; and Oost, Placidia, p. 87, "eventually probably most of the barbarian bands joined up with the Goths," cf. pp. 82–92, 132; see also Chrysos, "Gothia Romana"; and Teillet, Goths. And note SHA Claud. 6.2; and Burns, Ostrogoths, pp. 30–38, for "the elasticity within the Ostrogothic assemblage."

11. "manus ingens diversorum ... immanium hostium Vandalorum et Alanorum commixtam secum habens Gothorum gentem, aliarumque diversarum personas" (VAugustini 28.4). For the lack of cultural differentiation of the Alans, see also Bachrach, Alans, pp. 74–119.

12. See Thompson, Romans, pp. 18–19. Other groups, such as the Franks and Alamanni, were coalitions of different groups to begin with; see Wightman, Belgica, p. 193.

13. See, e.g., MacBain, "Odovacer the Hun?" Another barbarian potentate of mixed ancestry was the generalissimo Ricimer (PLRE II, p. 942; Papini, Ricimero).

14. See Lebel, "Vestiges," p. 92, for the " 'fusion' entre les immigrants germaniques et les populations indigènes de la Gaule"; McCormick, "Clovis," p. 155, for barbarians "operating largely within the structures and traditions of imperial civilization"; and Goffart, "Invasions," p. 98: "the barbarians could think of few other goals than to defend the Roman status quo and fit themselves into it as best they could"; cf. also Bianchini, "Unione"; Gamillscheg, Romania Germanica; Geary, France, p. 57; and Grünert, Römer.

15. See Bang, Germanen; Claude, "Begründung"; Johne, "Germanen"; Scott, "Sentiments"; Stroheker, "Alamannen" and "Rolle"; and Waas, Germanen.

16. Olymp. fr. 40, "a multitude of barbarians from the union with Athaulf." But note also Thompson, "Visigoths," pp. 105–126, who attributes pro- and anti-Roman views to the Germanic "optimates" and "rank and file" respectively.

17. Oros. Hist.adv.pag. 7.43; see Wallace-Hadrill, "Gothia," pp. 219–220; King, Law, p. 2; and Thompson, "Visigoths," p. 111. For an earlier example of Visigothic ambivalence toward Romanitas, see Eunap. fr. 60. For discussion, see Chapter 4.

18. See Olymp. fr. 24; and Oros. Hist.adv.pag. 7.43, which suggests that Athaulf was murdered for his Romanophile stance. Such unions, however, tended to be frowned upon by both Romans and barbarians; see Chapters 4 and 12.

19. For this thesis, see Thompson, "Visigoths" and Romans, pp. 230–248. For Theoderic, see Chapter 7. For the Romanization of some Goths before 400, see Thompson, Visigoths, pp. 104–105, 125, 141. For Euric's attempts to convince the Gallo-Roman aristocracy that "he was as good as they," see Matthews, Aristocracies, pp. 343–344.

20. For barbarian adoption of Roman culture, see Thompson, *Romans*, pp. 3–19, 232–235; and Wightman, *Belgica*, p. 301, speaking of the north, "the distinction between Romans and barbarians [was becoming] more blurred."

21. See Oost, *Placidia*, pp. 119–123.

22. See Demandt, "Militäradel" and "Osmosis"; Heinzelmann, "Prosopographie et recherche," pp. 229–232; and Wolfram, *Intitulatio*.

23. See, for example, McCormick, "Clovis" and *Eternal Victory*; and Burns, "Theoderic," pp. 103–104, suggests that the Frankish king Childeric emulated a *magister militum*.

24. See, e.g., Goffart, *Barbarians and Romans*.

I. THE ARISTOCRATIC BACKGROUND OF LATE ROMAN GAUL

1. For general histories of Roman Gaul, see Drinkwater, *Roman Gaul*; Ebel, *Transalpine Gaul*; Hatt, *Histoire*; and Lot, *Gaule*.

2. For the senatorial aristocracy of the Principate, see Drinkwater, "Wealth," pp. 237–242, and "Iulii," pp. 817–850, who notes (p. 817) that "between Caesar and the writers of the fourth century yawns a divide which is often embarrasingly difficult to fill." See also Christol, "Origine," pp. 117–118; Colin, "Sénateurs"; and Pflaum, "Mettii," pp. 265–272; as well as Chapters 2 and 5.

3. See Drinkwater, "Attitudes," passim; Jacques, "Ordine"; and MacMullen, *Corruption*, pp. 21–26.

4. See Held, "Aristokratie"; Matthews, *Aristocracies*, pp. 51–98, and "Supporters"; and Stroheker, *Adel*, passim.

5. For the Roman aristocracy of the Republic and early Principate, see Gelzer, *Nobility*; Münzer, *Adelsparteien*; Sinko, *Der Romanorum viro bono*; Syme, *Revolution*; and Willems, *Le sénat*. For the Principate, see Barbieri, *L'Albo Senatorio*; Chastagnol, "Naissance"; de Laet, *Samenstelling*; Gelzer, "Nobilität"; Hammond, "Composition"; Hill, "Nobilitas"; Lambrechts, *Composition*; Otto, "Nobilität"; and Talbert, *Senate*. For the later Roman Empire, see Arnheim, *Aristocracy*; Arsac, "Dignité"; Chastagnol, "L'évolution," *Sénat*, and "Modes"; Jones, *LRE*; Lécrivain, *Sénat*; Malcus, *Sénat*; Matthews, *Aristocracies*; McGeachy, *Aristocracy*; Stroheker, *Adel*; and Sundwall, *Studien* and *Abhandlungen*. For the Middle Ages, see Bouchard, "Origins"; Genicot, *Noblesse*; Martindale, "Aristocracy"; Reuter, *Nobility*; Schmid, "Structure"; and Wes, *Ende*.

6. See Brennan, "Senators"; Gilliard, "Senators"; Heinzelmann, *Bischofsherrschaft*; Held, "Aristokratie"; Kurth, "Sénateurs"; Pietri, "Ordine"; Prinz, "Aristocracy"; and Stroheker, "Senatoren."

7. At this time, it seems that the term *senator* was applied only to the most junior members of the Senate (see Talbert, *Senate*, pp. 249–250); senior members were described as *consulares* and *praetorii*. See also Bleicken, "Nobilität"; Brunt, "Nobilitas"; and Moebus, "Nobilitas."

8. For nobles as an elite group, see Barnes, "Nobility"; for the senate as a whole, see Amm. 16.10.13,21, 16.12.24; and Symm. *Rel.* 3.7.

9. For such in Gregory of Tours, see Dill, *Gaul*, p. 226; on the late use of *nobilis*

see also Gilliard, "Senators," pp. 692–693; and Martindale, "Aristocracy," pp. 5–45. For the later medieval period, some historians distinguish between the terms *aristocrat* (as a de facto status), and *noble* (as a de iure status); see Martindale, "Aristocracy"; Genicot, "Recent Research"; James, *Origins*, p. 125; and Reuter, *Nobility*.

10. See note 5 above.

11. For the terminology applied to leaders, see MacMullen, *Corruption*, pp. 205–208. Note that in the Burgundian kingdom of c. 500, there were three classes, viz., the Burgundian and Roman aristocrats (*optimates, nobiles*), the freeborn (*mediocres*), and the least significant class (*minores personae*) (see *Lex Burg.* 2.2,26.1–3).

12. The necessary distinction between members of the senatorial order and members of the Senate of Rome is not always made clear (see, e.g., Gilliard, "Senators," pp. 688–689).

13. See Jones, *LRE*, pp. 523–562; and MacMullen, *Corruption*, p. 63. Some older uses also survived, such as *vir egregius* (*VHonorati* 19); see Jones, *LRE*, pp. 525–526. Other terms included *gloriosissimus* and *magnificentissimus*.

14. See Arnheim, *Aristocracy*, p. 19.

15. See Bury, *LRE*, p. 18ff; Chastagnol, "L'évolution," pp. 305–314; Jones, *LRE*, p. 329ff, 523–532; Piganiol, *L'Empire*, p. 381ff; and Stein, *Geschichte*, p. 37ff.

16. See Achard, "Boni"; and Sinko, *Viro bono*.

17. "ex omnibus provinciis optimates viros" (Naz. *Pan.lat.* 10/4.35.2). See also Symm. *Epist.* 1.52, "pars melior humani generis senatus."

18. "bonorum pars magna" (*Epist.* 2.13.5). For *boni* and *optimi*, see also *Epist.* 8.1.1, 3.6.2, 7.9.11, 3.11.1, 5.20.1, 3.2.4, 4.15.1, 7.12.4, 5.10.2, 5.16.2, 2.6.1, 5.11.2, 1.4.2, 1.7.3, 1.11.7, 2.6.1, 2.6.2, 3.11.1, 4.4.3, 4.5.2, 4.22.5, 4.25.4, 5.7.6, 5.13.4, 7.8.3, 7.9.22, 7.13.4, 7.14.1,9, 9.1.3.

19. "erant quidem in senatu plerique opibus culti genere sublimes, aetate graves consilio utiles, dignitate elati dignatione communes" (*Epist.* 1.9.2). Elsewhere, Sidonius listed aristocratic concerns as "patrimony, descendents, and reputation" (ibid. 9.6.1). See also Valer. *Hom.* 14.4: *PL* 52.

20. For the criteria of aristocracy in the later Roman Empire, see note 5 above, and in particular Arnheim, *Aristocracy*, pp. 6–8, 12, 18; Jones, *LRE*, pp. 523–524; and Stroheker, *Adel*, p. 70. For the importance of education to the Gallic aristocracy, see Prinz, *Mönchtum*, p. 59, and Chapter 10.

21. Some also simply appropriated status; see MacMullen, *Corruption*, p. 63; and Reinhold, "Usurpation." In the late fourth century, the Gallic poet Ausonius described the three classes of individuals who had a claim on high office: "men of military glory," "men of ancient nobility," and "men noteworthy for loyalty and proven in office" (*Grat.act.* 4). By the fifth century, however, the military route was open primarily to barbarians, and had been essentially shut off for Roman senators.

22. See Arnheim, *Aristocracy*, pp. 8–12.

23. "stemmata quid faciunt, quid prodest . . . longo sanguine censeri?" (*Sat.* 8.1–2).

24. "impulsu fortasse boni sanguinis, qui se semper agnoscit" (*Orat.* 8.3). For

the importance of family background in marriages, see Sid.Apoll. *Epist.* 2.4.1–2; and Aus. *Par.* 22.9–10.

25. "qui genus, unde domo?" (*Aen.* 8.114; *Epist.* 1.11.5); see Stroheker, *Adel*, p. 60.

26. "qui genus, unde patres?" (*Carm.* 4.90).

27. "neque te novi, unde sis" (*HF* 4.46).

28. "non vilis, cuius et nomen et genus scitur" (*Etym.* 10.184).

29. For social mobility, see Chastagnol, " 'Latus clavus' "; Gilliard, "Senators," pp. 694–697; Hopkins, "Social Mobility"; and MacMullen, "Mobility." Note also Brown, *Religion*, pp. 125–126, "Late Roman society was dominated by the problem of the conflict between change and stability in a traditional society." For Gallic new men, see also Chapter 11.

30. See Arnheim, *Aristocracy*, pp. 18–19. For Gallic new men, see Stroheker, *Adel*, p. 60; and Chapter 11.

31. "propago generis, quanto longius recedit a novis, tanto altius tendit ad nobiles" (*Orat.* 7.4).

32. "mussitat quidem iuvenum nostrorum calcata generositas" (*Epist.* 1.3.2).

33. "plus . . . provectus est, quam status sui seu per censum seu per familiam forma pateretur" (*Epist.* 7.2.1).

34. Note Symmachus' comment to the Gallic *novus homo* Ausonius (*Epist.* 1.31.1), "neminem esse mortalium quem prae te diligam." For Ausonius' success, see Arnheim, *Aristocracy*, p. 19. For Symmachus' own family background, see *PLRE I*, pp. 865–870; and Paschoud, *Roma*, pp. 73, 96.

35. *Orat.* 6.

36. "non avitas largitiones, non uxorias gemmas, non paternas pecunias numeravisti . . . dote meritorum"; also as a result of his "inspecta sinceritas, spectata sedulitas, admissa sodalitas" (*Epist.* 1.4.1).

37. See Jones, *LRE*, p. 550, where families of parvenus "become almost as noble as the ancient aristocratic houses."

38. "non ex toto malus est, qui bonis iungitur" (Ruric. *Epist.* 1.12).

39. "inter summates viros . . . vestri mentio fuit. omnes de te boni in commune senserunt omnia bona . . ." (*Epist.* 7.14.1). See also *Epist.* 7.8.3, 3.11.1, and 9.9.16: "te beatissimum boni omnes . . . concelebrabunt."

40. "tanta est enim integri vis amoris, ut in amico nil displiceat" (*Epist* 2.35). Note, however, Sidonius' description of his irascible friend Lampridius, "nullus sic amicus qui posset effugere convicium" (*Epist.* 8.11.4).

41. "multorum plus quam bonorum odia" (*Epist.* 1.11.7). For Arvandus, see Chapter 8. For contrasts of the *mali* with the *boni*, see Sid.Apoll. *Epist.* 4.25.4, 4.4.3, 5.7.6, 5.13.4, 7.8.3, 7.13.4, 7.5.5, 7.9.11; and Salv. *De gub.* 5.4–5.

42. Such distinctions, of course, were nothing new. In a discussion of "those whom desire for the same things, hatred of the same things, and fear of the same things brings together," Sallust had noted, "haec inter bonos amicitia, inter malos factio est" (*Bell.Iurg.* 31.14–15).

43. For various expressions of status, see MacMullen, *Corruption*, pp. 60–121.

44. "non nequiter te concilii tempore post sedentes censentesque iuvenes inglorium rusticum, senem stantem latitabundum pauperis honorati sententia

premat, cum eos . . . videris dolens antecessisse?" (*Epist.* 1.6.4). The "council" presumably was the annual "Council of the Seven Provinces" (see Chapter 2). Eutropius did in fact subsequently become Prefect of Gaul (ibid., 3.6).

45. *Epist.* 7.12 (the former prefect Tonantius Ferreolus); 9.11 (Lupus of Troyes).

46. For late Roman *amicitia,* see, e.g., Matthews, *Aristocracies,* pp. 5–12.

47. "gratiam non captat omnium sed bonorum, non indiscreta familiaritate vilescens" (*Epist.* 7.9.22). Note also *Epist.* 3.2.4, 7.12.4.

48. See Sid.Apoll. *Epist.*3.5.3 ("fide amicus"), 1.7.3, 8.8.2. On this aspect of Roman friendship, see Arnheim, *Aristocracy;* and MacMullen, *Corruption,* passim.

49. "quotiens in boni cuiusque adscitur amicitias, non amplius consequatur beneficii ipse quam tribuat" (*Epist.* 2.6.1).

50. For the *iura* or *leges amicitiarum;* see Sid.Apoll. *Epist.* 4.1.5, 4.2.2, 4.3.1, 4.7.1, 4.13.3, 4.24.2, 7.6.1, 7.11.1, 7.17.1; Claud.Mamert. *Epist. apud* Sid.Apoll. *Epist.* 4.2.2; and Ruric. *Epist.* 2.62.

51. "non vitae merito sed amicitiarum privilegio" (*Epist.* 2.12).See also Sidonius, "ergo si de moribus tuis deque amicitiis iuste meliora praesumo . . ." (*Epist.* 4.23.3) and "gratias ago magnas . . . quod statuistis de amicitia mea . . . praesumere" (*Epist.* 1.10.1).

52. "amicus homini fui supra quam morum eius facilitas varietasque patiebantur . . . salva fidei reverentia" (*Epist.* 1.7.1,3). Cf. Ruric. *Epist.* 2.28, "amicus relinquendus non est."

53. "atqui praesule deo tenues nobis esse amicitias nec inimici fingere queunt" (*Epist.* 9.9.5).

54. "idem sentimus culpamus laudamus" (Sid.Apoll. *Epist.* 4.1.1). For the importance of shared sentiments, note Sidonius' "amicus animorum similitudine" (*Epist.* 4.4.1). Avitus of Vienne expressed a similar opinion: "communi quidem sed veraci sermone vulgatum est, quod sese mutuae dilectionis intuitu concordantium cernant motus animorum" (*Epist.* 52: *MGH AA* 6.2.81). And Ruricius of Limoges twice repeated the aphorism that "amicos duos unam animam habere" (*Epist.* 2.1, 2.10; cf. 2.29).

55. "veneror in actionibus tuis quod multa bono cuique imitabilia geris" (*Epist.* 5.11.2).

56. "quod est ad amicitias ampliandas his validius efficaciusque, in singulis quibusque personis vel expetendis aequaliter vel cavendis iudicii parilitate certavimus . . ." (*Epist.* 3.1.1; cf. 7.9.23).

57. "ego vero notitiam viri familiaritatemque non solum volens sed et avidus amplector, quippe qui noverim nostram quoque gratiam hoc obsequio meo fore copulatiorem" (*Epist.* 1.10.1; cf. 9.11.8; Ruric. *Epist.* 2.36,48). Enmities, too, were expected to be shared, and this could cause problems: see Faust. *Serm.* 6 (*CSEL* 21.244).

58. "quos laudabili familiaritate coniunxerat litterarum dignitatum periculorum conscientiarum similitudo" (*Epist.* 5.9.1).

59. "duco . . . ut quantas habemus amicitiarum causas, tantas habeamus ipsi amicitias . . . imbuamusque liberos invicem diligentes idem velle nolle refugere sectari" (ibid. 5.9.1,4). He also noted, "nil decuerit plus cavere, quam ne parentum

antiquorumque nostrorum per nos forte videatur antiquata dilectio. ad hoc in similem familiaritatem praeter hereditariam praerogativam multifaria opportunitate compellimur" (*Epist.* 5.9.3; cf. 6.7).

60. "dilectio, quae nobis a parentibus relicta, a magistro tradita, vitae communione firmata est" (*Epist.* 1.12; cf. 1.15).

61. For personal and corporate conflicts in the ecclesiastical world of fifth-century Gaul, see Mathisen, *Factionalism*, passim.

62. For the "enlarged senatorial order," based on both office and birth, of the early fifth century, see Jones, *LRE*, pp. 528–529, 545. For the inclusion of all *honorati* in the aristocracy, see ibid., pp. 536–537, 766.

63. Nevertheless the aristocrats always would have been in the minority. Salvian also could comment that an aristocrat was "one man in a great mob" (*De gub.* 3.10). Attempts to quantify the number of western senators have been based upon fairly restrictive criteria. Sundwall, *Studien*, p. 150, for example, suggests that c. 400 there were approximately three thousand western senators. Stroheker, *Adel*, p. 61 n.97, has about one hundred known Gallic senators for c. 450/500, and suggests a total of six to eight hundred.

64. For the application of exalted titulature to those of curial origin in fifth-century Gaul, note the appearance of *splendidi* (*VGermani* 1, *VHonorati* 22, Salv. *De gub.* 4.7). Note also Sidonius' descriptions of Arvandus as "plebeiae familiae ... redditus" (*Epist.* 1.7.11) and Paeonius as "non eminentius quam municipaliter natus" (ibid. 1.11.5). Both clearly belonged to the aristocracy. There probably was not now such a great chasm between the *curiales* and the "imperial senatorial class" as supposed, e.g., by Gilliard, "Senators," p. 688.

65. Note Sidonius' comment to a friend, "sunt nobis ... novo nostrorum temporum exemplo amicitiarum vetera iura" (*Epist.* 7.6.1). See also ibid. 4.11.7, "vix reservatur imaginaria fides vel superstitibus"; and *Sermo in natalis sancti Stephani* (perhaps by Faustus of Riez): *CSEL* 21.234, "sed quod peius est, aliquotiens non solum non diligimus inimicos, sed nec amicis quidem fidem integram custodimus."

2. GAUL, ITALY, AND ISOLATIONISM IN THE FIFTH CENTURY

1. For the suggestion that most Gauls were "content to stay at home," see Drinkwater, "Attitudes," p. 138; cf. idem., *Roman Gaul*, pp. 48, 114, 202; and Matthews, *Aristocracies*, p. 350ff. Drinkwater calls this attitude "Gallicanism" resulting from "contentment," rather than "nationalism" or "separatism."

2. See Drinkwater, *Gallic Empire*; and Koenig, *Usurpatoren*.

3. See Chadwick, *Poetry*, p. 27; Held, "Aristokratie"; Matthews, *Aristocracies* and "Supporters"; and Stroheker, *Adel*, p. 17ff.

4. Note Ausonius' *Gratiarum actio* to Gratian, in thanksgiving for his consulate and other honors. Ausonius (ibid. 1), however, also refers to the "licentia poetarum" used in such instances.

5. "quanto felicior nostra conditio? quanto beatitudo praestantior? non spica triticea, non viles uvarum racemi, sed opes atque divitiae nihil laborantibus ingeruntur: provinciae, praefecturae, fasces sponte proveniunt ... quicumque in

administratione reipublicae innocentem se unquam et strenuum praebuit, in consortium munerum receptatur. regendis provinciis non familiarissimum quemque, sed innocentissimum legis. omnes a te augentur pecunia, locupletantur divitiis, honoribus honestantur" (*Pan.lat.* 11/3.23,25).

6. For the glory of Rome, see Paschoud, *Roma.* For the theme of renewal, see Hopkins, *Renewal;* Ladner, "Attitudes," pp. 11–14, and "Renewal"; and Solari, *Rinnovamenti.*

7. "urbem fecesti, quod prius orbis erat" (*De red.* 1.66).

8. "verticem mundi, patriam libertatis, in qua unica totius orbis civitate soli barbari et servi peregrinantur" (*Epist.* 1.6.2). For other similarities in both sentiment and word between Rutilius and Sidonius, see Ladner, "Attitudes," p. 23 n. 117.

9. The concept of isolationism should be separated from that of nationalism or separatism, as noted by MacMullen, *Enemies,* pp. 212–213; see also Drinkwater, note 1 above.

10. See Fontaine, "Christianisme."

11. "Galli, quibus insitum est leves ac degenerantes a virtute Romana et luxuriosos principes ferre non posse" (*SHA* 23.4.3); "more illo, quo Galli novarum rerum semper sunt cupidi" (*SHA* 24.3.7) (a sentiment also applied to Spanish women by the Gaul Sulpicius Severus [*Chron.* 2.46]: "mulieres novarum rerum cupidae"). Note also *SHA* 24.3.3, and 29.7.1, for a "Gallus, ex gente hominum inquietissima et avida semper vel faciendi principis vel imperii"; and see Drinkwater, "Attitudes," pp. 136–137.

12. See Oost, *Placidia,* pp. 77, 111; and Stroheker, *Adel,* p. 19. For the west as "a nursery of pretenders" until 425, see Goffart, "Rome," p. 292. See also Drinkwater, "Attitudes," p. 152; and Matthews, *Aristocracies,* p. 92.

13. "imperatorem semper eget: hunc ex se habet" (*Expositio totius mundi et gentium* 58).

14. "nec tamen, imperator, existimes cuncta me ad aurium gratiam locuturum, triumphis tuis Galli (stupeas licebit) irascimur: dum in remota terrarum vincendo procedis, dum ultra terminos rerum metasque naturae regna Orientis extendis, dum ad illos primae lucis indigenas, et in ipsum, si quod est, solis cubile festinas, invenit tyrannus ad scelera secretum . . . unde igitur ordiar, nisi a tuis, mea Gallia, malis?" (*Pan.lat.* 12/2.23–24). The eastern chronographer Theophanes noted the same neglect of both Gaul and Spain by Valentinian III in the 430s (*Chron.* 5931).

15. See Croke, "Arbogast."

16. Opinions on the withdrawal date vary. For 395, see Griffe, *Gaule* 1.337; Nesselhauf, "Verwaltung"; Palanque, "La date," pp. 359–365; R.-Alfoldi, "Datum"; Stroheker, *Adel,* pp. 19–20, 43; and Zeller, "Zeit," pp. 91–92. For 407, see Chastagnol, "Le repli," pp. 23–40, and Matthews, *Aristocracies,* p. 333 n. 1 (on which see Palanque, "Du nouveau," pp. 29–38). Franses, *Leo,* p. 16, suggests 392.

17. See, for example, Demougeot, "Gaule"; and Will, "Remarques."

18. See Mathisen, *Factionalism,* pp. 27–37.

19. See Mathisen, *Factionalism,* pp. 41–43; Matthews, *Aristocracies,* pp. 327–328; Oost, *Placidia,* p. 147; and Sivan, "Rutilius," pp. 531–532.

20. *C.Th.* 15.14.14 (1 March 416), "si qua . . . indigne invidioseque commissa sunt."

21. Haenel, *Corp.leg.* p. 238 no. 1171. See Matthews, *Aristocracies,* p. 334; Mathisen, *Factionalism,* pp. 19, 42; Stein, *Geschichte,* pp. 409–410; and Zeller, "Concilium." See also Carette, *Assemblées;* and Larsen, "Assemblies."

22. See Mathisen, *Factionalism,* p. 42; Matthews, *Aristocracies,* pp. 333–334; Nesselhauf, "Verwaltung," p. 34; *PLRE II,* pp. 1246–1247; Stroheker, *Adel,* p. 48ff; and Sundwall, *Studien,* p. 8ff.

23. See *Chron.gall.452* s.a.; see also MacMullen, "Enclaves"; and Introduction and Chapter 3.

24. See Oost, *Placidia,* p. 155, for the Gothic settlement as a "confirmation of [Gallic] resentment at the policy of the court of Italy." But for other interpretations, see Bachrach, "Settlement"; Goffart, *Barbarians;* and Thompson, "Settlement." See also Chapter 8.

25. "facta est servitus nostra pretium securitatis alienae . . . si vero tradimur . . . invenisse vos certum est quid barbarum suaderetis" (*Epist.* 7.7.2,5).

26. For the ultimate "failure" to unify Gallic and imperial interests, see Drinkwater, "Attitudes," p. 151; and Matthews, *Aristocracies,* p. 350ff.

27. "ex quo Theudosius communia iura fugato reddidit auctoris fratri . . . mea Gallia rerum ignoratur adhuc dominis ignaraque servit. ex illo multum periit, quia principe clauso, quisquis erat, miseri diversis partibus orbis vastari sollemne fuit. quae vita placeret, cum rector moderandus erat? contempta tot annos nobilitas jacuit: pretium respublica forti rettulit invidiam" (*Carm.* 5.354–362).

28. "nullus solidum integri ponderis . . . recuset exactor, excepto eo gallico, cuius aurum minore aestimatione taxatur" (*Nov.Maj.* 7.14: 6 November 458); see Demougeot, "Solidi"; and Depeyrot, "Solidi."

29. "Gallus civis" (Avitus), "Gallus comes et civis" (Agrippinus) (*Chron.* 163,217).

30. See Chapter 5.

31. "ratio est potentium personarum, quarum actores per provincias solutionem fiscalium neglegunt, dum . . . se in praediis retinent contumaces" (*Nov.Maj.* 2.4); see Gaudemet, "Abus," pp. 129–130; Schlumberger, "Potentes," pp. 92–93.

32. See Matthews, *Aristocracies,* pp. 1–12; and Clover, "Olybrius," p. 170 n. 4, "the two traditions of landowning and public life [were] increasingly incompatible." For religious reasons for doing so, see Paul.Nol. *Epist.* 8.3, 25; and Frend, "Paulinus," pp. 8–9. For the decline in the number of offices, see Matthews, *Aristocracies,* p. 347.

33. *Carm.* 7.465; cf. Sid.Apoll. *Epist.* 1.3.2, 1.4.2, 1.6.1, 3.6.2, 7.2.3,1, 8.8.3.

34. See Heinzelmann, *Bischofsherrschaft,* p. 83; Matthews, *Aristocracies,* pp. 320–321; Stroheker, *Adel,* p. 48; and Sundwall, *Abhandlungen,* p. 10.

35. "non minus est tuorum natalium viro personam suam excolere quam villam" (*Epist.* 1.6.3).

36. Sid.Apoll. *Epist.* 3.6; see *PLRE II,* p. 444.

37. "i nunc et legibus me ambitus interrogatum senatu move, cur adipiscendae dignitati hereditariae curis pervigilibus incumbam" (*Epist.* 1.3.1). See also ibid. 1.9.3, as well as Arnheim, *Aristocracy,* passim; and Seeck, *MGH AA* 6.1.xcvi and n. 138.

38. "ut sicut nos utramque familiam nostram praefectoriam nancti etiam patriciam divino favore reddidimus, ita ipsi quam suscipiunt patriciam faciant

consularem" (*Epist.* 5.16.4). For Sidonius' "patriotism," see Saunders, "Debate," p. 16.

39. "quo fit, ut deinceps pro republica optimus quisque possit ac debeat, si quid cuipiam virium est, quia securus, hinc avidus impendere, quandoquidem mortuo quoque imperatore laborantum devotioni quicquid spoponderit princeps, semper redhibet principatus" (*Epist.* 5.16.2, cf. *Epist.* 8.7).

40. See Chapter 6.

41. See Barnish, "Pigs," p. 168; Loyen, *L'esprit*, pp. 60–61; Matthews, *Aristocracies*, p. 19; and Stroheker, *Adel*, p. 3. Parts of this section were presented at the Sheffield Conference on Late Roman Gaul, April 1989.

42. "cum sis alacer domi, in aggredienda peregrinatione trepidum te iners desperatio facit" (*Epist.* 1.6.2).

43. Note Consentius of Narbonne, a tribune of Valentinian before 455; and the *palatini* Polemius Silvius (by 448) and Maximus (qq.v., *PLRE II*). Constantius: Priscus fr. 8; see *PLRE II*, p. 319; and Blockley, "Constantius." Magnus of Narbonne, consul in 460, presumably remained in Gaul. For Gauls in the central administration c. 395–414, note Minervius, Florentinus, Protadius, Cl. Postumus Dardanus, Claudius Lepidus, Lachanius, and Rutilius Namatianus (qq.v., *PLRE II*; see Chapter 5).

44. Note the Patrician and Master of Soldiers Messianus; the *cura palatii* Consentius of Narbonne; and the *tribuni et notarii* Sidonius Apollinaris, Avitus of Cottion, Eutropius, Gaudentius, Catullinus, Hesychius: see *PLRE II* s.vv. and Mathisen, "Avitus," "Third Regnal Year," and "Resistance" for these and others.

45. *PLRE II* s.v.; see Chapter 6.

46. See Mathisen, "Last Year."

47. *PLRE II* s.v.; see Chastagnol, "Sidoine."

48. Sid.Apoll. *Epist.* 1.7. The prosecutors of Seronatus shortly thereafter may have done likewise. For the cases of both, see Chapter 8.

49. Primarily bishops such as Victricius of Rouen (c. 405), Patroclus of Arles (417), Brictius of Tours (early 430s), Chelidonius of Besançon and Hilary of Arles (c. 445), Nectarius of Avignon and Constantius of Uzès (446/449), Ceretius of Grenoble (449/450), Ingenuus of Embrun (452/453, 465), Faustus of Riez and Auxanius (462), Antonius (463), and Saturninus of Avignon (465). Also the laymen Prosper and Hilarius (c. 430), the presbyter Ravennius, the presbyter Petronius, and the deacon Regulus, all of Arles (c. 446–451), the deacon John of Narbonne (460), the *v.s.* Pappolus (460), and the archdeacon Hermes of Narbonne (c. 455/456) (qq.v. in Mathisen, *Factionalism*).

50. Usually concerned with the imperial administration of Gaul, such as Majorian's visits in 458–459 and 461, Anthemius' invasion in 471, and Julius Nepos' embassies to Euric in 474. Other Italian business visitors included the deacon Leo of Rome in 440 (Prosp. *Chron.* s.a. 440; *PLRE II*, pp. 50–53), and some Italian artisans in the mid 440s (*VGermani* 31; Mathisen, "Last Year"). In the early 450s, moreover, a certain Petronianus was traveling about Gaul passing himself off as a deacon of the church of Rome (*MGH Epist.* 3.16).

51. "post auditoria gallicana intra urbem Romam iuris scientiam plenitudini perfectionis adiecit" (*VGermani* 1).

52. Symm. *Epist.* 4.54–56, 9.54: *PLRE II*, pp. 775, 895, 1233.

53. "misit Romam, non parcens sumptibus . . . ut ubertatem Gallici nitoremque sermonis, gravitas romana condiret" (*Epist.* 125.6). Another aspect of the Gallic "identity," even among foreigners, was this high opinion of Gallic culture; see Claud. *De quart.cons.Hon.* 582–583 ("doctis civibus"); Hieron. *Chron.* s.a.358; and Symm. *Epist.* 6.34, 9.88 ("Gallicanae facundiae").

54. Rutil.Namat. *De red.* 207–212; see Cameron, "Rutilius."

55. "dignus omnino, quem plausibilibus Roma foveret ulnis . . . quod procul dubio consequebare, si pacis locique condicio permitteret, ut illic senatoriae iuventutis contubernio mixtus erudirere" (*Epist.* 9.14.2–3).

56. *Epist.* 1.6.2.

57. Sid.Apoll. *Epist.* 3.6.1; Mathisen, "Sidonius."

58. "quia voluptuosum censeas quae lectione compereris eorum qui inspexerint fideliore didicisse memoratu" (*Epist.* 1.5.1).

59. Note Sid.Apoll. *Epist.* 1.5.9, 1.6.1; see Bardy, "Pélerinages."

60. *VLupicini* 11.

61. Greg.Tur. *HF* 2.16; perhaps in the context of Avitus' expedition.

62. Paul.Nol. *Epist.* 17.

63. Contrary to the suggestions of Jones, *LRE*, pp. 553–554; and Stroheker, *Adel*, p. 62.

64. Another category of travelers, refugees from the barbarians, will be discussed in Chapter 6.

65. See Walsh, *Paulinus*, passim.

66. For these visits, see Paul.Nol. *Epist.* passim.

67. *Epist.* 1.8, 8.7, 1.10.

68. Relationship: Ven.Fort. *Carm.* 4.5.7–8. Letters: *MGH AA* 8.

69. This situation changed in the post-Roman period, when the southern part of Gaul was incorporated into the Ostrogothic kingdom of Italy, and the Gauls Magnus Felix Ennodius, an expatriate, and Alcimus Ecdicius Avitus did include both Gauls and Italians among their correspondents (*MGH AA* 7 and 6.2 respectively).

70. *VGermani* 35–39.

71. *VHilarii* 16(22), *Nov.Val.* 8.1–2: see Mathisen, *Factionalism*, pp. 166–168.

72. Allard, "Sidoine sous les regnes," p. 427.

73. Greg.Tur. *HF* 2.11; Joh.Ant. fr. 202: see Mathisen, "Third Regnal Year."

74. Sid.Apoll. *Epist.* 1.5. Only later was he received into a senatorial home.

75. "si contempleris ad viciniam Rheni, a qua nunc et optimus princeps et magistratus potissimus abest, nullum nostrarum partium commeare" (*Epist.* 4.28). For Protadius, see Chapter 6.

76. "et tamen defensio mihi suppetit, quia nec profectiones commeantium notae sunt" (*Epist.* 4.30). He did admit elsewhere, however, that "fors fuat, an quis tantum viae ob rem privatam mihi ignoratus adripiat" (ibid. 4.28). Symmachus' letters eventually were delivered by Protadius' brother Minervius.

77. "tibi proficiscentium Romam maior facultas: primo quia in commune imperii caput undique gentium convenitur; tunc quod clementissimum principem

in hac parte degentem varia omnium desideria vel necessitates sequuntur" (*Epist.* 4.28).

78. Nor is there justification for the suggestions that Gauls continued to participate in the Roman senate on a regular basis (as assumed, e.g., by Barnish, "Transformation," pp. 134–139; and Twyman, "Aetius," passim) or that "Provence can be better considered in conjunction with northern Italy" (Van Dam, *Leadership,* p. 2). For other kinds of contacts, see Fagerlie, "Contact."

79. Sid.Apoll. *Epist.* 8.6.7; *Carm.* 7.521–583; *Epist.* 1.7. In earlier years, such councils had been limited to single provinces, as in the case of the meeting of Gallia Lugdunensis in 220 (see *CIL* 13.3162; Pflaum, *Marbre*). Cf. Sid.Apoll. *Epist.* 1.6.4.

80. See Chapter 5.

3. THE BARBARIAN SETTLEMENT: IMPRESSIONS OF HARASSMENT, INTERFERENCE, AND OPPRESSION

1. See Vercauteren, "Ruine."

2. "florentissimas quondam antiquissimasque urbes barbari possidebant, Gallorum illa celebrata nobilitas aut ferro occiderat aut immitibus addicta dominis serviebat" (*Pan.lat.* 9/3.4). Libanius (*Orat.* 18.33–35) attributed these barbarian depredations to Constantius' attempts to defeat Magnentius.

3. See Wightman, *Belgica,* pp. 300–301.

4. Only a few modern writers accept these claims at face value; see Griffe, *Gaule* 2.11ff.

5. Jer. *Epist.* 123.16: *PL* 22.1057–1058; for similar, see Duchesne, *Fastes* 3.81.

6. "quo scelere admisso, pariter periere tot urbes? / tot loca, tot populi, quid meruere mali? / si totus Gallos sese effudisset in agros / oceanus, vastis plus superesset aquis . . . caede decenni / Vandalicis gladiis sternimur et Geticis / non castella petris, non oppida montibus altis / imposita, aut urbes amnibus aequoreis / barbarici superare dolos atque arma furoris / evaluere omnes, ultima pertulimus . . . maiores anni ne forte et nequior aetas / offenso tulerint quae meruere deo / quid pueri insontes, quid commisere puellae / nulla quibus dederat crimina vita brevis? / quare templa dei licuit popularier igni? / cur violata sacri vasa ministerii? / non honor innuptas devotae virginitatis / non texit viduas religionis amor." (*Carm.de prov.dei* 25–48: *PL* 51.618). For the suggestion that Prosper of Aquitania was the author of this poem, see *Clavis,* p. 94.

7. "denique expugnata est quater urbs Gallorum opulentissima" (*De gub.* 6.13–15).

8. "uno fumavit Gallia tota rogo" (*Comm.* 2.184: *CSEL* 16.234). See also *Carm.de prov.dei* 17–60; and Ennod. *VEpiph* 98, "tota civitas quasi rogus effulgurat."

9. "cum, transito Rheno saevissimos eius impetus multae Gallicanae urbes experirentur . . ." (Prosp. *Chron.* s.a. 451). According to Fredegarius, *Chron.* 2.53, however, Attila invaded "parcens civitatebus Germaniae et Galliae."

10. See Favez, "La Gaule"; Hamman, "L'actualité"; Ianelli, *Caduta;* Lagarrigue, "Salvian"; and Pricoco, "Barbari."

11. See Wightman, *Belgica*, p. 301: "accounts are more dramatic than clear."

12. "et habet adiacentem gentem barbaram Gothorum" (*Exposit.* 58).

13. "vidi siquidem ego Treviros ipse, homines domi nobiles, dignitate sublimes ... quamvis enim depopulatis iam atque nudatis aliquid supererat de substantia ..." (*De gub.* 6.13). See Wightman, *Trier,* p. 250.

14. "sic aemulorum sibi in medio positi lacrimabilis praeda populorum, suspecti Burgundionibus, proximi Gothis, nec impugnantum ira nec propugnantum caremus invidia" (*Epist.* 3.4.1).

15. Contrary to the views of Saunders, "Debate," p. 16. For travel difficulties, see Stevens, *Sidonius,* p. 77; and delle Corte, "Albingaunum," pp. 92–94; note also Sid.Apoll. *Epist.* 5.13.1.

16. "diros metuunt ac vicinos Alamannorum incursus, qui inopinatis viantibus non congressione in comminus, sed ritu superventuque solerent inruere bestiali ..." (*VEugendi* 17). For the value of the *vita,* see Martine, *Vies.*

17. Sid.Apoll. *Epist.* 9.9.6–7.

18. "qui quo minus assidue conspectus tui sacrosancta contemplatione potiatur, nunc periculum de vicinis timet, nunc invidiam de patronis" (*Epist.* 7.11.1). Note also visits prevented or delayed by "miseris ... causis" (4.2.1), by the "statum publicum" (4.4.2), "tempore timoris publici ... ad tempestuosos hostium incursus" (4.6.2–3), "turbine dissidentium partium" (5.12.1), or "diversarum sortium iure" (9.5.1). In *Epist.* 5.12.1, Sidonius also attributes his failure to correspond to "aliena impotentia," "impotence caused by others," a telling—and probably galling—admission of the barbarian impact.

19. "patronus indulgeat, advolaturi, ut rebus amicitia vegetetur, quae verbis infrequentata torpuerat" (*Epist.* 4.10.2).

20. See Chapter 10.

21. Sid.Apoll. *Epist.* 9.3.2, c. 475.

22. As when Sidonius wrote to his relative Apollinaris, "verbo quaepiam cavenda mandaveram" (*Epist.* 4.6.1). For verbal messages, see also Matthews, *Aristocracies,* p. 8.

23. See Barnish, "Transformation," p. 141.

24. "... gemit ille talentis / argenti atque auri amissis, hunc rapta supellex / perque nurus Geticas divisa monilia torquent. / hunc pecus abductum, domus ustae, potaque vina / afficiunt, tristes nati, obscenique ministri ... / at tu, qui squalidos agros desertaque defles / atria ..." (*Carm.de prov.dei* 903–907, 913–914).

25. "nec fas ulterius longas nescire ruinas" (*De red.* 1.27); see *PLRE II,* pp. 770–771; Rouche, *Aquitaine,* p. 22; and Stroheker, *Adel,* p. 193. Not all such ruin, however, was caused by the barbarians: see Sid.Apoll. *Epist.* 3.5.2; and Chapter 5.

26. For Sidonius' loss in this way, see *Epist.* 8.9.2. See also *Lex Burg.* 54, where Burgundians who "had received land ... either by the gift of our predecessors or of ourselves" were not eligible to receive additional land through the process of *hospitalitas.*

27. See Barnish, "Taxation"; Lot, "Régime"; and Thompson, "Visigoths," pp. 118–121.

28. "deserta Valentinae urbis rura Alanis ... partienda traduntur" (*Chron.gall.452* no.124). Note also *Pan.lat.* 7/6.6, where the "Frankish nations" are

"in desertis Galliae regionibus collocatae" in the fourth century. See also Goffart, *Barbarians*, p. 112ff.

29. Goffart, *Barbarians*, suggests that tax proceeds rather than actual lands were distributed; on this see also Durliat, "Salaire." These suggestions, even if valid, seem to give insufficient attention to the process by which Gallic properties came into the hands of individual barbarians.

30. Paul.Pell. *Euch.* 285–290. For barbarian patronage, see Chapter 7; and Burns, "Ennodius," p. 164, for similar regarding the settlement of barbarians around Arles in 509. See also Ennod. *Epist.* 9.23,29.

31. "inter barbaricas hostili iure rapinas" (*Euch.* 423, cf. 239, 288, 317, 330, 408–409). For other Gothic exactions, see *VViviani* 4: *MGH SRM* 3.96–98; and *VOrientii* 5: *AASS* May I, p. 63.

32. *Euch.* 498–515.

33. See Mathisen, "Aquitania"; and Jullian, *Gaule* 8.138. Barnish, "Transformation," p. 137, however, sees the family as an example of "long term social and demographic stability."

34. "patria careant et in comparatione praeteritarum opum pauperes vivant" (*De gub.* 7.5).

35. "Alani, quibus terrae Galliae ulterioris cum incolis dividendae a patricio Aetio traditae fuerant, resistentes armis subigunt et expulsis dominis terrae possessionem vi adipiscuntur . . ." (*Chron.gall. 452* s.a. 442). See Bachrach, "Alans," pp. 481, 488.

36. *Lex Burg.* 38.7, translation cited from Drew, *Burgundian Code.*

37. "Sichlarius . . . dixitque abbati, 'dona mihi hoc molendinum . . . et quod volueris repensabo,' cui ille, '. . . nunc non possumus ipsum donare, ne fratres mei fame pereant,' et ille, 'si vis,' inquit, 'ipsum bona voluntate tribuere, gratias ago, sin aliud, vi ipsum auferam" (Greg.Tur. *VPat.* 18.2).

38. See Ennod. *Epist.* 2.23. For barbarian appropriations of Gallo-Roman ecclesiastical property, see *VEparchi* 2.16; *VGerm.Par.* 5; Greg.Tur. *Glor.mart.* 79 and *Glor.conf.* 70; *VDomnoli* 9.

39. Matthews, *Aristocracies*, p. 347, suggests that the "virtual disappearance of the administrative services . . . implies the loss of those middling careers in administration which, for hundreds of lesser men, had been the substance of the political life." See also Wightman, *Belgica*, p. 306. For some possible survivals of these offices, see Chapter 8.

40. For Gallo-Roman office-holding in barbarian administrations, see Chapter 11.

41. *Carm.de prov.dei* 53–60; see McHugh, *Carmen*, pp. 19–20.

42. See, for example, *VAuctoris, VLupi, VMelanii,* and *VServatii.*

43. For barbarian intervention in church affairs at Gallic request, see Chapter 7.

44. See Saunders, "Debate," p. 16; and King, *Law*, pp. 4–6.

45. *Epist.* 7.6.7.

46. See Griffe, "L'épiscopat," p. 263 and *Gaule* 2.63–107; Mathisen, *Factionalism*, pp. 269–270; and Pricoco, *L'isola*, p. 227 n. 122.

47. Sidonius: *Epist.* 4.10.1, 4.22.4, 8.3.1, 8.9.1, 9.3.3. Crocus: Sid.Apoll. *Epist.* 7.6.9; Duchesne, *Fastes* 1.311. Faustus: Faust. *Epist.* 2, 5, 16; Ruricius *Epist.* 1.1–2. Marcellus:

AASS April vol. 1., pp. 824–826. It has been assumed (e.g., Courcelle, *Histoire*, p. 202; Rouche, *Aquitaine*, p. 46) that Ruricius of Limoges was exiled to Bordeaux, but the only source (Ruric. *Epist.* 1.17.5) makes no mention of Bordeaux, and appears to refer only to a metaphorical exile (as in Chapter 9): see Krusch, *MGH AA* 8.lxiii, for discussion.

48. "legibus Christianis insidiaturum" (*Epist.* 7.6.6).

49. "gravem in Galliis super Christianos . . . persecutionem" (*HF* 2.25). For the Gothic "persecution," see Brugière, *Littérature*, pp. 259–260; Griffe, *Gaule* 2.82–93; and King, *Law*, pp. 4–5.

50. "ob saevitiam scilicet vastantium Gallias barbarorum" (*Gest.epp.autiss.* 8).

51. The "persecution" is downplayed by Wallace-Hadrill, "Gothia," p. 234; Kidd, *Church*, p. 377; and Stroheker, *Eurich*, pp. 43–61. For the extensive interference by the Vandals in the North African church, see Jones, *LRE*, pp. 262–264.

52. Sid.Apoll. *Epist.* 7.6.2. Is the representation, on western imperial coinage, of the Arian barbarians as the serpent of the Old Testament, as suggested by Demougeot ("Image," pp. 141–143 and "Symbolique," p. 99), merely conventional, or indicative of deeper concern?

53. "infanda Arrianorum haeresis, quae se nationibus barbaris miscuit . . ." (*Chron.gall.452* no. 138, s.a. 451).

54. And in Vincentius of Lérins' account of persecutions by the Arians (*Comm.* 1.4), written in the 430s, the barbarian adherents are not even mentioned. See also *Carm.de prov.dei* 5.27–60; Faustus, *De spir.sanct.* 1.1,3, 2.2–4, *Epist.* 2/3 (possibly his *Contra Arrianos et Macedonianos* mentioned in Gennad. *Vir.ill.* 86) and 3/20.1,25; 4/14.3, 7/17.20; Salv. *De. gub.* 7.9; Vinc. *Comm.*4.11; *VCaesarii* 1.23.

55. *MGH AA* 6.2.

56. *Breviarium adversus haereticos*: Morin, *Opera*, pp. 182–208.

57. "utique habent potestatem heretici, sed praecipue Arriani" (*Expositio in apocalypsim*: Morin, *Opera*, p. 245).

58. Sid.Apoll. *Epist.* 7.8.3. It is unclear whether these Arians of Bourges were Romans or Goths. Salvian's statement (*De gub.* 5.3), "de Romanis haereticis, quorum innumera multitudo est," should not be interpreted as a reference to Arians (as in King, *Law*, p. 5 n. 2); indeed, his context indicates they were not (he says they cannot be compared either to Romans or barbarians).

59. In Spain, however, the Suevi seem to have acted more aggressively. Hydatius (*Chron.* no. 232) notes, "Ajax, natione Galata effectus apostata et senior Arrianus inter Suevos . . . hostis catholicae fidei . . . emergit. a Gallicana Gothorum habitatione hoc pestiferum . . . virus advectum." Ajax' name and ethnic designation indicate that he was a Greek, not a Gaul. Nor do the Romans seem to have striven to convert the barbarians: see Thompson, *Romans*, p. 241; and Prosper, *Gentium* 2.33: *PL* 51.717ff.

60. See Mathisen, *Factionalism*, p. xi and passim; and Goffart, "Rome," p. 296 n. 61; see also Chapter 4. For a more adversarial relationship, see Thompson, "Christianity," pp. 56–78; and Van Dam, "Images," p. 8 (cf. p. 13), for "challenges from heretical barbarians."

61. See Mathisen, *Factionalism*, p. 211.

62. See Chapter 12.

63. For the ransoming of captives, see Chapter 9.

64. *Carm.de prov.dei, Poema coniugis ad uxorem* (*PL* 51.611ff); see note 6 above.

65. *Carm.de prov.dei* 57–58.

66. "qui centum quondam terram vertebat aratris, aestuat ut geminos possit habere boves" (*Poema coniugis ad uxorem* 17–18). See Chadwick, *Poetry*, pp. 122–124.

67. *VEugendi* 5. For his epitaph, see *PL* 59.278.

68. Ennod. *Epist.* 9.9.

69. Faust. *Epist.* 4, 5, 7; see Chapter 6.

70. "ut diversarum homines provinciarum cuiuslibet sexus condicionis aetatis, quos barbaricae feritatis discursus captiva necessitate transduxerat, invitos nemo retineat" (*Sirm.* 16 [10 December 408], cf. *C.Th.* 5.5.2 [10 December 409]). Note also *Nov.Val.* 33 [31 January 451], repeating a ban on the sale of freeborn Romans to barbarians; and see Thompson, "Collaborators."

71. Elsewhere in the empire, note the cases of Alaric (Zos. *Hist.nov.* 5.36.1, 2], Fl. Aetius (*PLRE II*, pp. 21–22), and Theoderic the Ostrogoth (ibid., p. 1078); cf. Oros. *Hist.adv.pag.* 7.43. See also Aymard, "Otages."

72. *Euch.* 353–381.

73. *Euch.* 379–380.

74. "nobilis obses" (Sid.Apoll. *Carm.* 7.215–220); see *PLRE II*, p. 1087.

75. Sid.Apoll. *Carm.* 5.572, "obside percepto." It is unclear from Sidonius' context just who the hostages were. Given that Lyons had been in revolt against Majorian, Sidonius' vagueness may have been intended to camouflage the Roman identity of at least some of the hostages. And in Spain, an exchange of hostages between the Romans and Suevi was arranged in 433 "sub interventu episcopali" (Hyd. *Chron.* no. 100).

76. "Adovacrius de Andegavo et aliis locis obsides accepit" (Greg.Tur. *HF* 2.18). He generally is assumed to be Odovacar, later patrician and king of the Germans in Italy (see *PLRE II*, pp. 791–2).

77. See Matthews, "Hostages," pp. 38–41, and note pp. 40–41 for "the implications of hostage exchange for the mutual understanding between Romans and barbarians."

78. Greg.Tur. *HF* 3.15.

79. "barbaricus carcer" (Sid.Apoll. *Epist.* 7.9.20).

80. *VViviani* 4: *MGH SRM* 3.96–98.

81. "super Eucherium vero senatorem calumpnias devolvit, quem in carcere positum nocte extrahi iussit, ligatumque iuxta parietem antiquum, ipsum parietem super eum elidi iussit" (Greg.Tur. *HF* 2.20). On Victorius, see also Chapter 6.

82. Sid.Apoll. *Epist.* 3.8.

83. See Chapter 12.

84. "natione foederatorum non solum inciviliter Romanas vires administrante verum etiam fundamentaliter eruente" (*Epist.* 3.8.2).

4. THE INTELLECTUAL RESPONSE: CONFLICTING PERCEPTIONS OF THE BARBARIANS

1. For various perceptions of barbarians, see Brezzi, "Romani"; Caló Levy, *Barbarians;* Christ, "Römer und Barbaren"; de Mattei, "Concetto"; Fischer, *Völkerwanderung;* Gärtner, "Rome"; Goetz, "Orosius"; Jones, "Image"; Labuske, "Barbaren"; Langlois, "Invasions"; Paschoud, "Romains"; Saddington, "Attitudes"; Sterzl, *Romanus-Christianus-Barbarus;* Viscido, "Barbarus"; and Vogt, "Barbaren."

2. For the use of these terms, see Chauvot, "*Barbaricum*"; Christ, "Römer," pp. 279–282; Clover, "Boniface," pp. 80–81; Goffart, "Rome," p. 281; Kahane, "*Barbarus*"; Matthews, "Hostages," p. 43; and Zeiller, "*Romania*."

3. For the lack of concern of some Gallic ecclesiastics with the barbarians before the 460s, see Mathisen, *Factionalism,* pp. xii-xiii. For the scant attention given to barbarians in Salvian's letters, see Opelt, "Briefe."

4. Translations, which would obscure the effect and are irrelevant to the argument, are deemed unnecessary for these lists.

5. *Domestica* 5.34–37.

6. Hieron. *Epist.* 123.16.

7. See also *Pan.lat.* 12/2.5: "Sarmatica . . . Bataviam . . . Saxo . . . Scotum . . . Alamanus . . . Maurus . . ."; 12/2.11, "Gothus . . . Hunnus . . . Alanus . . ."; 12/2.22, "Indus . . . Bosporanus . . . Arabs . . . Gothos . . . Scythis . . . Albani . . . Persis . . ."

8. Bachrach, "Alites," however, accepts the list as genuine. For other Sidonian lists, see *Carm.* 7.230–237, 369–373; *Epist.* 8.9.5 *carm.*21–50.

9. Avit. *App.* 22 = *Anth.lat.* no. 349. For similar, see also Ven.Fort. *VGerm.Par.* 193; and Paul.Diac. *Hist.Lang.* 2.26.

10. "bellicum strepunt nomina, et immanitas barbariae in ipsis vocabulis adhibet horrorem" (*Pan.lat.* 10/4.18).

11. For "anachronistic names" as a means of keeping barbarians "in check," see Goffart, "Rome," p. 277.

12. See Geary, *France,* pp. 39–43, where barbarians are "described with almost monotonous similarity." For the question of barbarian ethnicity, see Introduction.

13. For "the term barbarian, with its connotations of inferiority," see Goffart, "Rome," p. 297. See also Brezzi, "Impero," pp. 260–262; Dauge, *Barbare,* passim; Demougeot, "Image"; Ladner, "Attitudes," p. 23; and Thompson, "End," pp. 21–22. For earlier Roman views of foreigners, see Balsdon, *Aliens,* pp. 215–259.

14. See Chapter 1.

15. "qua causa etiam civiles motus longe atrociores orti" (*Liber de caesaribus* 33.6–7). Note also *SHA* 24.3, "Gallienus . . . amore barbarae mulieris consenesceret."

16. "femina singularis exempli et familiae nobilis, gentis tamen Gothicae" (*SHA* 29.15); see Burns, "Barbarians"; and Clover, "Olybrius," p. 172.

17. *C.Th.* 3.14.1 (28 May 370/373), "nulli provincialium, cuiuscumque ordinis aut loci fuerit, cum barbara sit uxore coniungium, nec ulli gentilium provincialis femina copuletur . . . quod in his suspectum vel noxium detegitur . . ."

18. See Burns, "Frontier Policy," p. 397; Clover, "Olybrius," pp. 171–172; Demandt, "Osmosis," pp. 75–85; and Demougeot, "*Conubium,*" pp. 70–74, and "Restrictions," p. 383; for mixed marriages being "frowned on by the Church," see Oost, *Placidia,* p. 127. For such policies in barbarian Europe, see Chapter 12.

19. "soror imperatoris augusta Placidia primum captiva, deinde uxor regis quidem sed barbari statum temporum decolorat" (*Narratio de imperatoribus domus Valentinianae et Theodosianae: MGH AA* 9.630).

20. "livida coniunx . . . suffusaque bili / coxerat internum per barbara corda venenum" (*Carm.* 5.126–128; cf. ibid. 203–204 and Merobaudes, *Carm.* 4.15–18). See Clover, *Merobaudes,* pp. 30–31 (as a Visigoth); *PLRE II,* pp. 856–857. And Aetius' son-in-law is said to have been the barbarian—perhaps a Hun or Goth—Thraustila (ibid., pp. 1117–1118). For Aetius, see Zecchini, *Aezio.*

21. "dum exercitum negligeret et paucos ex Alanis . . . anteferret veteri ac Romano militi, adeoque barbarorum comitatu et prope amicitia capi, ut nonnumquam eodem habitu iter faceret, odia contra se militum excitavit" (*Epit.de caes.* 47.6). For the use of Germanic garb by the emperor Caracalla (211–217), see Herodian, *Hist.* 4.7.3–4. The Roman army itself in fact became heavily barbarized; see Jones, *LRE,* pp. 611–613, 665–668.

22. "ipse inter medios, ne qua de parte relinquat / barbariem, revocat fulvas in pectora pelles / nec pudet . . . sumere deformes ritus, vestemque Getarum, / insignemque habitum Latii mutare togaeque. / Maerent captivae pellito judice leges" (Claud. *In ruf.* 2.78–85). On the wearing of barbarian dress, see also *Gest.conc.Aquil. Epist.*2: *CSEL* 82.103–323; and note McCormick, "Clovis," p. 177.

23. "Gothos saepe fallaces et perfidos . . . illis enim sufficere mercatores Galatas, per quos ubique sine condicionis discrimine venundantur" (Amm. 22.7.8). For similar views of Goths being fit for slavery, see Synesius, *On Kingship,* 13–14. Ladner, "Attitudes," p. 21, notes that pagans such as "Rutilius Namatianus represent the persistence of undiluted anti-barbarian feeling."

24. See, for example, *Pan.lat.* 10/4.18 (Nazarius of Bordeaux to Constantine I), "hi omnes [barbari] . . . conspiratione foederatae societatis exserant"; see Ladner, "Attitudes," pp. 15–20.

25. "crinigeri . . . patres, pellita Getarum / curia" (*De bell.goth.* 481–482).

26. "sed tantum distant Romana et barbara, quantum / quadrupes abiuncta est bipedi vel muta loquenti / quantum etiam qui rite dei praecepta sequuntur / cultibus a stolidis et eorum erroribus absunt" (*Contra Symmachum* 2.816–819). See also Ambrose *De virg.* 1.4.14: *PL* 16.203; Velleius Paterculus, *Hist.rom.* 2.117.3, "[Germani] qui nihil praeter vocem membraque haberent hominum"; and Jord. *Get.* 122, "quasi hominum genus."

27. "ergo age, sacrilegae tandem cadat hostia gentis: / summittant trepidi perfida colla Getae. / ditia pacatae dent vectigalia terrae / impleat augustos barbara praeda sinus" (*De red.* 1.141–144).

28. See Sid.Apoll. *Carm.* 5.563, 7.219,349, 12, *Epist.* 1.7.6, 2.1.2, 5.5.3, 5.8.3, and 8.2.2.

29. "veterum coetus . . . Getarum / . . . squalent vestes . . . altatae . . . pelles" (*Carm.* 7.403,452–456). See also *Carm.* 5.563 for the Goths as a "pellitus . . . hostis."

30. *Carm.* 12.11–14; see Loyen, "Résistants," pp. 446–447. For Sidonius' dislike of barbarians, see Stevens, *Sidonius,* p. 49; Loyen, *L'esprit,* pp. 52–55; Moss, "Policies," p. 712; Rutherford, *Sidonius,* pp. 71–73; and Wallace-Hadrill, "Gothia," p. 224. For other views, see Brugière, *Littérature,* p. 200; Rousseau, "Search," p. 374.

31. "vicinantes impluvio cubiculi mei duae quaepiam Getides anus, quibus nil umquam litigiosius bibacius vomacius erit" (*Epist.* 8.3.2). For barbarian drunkenness, see also Ambrose, *De Helia et ieiunia* 54.

32. *De gub.* 5.5. For the equation of barbarians with brigands, see Thompson, *Romans,* pp. 234ff; and Amm. 17.10.5, 17.27.1; Eunap. fr. 11; and Zos. *Hist.nov.* 3.6.4, 7.1–3.

33. "occultos hostes . . . novos barbaros pacificum habitum mentientes" (*Praedestinatus* prol.: *PL* 53.627). For other applications of the term "barbarian" to native Romans, see Clover, "Boniface," pp. 84–85.

34. "quos [sc. Arvernos] . . . barbaros deinceps esse vetuisti" (*Epist.* 3.3.3).

35. On perceptions of decline, see Croke, "476"; and Demandt, "Das Ende."

36. "recentium inclytorumque regnorum apud nos iam quaedam fabula est, omnia illa, quae hic erant magna, modo iam nulla sunt. nihil, ut puto, immo, ut certo scio, ex illis opibus, honoribus, regnis, secum abstulerunt, nisi (si qua in his fuit) fidei pietatisque substantiam" (*PL* 50.717); see Cristiani, *Eucher.*

37. "senuisse iam saeculum . . . mundo senescente" (Cyprian, *Epist.ad Demet.* 3–4: *PL* 4.546); "mundi iam senescentis" (Sid.Apoll. *Epist.* 8.6.3).

38. *Epist.* 7.1.3.

39. Hyd. *Chron.* 73 ("signa . . . terrifica" at Béziers, s.a. 419); 151 ("multa anno signa procedunt . . . visa quaedam in caelo" near Autun, s.a. 451).

40. "postrema mundi aetas referta est malis tamquam morbis senectus. visa sunt, videnturque jamdudum ista cano saeculo, fames, pestilentia, vastitas, bella, terrores. hi sunt in ultimis jam annis languores sui. hinc saepe illa coeli cernuntur signa, motusque terrarum, permutatae temporum vices, monstrosae animantium fecunditates: quae omnia adhuc procedentis prodigia sunt temporis, sed jam deficientis" (*Epist.ad Valer.* p. 722). See also Ruric. *Epist.* 2.17, "imminente iam praesentis aevi termino et senii die usquequaque vicino."

41. "has nobis inter clades ac funera mundi / mors vixisse fuit" (*Carm.* 7.537–538). Cf. the alliterative *Poem.coniugis ad uxor.* 26, "mille modis miseros mors rapit una homines."

42. "si Romana respublica in haec miseriarum extrema defluxit, ut studiosos sui numquam remuneretur . . . quandoquidem facile clarescit rempublicam morari beneficia vos mereri. mirandum . . . non sit . . . si nobilium virorum militariumque . . . non tam defuerint facta quam praemia" (*Epist.* 3.8.1–2).

43. "Romanarum rerum . . . adversitas" (*Epist.* 4.14.1–2).

44. "latina . . . arma naufragium" (*Epist.* 8.2.1).

45. "non enim diutius ipsi maiores nostri hoc nomine gloriabuntur, qui minores incipiunt non habere" (*Epist.*7.7.5). Elsewhere, however, Sidonius also could attempt to forestall this dire eventuality by expressing the hope that a newly married couple would have "one or two sons" before embarking on the preferred life of chastity (*Epist.* 9.6.3–4). For the possible aristocratic failure to reproduce, see

Barnish, "Transformation," p. 144. Most Gauls, however, seem to have followed Sidonius' advice.

46. "ubi namque sunt antiquae Romanorum opes ac dignitates? fortissimi quondam Romani erant, nunc sine viribus; timebantur Romani veteres, nos timemus; vectigalia illis solvebant populi barbarorum, nos vectigales barbaris sumus . . . o infelicitates nostras! ad quid devenimus! et pro hoc gratias barbaris agimus, a quibus nos ipsos pretio comparamus. quid potest esse nobis vel abiectius vel miserius?" (De gub. 6.18, cf. 6.9). For Salvian as "un véritable agent de propagande de la suprématie barbare," see Loyen, "Résistants," p. 441. At the end of the fourth century, the military writer Flavius Vegetius Renatus had his own explanation for the barbarian successes: speaking of the ars bellica, he sorrowfully opined, "hanc solam hodieque barbari putant esse servandam" (Epit.rei mil. 3.10).

47. Pacatus, Pan.lat. 12/2.4; see Demougeot, "Restrictions," p. 383, and "Modalités"; Loyen, "Résistants," p. 440; Ladner, "Attitudes," pp. 8–10; Loyen, "Débuts," p. 414; Oost, Placidia, p. 155; Straub, "Geschichtsapologetic"; and Thompson, "Visigoths."

48. "foedifragem gentem" (Epist. 6.6.1). For Sidonius as being "sous l'illusion du foedus" between the Romans and Goths in the 460s, see Loyen, "Résistants," p. 446.

49. "tyrannopolitarum" (Epist. 5.8.3).

50. The chronicle was composed in the fifteenth year of the Priscillianist controversy (Chron. 2.51), that is, in the late 390s, and concluded in the consulate of Stilicho (A.D. 400: Chron. 2.9).

51. "dividendum esse Romanum regnum . . . praefigurant: quod aeque impletum est, siquidem cum non ab uno imperatore, sed etiam a pluribus semperque inter se armis aut studiis dissentientibus res Romana administretur" (Chron. 2.3).

52. "denique commisceri testum atque ferrum numquam inter se coeunte materie commixtiones humani generis futurae a se invicem dissidentes significantur, siquidem Romanum solum ab exteris gentibus aut rebellibus occupatum aut dedentibus se per pacis speciem traditum constet, exercitibusque nostris, urbibus atque provinciis permixtas barbaras nationes, et praecipue Iudaeos, inter nos degere nec tamen in mores nostros transire videamus."

53. Philostorg. HE 12.4: Bidez, p. 143; see Bury, LRE, p. 197 n. 1.

54. "in quo prophetia Danihelis putatur impleta, ut ait filiam regis Austri sociandam regi Aquilonis, nullo tamen eius ex ea semine subsistente" (Hyd. Chron. 57 s.a. 414), cf. Dan. 11.6 ["the daughter of the king of the south shall come to the king of the north to make peace, but she shall not retain the strength of her arm, and he and his offspring shall not endure": Revised Standard Version]; for discussion, see Bury, LRE, p. 197 n. 1; and Oost, Placidia, p. 125.

55. Hist.adv.pag. 7.40.2.

56. Carm. 7.496–498.

57. "mihi Romula dudum / per te iura placent . . . Romae sum te duce amicus, / principe te miles" (Carm. 7.495–496,511–512).

58. See Chapter 10.

59. Oros. Hist.adv.pag. 7.43; see Wallace-Hadrill, "Gothia," pp. 219–220; King,

Law, p. 2; Oost, *Placidia*, p. 122; and Thompson, "Visigoths," p. 111. For an earlier example of Visigothic ambivalence toward *Romanitas*, see Eunap. fr. 60.

60. "multa experientia probavisset neque Gothos ullo modo parere legibus posse propter effrenatam barbariem neque reipublicae interdici leges oportere, sine quibus respublica non est respublica . . . de restituendo in integrum augendoque Romano nomine Gothorum viribus."

61. And for the commonplace contrast of Roman law and order to barbarian lawlessness and disorder, see Oost, *Placidia*, p. 125; and Pavan, *Politica*, pp. 15–19.

62. "barbaros vitas quia mali putentur, ego, etiamsi boni" (*Epist.* 7.14.10).

63. In general, note Goffart, "Theme," p. 96, "There was no lack of hostility toward barbarians in the fourth and fifth centuries, but neither was there a barrier to their becoming respectable."

64. Note Salv. *De gub.* 6.8, 7.6, 7.9. Ladner, "Attitudes," p. 21, notes that western ecclesiastics "did not escape the necessity of living in close proximity to the Germanic barbarians and had therefore to overcome anti-barbarianism." See also Brezzi, "Impero" and "Romani" passim; and Straub, "Geschichtsapologetik."

65. "ad Scythiae proceres regesque Getarum / respice, queis ostro contempto et vellere Serum / eximius decor est tergis horrere ferarum" (*Carm.de prov.dei* 143–145).

66. Salv. *De gub.* 7.15, see also 4.14; translation cited from O'Sullivan, *Writings*, p. 207. And Augustine, after the sack of Rome in 410, attributed some virtues to the barbarians: see *De civ.dei* 1.1,7, 3.29, 5.23; see also Brezzi, "Impero," pp. 262–264; and Cleland, "Salvian."

67. See Introduction.

68. Salv. *De gub.* 4.13,16,19; see Brezzi, "Impero," pp. 265–266; and Ladner, "Attitudes," pp. 23–24, "the barbarians . . . often stand on a much higher moral level." See also Oros. *Hist.adv.pag.* 7.41.

69. For barbarians as the "scourge of God," see Oros. *Hist.adv.pag.* 7.22.6.

70. "vos nec contriti ab hoste luxuriam repressistis: perdidistis utilitatem calamitatis, et miserrimi facti estis, et pessimi permansistis" (*De civ.* 1.33).

71. Salv. *De gub.* 6.12, cf. 4.2, 4.9, 4.12, 5.4, 5.8, 7.12–13. See also *Carm.de prov.dei* 89–90, "nec tantus dolor est Scythicis consumier armis, quantus ab infidis cordibus ista seri"; see also ibid., 897–900, 908–918.

72. See Chapter 3.

73. *De civ.* 1.1,7, 3.29, 5.23: they showed mercy "propter Christum."

74. "grandi sedulitate . . . servet istam pro consuetudine potius quam pro ratione reverentiam" (*Epist.* 1.2.4).

75. "vir, femina, servus / liber, Iudaeus, Graecus, Scytha, barbarus, omnes / in Christo sumus unum . . ." (*Carm.de prov.dei* 456–457).

76. "barbari exsecrati gladios suos ad aratra conversi sunt residuosque Romanos ut socios modo et amicos fovent" (*Hist.adv.pag.* 7.41).

77. *Carm.* 7.411–418.

5. GALLIC TRADITIONALISTS AND THE CONTINUED
PURSUIT OF THE ROMAN IDEAL

1. For such in Gaul and elsewhere, see Brown, *World*, passim; Bury, *LRE*, p. 330; Drinkwater, "Attitudes," p. 152; Jones, *LRE*, p. 529; Lécrivain, *Senat*, pp. 65–67; Matthews, *Aristocracies*, pp. 92, 257, 308, 320–321, 340–341, 349–351; Oost, *Placidia*, pp. 77, 147; Stein, *Geschichte*, pp. 409, 544; Stevens, *Sidonius*, p. 28; Stroheker, *Adel*, pp. 3, 19, 48–62; and Sundwall, *Studien*, pp. 8–14. For this as the normal condition of Roman Gaul, see Drinkwater, "Attitudes," pp. 138–151, and *Roman Gaul*, pp. 48, 114, 202; and Matthews, *Aristocracies*, p. 350ff. In the 430s, *clarissimi* and *spectabiles* even were encouraged to stay at home (*CJ* 12.1.15).

2. See Cicero, *De inventione* 2.56.168, "potentia est ad sua conservanda et alterius attenuenda idonearum rerum facultas." See also Drinkwater, "Patronage"; Ensslin, "Auctoritas"; MacMullen, *Corruption*, passim; Schlumberger, "*Potentes*"; Mitteis, " 'Potentiores' "; and Wallace-Hadrill, "Gothia," p. 222.

3. "nec pompa minor polleret honoris / instructa obsequiis et turba fulta clientum" (*Euch.* 436–437; see also ibid. 264–265, "namque et quanta mihi per te conlata potentum / gratia praestiterit . . .").

4. "denique si aliqua potens persona contra nos iniuriam faciat, si etiam nos in faciem maledicat, nec respondere aliquid asperum, non dicam vicem reddere ausi sumus. quare hoc? ne ab illa persona potente adhuc maiora quam pertulimus patiamur . . . si ergo potens persona contra nos saeviat, tacemus et nihil dicere ausi sumus, si vero aut aequalis aut forte inferior vel levem contumeliam fecerit . . . consurgimus et aut in praesenti iniuriam nostram vindicavimus aut certe ad maiorem vicem reddendam nostrum animum praeparamus, quid est hoc, quod quando persona potens nobis iniuriam contulit, patienter accipimus, quando inferior nimio furore succendimur?" ("Sermo in natali sancti Stephani": *CSEL* 21.232–236).

5. " 'facito ut sim privatus et potens . . . liceat mihi spoliare non debentes, caedere alienos, vicinos autem et spoliare et caedere.' Lar: 'latrocinium non potentiam requiris' . . ." (*Querolus* 1.2).

6. This section often has been thought to deal with the Bacaudae; see Thompson, "Peasant Revolts," pp. 18–19; MacMullen, *Enemies*, pp. 211–212; and Van Dam, *Leadership*, pp. 46–47. The Bacaudae, however, are nowhere named, and "the Loire" may simply be a generic reference to backwoods areas where imperial power was weak and local potentates (*privati*) had appropriated authority.

7. See Schlumberger, "*Potentes*," pp. 96–98.

8. "maximus iniustis locus invenietur in orbe / oppressis autem pars prope nulla bonis / qui fuerit violentus, atrox, versutus, avarus / cuius corde fides cesserit, ore pudor / hunc omnes mirantur, amant, reverentur, honorant / huic summi fasces, huic tribuuntur opes . . . / falsa valent in iudiciis, et vera laborant / insontes sequitur poena, salusque reos" (*Carm.de prov.dei* 67–80).

9. *De gub.* 3.10. He also could assert, "ut pauci inlustrentur, mundus evertitur: unius honor orbis excidium est" (*De gub.* 4.4). On the attitudes of Salvian, see Badewien, *Geshichtstheologie*; Hamman, *Salvien*; Ianelli, *Caduta*; and Thouvenot, "Salvien."

10. "quae enim sunt non modo urbes, sed etiam municipia atque vici, ubi non quot curiales fuerint, tot tyranni sunt? quamquam forte hoc nomine gratulentur, quia potens et honoratus esse videatur" (De gub. 5.4); see Lepelley, "Curiales"; see also Wightman, Belgica, p. 256. For allowable kinds of ambition, see Valer. Hom. 13.7: PL 52.

11. "omnes dominos constat quidem esse et manifestissimum est malos" (Quer. 49).

12. "felices dici mos est, quos blanda potestas / in summos apices tumidorum evexit honorum / quos magni quaestus ditarunt, et quibus amplos / congessit reditus totum res fusa per orbem. / laudantur vestes pretiosae, et pulchra supellex, / magnae aedes, famuli innumeri, vigilesque clientes . . ." (Carm.de prov.dei 860–865).

13. See C.Th. 13.11.9 (9 March 398), about those "qui per potentiam fundos opimos ac fertiles occuparunt." For Gaul, see Drinkwater, "Attitudes," pp. 146–150, and Roman Gaul, pp. 173,181; and Wightman, Belgica, pp. 253–265; see also Applebaum, "Rural Pattern"; Barnish, "Transformation," pp. 140–149; Gaudemet, "Abus," p. 131; Matthews, Aristocracies, p. 79f; Percival, "Aspects" and Villa, p. 71; and Schlumberger, "Potentes."

14. "potentum magnitudinem . . . patrocinia maiorum" (De gub. 5.8).

15. "armatur vicinitas frequenter ad litem, unde est, nisi quod hic forte terminos transcendere, et cespitem iuris alieni cogitat occupare?" (Hom. 20.3). Cf. Basil, Hom.in divit. 5 (P.G. 31. 293–296). Some property owners even fenced off, or planted crops in, the public roads (Lex Burg. 27.3).

16. For Paulinus' lack of ambition, see Euch. 200–216.

17. Euch. 424–425, cf. 510–511.

18. Attendance by clients: Carm.de prov.dei 865; Paul.Pell. Euch.436–437; Sid.Apoll. Epist. 1.11.3–4; Valer. Hom. 14.4; see also Clover, "Olybrius," pp. 169–170.

19. See Salv. De gub. 5.8–9; Nov.Maj. 3, 7; C.Th. 5.5.2 = Sirm. 16; and Haenel, Corp.leg. p. 281; see also Arnheim, Aristocracy, p. 161; Matthews, Aristocracies, p. 346; and Stroheker, Adel, p. 60.

20. See Krause, "Städtpatronat"; and Zulueta, "Patronis." For patrocinium as "the greatest evil," see Charanis, "Structure," p. 41.

21. For terminology, see MacMullen, Corruption, pp. 69–70, 101–103.

22. For a suggested relationship between secular and ecclesiastical gratia, see Myres, "Pelagius," pp. 21–36.

23. See Schlumberger, "Potentes," p. 99; and Wightman, Belgica, p. 265.

24. See Sid.Apoll. Epist. 3.6.3, 5.9.1–3, 5.16.4.

25. Note Cl. Lupicinus (CIL 13.921) and Dalmatius (ILS no. 8987) (qq.v. in PLRE I-II); see also Matthews, Aristocracies, pp. 23–28.

26. See, in general, Arnheim, Aristocracy, pp. 6–7, 156; Liebs, "Amterpatronage"; Matthews, Aristocracies, pp. 1–31; and MacMullen, Corruption, pp. 148–164.

27. "ut scilicet memineris eo tempore, quo personam publicam portas, gratiae te privatae memorem semper esse oportere" (Epist. 4.14.1; see also 2.3; 3.6; 4.14; 5.18).

28. For patronage during the earlier empire, see Harmand, *Patronat;* and MacMullen, *Corruption,* passim.

29. For such by Sidonius, see *Epist.* 2.5, 3.9, 3.10, 4.22. For the "mechanical" nature of letters of recommendation, see MacMullen, *Corruption,* p. 98.

30. See MacMullen, *Corruption,* p. 99; and Wood, "Disputes," pp. 8, 22.

31. Greg.Tur. *HF* 2.24.

32. Eugenia: *CIL* 12.481; *PLRE II,* p. 416. Firminus and Gregoria: *VCaesarii* 1.8; *PLRE II,* pp. 471, 520.

33. Syagria: *VEpiphanii* 173; *PLRE II,* p. 1041. Eugenia: *CIL* 12.481. Note also Gemellus, presumably as an Ostrogothic agent (Avit. *Epist.* 35). For such by ecclesiastics, see Chapter 9.

34. See *CIL* 12.5336; *ILS* 1293–1296; and Sid.Apoll. *Epist.* 3.12, 4.15.1.

35. "ecclesiarum monasteriorumque per eleemosynam mater" (*VEugendi* 12); also called the "thesaurus ecclesiae" (*VEpiphanii* 173).

36. See Mathisen, *Factionalism,* p. 36.

37. *Corp.chr.lat.* 148.80–81.

38. Contrary to the suggestion of Van Dam, *Leadership,* p. 175, that Avitus was "forgotten." For the devotion of Avitus and his family to St. Julian, see Greg.Tur. *HF* 2.7,11; Sid.Apoll. *Carm.* 24.16–19, *Epist.* 4.6.2, 7.1.7.

39. Sid.Apoll. *Carm.* 7.207–214.

40. "foedera regum" (*Carm.* 7.214, cf. 7.311, 475–480); see Bayless, "Avitus."

41. "vel iam privatus" (Sid.Apoll. *Carm.* 7.14–225, 308–310, 353). Treaty: Demougeot, "Septimanie," p. 31; and Loyen, "Débuts," p. 411. Huns: Demougeot, "Attila," pp. 31–32. Note also his intercession, c. 425, on behalf of the Roman hostage Theodorus (see Loyen, "Débuts," pp. 406–409; and Chapter 3) and his role in the renewal of the treaty with the Visigoths in 439.

42. "spernis amicum / plus quam Romanum gerere" (*Carm.* 7.224–225).

43. "ab Arelatensium portis . . . te prandio removisse" (Sid.Apoll. *Epist.* 7.12.3); see Charaux, *Tonantius.*

44. Sid.Apoll. *Carm.* 5.574–585, *Epist.* 1.9.5.

45. Sid.Apoll. *Epist.* 3.1.4–5; see Demougeot, "Septimanie," pp. 17, 30.

46. "pro hac civitate stetit vel ante pellitos reges vel ante principes purpuratos" (Sid.Apoll. *Epist.* 7.9.19).

47. "Gothos rursum mihi dira minari" (*Euch.* 362).

48. See Arnheim, *Aristocracy,* pp. 146–147; Matthews, *Aristocracies,* p. 341; Paunier, "Refuge"; Percival, *Villa,* p. 175ff; Samson, "Castle"; Stroheker, *Adel,* pp. 59–60; Thompson, *Romans,* p. 122; and Wightman, *Belgica,* pp. 253–260.

49. *Mos.* 284, cf. 318–330. Ausonius also, however, reassuringly claimed that such establishments were used only for "storage." See also *Carm.de prov.dei* 25–48.

50. "castellum . . . Alpinis rupibus cinctum" (*Epist.* 4.15.3); cf. "solidae domus ad hoc aevi inconcussa securitas" (*Epist.* 4.6.2, cf. 8.4.1).

51. "delectat . . . an fortasse montana sedes circum castella et in eligenda sede perfugii quandam pateris ex munitionum frequentia difficultatem?" (*Epist.* 5.14.1).

52. Sid.Apoll. *Carm.* 22, *Epist.* 8.11.3, 8.12.5–8. In the late fourth century, a *praepositus* Leontius, perhaps even a relative, built a "burgum a fundamentis" in Noricum (*CIL* 3.567a = *ILS* no. 774). For a *burgus* as a small fort, see *C.Th.* 12.19.2 and *CJ* 1.27.2.4; see also Isid.Hisp. *Etym.* 9.2.99, 9.4.28; and Burns, "Frontier Policy," pp. 396–397.

53. "non illos machina muros / non aries, non alta strues vel proximus agger / non quae stridentes torquet catapulta molares, / sed nec testudo nec vinea nec rota currens / iam positis scalis umquam quassare valebunt" (*Carm.* 22.121–125).

54. "qui hostium terrore compulsi ad castella se conferunt" (*De gub.* 5.8). See also *Carm.de prov.dei* 35–36, for protection by "non castella petris, non oppida montibus altis / imposita."

55. See Wightman, *Belgica,* p. 258; and von Petrikovits, "Fortifications." For a comparison to Celtic hill forts, see Matthews, *Aristocracies,* p. 346; and Wightman, "Social Structure," p. 20.

56. The name may be an allusion to Augustine's "Civitas dei." See Marrou, "Un lieu"; and Chatillon, "Dardanus."

57. "loco, cui nomen Theopoli est, viarum usum, caesis utrimque montium laterib[us] praestiterunt, muros et portas dederunt, quod in agro proprio constitutum tuetioni omnium voluerunt esse commune" (*CIL* 12.1524 = *ILS* 1279).

58. For other examples, note *Chron.gall.511* s.a. 477; Ennod. *Opusc.* 5.20: *MGH AA* 7.303; Greg.Tur. *Glor.conf.* 46; Paul.Pell. *Euch.* 528; Ven.Fort. *Carm.* 3.12, 3.20; *VHilar.Arel.* 6[9]); *VSeverini* 11.1–2, 25.2, 40.1. Namatius of Vienne also was called a "perfugium miseris" (Avit. *Appendix* 11.24: *MGH AA* 6.2).

59. See Chapter 9. Note also city fortifications: see Butler, "Town Walls."

60. Themistius, *Oratio* 8, translation from Goffart, "Rome," p. 290; see also Dagron, "Thémistios," pp. 101–104; and Daly, "Themistius."

61. See Goffart, "Rome," pp. 292–295; and Moss, "Policies."

62. See Thompson, "Settlement"; and Bachrach, "Alans" and "Settlement."

63. See, in particular, Thompson, *Romans,* p. 179, cf. pp. 239–240, for the "degree of apathy on the part of the civilians, that inability to combine, plan, and attack, which is all too obvious."

64. See, for Gaul and Spain, Rouche, *L'Aquitaine,* p. 45; and Thompson, "End," pp. 22–26. For Italy during the Gothic wars, see Cass. *Var.* 12.5; Procop. *Bell.goth.* 7.18.20–23, 22.20ff, 30.6.

65. For popular resistance in general, see MacMullen, *Corruption,* p. 52.

66. See Sid.Apoll. *Epist.* 1.6.2, 3.3.3, 4.20.1, 5.12.1; see also Bachrach, "Alans," p. 485; and Rattenbury, "Armored Force." As to the Italian senators, Aurelius Victor noted for the period c. 280, "oblectantur otio simulque divitiis pavent, quarum usum affluentiamque aeternitate maius putant, munivere militaribus et paene barbaris viam in se ac posteros dominandi" (*Liber de caes.* 37.7).

67. "omnis autem regio viros habet fortes et nobiles in bello" (*Expos.* 58).

68. See Chapter 3.

69. See, Fred. *Chron.* 2.53; Greg.Tur. *HF* 2.7; and Sid.Apoll. *Epist.* 8.15.1; see also Banniard, "L'aménagement," pp. 5–38.

70. *VEuspicii: AASS* July V, pp. 74–76.

71. Sid.Apoll. *Carm.* 7.246ff.

72. "collegisse te privatis viribus publici exercitus speciem parvis extrinsecus maiorum opibus adiutum" (*Epist.* 3.3.7). It is unclear who these outside *maiores* were, whether local senators, those from other cities (such as Lyons), other barbarians (such as the Burgundians), or even the imperial government.

73. Sid.Apoll. *Epist.* 5.6.2; see Chapter 8.

74. Greg.Tur. *Virt.Iul.* 7, probably to be identified with the illustrious Helladius of Avit. *Epist.* 84. For similar examples of local resistance involving ecclesiastics, see Chapter 9.

75. For these individuals, see Wightman, *Belgica,* p. 304.

76. See Mathisen, *Factionalism,* pp. 217–219.

77. Greg.Tur. *HF* 2,18,27,41; Fred. *Chron.* 3.12,15; *LHF* 8–9. See *PLRE II,* pp. 1041–1042 and 851–852 (with Paul as a possible *magister militum*) respectively. *LHF* 9 also styles Syagrius a "patricius Romanorum." See also James, "Syagrius"; and Schmidt, "Ende."

78. Sid.Apoll. *Epist.* 4.17; he apparently was a man of some education, see Chapter 10.

79. See Heinzelmann, "Recherche," pp. 230–231; and Wightman, *Trier,* p. 251. It also may be that Arbogastes already was reporting to the Franks. He was a friend of Sidonius Apollinaris (Sid.Apoll. *Epist.* 4.17) and of Auspicius of Toul (*MGH Epist.* 3.135–137 no. 23 = *MGH Poet.* 4.2.614).

6. FLIGHT AND DISLOCATION, EMIGRANTS AND EXILES

1. Some of the conclusions of the first section of this chapter appeared in *Phoenix* 38 (1984), pp. 159–170, under the title "Emigrants, Exiles, and Survivors: Aristocratic Options in Visigothic Aquitania."

2. Related to this was the pursuit of isolation and the ascetic ideal; see Fontaine, "L'ascétisme," pp. 87–115; Heinzelmann, *Bischofsherrschaft,* pp. 73–98, 185–211; Nagel, *Askese;* Nürnburg, *Askese;* and Pricoco, *L'isola,* pp. 25–59, 131–186.

3. "admonemus ergo vos . . . nostri temporis homines, ut his mundi turbinibus ad domum dei certatim unusquisque confugiat" (*Serm.* 26: *CSEL* 21.328–330, cf. *Serm.* 2: *CSEL* 21.229). Note also "sic et monachus devictis et superatis mundi huius criminibus quasi periculosis fluctibus, cum ad portum monasterii venerit" (*Serm.* 24: *CSEL* 21.319); and Ruric. *Epist.* 1.17; and Paul.Nol. *Epist.* 51.2, for escape "ab istius mundi strepitu."

4. "urbium frequentiam turbasque vitantes remotioris villulae et in ea secretum monasterii incolamus habitaculum . . ." (*Comm.* 1). And Honoratus of Arles settled on a "vacantem itaque insulam ob nimietatem squaloris et inaccessam venenatorum animalium metu" (*VHonorati* 3[15]).

5. "carcere si caeco claudar, nectarque catenis / liber in excessu mentis adhibo deum / si mucrone paret cervicem abscindere lictor / impavidum inveniet: mors cita, poena brevis / non metuo exsilium, mundus domus omnibus una est" (*Poem.coniug.ad uxor.* 93–97).

6. "iustus . . . in totis mundi partibus exsul agit" (*Carm.de prov.dei* 73–76).

7. "cum vos persecuti fuerint in una civitate, fugite in aliam" (*Hist.adv.pag.* 7.41; cf. *Matth.* 10.23).

8. *Hist.adv.pag.* 5.2; see also Thompson, "End," pp. 23–24.

9. See Jones, *LRE*, p. 1059, "more usually, those who could fled to safer places."

10. See, inter alios, Brown, "Patrons," pp. 65, 70; Clover, "Symbiosis," p. 59; Dill, *Last*, p. 160; Hodgkin, *Italy* 4.421, 534; Jones, *LRE*, pp. 249, 1059; Matthews, *Aristocracies*, pp. 286, 300, 308; and Thompson, *Romans*, pp. 208–217.

11. See Benoit, "Hilarianum," p. 183; Ewig, *Trier*, p. 106; Prinz, *Mönchtum*, p. 48, and "Aristocracy," pp. 155–156; Stroheker, *Adel*, pp. 19–20; Wightman, *Belgica*, pp. 254–255, 302–308, and *Trier*, p. 250, where the emigrants consist of "all people who had, or thought they could find, a means of livelihood elsewhere." For the expulsion of northern officials, see Zos. *Hist.nov.* 6.3.1–3; see also Stevens, "Marcus, Gratian, and Constantine."

12. "ad viciniam Rheni . . . nullum nostrarum partium commeare . . ." (*Epist.* 4.28). See Chapter 2.

13. See Gabba and Tibiletti, "Signora."

14. See Stroheker, *Adel*, p. 19 and s.vv. in prosopography, and *PLRE I* s.vv. For their origin, see Symm. *Epist.* 4.30 (to Protadius), "et tu non iisdem sedibus inmoraris, dum aut Treviros civica religione aut Quinque Provincias otii voluntate commutas." See Matthews, "Supporters," p. 1096, and *Aristocracies*, p. 262 n. 2 (for Trier). The phrase "civica religione" does indicate that Trier was their home. For the date, see Chapter 2.

15. *A.E.* (1953) no. 200, "inde iter Italiam magno cumulandus honore ni luctu tristem linquens Eventius urbem neu vitae merito sanctis sociandus obisset." See *PLRE II*, p. 413; and Marrou, "L'épitaphe." Matthews, *Aristocracies*, p. 275 n. 3, questions whether Eventius was a refugee.

16. *ILS* no. 266. The only other Arcontius known for Gaul is a subdeacon of Angers c. 460/470 (*PL* 58.66–68), and Remus' name suggests, perhaps, a connection to Rheims.

17. See *PLRE II*, p. 851; and Wightman, *Belgica*, p. 306.

18. See Duchesne, *Fastes* 1.264. His *vita* (*Analecta bollandiana* 11[1892], pp. 374–383) describes him as an "incola civitatis Remensis."

19. See Benoit, "Fragments"; and *PLRE I*, p. 921.

20. See *CIL* 12.674 = *ILCV* 88; and *PLRE I*, p. 389.

21. *CIL* 12.2128.

22. See Greg.Tur. *HF* 1.46; perhaps to be identified with Marius Artemius, *vicarius Hispaniarum* in 369–370 (*PLRE I*, p. 113).

23. *AASS* August IV p. 441ff.

24. *VSeverini* 2.

25. See Mathisen, *Factionalism*, passim; and Prinz, *Mönchtum*, pp. 47–59.

26. See Mathisen, *Factionalism*, pp. 76–80.

27. Salv. *Epist.* 1.

28. See Prinz, "Lerinum als 'Flüctlingskloster' der nordgallischen Aristokratie," *Mönchtum*, pp. 147–158.

29. As did Antiolus, bishop of an unknown northern see; see Mathisen, *Factionalism*, pp. 78–80, 89–90.

30. "tunc primum illam esse patriam, quam fugiendam dudum crediderat, agnovit" (VHonorati 5[24]).

31. See Mathisen, Factionalism, pp. 77–78.

32. Contrary to Jones, LRE, p. 1060, "we hear of no similar exodus from Gaul." Aquitania here refers to the Visigothic kingdom, for which see Matthews, Aristocracies, pp. 314–345; Rouche, Aquitaine, pp. 19–56; and Thompson, Romans, pp. 23–57.

33. See Chapter 2.

34. De red. 1.208–211. See Matthews, Aristocracies, p. 328 n. 3; Stroheker, Adel, pp. 197–198; and Wightman, "Peasants," p. 113, and Belgica, p. 267.

35. "errantem Tuscis considere compulit agris / et colere externos capta Tolosa lares" (De red. 1.495–496). See Courcelle, Histoire, p. 68, who dates the move to c. 413.

36. "substituit patriis mediocres Umbria sedes / virtus fortunam fecit utramque parem. / mens invicta viri pro magnis parva tuetur . . ." (De red. 1.551–553).

37. See Matthews, "Supporters," p. 1096, and Aristocracies, pp. 261–262, 326–327; on Protadius' origins, see also above.

38. "natales puer horruit Cadurcos / plus Pandionias amans Athenas" (Carm. 9.281–282). PLRE II, p. 1237, suggests only that he "possibly visited Athens," but Sidonius' context leaves no doubt; he discussed three poets with one thing in common: all moved away from home.

39. For the decline of Ausonius' family under the barbarians, see Jullian, Gaule 8.138. For contra, see Barnish, "Transformation," p. 137.

40. ". . . quorum mihi plurima saepe adversa experto rursum suasere moranti linquendas patriae sedes quantocius esse—quod fecisse prius fuerat magis utile nobis—illa ut contento peteremus litora cursu, pars ubi magna mihi etiamnunc salva manebat materni census, complures sparsa per urbes Argivas atque Epiri Veterisque Novaeque" (Euch. 408–415). For Paulinus, see Chapter 3.

41. Euch. 494–495.

42. "perpetuum exilium . . . exul inops" (Euch. 491, 542).

43. Euch. 520–563.

44. "excedens patria communi clade careret" (Euch. 327).

45. Ausonius' official duties are implied by his use of the balteus, punicea tunica, and cursus publicus (Hieron. Epist. 118.1). Jerome's reference to Ausonius as Julianus' "frater" presumably refers to a physical rather than a spiritual bond, because neither of them was an ecclesiastic.

46. For the younger Ausonius, see PLRE II, p. 139; Seeck, MGH AA 6.1.lxxv–lxxvii; Martindale, "Addenda," p. 247; and Stroheker, Adel, p. 152, who suggests the relationship.

47. For this pattern of nomenclature, see Heinzelmann, Bischofsherrschaft, pp. 19–22; Mathisen, "Epistolography," pp. 99–100; and Seeck, MGH AA 6.1.lxxi–lxxvii.

48. Euch. 518–521.

49. "consecuta rei familiaris damna, vastationem totius barbaro hoste provinciae, et in communi depopulatione privatas possessionum tuarum ruinas" (Hieron. Epist. 118.2).

50. Ibid. 5–6.

51. As a Dalmatian: *PLRE II*, p. 637. As a Gaul: Stroheker, *Adel*, p. 186.

52. He ultimately may have settled in Italy: a *vir inlustris* Ausonius complained to the emperor Severus in 465 about the marital practices of the slaves and *coloni* in Rome (*Nov.Sev.* 2).

53. Hieron. *Epist.* 122, 120; Oros. *Hist.adv.pag.* 7.43.

54. "sed impeditum est desiderium meum per totas iam Hispanias hoste diffuso" (*PL* 41.805). Brown, "Patrons," p. 71, refers to such travelers as "quite as much refugees as pilgrims."

55. Hieron. *Epist.* 109; Gennad. *Vir.ill.* 36.

56. See Mathisen, *Factionalism*, pp. 124–139; and Markus, "Prosper." Prosper has been suggested as the author of the aforementioned *Poema coniugis ad uxorem* and *Carmen de providentia dei;* see Chadwick, *Poetry*, pp. 122–123; Duckett, *Writers*, pp. 97–101; Duval, *Gaule*, pp. 743–744; Griffe, *Gaule* 2.21–23; and Schanz, *Geschichte* 4.2.493–495.

57. Gennad. *Vir.ill.* 89; *PLS* 3.379ff.

58. For the withdrawal of Paulinus of Nola from Gaul, see Matthews, *Aristocracies*, p. 152; Moricca, "Morte Violenta"; and *PLRE I*, pp. 681–683.

59. Greg.Tur. *HF* 2.1, 10.31.

60. "tam nobilis sanctitate quam sanguine" (*VEpiphanii* 35).

61. *PLRE II*, pp. 393–394.

62. Sidonius does mention a poet Quintianus who moved from Liguria, on the border between Gaul and Italy, to Gaul c. 430 in the train of Aetius (*Carm.* 9.289–295).

63. See Stevens, *Sidonius*, pp. 140, 195–196; and Stroheker, *Adel*, pp. 145, 223–224. The Visigoths are thought to have had a more adversarial relationship with the imperial government than the more pro-Roman Burgundians and Franks; see Jones, *LRE*, p. 259.

64. Sid.Apoll. *Epist.* 5.16.1–2,4; Jord. *Get.* 240–241. Circa 507/511, the Ostrogothic king Theodoric ordered, "ut Ecdicii filios, quos in urbe primitus residere censuimus, ad patriam cum genitoris sui funere . . . remeare iubeatis" (Cass.*Var.*2.22). Since both other holders of the rare name Ecdicius listed in *PLRE II* (pp. 383–384) are Gallic, the foreign Ecdicius who died in Rome may have been the Arvernian, a conclusion supported by the date of their return, just after the Gothic defeat at Vouillé in 507, which would have eliminated the possibility of Visigothic reprisals against them.

65. *VDan.Styl.* 60. Note also a "quaedam vero puella ab urbe Tolosa praeclaris orta natalibus" who supposedly went to Rome during the reign of Alaric II (484–507) to be cured of an illness (*VRemedii* 16ff: *MGH AA* 4.2.64–67).

66. "parate exulibus terram, capiendis redemptionem, viaticum peregrinaturis" (*Epist.* 7.7.6).

67. See Chapter 3.

68. Sid.Apoll. *Epist.* 9.10, to the bishop Aprunculus, who himself subsequently fled to Clermont in order to escape the Burgundians.

69. Greg.Tur. *Glor.mart.* 44, *HF* 2.20.

70. "in exsilium apud urbem Mediolanensem" (Greg.Tur. *Glor.mart.* 44).

71. "patria gravi sumus exire necessitate conpulsi, et casus qui vos extorres de patria fecit nos etiam conpolit exolare" (*PLS* 3.831–832); see C. Turner, *J.Th.S.* 30(1929), p. 27; and Morin, "Castor et Polychronius." The letter does not give any specific locations. Polychronius presumably is the bishop of Verdun of that name who was a disciple of Lupus of Troyes (*VLupi* 11: *MGH SRM* 3.123, see Duchesne, *Fastes* 3.69–70). The only bishop Castor attested for the fifth century was at Chartres (ibid. 2.424).

72. Duchesne, *Fastes* 2.424–425.

73. See Duchesne, *Fastes* 2.424–425; and Wightman, *Belgica*, pp. 304, 306, and *Trier*, pp. 250–251. Auspicius of Toul earlier had suggested that Arbogastes would make a good cleric: "quod te iam sacerdotio / praefiguratum teneo" (*Epist.ad Arbog.* sec. 38, cf. sec. 39).

74. See Sid.Apoll. *Epist.* 4.17 and Auspic. *Epist.ad Arbog.* sec. 40 (*MGH Epist.* 3.140); see also Duchesne, *Fastes* 2.193 n. 1, 3.37; Wightman, *Belgica*, p. 304.

75. As in the third century and later, when refugees occupied caves in the Rhone valley; see Gagnière and Granier, "L'occupation."

76. "pollutionem eorum evitans . . . e laribus propriis commigravit" (*VMariani* 1: *AASS* April II p. 758; cf. *Gest.epp.Autiss.* 8: *PL* 138.229).

77. "depraedationis Gothicae turbinem vitans" (Sid.Apoll. *Epist.* 6.10.1–2).

78. "ut ille crudelissima morte non privaretur vita, ipse extorris est factus e patria" (*Epist.* 2.8). Given that he had taken refuge in Aquitania and the south, Possessor may have been another displaced northerner.

79. *Epist.* 6.4.

80. "pro absolutione uxoris per diversarum regionum est iactatus exsilia" (Victorinus of Fréjus *apud* Faust. *Epist.* 7: *MGH AA* 8.271).

81. "harum autem portitorem sanctum presbyterum Florentium . . . quoniam pro germanae suae absolutione peregrinatur, insinuo . . ." (*Epist.* 5: *MGH AA* 8.270).

82. "qui in Lugdunensi pertulit captivitatem . . . et quia in se aliquatenus absolutus, in uxoris vel filiorum tenetur servitute captivus. . ." (*Epist.* 4: *MGH AA* 8.270).

83. "et quidem mirari possim, quod hoc non omnes omnino facerent tributarii pauperes et egestuosi, nisi quod una tantum causa est, qua non faciunt, quia transferre illuc resculas atque habitatiunculas suas familiasque non possunt" (*De gub.* 5.8).

84. See *C.Th.* 15.14.14 (1 March 416), granting immunity to those "qui evadendi forsitan non habuerant facultatem"; see Chapter 7.

7. BETWEEN *ROMANIA* AND *BARBARIA:* THE BARBARIAN ALTERNATIVE

1. "sub clade barbaricae depopulationis, si qua aut per fugam aut per congregationem infelicium populorum indigne invidioseque commissa sunt, ad invidiam placatarum legum a callidis litigatorum objectionibus non vocentur. habeant omnium criminum impunitatem, qui evadendi forsitan non habuerant facultatem . . .

non enim crimen dicitur, quod mortis adegit impulsus" (*C.Th.* 15.14.14: 1 March 416, at Ravenna).

2. For a general discussion of types of collaborators with barbarian invaders (few, however, in Gaul), see Thompson, "Invaders," pp. 71–86; and Ladner, "Attitudes," p. 2. Elsewhere, too, imperial policies benefited those affected by the barbarian invasions: *Nov.Val.* 35.12 (15 April 452) removed the thirty-year limitation on legal actions for Africans "qui se probaverint necessitatem Wandalicam pertulisse."

3. "porro aliae [sc. urbes], quas a vastitate barbarica terrarum intervalla distulerant, judicum nomine a nefariis latronibus obtinebantur, ingenua suberant indignis cruciatibus corpora, nemo ab injuria liber, nemo intactus a contumelia, nisi qui crudelitatem praedonis pretio mitigasset, ut jam barbari desiderarentur, ut praeoptaretur a miseris fortuna captorum" (*Pan.lat.* 11/3.4).

4. "si legatus aliquis vel sacerdos intercessurus pro civitate captiva largius pretium deferat et universum captivitatis populum de manu eius recipiat, qui belli iure retinebat, et omnis omnino relaxetur lex ac necessitas servitutis, et inter haec, si forte illic aliquos de captivis vel oblectatio consuetudinis vel male blandus praedo sollicitet, gratuitum beneficium unusquisque voluntatis suae servus recuset, numquid minoravit gratiam pretii contemptus ingrati?" (*De gratia* 1.16).

5. On this phenomenon, see also Chapter 12.

6. "itaque unum illic Romanorum omnium votum est, ne umquam eos necesse sit in ius transire Romanum. una et consentiens illic Romanae plebis oratio, ut liceat eis vitam, quam agunt, agere cum barbaris. et miramur, si non vincuntur a nostris partibus Gothi, cum malint apud hos esse quam apud nos Romani. itaque non solum transfugere ab eis ad nos fratres nostri omnino nolunt, set ut ad eos confugiant, nos relinquunt" (*De gub.* 5.8).

7. "ut multi eorum, et non obscuris natalibus editi et liberaliter instituti, ad hostes fugiant, ne persecutionis publicae adflictione moriantur, quaerentes scilicet apud barbaros Romanam humanitatem, quia apud Romanos barbaram inhumanitatem ferre non possunt . . . malunt tamen in barbaris pati cultum dissimilem quam in Romanis iniustitiam saevientem. itaque passim vel ad Gothos vel ad Bacaudas vel ad alios ubique dominantes barbaros migrant, et commigrasse non paenitet, malunt enim sub specie captivitatis vivere liberi quam sub specie libertatis esse captivi . . ." (*De gub.* 5.5).

8. "plerique et honesti et nobiles et quibus Romanus status summo et splendori esse debuit et honori, ad hoc tamen Romanae iniquitatis crudelitate compulsi sunt, ut nolint esse Romani. et hinc est, quod etiam hi, qui ad barbaros non confugiunt, barbari tamen esse coguntur" (*De gub.* 5.5). See Ladner, "Attitudes," p. 24 n. 122.

9. See Chapter 6. For similar in Spain, see Oros. *Hist.adv.pag.* 7.41.1, who in 417 mentioned "quidam Romani, qui malint inter barbaros pauperem libertatem quam inter Romanos tributariam sollicitudinem sustinere." For the empirewide phenomenon of members of the less-privileged social orders making common cause with invaders, see Thompson, "Invaders," pp. 71–87.

10. For this phenomenon, see Czuth, "Rolle," p. 8; and Thompson, "End," pp. 25–26.

11. "qui per injuriam compulsorum rurales habitationes et solitudines expetunt

. . . [fugientes] ab improbitatibus insolentum" (*Nov.Maj.*3); see also *Nov.Maj.* 7 for decurions who "occultas latebras et habitationem eligerent ruris alieni."

12. "discessu primorum populariumque" (*Epist.* 7.1.3); in this instance, the citizens eventually returned.

13. "Eudoxius arte medicus . . . in Bacauda id temporis mota delatus ad Chunos confugit" (*Chron.gall.452.* no. 133 s.a. 448: *MGH AA* 9.662), see *PLRE II*, p. 412.

14. Priscus fr. 8; for translation see Bury, *LRE* 1.284. For other eastern examples of Romans, none of them noble, fleeing to or joining the barbarians, see Thompson, "Invaders," pp. 75–79.

15. For similar, see Thompson, "Invaders," p. 85; on the Alamannic invasion of 354–355, see Amm. 14.10.8, 29.4.7.

16. "nunc inter barbaros in Hispania egens exulat" (Oros. *Hist.adv.pag.* 42.5, cf. Olymp. fr. 16; and *PLRE II*, p. 745). Thompson, "End," p. 25, suggests that the Spanish noblemen Ospinio and Ascanius "fled" to the Suevi, but they may simply have been collaborators.

17. Olymp. fr. 24: *PLRE II*, pp. 591, 882, 961; see Matthews, *Aristocracies*, pp. 316–317; and Oost, *Placidia*, pp. 127–129. Ingenius was called "a leader [protos] of those in the city"; see Thompson, "Visigoths," p. 114. Jordanes (*Getica* 31) claims that the marriage took place in Fréjus; see also Oros. *Hist.adv.pag.* 7.40,43.

18. Olymp. fr. 24, see *PLRE II*, p. 257. Such individuals, however, may have justified their activities as being in support of the Roman Priscus Attalus rather than of the Goth Athaulf.

19. Oros. *Hist.adv.pag.* 7.43.4; as to the identity of this person, *PLRE II*, p. 1232, proposes Ingenius, while Matthews, *Aristocracies*, pp. 73, 317, 322, and *Latomus*, pp. 1085–1099, suggests the medical writer Marcellus of Bordeaux (*PLRE I*, pp. 551–552). For the incident, see Chapter 4.

20. "cernamus plures Gothico florere favere" (*Euch.* 307).

21. "rege mandante" (Sid. *Epist.* 4.8.1–5). Evodius: *PLRE II*, pp. 421–422.

22. Sid.Apoll. *Epist.* 8.9.1–5: *PLRE II*, pp. 656–657. Note also the *VVasii* (*AASS* April II p. 421), where Vasius of Saintes was able to recover his inheritance with the help of Alaric II.

23. *Epist.* 1.2 (on which, see Sivan, "Sidonius"); see also *Epist.* 2.1.2, 4.24.2, and 8.9.1–5 for Sidonius' business at court, and note *Epist.* 4.22.1 for Sidonius' friend Hesperius' business there. See also Matthews, *Aristocracies*, p. 334.

24. "Romanae columen salusque gentis" (*Carm.* 23.71). For Theoderic as "fidus Romano . . . imperio," see Hydatius, *Chron.* 170; cf. Sid.Apoll. *Carm.* 7.495–496,501–512. See also Stevens, *Sidonius*, p. 74; Thompson, "Visigoths," p. 126; and Wallace-Hadrill, "Gothia," p. 222.

25. "etiam ego aliquid obsecraturus feliciter vincor, quando mihi ad hoc tabula perit, ut causa salvetur" (*Epist.* 1.2.8).

26. *Epist.* 8.9.5 *carm.* 21–54.

27. *Epist.* 5.7.7.

28. "regem praesentem prandia tua, reginam laudare ieiunia" (Sid.Apoll. *Epist.* 6.12.3).

29. "insuper ipse etiam, velut ad solacia nostra / qui superest, actu simul eventuque sinistro / inter amicitias regis versatus et iras / destituit prope cuncta pari

mea commoda sorte" (Euch. 512–515). This unnamed son is omitted from both PLRE II and Stroheker.

30. See Chapter 3.

31. See Perrenot, "Etablissement," p. 70, for Gallo-Romans for whom "l'hospitalité fut spontanée et bénévole."

32. Paul.Pell. Euch. 328–398. The lands seem to be alluded to in vv. 396–398, "auxiliares [sc. Alani] / discessere, fidem pacis servare parati / Romanis, quoque ipsos sors oblata tulisset"; for this interpretation, see Bachrach, "Another Look," pp. 354–356; and Lot, "Régime," p. 1007. White, Ausonius 2.334, however, translates "sors" as "chance"; see also Goffart, in Wolfram and Schwarcz, Anerkennung, pp. 83–84.

33. "Burgundiones partem Galliae occupaverunt terrasque cum Gallis senatoribus diviserunt" (Mar.Avit. Chron. s.a. 456: MGH AA 11.225); see Mathisen, "Resistance," pp. 604–605; and Durliat, "Salaire," pp. 50–51.

34. "per legatis invitati a Romanis vel Gallis, qui Lugdunensium provinciam et Gallea comata, Gallea domata et Gallea Cesalpinae manebant, ut tributa rei publice potuissent rennuere, ibi cum uxoris et liberes visi sunt consedisse" (Fred. Chron. 2.46: MGH SRM 2.68). For other interpretations of these passages, see Goffart, "Rome," p. 301, and Barbarians, pp. 107–108.

35. "inter barbaricas hostili iure rapinas / Romanumque nefas, contra omnia iura licenter / in mea grassatum diverso tempore damna" (Euch. 423–425).

36. Cod.Eur. 312.

37. "nam quosdam scimus summa humanitate Gothorum / hospitibus studuisse suis prodesse tuendis" (Euch. 289–290).

38. "ipsis barbaris mercennariis ministris ac defensoribus uteretur" (Hist.adv.pag. 7.41).

39. See also Barnish, "Taxation," p. 191.

40. Lex Burg. 22. Translations are based upon those in Drew, Burgundian Code.

41. Lex Burg. 55.

42. For similar, see Mathisen, Factionalism, pp. 206–217.

43. Hil. Epist. "Miramur fraternitatem": MGH Epist. 3.22–23. See Demandt, "Magister," cols. 690–691; Demougeot, "Septimanie," pp. 18, 31; Duchesne, Fastes 1.128–130; Griffe, Gaule 2.183–185; and Langgärtner, Gallienpolitik, pp. 93–95.

44. "a diacono Iohanne, qui a magnifico viro filio nostro Friderico litteris suis nobis insinuatus est . . ." (Hil. Epist. "Miramur fraternitatem": MGH Epist. 3.22–23).

45. Fridericus: PLRE II, p. 484. See Langgärtner, Gallienpolitik, pp. 94, 98–99 n. 29; Demandt, "Magister," pp. 690–691; and Griffe, Gaule 2.135–170.

46. Hydatius, Chron. 217; see Mathisen, "Resistance," pp. 614–618.

47. Narbonne recently had fiercely resisted the Visigoths, see Sid.Apoll. Carm. 7.475–480; 22 epist. 1; 23.59–79.

48. Sid.Apoll. Carm. 23.436–487; see Mathisen, "Resistance," pp. 598–604; and the appropriate entries in PLRE II.

49. Death of Fridericus: Chron.gall.511 no. 638 (MGH AA 9.664); Hyd. Chron. 218 (ibid.11.33); and Mar.Avit. Chron. s.a.463 (ibid.11.225).

50. "quantum enim filii nostri, viri illustris, magistri militum Gunduici sermone

est indicatum, praedictus episcopus invitis Deensibus . . . hostili more, ut dicitur, occupans civitatem, episcopum consecrare praesumpsit . . ." (Hil. *Epist.* "Qualiter contra sedis": *MGH Epist.* 3.28–29). See Demandt, "Magister," col. 694; Demougeot, "Septimanie," p. 31; Duchesne, *Fastes* 1.129–131; Griffe, *Gaule* 2.163, 270; and Langgärtner, *Gallienpolitik*, pp. 98–101. Thiel, *Epistolae*, p. 147 n. 3, interprets the appellation *filius noster* to mean that Gundioc was a Catholic at the time.

51. See Duchesne, *Fastes* 1.129.

52. Gundioc: *PLRE II*, pp. 523–524. Gundioc also was an ally of the Visigoths (*Auct.Prosp.Haun.* s.a. 457: *MGH AA* 9.305). See Demandt, "Magister," p. 694.

53. See the *VMarcelli*: "igitur, ut adsolet in electione pontificis, dum unus petitur, pars populi vertitur in alterum . . ." (Dolbeau, "Marcel," p. 115; Kirner, *Due vite*, p. 304). Duchesne, *Fastes* 1.129, suggests that Gundioc and Fridericus were attempting to rid themselves of patriotic pro-Roman bishops.

54. See Lot, *End*, p. 394, "delation thrived."

55. See Fanizza, *Delatori* (for earlier times); and MacMullen, *Corruption*, pp. 91–92 (as "sycophants").

56. "extinctores delatorum, extinctores calumniarum" (*C.Th. Gest. sen.*). According to the jurist Marcian (*Dig.* 49.14.18.2), "clarissimi viri deferre non possunt." Some emperors, however, allowed them to do so (e.g., Dio 58.21.6, on Tiberius).

57. "nemo delationes metuat" (*Nov.Maj.*1).

58. "quisque est iste, domine imperator, publice accuset" (*Epist.* 1.11.13).

59. On Paeonius, see Mathisen, "Resistance."

60. "quod beatissimum, nulla mentio de potestatibus aut de tributis, nullus sermo qui proderetur, nulla persona qui proderet" (*Epist.* 5.17.5)

61. "gurges de sutoribus fabularum, de concinnatoribus criminum, de sinistrarum opinionum duplicatoribus . . . laudator in prosperis, delator in dubiis" (*Epist.* 3.13.2,10, cf. 3.13.10, "quas domorum nequiverit machinis apertae simultatis impetere, cuniculis clandestinae proditionis impugnat"). Avitus of Vienne similarly cautioned Apollinaris, "cavete attentive malos et linguarum mordacium dolis sibilantibus blandimenta venenaque machinantibus docti post experimenta non credite" (*Epist.* 52). These warnings, along with his association with Victorius (Chapter 6), suggest that Apollinaris ran with a bad crowd.

62. "hi sunt . . . quos se iamdudum perpeti inter clementiores barbaros Gallia gemit" (*Epist.* 5.7.1).

63. "vir nobilissimus genere, ex Hispaniis, praedives facultatibus, invidiam pessimi accusatoris incurrit" (*Vorientii* 5: *AASS* May I p. 63). In some cases, this being one example, the nationality of the accuser is not clear.

64. *VLupicini* 10; see Chapter 11.

65. "flexuosa calumniarum fraude circumretit" (*Epist.* 5.13.2); "calumniatur ut barbarus" (ibid. 2.1.2).

66. "ne quam tibi calumniarum turbo barbaricus aut militaris concinnaret improbitas" (*Epist.* 5.6.1).

67. "confirmat . . . Chilperico victorissimo viro relatu venenato quorumpiam sceleratorum fuisse secreto insusurratum tuo praecipue machinatu oppidum Vasionense partibus novi principis applicari . . ." (*Epist.* 5.6.2). See Brugière, *Littérature*, p. 264; Stevens, *Sidonius*, pp. 157, 210–211; and Stroheker, *Adel*, p. 98.

68. "hi . . . quos se iamdudum perpeti inter clementiores barbaros Gallia gemit . . . hi sunt, quos timent etiam qui timentur. hi sunt, quos haec peculiariter provincia manet, inferre calumnias deferre personas afferre minas auferre substantias" (*Epist.* 5.7.1).

69. "aures mariti virosa susurronum faece completas . . . eruderat" (*Epist.* 5.7.7). For another example of influencing the king through his wife, note the example of Evodius above.

70. "indagavimus tandem, qui . . . criminarentur, si tamen fidam sodalium sagacitatem clandestina delatorum non fefellere vestigia" (*Epist.* 5.7.1).

71. "barbaris paene in conspectu omnium sitis nullus erat metus hominum, non custodia civitatum" (*De gub.* 6.14).

8. CONFLICTING LOYALTIES: COLLABORATORS, TRAITORS, AND THE BETRAYAL OF TERRITORY

1. Spain: Hyd. *Chron.*, passim; and note *Chron.* 200–207 for two noble Spanish *delatores* who assisted the Suevi in the betrayal of the city of Aquae Flaviae and the kidnapping of a bishop (see Thompson, "End," p. 25). For the betrayal to the Huns of Margus on the Danube by its bishop in 441, see Prisc. fr. 2.

2. "Treverorum civitas factione uni ex senatoribus nomen Lucii a Francis capta et incensa est" (*Chron.* 3.7).

3. *VAusonii* 10: *Analecta bollandiana* 5 (1886), pp. 310–311.

4. "Sangibanus namque rex Alanorum metu futurorum perterritus Attilae se tradere pollicetur et Aurelianam civitatem Galliae, ubi tunc consistebat, in eius iura transducere" (Jord. *Get.* 194: *MGH AA* 5.108).

5. See Bachrach, "Alans," p. 483; and Demougeot, "Attila," pp. 30–32.

6. "factio servilis paucorum mixta furori / insano iuvenum [nequam] licet ingenuorum, / armata in caedem specialem nobilitatis" (Paul.Pell. *Euch.* 334–336).

7. "instantemque mihi specialem percussorem / me ignorante alio iussisti [sc. deus] ultore perire" (*Euch.* 339–340).

8. Sid.Apoll. *Epist.* 3.2.2.

9. *Epist.* 5.12.1: "ad arbitrium terroris alieni . . . in hoc solum captivus adduceris"; perhaps he was connected to the Calminius named in a late saint's life as *dux Aquitaniae* under Justinian c. 530 (*VCalminii: AASS* August III p. 756); see Mathisen, "*PLRE II*," pp. 368–369. Note also Trygetius of Bazas, who had been on campaign outside Cadiz (*Epist.* 8.12.2) in either Roman or Visigothic service (*PLRE II*, p. 1129).

10. "fuerant qui in pace recepti / non aliter nobis quam belli iure subactis" (*Euch.* 312–314). Thompson, "Invaders," pp. 82–83, cites Nicopolis in Thrace in the late 370s as the only other example of a Roman city willingly going over to the barbarians. Salvian, however, reported that at a city near Trier, perhaps Mainz, greed and drunkeness was so rife "ut principes . . . ne tunc quidem de conviviis surgerent, cum iam urbem hostis intraret" (*De gub.* 6.13).

11. "multis ficta fides, multis periuria, multis / causa fuit mortis civica proditio" (*Comm.* 2.173–174).

12. "si qui tradendis vel capiendis civitatibus fuerint interfuisse detecti, non solum a communione habeantur alieni, sed nec conviviorum quidem admittantur esse participes" (*Corp.chr.lat.* 148.138).

13. "tuo praecipue machinatu oppidum Vasionense partibus novi principis applicari . . ." (*Epist.* 5.6.2).

14. "cum iam terror Francorum resonaret in his partibus, et omnes eos amore desiderabili cupirent regnare, sanctus Aprunculus Ligonicae civitatis episcopus apud Burgundiones coepit haberi suspectus. cumque odium de die in diem cresceret, iussum est, ut clam gladio feriretur" (Greg.Tur. *HF* 2.23).

15. "suspectus habitus a Gothis, quod se Francorum ditionibus subdere vellet, apud urbem Tholosam exilio condempnatus, in eo obiit" (Greg.Tur. *HF* 10.31, cf. 2.26). Elsewhere (*HF* 2.29), Gregory claims that Volusianus was exiled to Spain.

16. "et ipse pro memoratae causae zelo suspectus habitus a Gothis in exilio deductus vitam finivit" (Greg.Tur. *HF* 10.31).

17. "orto inter cives et episcopum scandalo, Gothos qui tunc in antedicta urbe morabantur suspicio attigit, quod se vellet episcopus Francorum ditionibus subdere, consilioque accepto, cogitaverunt eum perfodere gladio" (Greg.Tur. *VPat.* 4.1, cf. *HF* 3.2); see Griffe, "L'épiscopat," pp. 281–282.

18. "veneno enim saevissimae accusationis armatus, suggessit per auricularios Alarico regi, quod beatissimus Caesarius, quia de Galliis haberet originem, totis viribus affectaret territorium et civitatem Arelatensem Burgundionum ditionibus subiugare" (*VCaesarii* 1.21: *MGH SRM* 3.465). *Gallia* presumably refers to the northern Gallic diocese, as opposed to *Septem provinciae* in the south: Caesarius was a native of Chalon-sur-Saône. Arvandus, too (see below), was betrayed by his secretary (Sid.Apoll. *Epist.* 1.7.5).

19. See Griffe, "L'épiscopat," p. 283, for Caesarius' "collaboration" regarding the Council of Agde in 506.

20. "tunc quidam e clericis concivis et consanguineus ipsius, captivitatis timore perterritus et iuvenili levitate permotus . . . funiculo per murum sese nocte submittens, ultro offertur in crastino secleratissimus obsidentibus inimicis" (*VCaesarii* 1.29: *MGH SRM* 3.467).

21. "iterum accusatione confecta, extrahi ab Arelate antistitem facit et in Italia sub custodia Ravennam usque perduci" (*VCaesarii* 1.36: *MGH SRM* 3.470); see Levillain, "Rivalités," pp. 566–567.

22. See the next chapter for the role of Gallic bishops.

23. "ita ut de Novempopulana, et Secunda Aquitania, quae provinciae longius constitutae sunt, si earum iudices occupatio certa tenuerit, sciant, legatos iuxta consuetudinem esse mittendos" ("Saluberrima magnificentiae": Haenel, *Corp.leg.* no. 1171 p. 238).

24. See Matthews, *Aristocracies,* p. 336

25. And with regard to Spain, Thompson, "Visigoths," p. 19, doubts whether "the provincial administration ever went out of existence in the fifth century."

26. *De gub.* 6.15, "pauci nobiles . . . circenses ab imperatoribus postulabant."

27. *VGermani* 7; see Mathisen, "Addenda," p. 376. For the office, see *Not.dig. occ.* 45.

28. can.7: *Corp.chr.lat.* 148.138.

29. "relicto officii sui ordine, laicam voluerit agere vitam, vel se militiae tradiderit" (can.5: *Corp.chr.lat.* 148.145).

30. "negotium criminale" (*Epist.* 6.4.3).

31. Sid.Apoll. *Epist.* 5.13.1, at an otherwise unknown place called Clusetium; see *PLRE II*, p. 403. Note also Pannychius, who, responsible for local peacekeeping and tax supervision, perhaps was a *comes civitatis* (at Bourges?) as late as 469 (Sid.Apoll. *Epist.* 5.13.4, 7.9.18, 9.7): see *PLRE II*, p. 829; Stroheker, *Adel*, no. 276; and Mathisen, "*PLRE II,*" p. 380.

32. See Chapter 5; and Wightman, *Belgica*, p. 307.

33. See Remigius, *Epist.* 2 = *Epist.aust.* 2: *MGH Epist* 3.113, "rumor ad nos magnus pervenit administrationem vos Secundae Belgicae suscepisse"; see Jones, *LRE*, p. 261. Note also Procopius' curious report (*Bell.goth.* 1.12–18) about the preservation of Roman military practices under the Franks in the area of Armorica in the sixth century.

34. "qui secreta dirigentium principum venditantes ambiunt a barbaris bene agi" (*Epist.* 3.7.3).

35. Olymp. fr. 17: Müller, *FHG* 4.61. Barbarians: Bachrach, "Alans," pp. 478–479, 488; Byvanck, "Burgondes," p. 77; and Sundwall, *Studien*, pp. 9–12.

36. See Matthews, *Aristocracies*, pp. 313–315; and Oost, *Placidia*, p. 111. The Franks and Alamanni also were involved.

37. Paul.Pell. *Euch.* 293–296: see *PLRE I*, pp. 677–678. This position, nonexistent in the normal Roman administration, seems to have been a conflation of the offices of *comes sacrarum largitionum* and *comes rei privatae* (see *PLRE II*, pp. 1260–1263). Attalus: *PLRE II*, p. 181.

38. See Sid.Apoll. *Carm.* 7.394–571 for the role of the Goths; see also King, *Law*, p. 3 (wrongly dated to 456); and Mathisen, "Avitus."

39. "tractare solebam / res Geticas olim" (*Carm.* 7.471–472).

40. "Gallos scires non posse latere / quod possint servire Getae te principe" (*Carm.* 7.520–521).

41. See Sivan, "Sidonius."

42. For Avitus' reign, see Mathisen, "Avitus," "Resistance," and "Third Regnal Year."

43. "romanis fascibus livens, barbaris procul dubio favens, subreptione clandestina provincias a publica niteretur ditione deiscere" (*VLupicini* 11); see Mathisen, "Resistance," pp. 614–618.

44. Agrippinus' partisan Lupicinus of St. Claude lived in Burgundian territory.

45. "haec ad regem Gothorum charta videbatur emitti, pacem cum Graeco imperatore dissuadens ... cum Burgundionibus iure gentium Gallias dividi debere confirmans, et in hunc ferme modum plurima insana" (Sid.Apoll. *Epist.* 1.7.5, cf. Cass. *Chron.* s.a. 469); see Demougeot, "Septimanie," p. 19; *PLRE II*, pp. 157–158; and Stroheker, *Adel*, no. 37.

46. "Seronatum barbaris provincias propinantem" (Sid.Apoll. *Epist.* 7.7.2, see also 2.1.1, 5.13.1–4); see Demougeot, "Septimanie," pp. 19, 31–32; *PLRE II*, pp. 995–996; Schmidt, *Ostgermanen*, p. 487; Seeck, *Untergang*, p. 372; Stein, *Geschichte*, pp. 576–580; Stevens, *Sidonius*, p. 107; and Stroheker, *Adel*, p. 80 and no. 352.

47. *VLupicini* 11.

48. Hyd. *Chron.* 217. See Courcelle, *L'Empire,* p. 142; Demougeot, *Formation,* pp. 586, 628, and "Septimanie," pp. 18, 31; Ensslin, "Magister," p. 49; Mathisen, "Resistance"; Nesselhauf, "Verwaltung," p. 34; Rouche, *Aquitaine,* p. 34; and Vassili, "Agrippino."

49. "Arvandi amicitias quoquo genere incursas inter ipsius adversa vitare perfidum barbarum ignavum computabamus" (*Epist.* 1.7.6).

50. *Epist.* 1.7.6–7.

51. Sid.Apoll. *Epist.* 1.7.13; Cass. *Chron.* s.a. 469; Paul.Diac. *Hist.rom.* 15.2.

52. See Paul.Diac. *Hist.rom.* 15.2 (*MGH AA* 2.208), "Servandus [sic] Galliarum praefectus imperium temptans invadere iussu Anthemii principis in exilium trusus est." Wallace-Hadrill, "Gothia," p. 222, however, suggests that Arvandus (and Seronatus) "would have wished to see Euric a Gallic emperor."

53. For the "treason" of Arvandus and Seronatus, see Courcelle, *L'Empire,* pp. 143–144; Dill, *Gaul,* p. 24; and Loyen, "Résistants," pp. 437–450.

54. "ipse Catilina saeculi nostri" (*Epist.* 2.1.1).

55. *Epist.* 5.13.

56. "quem convictum deinceps res publica vix praesumpsit occidere" (*Epist.* 7.7.2).

9. THE ACQUISITION OF CHURCH OFFICE AND THE RISE OF AN ECCLESIASTICAL ARISTOCRACY

1. "si nullae a republica vires, nulla praesidia, si nullae, quantum rumor est, Anthemii principis opes, statuit te auctore nobilitas seu patriam dimittere seu capillos" (*Epist.* 2.1.4).

2. See Momigliano, "Caduta," p. 12, for an implied comparison between "Gallia Comata" and "Gallia 'Tonsurata.' "

3. See Chapter 5.

4. "sed aut idem sunt nobiles, qui et divites, aut si sunt divites praeter nobiles, et ipsi tamen iam quasi nobiles . . . ut nullus habeatur magis nobilis quam qui est plurimum dives . . ." (*De gub.* 3.10). For similar in Gregory of Tours, see Gilliard, "Senators," p. 693.

5. See Chrysos, "Nobilitierung," pp. 119–128; Heinzelmann, "Neue Aspekte" and *Bischofsherrschaft,* passim; Jerg, *Vir Venerabilis,* passim; Klauser, *Ursprung,* passim; Lotter, "Epitheta"; and O'Brien, *Titles,* passim.

6. See Arnold, *Caesarius,* pp. 15–16; Dill, *Gaul,* pp. 476–488; Heinzelmann, *Bischofsherrschaft,* pp. 35–36,123,221; Klauser, "Bischofe," passim; Prinz, *Stadtherrschaft,* passim; and Stroheker, *Adel,* pp. 72–73. For the "power of the episcopal name," see *De sept.ord.eccl.* 5: *PL* 30.154.

7. "ad veram et integram nobilitatem" (*In ord.episc.* 1: *MGH AA* 6.2.124). Later, Venantius Fortunatus referred to the episcopate as an "altera nobilitas" (*Carm.* 1.15.32–33).

8. "absque conflictatione praestantior secundum bonorum sententiam computatur honorato maximo minimus religiosus" (*Epist.* 7.12.4).

9. "natalibus nobilis, religione nobilior" (*VGermani* 22); see also *VFursei* 1;

VSigolenae 1; *VSolemnis* 2; *VWandregesili* 3; and Mathisen, *Ecclesiastical Aristocracy*, pp. 28–29.

10. "si qui ex nobilibus converti ad deum coeperit, statim honorem nobilitatis amittit" (*De gub.* 4.7). For similar, see Sid.Apoll. *Epist.* 7.12.4.

11. Note Cass.*Coll.* 11.10 for the "bonos et malos, iustos et iniustos"; see von Müller, *Gloria.*

12. "cum hic mali interdum bona capiant, boni malis afflictentur" (Euch. *Epist.ad Valer.* p. 725); cf. Euch. *De laud.erem.* 35, "apud alios malum sit malum fecisse, apud hos vero malum est bonum non fecisse."

13. "bonos et iustos viros semper persecutionem malorum sustinuisse" (Faust. *Serm.* 5: *CSEL* 21.240); "oremus pro bonis, ut semper ad meliora conscendant, pro malis, ut cito ad emendationem vitae . . . confugiant" (Faust. *Serm.* 3: *CSEL* 21.236).

14. "ubi bonorum ac malorum summa et inconfusa discretio est" (*Epist.ad Valer.* p. 717).

15. "optimus quisque in coelestes honores, in coelestes opes, terrenos honores, terrenas opes transfert" (*Epist.ad Valer.* p. 717).

16. "esto bonus, qui habes bona. bonae sunt divitiae, bonum est aurum, bonum et argentum, bonae familiae, bonae possessiones. omnia ista bona sunt, sed unde facias bene?" (*Serm.* 5: *CSEL* 21.241–242).

17. Sulp.Sev. *VMartini* 10; see Arnold, *Caesarius*, p. 15; Beck, *Pastoral Care*, pp. 6–30; Brown, *World*, p. 174; Brugière, *Littérature*, p. 263; Dill, *Last Century*, p. 216; Gassmann, *Episkopat*; Gilliard, "Bishops," pp. 159–166; Heinzelmann, "L'aristocratie," pp. 75–90 and *Bischofsherrschaft*, passim; Loyen, *L'esprit*, p. 41; Mathisen, "Hilarius" and "Petronius"; Matthews, *Aristocracies*, p. 185; Prinz, "Aristocracy" and *Mönchtum*, p. 59ff; Stroheker, *Adel*, p. 75; and Wieruszowski, *Zusammensetzung*, passim. Stroheker (*Adel*, p. 8) compares Gallic aristocratic bishops to Druids in pre-Roman Celtic society.

18. See Arnheim, *Aristocracy*, p. 106.

19. "antiquam natalium praerogativam" (*Epist.* 4.25.2); "parentes ipsius aut cathedris aut tribunalibus praesederunt" (ibid. 7.9.17).

20. "propter . . . saeculi dignitatem" (*Glor.conf.* 75). An even later source told of a bishop elected "Romanae nobilitatis . . . merito" (*VThuribii* 1).

21. For hereditary claims to secular office, see Chapter 5.

22. "nonnulli episcopatum . . . non divinum munus sed haereditarium putant esse compendium, et credunt, sicut res caducas atque mortales, ita sacerdotium, velut legali aut testamentario iure, posse dimitti. . ." (*Epist.* "Quoniam religiosus": Thiel, p. 162). This reading seems preferable to the "legati aut testamenti" of other manuscripts.

23. Note Sidonius' comment to Graecus of Marseilles, "vos vero Eustachium pontificem tunc ex asse digno herede decessisse monstrabitis . . ." (*Epist.* 7.2.9).

24. "nutriret sine dubio sibi successorem, et cui germana propinquitate fratris proprio iure veniret privata possessio, non transiret ad alterum eius sacerdotium" (*VMarcelli* 1: *AASS* April I 824–826).

25. "ordo sacerdotum cui fluxit utroque parente / venit ad heredem pontificalis apex" (Ven.Fort. *Carm.* 8.7–8: *MGH AA* 4.2.84). For the importance of the female line, see Heinzelmann, "Prosopographie," pp. 233–234.

26. See Barnish, "Transformation," p. 138; Brown, "Patrons," p. 61; Brugière, *Littérature*, pp. 265ff; Dill, *Gaul*, pp. 310–329; Heinzelmann, *Bischofsherrschaft*, pp. 211–232, and "Aristocratie," p. 80; Stroheker, *Adel*, pp. 118–119; and Wieruszowski, "Zusammensetzung," pp. 50–56.

27. By now, the late fourth-century opposition to such conversions (see Amb. *Epist.* 58.3, and Arnheim, *Aristocracy*, p. 87) had vanished. See Griffe, "Pratique."

28. "plus ego admiror sacerdotalem virum quam sacerdotem" (*Epist.* 4.9.5).

29. See *Epist.* 4.24.3; but did Sidonius really eat the moss from the walls of Clermont (*Epist.* 7.7.3)? On Gallic asceticism, see Consolino, *Ascesi*; Fontaine, "L'ascétisme," pp. 87–115; Heinzelmann, *Bischofsherrschaft*, pp. 73–98, 185–211; Pricoco, *L'isola*, pp. 25–59, 131–186; Prinz, *Mönchtum*, pp. 47–54; Rousseau, *Ascetics*; and Turbessi, *Ascetismo*; see also Van Dam, "Images," p. 12, "the connection between holiness and aristocracy became a common feature in the self-promotion of families and individuals."

30. "sperans congruentius tuum salve pontificum quam senatorum iam nominibus adiungi, censuitque iustius fieri si inter perfectos Christi quam si inter praefectos Valentiniani constituerere . . ." (*Epist.* 7.12.4, cf. 2.1.4, 4.15.2, 8.4.4).

31. Note, for example, the priests Maximus and Faustinus (Sid.Apoll. *Epist.* 4.24, 4.4.1, 4.6.1) and the abbot Auxanius (ibid. 7.17.4); see also Ruric. *Epist.* 2.12–13, 2.32; and Paul.Pell. *Euch.* 508–509.

32. See Arnheim, *Aristocracy*, pp. 106, 187; Arnold, *Caesarius*, pp. 15–16; Beck, *Pastoral Care*, pp. 6ff, 21–22; Brown, "Patrons," p. 61, and *World*, p. 131; Brugière, *Littérature*, p. 213; Dill, *Gaul*, pp. 220, 479, and *Last Century*, p. 216; Duchesne, *Fastes* 1.112–113; Griffe, *Gaule* 2.181; Heinzelmann, *Bischofsherrschaft*, pp. 12, 211–231, "L'aristocratie," p. 275, and "Prosopographie," p. 233; Loyen, *L'esprit*, p. 41; Matthews, *Aristocracies*, p. 346; Mathisen, *Ecclesiastical Aristocracy*, passim; Oost, *Placidia*, p. 147; Pricoco, *L'isola*, pp. 65–73; Prinz, *Mönchtum*, pp. 48, 57–62, and *Stadtherrschaft*, pp. 8–9; Stroheker, *Adel*, pp. 8–9, 72–75, 92, 106ff; Wieruszowski, "Zusammensetzung," pp. 1–2, 50–63; and Woodward, *Nationalism*, p. 77.

33. The suggestion of Wallace-Hadrill, "Gothia," p. 224, that "the civil service lost its best recruits to the church," fails to consider that few state offices were available and that many Gallic senators were no longer interested in them anyway. Nor is there much support for the suggestion of Barnish, "Transformation," p. 140, that bishoprics gave Gallic nobles "a means of providing for unwanted heirs": the bishopric was the grand, rather than the consolation, prize. For ordination as a means of preserving inheritances for a single family member, see Barnish, "Transformation," pp. 139–145; cf. *Nov.Maj.* 6, 11.

34. "militia illis in clericali potius quam in Palatino decursa comitatu" (*Epist.* 7.2.3).

35. "laicalem an ecclesiasticam expeteret dignitatem" (*VDomitiani* 2).

36. See Mathisen, *Factionalism*, p. 199.

37. Duchesne, *Fastes* 2.34; he may be the Eparchius who signed the Gallic episcopal letter to Leo of Rome of 451/452 (*Corp.chr.lat.* 148.107–110).

38. For the importance of literary pursuits, see Chapter 10. See also de Montauzan, "Saint-Eucher"; Glorie, "Culture"; and Kaufman, "Rhetorenschulen."

39. See Mathisen, *Factionalism*, passim. Eucherius of Lyons, for example, praised the education and literary abilities of senators who had become bishops (*Epist.ad Valer.* pp. 718–719), and he told of pursuing philosophy "in illius eremi deambulacris tamquam in suis gymnasiis" (*De laud.erem.* 32).

40. At the most basic level, Gallic bishops had to be "litteratus" (*Stat.eccl.ant.* 1: *Corp.chr.lat.* 148.164). Likewise, in 465 Hilarus of Rome had decreed, "inscii quoque litterarum . . . ad sacros ordines adspirare non audeant" (Thiel, p. 161). See Heinzelmann, "Aristocratie," p. 83.

41. See Brezzi, "Impero," pp. 266–267; Chaffin, "Maximus"; Dill, *Gaul*, pp. 3, 476–487, 502; Grahn-Hoek, *Oberschicht*, p. 183; Heinzelmann, *Bischofsherrschaft*, p. 213; Oost, *Placidia*, p. 147; Prinz, *Mönchtum*, p. 59, and *Stadtherrschaft*, p. 4ff; Stroheker, *Adel*, pp. 69ff, 92ff; Wallace-Hadrill, "Gothia," pp. 223–224; and Wightman, *Belgica*, p. 306.

42. See Rousseau, "Spiritual Authority."

43. For a bishop's ability to unite the interests of both his family and his city, see Barnish, "Transformation," p. 139; and Van Dam, *Leadership*, pp. 153–156.

44. "vici omnes, municipia, civitates, quot sese per itineris eius tramitem porrigebant, in occursum cum coniugibus ac liberis convolabant et continuatum plerumque agmen dum occurentes iungebantur prosequentibus, cohaerebat" (*VGermani* 21, cf. 14, 23, 30, 36).

45. "indiscreto sexu, confusa aetas" (*VEutropii*, p. 63).

46. "quam tu ab omni ordine sexu aetate stipatissimus ambiabare" (*Epist.* 3.2.1).

47. "omnis aetas ordo sexus" (*Epist.* 3.3.3).

48. "patronum proprium" (*VGermani* 46).

49. "religione potens," "potens meritis," "arbitrio iustitiaque potens": Duchesne, *Fastes* 1.188–189, 2.165–168. For the bishop as patron in the Celtic tradition, see Stroheker, *Adel*, p. 9; see also Heinzelmann, *Bischofsherrschaft*, pp. 123, 127; and Woodward, *Nationalism*, p. 77.

50. See Wightman, *Belgica*, p. 308: the bishop "enjoyed the authority of permanent magistracy and priesthood combined"; see also Declareuil, "Curies."

51. See Ewig, "Kirche"; Harries, *Bishops*; and Wightman, *Belgica*, p. 308; cf. Duchesne, *Fastes* 3.106–114, 130–137.

52. "nulli penitus nisi soli episcopi regnant; periet honor noster et translatus est ad episcopos civitatum" (Greg.Tur. *HF* 6.46).

53. See Faust. *Serm.* 27 (*CSEL* 21.331) for an appeal to Augustine, "patrono nostro peculiari"; see Corbett, "Saint as Patron"; Heinzelmann, *Bischofsherrschaft*, passim; Higounet, "Saints"; and Van Dam, "Images," p. 7, who sees saints as successors to "emperors, magistrates, and generals." Even a deceased child could be called a patron; see Ruric. *Epist.* 2.3, and 2.39: "patronum haberetis ex filio."

54. "orate ut apud dominum meum qualemcunque locum habeam, nam pro Arausicis meis non cessabo orare, auxiliante deo" (*VEutropii* p. 64).

55. The east: see Brown, "Holy Man"; and Fowden, "Holy Man." Gaul: see Greg.Tur. *HF* 8.15 for a would-be Gallic stylite who was reprimanded by local bishops; see also Mathisen, *Factionalism*, p. xii.

56. See the *VGenovefae*; and Croidys, *Sainte Geneviève et les barbares.*

57. See Bratton, *Tours.*

58. See, for example, *VAvit.Miciac.* 21 (*AASS* June IV p. 289); and *VMaxim.Trev.* 9.

59. See Beck, *Pastoral Care,* p. 15, "cliques formed in support of one aspirant or another."

60. *Euch.* 410–457.

61. Sid.Apoll. *Epist.* 7.9.18; note also the unsuccessful nobles at Troyes at the same time (ibid. 4.25.2).

62. "in honoribus vero huius mundi . . . quae aestimari dignitas potest rerum, cum ad hanc promiscue cum bonis mali ambitione conscendant" (*Epist.ad Val.* p. 716).

63. "nunc episcopatus pravis ambitionibus appetuntur" (*Chron.* 2.32).

64. "sunt enim multi qui sequentes vota populorum, disciplinam ecclesiae non observant . . . peccantes, nobilitatem potius quam mores optimos benedicunt" (*De septem ordinibus ecclesiae* 7: *PL* 30.160); see Mathisen, *Factionalism,* p. 268, and note also Jul.Pom. *De vit.cont.* 1.15, "ambitioni finem imponite."

65. "quia te non suscepit ecclesia distensa censu, ornata ministerio, inflata privilegio, comitatu nobilium inquieta . . ." (*VEutropi,* p. 56). And in the next century, the adviser of the young aristocrat, and later bishop, Leobinus said, "agnosco, frater, de minimis ad maiora te velle conscendere" (*VLeobini* 3[8]).

66. "cum ad officium clericatus rabida ambitione pervenerint, confestim cothurno elationis inflati, non solum supra coaevos digniores, sed etiam supra vetulos ac seniores delibuti ac delicati iuvenculi efferuntur, et nec primis saltim simplicibusque elementis imbuti, nituntur cathedris vel sacerdotio praesidere, qui adhuc pro elatione ac levitate iuvenali virgis indigent coerceri . . ." (*VRomani* 6); see Martine, *Vie,* pp. 262–263. For monks and abbots in the sixth century, see Prinz, *Mönchtum,* pp. 59–62.

67. "facit hoc nimia remissio consacerdotum nostrorum, qui pompam multitudinis quaerunt, ut putant ex hac turba aliquid sibi dignitatis acquiri. hinc passim numerosa popularitas etiam his locis, ubi solitudo est, talium reperitur, dum paroecias extendi cupiunt, aut quibus aliud praestare non possunt, divinos ordines largiuntur" (*Epist.* "Exigit dilectio": *PL* 20.669ff).

68. See Mathisen, *Factionalism,* pp. 51–57; see also Gundlach, "Streit."

69. "de custodia sollicitudo non de pervasione contentio, ne mercenariorum subeant notam" (*Epist.* 2.6).

70. "nec per saecularia patrocinia, nec per cuiuslibet excusationis obtentum, illicita praesumptione terminos concessae potestatis excedant . . ." (*Epist.* "Sedis apostolicae": *PL* 62.64–65).

71. "ut antistitum reverentia magis potestas saeculi putaretur, et tyrannopolitas esse se malint, qui vocabantur antistites, ac religione neglecta, sub hominum patrociniis constituti, publica magis quam divina curarent . . ." (Haenel, *Corp.leg.* no. 1266 p. 260: 11 March 473, at Rome, reissued to the prefects Dioscurus, Aurelianus, and Protadius on 29 April 473: Haenel, ibid.). Cf. Sidonius' reference (*Epist.* 5.8.3) to "tyrannopolitarum."

72. "in hoc igitur conscio securitatis suae otio mens spebus suis laeta requieverat

... tamen per ministerium impositi sacerdotii etiam ceteris praedicabat, munus suum ad officium publicae salutis extendens ..." (*De trinitate* 1.14: *Corp.chr.lat.* 62.15). See also Aug. *Retract.* 1.1.1 (*CSEL* 36.11) for "Christianae vitae otium."

73. See Auer, "Militia Christi"; Emonds, "Topos"; and von Harnack, *Militia Christi*.

74. "intellexit quoque hoc onus esse sacerdotii ipsius dignitatem" (Greg.Tur. *VPat.* 17.1).

75. For Gaul, note *Sirm.* 6 (A.D. 425); *Nov.Val.* 35 (A.D. 452); and Avit. *Epist.* 61. For a detailed list, see Joannou, "Législation"; see also Heinzelmann, *Bischofs-herrschaft*, pp. 179–183; Morrison, *Authority*, p. 48ff; and Noethlichs, "Einfluss-nahme" and "Materialien."

76. *C.Th.* 16.2.12 (355), *Sirm.* 3 (384), *C.Th.* 1.27.2 (408), 16.2.41 (412), 16.2.47 (425), *Sirm.* 6 (425), *Nov.Val.* 35 (452), cf. *C.Th.* 16.11.1, *CJ* 1.4.7. For ecclesiastical requirements, see *Conc.Venet.* 9 (*Corp.chr.lat.* 148.153). See also Larde, *Tribunal;* Selb, *Audientia.*

77. *C.Th.* 4.7.1 (321). In Italy, however, bishops later sponsored "fairs" at which children were sold for "urbana servitia" (see Barnish, "Pigs," p. 171).

78. Empire: *C.Th.* 9.45.1,4 (392 and 431), 5 (= *CJ* 1.12.4) (432), *Sirm.* 13 (419). Barbarian kingdoms: Ruric. *Epist.* 2.19(20).

79. See *C.Th.* 9.16.12 (409) for the burning of heretical books.

80. *Sirm.* 6; see *VGermani* 12, 27; see also Mathisen, *Factionalism*, pp. 101–102, 139–140.

81. The empire: *C.Th.* 9.40.16 (A.D. 398), 9.3.7 (A.D. 409); and *Sirm.* 13 (A.D. 419). For the need for such service, note Sidonius' reference to "catervatim ... vincti ... vincula trahentes" (*Epist.* 5.13.3) in Aquitania c.470.

82. See *C.Th.* 9.40.17 (A.D. 419).

83. "ut clausos carcere liberaret, exiliis datos restitueret, bona adempta rehiberet" (Sulp.Sev. *Dial.* 2.7); perhaps the basis of Greg.Tur. *Virt.Jul.* 4.

84. "iussit omnes qui in carcere tenebantur absque aliqua tarditate dimitti" (*VAniani* 3); see also *VAmbrosii* 38; *VGermani* 36; Valer. *Hom.* 4.6; and *C.Th.* 9.40.17.

85. Sid.Apoll. *Epist.* 6.12.5, "peculiari sumptu"; *VEutropi* p. 61.

86. See Chapter 5.

87. See Chapter 10.

88. The consecration of new churches, even those built at the expense of an outside bishop or a layman, was reserved for the local bishop (*Corp.chr.lat.* 148.80–81,121–122).

89. See Vieillard-Troiekouroff, *Monuments.*

90. "extinctor iurgii" (*VCaesarii* 1.45); "in mediatione iugiter permanere" (*VHilarii* 8[11]).

91. See Sid.Apoll. *Epist.* 3.2, 4.23, 6.2–5, 6.9, 6.11; Faust. *Epist.* 5; Ruric. *Epist.* 2.7–8, 2.12, 2.20, 2.47–8, 2.51, 2.56–57; Avit. *Epist.* 49; and *VJoannis* 16.

92. *VGermani* 19, 24; *VHilarii* 10[13]): "nam cum saepius praefectum temporis illius secrete monuisset ut ab iniustis iudiciis se temperaret."

93. See Stevens, *Sidonius,* p. 38. Note also Lupicinus of St. Claude's support of Agrippinus after the latter had been accused of treason by Aegidius (*VLupicini* 11: see Chapter 8).

94. *VGermani* 28ff: "freni habenas invadit."

95. *VLupi* 5: see Demougeot, "Attila," pp. 28–30. Note also cases involving the Alamanni (*VLupi* 10; *VEugendi* 17), Burgundians (*VEpiphanii* 32; *VLupicini* 10; Greg.Tur. *VPat.* 1.10), Franks (*VEuspicii*, passim), and Visigoths (Hyd. *Chron.* 219; *VOrientii* 5; *VViviani* 4ff).

96. *VAniani* 4: MGH SRM 3.110; when he arrived, there were already other bishops there with petitions of their own. See Demougeot, "Attila," pp. 30–33; Czuth, "Rolle"; Loyen, "Aignan"; and Matthews, *Aristocracies*, p. 332. Similarly, c. 431 the Spanish bishop Hydatius undertook an embassy to Aetius because of the raids of the Suevi (Hyd. *Chron.* 96).

97. *VViviani* 4: MGH SRM 3.96; see Lot, "Vita Viviani."

98. For secular treaty-making, see Chapter 5.

99. Salv. *De gub.* 7.9; *VOrientii* 5; see Lécrivain, "Orientius."

100. Fred. *Chron.* 2.53. A peace between the Suevi and the Galicians in Spain was made in 431 "sub interventu episcopali" (Hyd. *Chron.* 100). These bishops apparently acted on their own authority.

101. *VEpiphanii* 81ff.

102. "inter dissidentes principes solus esset qui pace frueretur amborum" (*VEpiphanii* 114, see also 32, 52, 70, 106ff, 136, 182).

103. "per vos mala foederum currunt, per vos regni utriusque pacta condicionesque portantur" (*Epist.* 7.6.10); for discussion see Mathisen, *Factionalism*, pp. 268–271.

104. "ad montis perfugium Latiscone . . . patentibus campis expositam nec armis munitam nec muris" (*VLupi* 5–6: MGH SRM 7.297–298).

105. Greg.Tur. *Glor.conf.* 22. Note also a *castellum* near Tours used by monks in the early fifth century (Sulp.Sev. *Dial.* 3.8).

106. See Greg.Tur. *HF* 2.23, 2.32, 3.19, 3.34, 4.16, 5.5, *Glor. mart.* 50, *VPat.* 7; and *LHF* 16; see also Dill, *Gaul*, p. 264. For Aprunculus' nocturnal escape from Dijon, see Chapter 8.

107. "gratum arbitratus sum ut situm loci Divionensis, in quo maxime erat assiduus, huic inseram lectioni: est autem castrum firmissimis muris in media planitiae et satis iocunda conpositum . . . a meridie habet Oscara fluvium . . . totum munitionis locum placida unda circumfluens . . . quattuor portae a quattuor plagis mundi sunt positae, totumque aedificium XXXIII turres exornant, murus vero illius de quadris lapidibus usque in viginti pedes desuper a minuto lapide aedificatum habetur, habens in altum pedes XXX in latum pedes XV, qui cur civitas dicta non sit, ignoro" (*HF* 3.19).

108. For Dijon as a later stronghold for bandits, see *VLauteni* 10: "aliquando vero a Divionensi castro veniebant raptores cum praeda."

109. A poem of Venantius Fortunatus (*Carm.* 3.20), to bishop Felix of Bourges c. 575, was "scriptum in turrem eius"; and of Nicetius of Trier, Venantius said (*Carm.* 3.12.19–24), "condidit optatus pastor ovile gregi / turribus incinxit ter denis undique collem / praebuit hic fabricam, quo nemus ante fuit / vertice de summo demittunt brachia murum / dum Mosella suis terminus extet aquis."

110. "obsessa postmodum a Wandalis civitate in castrum se recepit, quod multo antea imperator ei dono dederat Theodosius iunior. castrum hoc vocatur Ruffeium

iuxta Marniacum. illic multos invenit fideles, immanitatem barbarorum fugientes" (*VAntidii: AASS* June VI pp. 36–37).

111. "Provinciae loca hostis cruentus invaderet. qui etiam universa loca bellantium vigore vastabant, et captivitates perpetrabant, insanientesque ad castrum Toronna, quod sanctus Paulus episcopus firmaverat, ire festinaverunt ubi cum iam populus inclusus" (*VPaul.Tricast.* 10). This event occurred after the death of Paulus, on whom see Mathisen, *Factionalism*, p. 288.

112. *VGermani* 17–18.

113. *VAniani* 4ff; *VViviani* 4.

114. Sid.Apoll. *Epist.* 2.1, 3.2–3, 3.7.4, 7.7; see Loyen, "Résistants," p. 448; and King, *Law*, pp. 4–5.

115. See Elert, "Redemptio"; le Blant, "Rachat"; Thompson, "Invaders," pp. 71–74; and Klingshirn, "Charity," p. 184, who cites Cyprian of Carthage: "I was in the prison of captivity, and locked up and bound I lay in the hands of barbarians, and you freed me from that prison of servitude" (*Epist.* 62.4: *CSEL* 3.2).

116. See Amb. *De off.min.* 2.15,28: *PL* 16.128–129; Sid.Apoll. *Epist.* 4.11.4; Avit. *Epist.* 12, 32(35); Faust. *Epist.* 10, *Serm.* 17: *CSEL* 21.290; Greg.Tur. *VPat.* 7.4; Jul.Pom. *Vit.cont.* 1.25; Max.Taur. *Serm.* 18, 26; Valer.Cemel. *Hom.* 4.6, 7.1,5–6, 9.5; *VAmbrosii* 38; *VCaesarii* 1.38ff; *VEptadii* 7; *VHonorati* 20; *VLupi* 8, 10; and *VSeverini* 4(18), 6(25, 27), 11(51).

117. "consuetudo Romanorum Gallorum Christianorum: mittunt viros sanctos idoneos ad Francos et caeteras gentes cum tot millia solidorum ad redimendos captivos baptizatos" (*Epist.ad Corot.* 7(14): *PL* 53.817).

118. Sulp.Sev. *Dial.* 3.14.

119. *VHilarii* 8(11), "argenti omnes basilicae."

120. *VLupicini* 10; see Chapter 11.

121. "in Arelato vero Gothis cum captivorum inmensitate reversis, replentur basilicae sacrae, repletur etiam domus ecclesiae constipatione infidelium . . . donec singulos redemptionis munere liberaret, expenso argento omne quod venerabilis Eonius antecessor suus ecclesiae mensae reliquerat" (*VCaesarii* 1.32); see Klingshirn, "Charity," pp. 189–191.

122. "captivos de ultra Druentiam, maximeque Arausici oppidi" (*VCaesarii* 1.38); see Klingshirn, "Charity," pp. 191–192.

123. "cum . . . undique captivi Arelato redimendi non frustra exhiberentur, magna multitudo redemptorum ingenuorum et multorum nobilium Arelato ab ipso viro sancto cotidie pascebantur" (*VCaesarii* 2.8); see Klingshirn, "Charity," p. 192.

124. Ennod. *VEpiph.* 136–174; and pope Gelasius wrote to Rusticus of Lyons in 494 about Epiphanius, "qui ad gentis suae relevandos et redimendos captivos ad partes vestras destinatur" (*Epist.* "Inter ingruentium": *PL* 59.138).

125. See *VGenovefae* 26; *VGerm.Par.* 163ff, 182–183; *VDomnoli* 12; and Greg.Tur. *VPat.* 7.3.

126. Victorinus of Fréjus *apud* Faust. *Epist.* 7; see Duchesne, *Fastes* 1.286.

127. "quia quod habuit pro fratris redemptione profudit . . . ut fratrem ab hostibus redderet liberum, se creditorum maluit esse captivum" (*Epist.* 2.8).

128. See Klingshirn, "Charity," pp. 184–185, 189.

129. See *Corp.chr.lat.* 148.61–134; and Mathisen, *Factionalism*, pp. 283–289.

130. See *Corp.chr.lat.* 148.135–158.

131. See *Corp.chr.lat.* 148.159–160; and Mathisen, *Factionalism*, pp. 256–264.

132. See Mathisen, *Factionalism*, pp. 101–116 and passim.

133. Except for the tentative Germanic involvement in ecclesiastical elections in Narbonne and Die in the 460s: see Chapter 7.

134. *Epist.* "Perlata ad nos": *Corp.chr.lat.* 148.107.

135. See Mathisen, *Factionalism*, p. xii.

136. See Heinzelmann, *Bischofsherrschaft*, passim; and Stroheker, *Adel*, pp. 71–75.

137. See Aug. *De civ.dei* 1 and Salv. *De gub.* 7.9, who said of the Visigoths, "illi etiam in alienis sacerdotibus deum honorarent." Under the empire, too, the person of bishops was respected: see *C.Th.* 11.39.10 and *Sirm.* 3.

138. *Carm.de prov.dei* 53–60. And for the upsurge in social violence in general in the sixth century, see Chapter 12.

139. *VAniani* 9; *VAusonii* 10.

140. Sid.Apoll. *Epist.* 7.9.18; see Chapter 3.

141. Sidonius: Sid.Apoll. *Epist.* 4.10.1, 4.22.4, 8.9.2–3, 9.3.3; Simplicius: ibid. 7.6.9, 7.9.16–25.

142. See Brezzi, "Impero," p. 264.

10. THE PURSUIT OF LITERARY STUDIES: A UNIFYING ELEMENT

1. For literary pursuits as an adjunct of senatorial *otium*, see Brown, *World*, p. 115; Dill, *Last Century*, p. 192; Matthews, *Aristocracies*, pp. 1–12; and Stroheker, *Adel*, p. 65. For the topos of Gallic literary abilities, see, e.g., Claud. *Pan.IVcons.Hon.* 582–583.

2. "splendore liberalium doctrinarum minus quam nobilem decuerat institutus" (14.6.1).

3. "ne primis quidem apicibus sufficienter initiatus" (*Epist.* 2.1.2); for Seronatus, see Chapter 8.

4. Some of the views of this section were presented in *Classical Philology* 83(1988), pp. 45–52, under the title "The Theme of Literary Decline in Late Roman Gaul."

5. Assumed by MacMullen, *Corruption*, Chapter 2, for the empire as a whole. For Gaul, see Auerbach, *Literary Language*, p. 258; Chadwick, *Poetry*, pp. 296, 303; Dill, *Last Century*, pp. 438–439; Duckett, *Writers*, pp. 12–13; Glover, *Life and Letters*, p. 11; Loyen, *L'esprit*, pp. 55, 166; Raby, *Poetry*, pp. 76, 84; and Stevens, *Sidonius*, pp. 14, 78–81.

6. "illud appone, quod tantum increbruit multitudo desidiosorum ut, nisi vel paucissimi quique meram linguae Latiaris proprietatem de trivialium barbarismorum robigine vindicaveritis, eam brevi abolitam defleamus interemptamque: sic omnes nobilium sermonum purpurae per incuriam vulgi decolorabuntur" (*Epist.* 2.10.1).

7. "quis provocatus nunc ad facta maiorum non inertissimus, quis quoque ad

verba non infantissimus erit? namque virtutes artium istarum saeculis potius priscis saeculorum rector ingenuit, quae per aetatem mundi iam senescentis lassatis veluti seminibus emedullatae parum aliquid hoc tempore in quibuscumque, atque id in paucis, mirandum ac memorabile ostentant" (*Epist.* 8.6.3). Sidonius echoes the Christian topos of the aging world: cf. Cyprian of Carthage, in the middle of the third century, "senuisse iam saeculum, non illis viribus stare quibus prius steterat, nec vigore et robore eo valere quo antea praevalebat. . . . deficit . . . in artibus peritia" (*Epistula ad Demetrianum* 3, *PL* 4.546); see also Pliny, *Epist.* 8.12.1, "litterarum iam senescentium"; and Tac. *Dial.* 1.1.

8. "quapropter si quis post vos Latiae favet eruditioni . . . sodalitati vestrae . . . optat adhiberi. quamquam . . . pauci studia nunc honorant" (*Epist.* 5.10.4, cf. 9.7.2,4).

9. "bonarum artium iam inde a proavorum nostrorum saeculis facta iactura et animi cultum despuens quo solo praestat pecudi gens humana . . . video enim os romanum non modo neglegentiae sed pudori esse Romanis . . . sed haec in laudem tuam suggestui sunt, quia . . . professionis tuae par unus et solus es" (*Epistula ad Sapaudum*).

10. "quod paucis intellegentibus mensuram syllabarum servando canat" (*Carm.* 6 prol.).

11. "decedente atque immo potius pereunte ab urbibus gallicanis liberalibus cultura litterarum . . . ingemescebant saepius plerique, dicentes, 'vae diebus nostris, quia periit studium litterarum a nobis' . . ."

12. "fors fuat an . . . scriptor aequalis maiorum temporibus accesserit" (*Epist.* 8.3.6, see also 9.11.6, 9.15.1 *carm.* 53). When he asserted (*Epist.* 4.3.10) that his own literary efforts did not even meet the standards of those who "illitteratissimis litteris vacant," he was artfully alluding to Pliny, who modestly had stated (*Epist.* 1.10.9) "scribo plurimas, sed illitteratissimas litteras." See also Ruric. *Epist.* 1.3, 1.4.2, 2.17; and Verus, *VEutropii* praef.

13. For the Gallic literary output of this period, see Chadwick, *Poetry;* Curtius, *Literatur; Clavis* nos. 427–536, 957–1079, and passim; Duckett, *Writers;* Duval, *Gaule,* pp. 663–826; Manitius, *Literatur;* and Raby, *Poetry.* For lost works, see Duval, pp. 789–809; and Gennad. *Vir.ill.* passim. Note also Sidonius' disclaimer (*Epist.* 1.11.7), "As if I were the only person of my times who could write verse."

14. "a quo studia posterorum ne parum quidem, quippe in hac parte, degeneraverunt" (*Epist.* 5.5.1).

15. *De statu animae* praef.

16. *Epistula ad Sapaudum.* Classical writers, however, were not universally admired in Christian circles: Ruricius of Limoges' friend Taurentius wrote to him, "praeteritae calumniamur aetati, quod viros illos [sc. Cyprianum, Augustinum, Hilarium, Ambrosium] admiratione dignissimos haec saecula non tulerunt" (*apud* Faust. *Epist.* 8).

17. "si Augustinus post te fuisset, iudicaretur inferior" (*VHilarii* 11[14]).

18. "est quidem, fateor, versibus meis sententia tua tam plausibilis olim . . . ut poetarum me quibusque lectissimis comparandum putes, certe compluribus anteponendum" (*Epist.* 9.13.1).

19. Sid. Apoll. *Epist.* 4.3.2, 5.17.1, 4.22.2, 8.11.7; 9.15.1 *carm.* 26, 47–49. Sidonius (*Epist.* 4.3.6–7) also compared Claudianus to no less than thirty-eight Greek and Latin exemplars.

20. "quorum egomet studiorum quasi quandam mortem flebile velut epitaphio tumularem, nisi tute . . . resuscitavisses . . ." (*Epist.ad Sapaud.*).

21. "non modo ad innovandum quippiam, sed ne ad dediscendum quidem absque te uno disciplinae nobilis ullus adspirat" (*Epist.ad Sapaud.*).

22. "sed hoc temporibus istis sub tuae tantum vel contemplatione conscientiae vel virtute doctrinae. nam quis aequali vestigia tua gressu sequatur cui datum est soli loqui melius quam didiceris . . ." (*Epist.* 9.9.16; cf. 8.3.3, 4.3.6).

23. "granditer laetor saltim in inlustri pectore tuo vanescentium litterarum remansisse vestigia . . . experiere per dies, quanto antecellunt beluis homines, tanto anteferri rusticis institutos" (*Epist.* 4.17.2). Claudianus Mamertus used the same topos in the letter to Sapaudus cited above.

24. "nostro saeculo non ingenia deesse, sed studia" (*Epist.ad Sapaud.*).

25. Although some did still exist. See Marrou, *Education,* pp. 456–458; Haarhoff, *Schools;* Labroue, "L'école"; Matthews, *Aristocracies,* pp. 347–348; and Riché, "Survivance," pp. 421–436.

26. See Baldwin, "Literature."

27. For Ausonius, see Hopkins, "Social Mobility."

28. Contrary to the conclusion of Loyen, *L'esprit,* pp. 64–65.

29. "delectaris contuberniis eruditorum, ego turbam quamlibet magnam litterariae artis expertem maxumam solitudinem appello" (*Epist.* 7.14.10).

30. "conclamata sunt namque iudicio universali scientiae dignitas virtus praerogativa, cuius ad maximum culmen meritorum gradibus ascenditur" (*Epist.* 7.14.7).

31. Note also Claudianus Mamertus' comment to the rhetor Sapaudus, "Viennensis urbis nobilitatis antiquae, cuius tu civis et doctor . . . debitum solves" (*Epist.ad Sapaud.*).

32. "utique in tanta rerum confusione amitterent nobilitatem, si indicem non haberent" (*Epist.* 1.3.5–6); Ennodius, *Dict.* 9.5, similarly described the teacher as the "libertatis index, boni testimonium sanguinis, ingeniorum lima."

33. "tibi uni concessum est claritatem aut dare aut reparare maiorum" (Ennod. *Dict.* 8.4).

34. "nam iam remotis gradibus dignitatum, per quas solebat ultimo a quoque summus quisque discerni, solum erit posthac nobilitatem indicium litteras nosse" (*Epist.* 8.2.2); see Loyen, "Résistance," p. 450.

35. "cui procul dubio statuas dederant litterae, si trabeae non dedissent" (*Epist.* 5.5.1).

36. For the parallel importance of office and literary skills, see also Sid.Apoll. *Epist.* 8.6.2; and Auspicius of Toul, *Epist.ad Arbogast.*: MGH *Epist.* 3.135–137 no. 23 = MGH *Poet.lat.* 4.2.614. Official rank, of course, was preferred, if it was available: see Sid.Apoll. *Epist.* 1.6.5.

37. "neque enim tibi familiaritas tam parva cum litteris, ut per has ipsas de te aliquid post te superesse non deceat. . . . vivet in posterum nominis tui gloria" (*Epist.* 8.5.1).

38. "igitur incumbe, neque apud te litterariam curam turba depretiet imperitorum, quia natura comparatum est ut in omnibus artibus hoc sit scientiae pretiosior pompa, quo rarior" (*Epist.* 2.10.6).

39. Brown, "Christianization," p. 9, for example, suggests that in an earlier age senatorial Christians and pagans found "a common ground . . . in the classical culture of the age."

40. "amo in te quod litteras amas" (*Epist.* 2.10.1). See also Sid.Apoll. *Epist.* 1.1.3, 5.1.1, 5.10.1, 8.1.1, 8.5.1, 8.6.2, 8.10.1, 9.9.16, 9.11.5; Avit. *Epist.* 43, 51; and Ven.Fort. *Carm.* 3.28–29, 7.28.7.

41. "quam ille barbariem non mitigavit?" (*VHonorati* 3[17]; see Pricoco, *L'isola*, pp. 61–63. See Loyen, *L'esprit*, pp. 53, 65; Momigliano, "Caduta," p. 12; and Stroheker, *Adel*, p. 65. For the west in general, see Chastagnol, "L'évolution," p. 313; Croke, "Manufacture," p. 92; Dauge, *Barbare*, p. 317; Matthews, *Aristocracies*, p. 85; Momigliano, "Cassiodorus," p. 216; and Brown, *World*, p. 130: "shorn of their privileges, their wealth curtailed by confiscations, ruled by outsiders, the senators of the west showed in a rococo zest for Latin rhetoric, their determination to survive and to be seen to survive." Sidonius' rhetorical description of his Lyonese confrères as *rustici* (*Epist.* 7.14.1) hardly means that they were "uneducated persons who were hardly better than barbarians" (Auerbach, *Literary Language*, p. 256).

42. "inter barbaros litteras" (*Epist.* 2.1.2), cf. *Epist.* 1.8.2, where, equally irrationally, "federates study literature." See also Claud.Mamert. *Epist.ad Sapaud.:* "video . . . grammaticam uti quandam barbaram barbarismi et soloecismi pugno et calce propelli."

43. "sumens de matris sapientia quod libenter barbaros fugit, de virtute paterna quod litteris terga non praebuit" (*Epist.* 95); see Mathisen, "*PLRE II,*" p. 370.

44. Sidonius did write to the apparently Frankish, but thoroughly romanized, Count of Trier Arbogastes (*Epist.* 4.17), and to the abbot Chariobaudus (*Epist.* 7.16), whose name suggests a Germanic origin (cf. the master of soldiers Chariobaudus of c. 407: *PLRE II*, p. 283), and who is omitted from Stroheker's list of Sidonius' barbarian correspondents (*Adel*, p. 59 n. 92), which does include the Breton leader Riothamus (*Epist.* 3.9).

45. "secundus nobis animorum nexus accessit de studiorum parilitate" *Epist.* 4.1.1; cf. Ruricius of Limoges' comment to Sidonius' son Apollinaris (*Epist.* 2.26): "cuius vos esse filios non solum generositate prosapiae, verum etiam et eloquentiae flore, et omni virtutum genere comprobatis: quae bona vobis non tam doctrina contulit, quam natura."

46. See Sid.Apoll. *Epist.* 1.11.13–14, 5.17.5, 9.13.4–5.

47. See, e.g., Sid.Apoll. *Epist.* 2.9.5, for a discussion of Origen in the library of the former prefect Tonantius Ferreolus.

48. See Chadwick, *Poetry*, pp. 170–186; Loyen, *L'esprit*, pp. 77–98; and Mathisen, *Factionalism*, pp. 83–85,93–97, 135–138, 235–253.

49. "o convivia, fabulae, libelli, risus, serietas, dicacitates, occursus, comitatus unus idem" (*Carm.* 23.439–441).

50. For the exclusion of barbarians from Sidonius' circle, see Matthews, *Aristocracies*, p. 326. A few possible exceptions include Arbogastes (note 44 above);

Sidonius' assertion that Eparchius Avitus taught the young Theoderic II to memorize Vergil (*Carm.* 7.496–498); and Sidonius' composition of a poem for the Visigothic queen Ragnahilda (*Epist.* 4.8.5); note also Jerome's praise of the Gothic priests Sunnias and Fretela—were they orthodox or Arian?—for their Biblical studies (*Epist.* 106).

51. "idem sentimus culpamus laudamus in litteris et aeque nobis quaelibet dictio placet improbaturque" (*Epist.* 4.1.1).

52. "cuius lectio sicut mihi antiquum restaurat affectum, ita prae obscuritate dictorum non accendit ingenium" (*Epist.* 2.26). And Julius Severianus (perhaps the rhetor Severianus of Sid.Apoll. *Carm.* 9.311–317, *Epist.* 9.13.4, 9.15.1: *PLRE II*, pp. 999–1000) in the dedicatory letter of his *Ars rhetorica* also alluded to this problem: "adverti praeterea—videro quid ceteri sentiant—obesse dicentibus rhetoricae artis nimiam disciplinam."

53. See Auerbach, *Literary Language,* p. 258; Brown, *World,* pp. 130–131; Loyen, *L'esprit,* passim; and Hagendahl, *Ruricius,* passim.

54. See Sid.Apoll. *Epist.* 1.1.1, 2.10.1–2, 4.15, 8.1.1, 9.16; Paul.Pet. *Epist.ad Perp.*: *CSEL* 16.160–161; Uran. *Epist.ad Pacat.*: *PL* 53.858–866; Gennad. *Vir.ill.* 80; Vict. Aquit. *Curs.pasch.*: *P.L.S.* 3.380ff; Claud.Mamert. *De stat.anim.* praef.: *CSEL* 11.18–20; Faust. *De gratia* praef.: *CSEL* 21.3–4; Const. *Epist.ad Pat.*: *S.C.* 112.112; see Anderson, *Sidonius* 1.lx-lxi; Stevens, *Sidonius,* pp. 168–174; and Mathisen, "Sidonius," p. 168.

55. "namque in audentiam sermocinandi quem non ipse compellas? qui omnium, de me enim taceo, litteratorum, licet occuli affectent, sic ingenia producis . . ." (*Epist.* 9.11.9).

56. Poetry: Sid.Apoll. *Epist.* 2.10.1, 4.18.3, 5.1.2, 5.17.2, 5.21.1, 8.11.3, 8.12.4, 9.12.1, 9.13.2, 9.14, 9.15.1. Prose: Sid.Apoll. *Epist.* 1.11.1–2, 7.3, 7.9, 8.16.1; Const. *Epist.ad Cens.*; Ruric. *Epist.* 1.4,11, 2.18–19. Works of other authors: Agroec. *De orth.* 1: Keil, *Gram.lat.* 7.113; Sid.Apoll. *Epist.* 4.16, 5.15.1–2, 8.3.1, 8.6.18; Ruric. *Epist.* 1.6–8, 2.17,47; Faust. *Epist.* 8. For a circulation route, see Sid.Apoll. *Carm.* 24, on which see Demougeot, "Gabales," pp. 43–45; and Loyen, *L'esprit,* pp. 62–63.

57. "spero ut qualecunque est opusculum ipsum, nec vacanter editum nec omnimodis emendatum, viro sublimi ac piissimo, si dignamini, fratri nostro Apollinari publicare atque excusare dignemini . . ." (*Epist.* 43). Borrowers could be scolded for keeping a work too long: Sid. Apoll. *Epist.* 5.2.

58. "specialis apud deum patrone" (*CSEL* 16.160); "tamquam si patrono vel domino inseparabiliter pedisequus minister inhaereat" (*De grat.* prol.); and Ruricius of Limoges spoke to Sidonius of "vestris patrociniis" (*Epist.* 1.9).

59. "sed scilicet tibi parui tuaeque examinationi has non recensendas, hoc enim parum est, sed defaecandas, ut aiunt, limandasque commisi, sciens te inmodicum esse fautorem non studiorum modo verum etiam studiosorum" (*Epist.* 1.1.3).

60. "ad te igitur hoc opusculum mittitur, in quo laborabis plurimum, cui necesse est emendare ipsum qui aliquid emendare praesumpsit . . ." (*De orthographia* praef.: Keil, *Gram.lat.* 7.114). See also Ruric. *Epist.* 2.41, "ideo quae displicuerint emendabitis . . . potius quam prodetis."

61. "tu modo faxis uti memineris non absque cura tui prodi oportere, quod

publicari iubes . . . proinde consilium tuum adserito et defensitato, quoniam, se in his secus aliquid, ego conscriptionis periclitabor, sed tu editionis . . ." (*CSEL* 11.20). For such conventions, see Jansen, *Prefaces*, pp. 141–144.

62. "itaque, si quid mihi credis, si quid utrique consulis, indignum memoria, oblivione dignissimum volumen absconde, si vis et me ad arbitrium tuum oratoris famam et te probati iudicis obtinere personam" (*Epist.* 1.4).

63. "nullam mihi domi chartulam, nullum libellum, nullum epistolam reliquisti" (*Epist.* 3).

64. *Epist.* 7.18.1, 8.1.1, 8.16.3, 9.1.4, 9.16.2.

65. Sidonius complimented the *vir inlustris* Petronius, the dedicatee of the eighth book of his letters, "quod amicorum gloriae, sicubi locus, lenocinaris" (*Epist.* 8.1.1).

66. "quapropter esse te, in quadam tuendae opinionis meae quasi specula, decet curiosisque facti huiusce rationem manifestare quidque ad hoc sentiant optimi quique, rescripto quam frequentissimo mihi pandere" (*Epist.* 9.1.3).

67. "dicto mea, quod mihi sufficit, placet amicis" (*Epist.* 8.16.5).

68. Elsewhere, it is "boni omnes" who approve the works of Faustus of Riez (Sid.Apoll. *Epist.* 9.9.16, cf. 7.12.4, "secundum bonorum sententiam").

69. "ceterum quisquis ita malus est, ut intellegat bene scripta nec tamen laudet, hunc boni intellegunt nec tamen laudant" (*Epist.* 9.14.8).

70. "non doctrinam, non eloquentiam, sed nescio quid super homines consecutum" (*VHilarii* 11[14]).

71. "praeconio, quantum comperi, immenso praesentis opusculi volumina extollit" (*Epist.* 8.6.2); see also Sid.Apoll. *Epist.* 1.9, 2.10, 4.3,14,22, 5.5,8,10, 8.3,6,10, 9.3,9; Claud.Mamert. *Epist.ad Sapaud.*: *CSEL* 11.203–206; Ruric. *Epist.* 1.4. Only rarely, it seems, was work actually discussed critically, as when the rhetor Viventiolus berated Avitus of Vienne for supposedly perpetrating a barbarism; Avitus, in turn, wrote a lengthy response in his own defense (*Epist.* 57).

72. "audio, quod lectitandis epistulis meis voluptuosam patientiam inpendas" (*Epist.* 5.1.1).

73. "faventes audient cuncti, cuncti foventes" (*Epist.* 9.14.9; cf. 9.7.5).

74. "sed probe intellego quod moribus tuis hanc voluptatem non operis effectus excudit sed auctoris affectus, ideoque plus debeo, quia gloriae punctum, quod dictioni negares, das amicitiae" (*Epist.* 3.14.1).

75. "bonum creditis quod bonum vultis, et in consortium vestrae devotionis adsciscitis etiam quos de desipientibus legeritis" (*De vita s. Mart.* prol: *CSEL* 16.17); see also Sid.Apoll. *Epist.* 8.16.5, 9.13.1; and Ruric. *Epist.* 1.11: "epistula . . . si displiceret affatu, placeret affectu."

76. "ne quispiam nostrum, qui ceteris dixisset exilius, verecundia primum, post morderetur invidia" (*Epist.* 9.13.4–5).

77. "studiosis favere non invidere consuevit" (*Epist.* 1.8).

78. "dum me laudare non parum studes, laudari plurimum te vetares" (*Epist.* 8.10.1)

79. "sane moneo praeque denuntio quisquilias ipsas Clius tuae hexametris minime exaeques. merito enim conlata vestris mea carmina non heroicorum phaleris sed epitaphistarum neniis comparabuntur" (*Epist.* 1.9.7); cf. Sidonius' references

to his "animique vota destituta litteris" (9.15.1 *carm.* 53), or his "frequentia barbarismorum" (ibid. 9.11.6).

80. See Chadwick, *Poetry*, p. 14; Loyen, *L'esprit*, pp. 101-102; Peter, *Briefe*; Semple, "Sidonius," p. 143; Stevens, *Sidonius*, p. 6off; and Stroheker, *Adel*, p. 59. The correspondence often concerned literary matters: see Sid.Apoll. *Epist.* 1.11; 2.2,10; 3.14; 4.1-3,16; 5.5,8,10,15,17,21; 7.14; 8.2,5,9-11; 9.1,12-15; and passim.

81. For complaints about the distances, see Sid.Apoll. *Epist.* 2.11, 4.1-2, 7.10-11,14, 8.15, 9.4-5,8; Faust. *Epist.* 16; and Ruric. *Epist.* 2.10, 2.36, 2.51-52. For correspondents who had never met, see Sid.Apoll. *Epist.* 4.17, 8.13-14, 9.2; Ruric. *Epist.* 1.1.

82. "dilectio, quae ante cognitionem mutua[m] inter absentes epistulario inchoata sermone semper et fota est" (*Epist.* 2.16).

83. "non enim interest, utrum ex necessitate aut ex voluntate, dummodo inter se invicem qui se diligunt colloquantur et quos corpore locorum intervalla discriminant animorum ac sensuum colloquia fida coniungant" (*Epist.* 2.51).

84. "testor deum, quod post praesentiam tuam nihil mihi dulcius est, quam si colloquium desiderantissimae pietatis vel litterarum dignatione meruero" (*apud* Faust. *Epist.* 10). See also Ruric. *Epist.* 2.62; and Ven.Fort. *Carm.* 3.28, 7.28.7.

85. "praevaleant ingenia sua ... ad remotarum desideria provinciarum stilo adminiculante porrigere, per quem saepenumero absentum dumtaxat institutorum tantus colligitur affectus, quantus nec praesentanea sedulitate conficitur" (*Epist.* 7.14.2). He also referred to letters as the "fundamenta certantis amicitiae" (*Epist.* 2.11.1).

86. See, for example, *Epist.* 4.2.1, 4.4.2, 5.12.1, 9.5.1. For travel difficulties, see also Chapter 3.

87. "sed quoniam fraternae quietis voto satis obstrepit conflictantium procella regnorum, saltim inter discretos separatosque litterarii consuetudo sermonis iure retinebitur, quae iam pridem caritatis obtentu merito inducta veteribus annuit exemplis" (*Epist.* 7.11.1).

88. "quod perhorrescens ad epistularum / transtuli cultum genus omne curae / ne reus cantu petulantiore / sim reus actu" (*Epist.* 9.16.3 *carm.* 49-52); cf. *Epist.* 8.4.3, "modo tempus est seria legi, seria scribi"; see also Avit. *Carm.* 1 prol.: *MGH AA* 6.2.201-202.

89. "undique litterarum officia perlata sunt" (*VHonorati* 4[22]; cf. Paul.Nol. *Epist.* 39.2).

90. "familiaritatis officia" (*Epist.* 2.11.1); "per sola officia verborum amicitias ... excolere" (*Epist.* 7.11.1); cf. Ruric. *Epist.* 2.4, "ab epistulari officio."

91. "impendo tamen per litteras debitum sospitationis officium" (*Epist.* 2.63).

92. "non solum vos nullis officiis mutuis sed nec litteris requiramus" (*Epist.* 2.64).

93. Note Ruric. *Epist.* 2.27, "scribendi opportunitatem mihi perire non passus sum"; cf. *Epist.* 2.36, 2.49. For requests and demands for letters, and complaints when letters were not sent, see Sid.Apoll. *Epist.* 1.5.1, 3.7, 4.5, 4.10, 4.12.4, 4.14.4, 5.4.1, 5.4.2, 6.3.1, 6.6.2, 6.10.2, 8.9, 8.11.4, 8.14.8, 9.7, 9.9.1-2, 9.11.9; Sedatus of Nîmes *apud* Faust. *Epist.* 9-10; Ruric. *Epist.* 1.1, 1.5, 1.10, 2.18, 2.38, 2.40-41, 2.49.

94. "saepenumero scriptis vestris alii inpertiuntur, qui id ipsum nec ambiunt

quam egomet forsan nec merentur amplius, non arbitror amicitiae legibus inpune committi" (Epist. 4.2.2). For the relation between letters and friendship, see also Epist. 9.9.1.

95. "qui modus potest paginis, non potest poni ipse amicitiis" (Epist. 9.1.3). For the importance Sidonius' friends attached to their inclusion, see Sid.Apoll. Epist. 7.12.1, 8.5.1, 9.15.1.

96. For the numbers, see Mathisen, "Epistolography," p. 95.

97. "tu fac memineris docendi munus tibi a proavis et citra hereditarium fore . . . multiplex in te a maioribus profecta tuis doctrina confluxit" (Epist.ad Sapaud.).

98. "perorandi illud quoque celeberrimum flumen, quod non solum gentilicium sed domesticum tibi quodque in tuum pectus per succiduas aetates ab atavo Frontone transfunditur" (Epist. 8.3.3; cf. 8.11.2).

99. "paterni interpres eloquii . . . cuius vos esse filios, non solum generositate prosapiae, verum etiam et eloquentiae flore et omni virtutum genere comprobatis, quae bona vobis non tam doctrina contulit quam natura" (Epist. 2.26).

100. "recognovi illic, qua satis delectatus sum, manum vestram, qua plus, paternam declamationem, qua maxime, haereditarium benignatatem" (Avit. Epist. 51).

101. See Mathisen, "Epistolography."

102. "genere vel censu, aetas venustas pudor patrocinarentur" (Epist. 5.10.2).

103. See Brown, World, p. 43; and also Barnish, "Transformation," p. 148; Drinkwater, "Attitudes," p. 152; Mathisen, "Epistolography," passim; and Wightman, Belgica, p. 306. For Italy, note also Cass. Var. 9.22.5, on the Decii, "curia Romana completur paene vestra familia."

104. "qui aut litterarum aut altarium cathedras cum sui ordinis laude tenuerunt" (Epist. 7.9.24). For the family, see PLRE II, p. 821.

105. "nam quae mundi nobilitas, qui honores, quae dignitas, quae sapientia, quae facundia, quae litterae non se jam ad hanc coelestis regni militiam contulerunt?" (Epist.ad Valer. p. 718).

11. COMING TO TERMS WITH THE BARBARIANS

1. See Mathisen, Factionalism, pp. 217–218.

2. "nimium autem ingratus est liberatori, qui in patria degens loquitur dolore captivi; dicis ergo, quid nobis profuit orasse, et tota spiritus contritione laborasse? . . . ita dum contra deum superbo corde audemus haec dicere, digna nos ostendimus pertulisse. interrogemus conscientias nostras, si aliquem in nobis deus perfectum post castigationem primae hostilitatis invenerit . . ." (PLS 3.606).

3. "videamus autem quid nobis in ipsa hostilitate, quid nobis contulerint oblata communium precum, et praesidia invocata sanctorum, unde quasi praesens tempus illud ante oculos disponamus. ecce omnis terra ad potentissimae gentis fremitum contremiscit, et tamen Romano ad te animo venit, qui barbarus putabatur, et ex omni parte conclusa Romana barbaries . . . inter ista miraris te peccatis exigentibus

flagellari, cur potius innocentiam gladii, et patientiam non miraris armati? expugnatoris tui ferrum quale producitur ad pugnam, tale reconditur in vaginam, qualis est ante bellum, talis est post triumphum. ac sic fortissimus tanti moderatoris exercitus vincere scivit, hostis esse nescivit. itaque inter stupenda circa te beneficia dei tui gratias tibi referat celeberrimus triumphator, ut apud arma victricia quieti maneant victi, et illaesa libertas: propter te donetur victori incruenta felicitas" (PLS 3.606–607).

4. "nonne vos estis Burgundiones nostri?" (VEpiph. 160).

5. "Eorice, tuae manus rogantur / ut Martem validus per inquilinum / defendat tenuem Garumna Thybrim" (Epist. 8.9.5 carm. 42–44).

6. "rumor ad nos magnum pervenit, administrationem vos Secundae Belgicae suscepisse . . . consiliarios tibi adhibere debes, qui famam tuam possent ornare . . . et sacerdotibus tuis debebis deferre et ad eorum consilia semper recurre, quodsi tibi bene cum illis convenerit, provincia tua melius potest constare . . . paternas quascunque opes possides, captivos exinde liberabis et a iugo servitutis absolvas . . . cum iuvenibus ioca, cum senibus tracta, si vis regnare nobilis iudicari" (Epist.aust. 2: MGH Epist. 3.113). The letter usually is dated to c. 486, after Clovis' defeat of Syagrius of Soissons, although it may date to after Clovis' succession to Childeric as king of Tournai c. 481. Rheims, Soissons, and Tournai all were situated in the Roman province of Belgica Secunda.

7. See Chapter 12.

8. "turpiter falsa periculose vera dicuntur" (Epist. 4.22.5). For Sidonius' prudence, see Mathisen, "Sidonius."

9. Note, however, Epist. 2.64, where Ruricius speaks of Volusianus of Tours' "fear of the enemy" (presumably the Franks), but then downplays it by saying that he appears to fear his wife ("matrona") more!

10. VViviani 6; see Courcelle, "Diners"; and Lécrivain, "Episode."

11. "cui excusavit dixitque sibi non esse in more positum alienis aliquando prandiis vesci, perendie se magis velle proficisci" (VEpiph. 92).

12. VGermani 28.

13. Sometimes assumed to have been "an aristocratic Gallo-Roman landowner" (Geary, France, pp. 29, 35; cf. Martine, Vie, pp. 336–337 n. 2). For him as a Burgundian, see Griffe, Gaule 2.96; and Courcelle, Histoire, p. 138; see also Mathisen, "Ten Office Holders."

14. "dum pro adflictione pauperum, quos persona quaedam, honore dignitatis aulicae tumens, vi pervasionis inlicitae servitutis iugo subdiderat, coram viro inlustri Galliae quondam patricio Hilperico, sub condicione regia ius publicum tempore illo redactum est, adsertione piissima dei famulus nititur defensare . . ." (VLupicini 10).

15. "oppressor ille nefarius, iracundiae furore succensus, in naevum sanctissimi viri quasdam verborum spumas, iracundia suppletus, eructans, 'nonne,' ait, 'tu es ille dudum noster inpostor, qui ante hos decem circiter annos, cum civilitatem Romani apicis arrogans derogares, regioni huic ac patribus iam iamque inminere interitum testabaris? cur ergo, oro te, tam terribilia ostenta praesagii in nullo rei tristis probatione firmentur, vanus vates exponas?' " (VLupicini 10).

16. Geary, *France*, p. 29, however, supposes that Lupicinus was predicting "the ruin of the Roman Empire."

17. Perhaps the views of the accuser reflect ideas prevalent at the time of the authors (c. 520), and Lupicinus' those of the 460s.

18. "tum ille audacter, manum ad memoratum Hilpericum, virum singularis ingenii et praecipuae bonitatis, extendens, 'ecce,' ait, 'perfide ac perdite! iram quam tibi tuisque similibus praedicabam adtende. nonne cernis, degener et infelix, ius fasque confusum, ob tuis tuorumque crebra in innocentum pervasione peccatis, mutari muriceos pellito sub iudice fasces? tandem resipisce paulisper et vide utrum rura ac iugera tua novus hospes inexspectata iuris dispectione sibi non vindicet ac praesumat. quae tamen sicut te scire non abnuo vel sentire, ita personulam meam unco bicipiti, aut rege timidum aut eventu trepidum, stigmatis nota turpare decrevisse non denego' " (*VLupicini* 10). Cf. Sid.Apoll. *Epist.* 7.9.11, "pungentibus linguis maledicorum veluti bicipitibus hamis," for similar vocabulary used in another case of slander.

19. "quid plura? tanto est memoratus patricius veritatis audacia delectatus, ut hoc, adstantibus aulicis, ita divino iudicio accidisse exemplis multis ac longa disputatione firmaret. mox vero, vigoris regii sententia promulgata, liberos restituit libertati, et Christi famulum, oblatis ob necessitatem fratrum vel loci muneribus, honorifice fecit ad coenobium repedare" (*VLupicini* 10).

20. See also *VEpiph.* 85–92, 151–179; and the accounts in the *VGenovefae, VLupi,* and *VViviani.*

21. "ecce tunc conperimus armatorum mentes sanctitate superatas et cessisse precibus electi principem . . . quantum acutior fuit verborum quam ferri lammina, hinc lector agnosce: expugnavit sermo cui se gladii subduxerunt" (*VEpiph.* 176).

22. *Euch.* 572–581.

23. Sid.Apoll. *Epist.* 5.5.3, "Germanorum senectus . . . arbitrum te disceptatoremque desumit. novus Burgundionum Solon in legibus disserendis . . . decernis audiris." Momigliano, "Caduta," p. 17, has Syagrius learning "Gothic" rather than Burgundian. Note also the Spaniard, or Aquitanian, Cerasia, who learned German in order to convert the barbarians to Christianity (Eutrop. *De similitudine carnis peccati:* Morin, *Etudes,* pp. 107–150): "ethnicis vero et istis barbaris vestris non minus mente quam lingua . . . illa peculiariter exhibebas . . . lingua barbara hebraïcam adserere doctrinam"; see Courcelle, "Textes," pp. 30–31. On the other hand, the tribune Hariobaudes of 359, "sermonis barbarici perquam gnarus" (Amm. 18.2.2), presumably was a German.

24. See *PLRE II,* p. 1042; and Stroheker, *Adel,* p. 98, who also suggests that the poet Secundinus served as Chilperic's "Hofdichter."

25. "per servum [or stuprum] . . . traduntur" (*HF* 3.13).

26. Ibid.

27. Some of these conclusions were presented at the conference of the American Historical Association in December, 1988, under the title "Gallo-Roman Collaborators with the Barbarians: What Did They Do and When Did They Do It?"

28. Barnish, "Transformation," p. 142, suggests this happened because this route "promised many senators a hope of less expensive advancement."

29. *VOrientii* 3: *AASS* May I p. 63; Mathisen, "*PLRE II,*" p. 379; see also Salv.,

De gub. 7.9; and note also the Gaul Constantius, who c. 440 was sent to serve as the secretary of Attila (Priscus fr. 8: *PLRE II*, p. 319). The Visigothic chieftan Alaric also twice used bishops as ambassadors (Soz. *HE* 9.8).

30. It is assumed that Roman names indicate Roman origin, at least in the fifth and early sixth centuries; there seem to be no certain exceptions to this. For Germanic nomenclature, see Bach, *Namenkunde;* and Förstermann, *Namenbuch.*

31. Attalus: *PLRE II*, pp. 180–181. For the suggestion that other Gallo-Roman potentates also supported Attalus (and therefore, by inference, the Visigoths), see Oost, *Placidia,* p. 130.

32. "tyrannus Attalus absentem casso oneraret honoris nomine, privatae comitivam largitionis dans mihi" (*Euch.* 293–296).

33. "Nepotianus [one of the masters of soldiers] Theuderico ordinante Arborium accipit successorem" (*Chron.* 213; cf. 230); see *PLRE II*, p. 129.

34. For other possibilities, see Demougeot, "Septimanie," pp. 18, 31.

35. For various lists, none complete, see Bury, *LRE*, p. 344; Courcelle, *L'empire,* pp. 198–199; Griffe, "L'épiscopat," pp. 262–263; Stevens, *Sidonius,* p. 92; and Stroheker, *Adel,* p. 90.

36. Gregory of Tours (*HF* 2.20) dates Victorius' appointment to c. 470: in the fourth year of Euric's reign (466–484), and before the Visigothic attacks on Clermont of the early 470s; see *PLRE II*, pp. 1162–1164. Note also Sid.Apoll. *Epist.* 4.10.2; Greg.Tur. *VPat.* 3, *Glor.mart.* 44.

37. *Chron.gall.511.* no. 652. *PLRE II*, p. 1168, suggests that he may also have been *magister militum* in 473.

38. See Jones, *LRE,* p. 192; and *PLRE II*, p. 1296. Previous Visigothic *duces* who operated in Spain (not specifically called *duces Hispaniarum*), include Cyrila (458–459) and Suniericus (459–460) (ibid.). If, as *PLRE II*, p. 334, suggests, Cyrila's "name is not Germanic," he would be another Roman in Visigothic service at this time.

39. *Chron.gall.511* no. 653; see Thompson, "End," p. 19.

40. See *PLRE II*, p. 1168.

41. See Mathisen, "Ten Office Holders," pp. 125–127.

42. See Thompson, "End," p. 19.

43. "nuper vos classicum in classe cecinisse atque inter officia nunc nautae, modo militis litoribus Oceani curvis inerrare contra Saxonum pandos myoparones . . . victoris populi signa comitaris" (*Epist.* 8.6.13–18); see *PLRE II*, p. 771; Stroheker, *Adel,* no. 253.

44. *Not.dig.occ.* 36.

45. *Epist.* 5.11.2, "iudicas ut qui aequissime"; see *PLRE II*, p. 903; and Stroheker, *Adel,* p. 206.

46. See Ruric. *Epist.* 2.20,54; and Sid.Apoll. *Epist.* 2.11, 8.11.3; see also Stroheker, *Adel,* no. 332. *PLRE II*, p. 964, has the Rustici of Sidonius and Ruricius as two different individuals.

47. *PLRE II*, p. 5; Stroheker, *Adel,* no. 212, p. 187.

48. "consiliorum principis et moderator et arbiter, Leo nomine" (*VEpiphanii* 85).

49. "cotidie . . . per potentissimi consilia regis totius sollicitus orbis pariter negotia et iura, foedera et bella, loca spatia merita cognoscis" (*Epist.* 4.22.3). Leo also

was Euric's speechwriter: Sid.Apoll. *Epist.* 8.3.3, see also *Carm.* 9.311–314, 14 *epist.* 2, 23.441–444, *Epist.* 4.22.1–3, 9.3.2 *carm.* 20, and 9.15.1 *carm.* 19–20.

50. Greg.Tur. *Glor.mart.* 92.

51. For barbarian law codes, see Chapter 12.

52. Note Hispanus (*PLRE II*, p. 566: Ruric. *Epist.*2.45); Elaphius (*PLRE II*, p. 387; Stroheker, *Adel*, no. 111: Ruric. *Epist.* 2.7; Sid.Apoll. *Epist.* 4.15); Praesidius (*PLRE II*, p. 903; Stroheker, *Adel*, p. 206: Ruric. *Epist.* 2.12); Anianus (*PLRE II*, p. 90; Stroheker, *Adel*, no. 18: *C.Th.* vol.1 pt.1 pp. xxxiv–v); Timotheus (*PLRE II*, p. 1121; Stroheker, *Adel*, no. 352: *C.Th.* vol.1 pt.1 pp. xxxiii–iv); Goiaricus (*PLRE II*, p. 517 [possibly a German]: *C.Th.* vol.1 pt.1 pp. xxxii–v); Eudomius (*PLRE II*, p. 409; Stroheker, *Adel*, no. 122: Caes. *Epist.ad Ruric.* 7; Ruric. *Epist.* 2.39); Apollinaris (*PLRE II*, p. 114; Stroheker, *Adel*, no. 22: *HF* 2.37; Avit. *Epist.* 51); and Avitus (*AASS* June IV p. 292).

53. See note 13 above. The supposed *consiliarii* Lucanus and Placidus of Gundobad in 499 are attested only in a forged document: see *PLRE II*, pp. 690, 890; and Mathisen, "Addenda" s.v.

54. Sid.Apoll. *Epist.* 5.18; see *PLRE II*, p. 179; and Stroheker, *Adel*, pp. 98–99.

55. "cui et rerum et verborum fides ab illo [sc. Gundobado] semper tute mandata est . . . cum quo confert quotiens" (*VEpiphanii* 168).

56. Avit. *Epist.* 53, 94–96; *PLRE II*, pp. 542–543. Stroheker, *Adel*, p. 98, suggests that Heraclius was the "court poet."

57. Avit. *Epist.* 9, 46a, 47, 48, 49; perhaps also Ennod. *Epist.* 4.22; see *PLRE II*, pp. 658–659.

58. See Avit. *Epist.* 94; and Mathisen, "Ten Office Holders," p. 127. He may be the Laurentius of the previous note.

59. "ex officio regis Sigismundi . . . qui super omnem dominationem fisci principatum gerebat" (*VApollin.Valent.* 2; see *Corp.chr.lat.* 148A.39–41); see also Mathisen, "*PLRE II*," p. 384.

60. *Lex Burg. addit.* 21.11 also refers to "counts, Burgundian as well as Roman."

61. See Chapter 5.

62. See McCormick, "Clovis," p. 170, for "army commanders [as] the privileged point of contact between two cultures in the process of osmosis."

63. See *PLRE II*, p. 200; and Mathisen, "Hagiographical Addenda," p. 451.

64. See Selle-Hosbach, *Prosopographie*, passim; and Prinz, "Aristocracy," pp. 155–156.

65. "denique Franci, hunc eiectum, Egidium sibi . . . unanimiter regem adsciscunt, qui cum octavo anno super eos regnaret . . ." (Greg.Tur. *HF* 2.12; cf. Fred. *Chron.* 3.11; and *LHF* 7). See *PLRE II*, p. 12; and Grahn-Hoek, *Oberschicht*, pp. 134–136.

66. See Goffart, *Barbarians*, p. 115; Jones, *LRE*, pp. 253–262; Loyen, "Résistants," pp. 445–446; Saunders, "Debate," p. 17; Stroheker, *Adel*, pp. 98–99; Thompson, *Romans*, p. 56; and Wallace-Hadrill, "Gothia," pp. 220, 226.

67. For new men, see Chapter 1.

68. "invident . . . originem nobilibus . . . hi sunt, qui novis opibus ebrii . . . per utendi intemperantiam produnt imperitiam possidendi" (*Epist.* 5.7.3–4). Note also

Sidonius' picture of a noble forced to give precedence to "a poor man who has gained office" (*Epist.* 1.6.4).

69. "his moribus obruunt virum non minus bonitate quam potestate praestantem. sed quid faciat unus, undique venenato vallatus interprete?" (*Epist.* 5.7.6).

70. See *PLRE II*, p. 817; and Mathisen, "Resistance."

71. "municipaliter natus" (*Epist.* 1.11.5); perhaps an ancestor of Paeonius, Count of Auxerre in the sixth century (Greg.Tur. *HF* 4.42).

72. "plebeiae familiae" (*Epist.* 1.7.11); see *PLRE II*, pp. 157–158 and 495 respectively. For Paeonius and Arvandus as "climbing parvenus," see Barnish, "Transformation," p. 137.

73. See Mathisen, "Family," passim.

12. THE FINAL RESOLUTION: ARISTOCRATIC OPTIONS IN POST-ROMAN GAUL

1. See Candidus fr. 1: *FHG* 4.136; see Schmidt, "Anfangen," p. 315 n. 2.

2. See Goffart, "Rome," p. 301; and Ladner, "Attitudes," p. 25.

3. See Banniard, "L'aménagement," pp. 5–38.

4. Contrary to the suggestion of Jones, "Constitutional," p. 130.

5. "Burgundionibus leges mitiores instituit, ne Romanis obpraemerent" (*HF* 2.33).

6. See Jones, *LRE*, pp. 239, 264; King, *Law*, passim; Ladner, "Justinian," p. 191; Stroheker, *Adel*, pp. 88–91, 100; and Wallace-Hadrill, "Gothia," p. 226.

7. "leges . . . Theodoricianas" (*Epist.* 2.1.3; see also *Carm.* 7.495–496, where Theoderic says, "mihi Romula dudum . . . iura placent"); see Beyerle, "Frühgeschichte"; Demougeot, "Septimania," pp. 18–19; King, *Law*, p. 7; Lear, "Public Law"; and Vismara, *Edictum Theodirici*, who attributes the "edict" to the Visigoth Theoderic I.

8. "omnes autem cau[sa]s, quae in regno bonae memoriae patris [no]stri, seu bonae seu male actae sunt, [no]n permittimus penitus conmoveri" (*Codex Euricianus* no. 177: *MGH Leges* 1.5). Only about 60 of the original 350 clauses survive, many of them fragmentary; see King, *Law*, pp. 6–10; and Wormald, "Lex scripta." For the jurist Leo of Narbonne as the editor of the laws, see Demougeot, "Septimanie," p. 19; Beyerle, "Frühgeschichte," pp. 6–8, suggests Marcellinus of Narbonne.

9. Clause 277 of the *Codex Euricianus*, for example, placed a fifty-year statute of limitations on claims regarding land distributions, which conceivably could have gone all the way back to 418.

10. See King, *Law*, p. 6; and Wallace-Hadrill, "Gothia," p. 227.

11. See *Cod.Eur.* 277, cf. 274–276, 312; see also Weber, "Stadt."

12. "antiquos vero terminos [sic] stare iubemus, sicut et bonae mem[ori]ae pater noster in alia lege praecepi[t]" (*Cod.Eur.* 277).

13. *Epist.* 8.9.3.

14. See Nehlson, "Alarich."

15. In the same year, Alaric allowed the first synod of Catholic bishops in the Gothic kingdom (see below). For Alaric's eleventh-hour cooperativeness, see also the *VVasii: AASS* April II p. 421.

16. "ut omnis legum Romanarum et antiqui iuris obscuritas adhibitis sacerdotibus ac nobilibus viris in lucem intellegentiae melioris deducta resplendeat et nihil habeatur ambiguum . . . venerabilium episcoporum vel electorum provincialium nostrorum roboravit adsensus" (*C.Th.* vol.1 pt.1 pp. xxxiii–xxxv).

17. See *MGH Leges* 1.2.1; and Drew, *Burgundian Code.* Syagrius: Sid.Apoll. *Epist.* 5.5.3–4; and Chapter 11.

18. Translations from Drew, *Burgundian Code.*

19. *Lex Burg.* 17.1: "All cases which involve Burgundians and which were not completed before the 'pugna Mauriacensis' are declared dismissed."

20. *Lex Burg.* 79.1.

21. *Lex Burg.* 79.2–3. Similar requirements were in the *Codex Euricianus.*

22. *Lex Burg.* 84. No sales to outsiders ("extranei") were permitted.

23. *Lex Burg.* 21.2.

24. See Gaudemet, "Survivances"; Grahn-Hoek, *Oberschicht*, pp. 31–38; Stein, "Romanus"; and Zöllner, *Geschichte*, pp. 116–120.

25. *Lex Burg.* 12.1.

26. *C.Th.* 3.14.1; see Demougeot, "Restrictions," p. 383; and Chapter 4.

27. "exclusa sceptris Geticis" (*Carm.* 5.204).

28. "quoniam non oportet cum omnibus hereticis miscere connubia, et vel filios vel filias dare, sed potius accipere, si tamen se profitentur christianos futuros esse catholicos" (no. 20[67]: *Corp.chr.lat.* 148.228). The most likely source of "heretics" would have been the barbarian Arians. The canon is included in a list appended to some manuscripts of the council.

29. See Blockley, "Marriages"; and Demougeot, "Conubium."

30. See Introduction.

31. *HF* 3.20–27; see Demougeot, "Conubium," p. 78. And for the marriage of the Ostrogoth Gento to a Roman, see Thompson, *Romans*, p. 235.

32. Here, one must note a Roman vogue for adopting Germanic names, as exemplified by Sidonius' young friend Burgundio (*Epist.* 9.14). For the following period, see Lot, *End*, p. 395: "The further we go in the sixth century, the more we find 'Romans' abandoning their Latin names to adopt Frankish ones . . . This was a fashion only, but a fashion is indicative of a state of mind."

33. *CIL* 12.11282.

34. *VMartini* 1.26.

35. Greg.Tur. *VPat.* 8.1, *HF* 6.11; see Heinzelmann, "Prosopographie," p. 610; and Stroheker, *Adel*, p. 180: Gundulphus suppposedly went on to become a *major domus* and then bishop of Tongres (*VGundulfi: AASS* July IV 159ff; *VArnulfi* 4: *AASS* July IV 435).

36. *VUrbani* 1ff: *AASS* Jan II 494ff; *VDomitiani* 10ff: *AASS* July I 44ff.

37. *MGH SS* 2.308ff.

38. Note *Lex Burg.* 44.1, "if the daughter of any native Burgundian . . . unites herself . . . with either barbarian or Roman . . ."; and *Lex Burg.* 79.1, "if anyone of our people [sc. Burgundian] has invited a person belonging to a barbarian nation

to live with him . . ." See also *Const.extrav.* 21.4, 21.6, *Lex Burg.* 17.5, 47.1, 55.3–4, 56.1, 60.1–3, 61; and note van Acker, *"Barbarus."*

39. "quid faciam ignoro, quia venerunt hi barbari super nos . . . lenire feritatem hominis huius" (*HF* 2.32).

40. See Riché, *Education;* and Roger, *Enseignement.*

41. "Asteriolus tunc et Secundinus magni cum rege habebantur; erat autem uterque sapiens et rhetoricis imbutus litteris" *HF* 3.33; see note 74 below.

42. See Schmitz, *"Tendenz."*

43. "cum in nomine domini ex permissu domni nostri gloriosissimi magnificentissimi piissimique regis . . . sancta synodus convenisset, ibique flexis in terram genibus, pro regno eius, pro longaevitate . . . deprecaremur, ut qui nobis congregationis permiserat potestatem, regnum eius dominus . . . extenderet . . ." (*Corp.chr.lat.* 148.192).

44. A second council, scheduled for Toulouse in 507, apparently did not meet; see Caes. *Epist.apud* Faust. *Epist.* 12; and Ruric. *Epist.* 2.39.

45. See Mathisen, *Factionalism,* pp. 101–116 and passim.

46. See above, Chapter 3.

47. See Claude, *"Bestellung";* and Schreibelreiter, *Bischof.*

48. "domno suo catholicae ecclesiae filio Chlothovecho gloriosissimo regi omnes sacerdotes, quos ad concilium venire iussistis . . . cum auctore deo ex evocatione gloriosissimi regis Clothevechi . . . fuisset concilium summorum antestitum congregatum . . ." (*Corp.chr.lat.* 148A.4); see Grahn-Hoek, *Oberschicht,* p. 184.

49. See Grahn-Hoek, *Oberschicht,* pp. 181–189; and Moorhead, *"Motives."*

50. Attested only rarely in the fifth century, as c. 456, when a local council at Narbonne was attended by *episcopi* and *honorati* (Leo, *"Epistolas fraternitatis":* PL 54.1199ff). See Speigl, *"Laien."*

51. "laicos permittimus interesse . . . a solis pontificibus ordinanda sunt" (*Corp.chr.lat.* 148A.23).

52. *Corp.chr.lat.* 148A.64–65. Three of these laymen, Syagrius, Pantagathus, and Namatius, may have gone on to become bishops in their own right, of Grenoble, Vienne, and Vienne again respectively.

53. "in conventu episcoporum et laicorum, qui interfuerant" (*Corp.chr.lat.* 148A.85). The qualifier would suggest that the attendance of laymen still was regarded as rather unusual. In this instance, however, no laymen subscribed.

54. See Brezzi, *"Impero,"* pp. 266–268; and the many studies of Griffe.

55. See Chapter 11.

56. "vestra fides nostra victoria est" (*Epist.* 46); see Brezzi, *"Impero,"* p. 267. In 497, even the bishop of Rome Anastasius wrote to Clovis advising him to support the church (*Epist.* "Tuum gloriose fili": Jaffé no. 745).

57. "quod si se rex praecellentissimus ab ecclesiae vel sacerdotum communione ultra suspenderit, locum ei dantes ad sanctae matris gremium veniendi, sancti antistetes se in monasteriis absque ulla dilatione . . . recipiant, donec pacem dominus integram . . . restituere . . . dignetur, ita ut non unus quicunque prius de monasterio . . . discedat, quam cunctis generaliter fratribus fuerit pax promissa vel reddita" (*Corp.chr.lat.* 148A.39).

58. See Cloché, "Elections."

59. "ut nullus saecularium ad clericatus officium praesumatur nisi aut cum regis iussione aut cum iudicis voluntate" (Corp.chr.lat. 148A.6); see also Caes. Serm. 78.3, for people "asking a king or judge or a powerful person for something they need very badly."

60. See Grahn-Hoek, Oberschicht; Jones, LRE, p. 264; Prinz, Klerus; and Wieruszowski, "Zusammensetzung."

61. See Jones, LRE, p. 264, "the Frankish kings . . . in general milked the churches unmercifully."

62. Epist. 3.12.1–3.

63. See Wallace-Hadrill, "Bloodfeud."

64. See Chapter 3.

65. Greg.Tur. HF 3.36.

66. Greg.Tur. HF 6.13.

67. "amatorque mulierum et gulae ac fornicationis omnique inmunditiae valde deditus" (Greg.Tur. HF 6.36).

68. Greg.Tur. HF 10.8.

69. Greg.Tur. HF 3.34–35.

70. Greg.Tur. HF 5.5.

71. Greg.Tur. HF 5.36.

72. Greg.Tur. VPat. 8.7.

73. "nisi ulciscar interitum parentum meorum, amittere nomen viri debeo et mulier infirma vocari" (Greg.Tur. HF 7.47, 9.19).

74. "quae usque ad hoc proficit, ut, oblitis verborum obiectionibus, propriis se manibus verberarent . . . ne in manus inimici conruerit" (Greg.Tur. HF 3.33).

75. Greg.Tur. HF 4.43, 6.7.

76. VGerm.Par. 5.

77. Greg.Tur. HF 7.23.

78. Greg.Tur. HF 8.43.

79. Greg.Tur. HF 8.43.

80. "non ideo, quia clericus factus sum, et ultor iniuriarum mearum non ero" (HF 8.39).

81. "coepit persequi ac interficere multos de his quos vir dei familiares habuerat . . . Gratias tibi ago, Iesu Christe, quod post mortem iniquissimi Nicetii super hunc tectum calcare promerui" (HF 4.36).

82. "eum a communione suspendi, non quasi ultor iniuriae meae, sed ut facilius eum ab hac insania redderem emendatum" (HF 8.40).

83. Note Epist. 3.5, 4.24, 5.19, 5.21, 6.2, 6.3, 6.4.

84. "maledicta sit domus haec, et maledicti habitatores eius in sempiternum, fiatque deserta, et non sit qui inhabitet in ea" (Greg.Tur. VPat. 4.3).

85. See Dill, Gaul, p. 43–49. The Salic Law listed 343 total crimes, of which 150 involved theft, 113 violence, 30 mutilation, and 24 outrage to women; nearly all were compensated for by a specific number of solidi.

86. Note how Sidonius had originally asked that Arvandus be punished "by the confiscation of his property" (Epist. 1.7.13).

87. See Jones, *LRE*, p. 265, "Gregory of Tours records the most appalling acts of lawless violence as a matter of course."

EPILOGUE

1. See Bachrach, "Alans," p. 488; Geary, *France*, pp. 109–116; Wightman, *Belgica*, pp. 306, 311, and "Attila," p. 42; and, in general, Reuter, *Nobility*.

2. See Battisti, "Latini"; Buchner, *Provence*; James, *Origins*, pp. 13–31; Rey, "Tradition"; and Ullmann, " 'Romani.' "

3. See Lot, *End*, p. 395.

4. *Passio s. Sigismundi: MGH SRM* 2.333, perhaps a result of the report that Gundobad had executed the supporters of Godegisel (Greg.Tur. *HF* 2.33, "interfectis senatoribus Burgundionibus, qui Godegiselo consenserant"; cf. Mar.Avit. *Chron.* s.a. 500: *MGH AA* 11.234).

5. *MGH SRM* 7.773, a manuscript of the ninth century. See also *VMaxim.Trev.* 10: *AASS* May VII p. 23; see also Lot, *End*, p. 395.

6. See Lot, *End*, p. 395.

7. See Fischer, "Continuity"; and Silber, *Royalty*.

8. Ruric. *Epist.* 2.26.

9. See *MGH AA* 8.lxix; and Mathisen, "Epistolography," pp. 108–109.

10. Beginning perhaps with the Romanized Frank Arbogastes c. 470; see Chapter 5. For the late sixth century, note the works of Gregory of Tours and, in particular, Venantius Fortunatus; and see Laistner, *Thought*, passim.

11. Greg.Tur. *HF* 5.44, 6.46. For Chilperic's "Hymni in sollemnitate s. Medardi episcopi," see *MGH Poet.lat.* 4.2.477–480.

12. For Gallic literary output of the sixth century and later, see Raby, *Poetry*, pp. 127–142, 153–158; Rusch, *Latin Fathers*, pp. 178–185, 207–209; and Wright and Sinclair, *Literature*, pp. 100–113, 121ff; see also Lesne, "Contribution." But for the seventh and eighth centuries as "an age of intellectual barrenness and decline," see Raby, *Poetry*, p. 146.

13. See Jones, *LRE*, pp. 239, 476–477, 762; and de Wretschko, "De usu."

14. See Clover, "Symbiosis," p. 60

15. See Clover, "Symbiosis," pp. 56, 60.

16. For the aristocracy of Roman North Africa, see Overbeck, *Untersuchungen*; for churchmen, see Mandouze, *Prosopographie*.

17. *VFulgentii* 4: *PL* 65.118; two of his sons later returned and successfully reclaimed part of the family property.

18. See Clover, "Symbiosis," pp. 59–60.

19. Clover, "Symbiosis," pp. 62–69.

20. Dracontius, *Satisfactio: MGH AA* 14.114–131; see *Clavis* nos. 1509–1514, pp. 252–253.

21. See *Clavis*, pp. 252–254; Rusch, *Latin Fathers*, pp. 190–197; Raby, *Poetry*, pp. 142–146; Schanz, *Geschichte*, pp. 567–586, passim. But for the same theme of literary

decline as in Gaul, see Laistner, *Thought*, pp. 83–84, "In Africa . . . a feeble flame of learning continued to flicker."

22. See Stevens, "Circle."

23. See in particular Vict.Vit. *Hist.persecut.*; see also Clover, "Symbiosis," p. 59; and Jones, *LRE*, pp. 263–264.

24. See Chadwick, "Contacts"; Morris, *Age of Arthur*; Thompson, *Germanus*; and Wood, "End."

25. For Gildas (c. 516–570), see Wright and Sinclair, *Literature*, pp. 97–98; and for St. Patrick, see Schanz, *Geschichte*, pp. 530–533.

26. See the extensive bibliography in Ferreiro, *Visigoths*; see also Blasquez, "Rejection and Assimilation"; Fontaine, "Romanité et hispanité" and *Isidore*; James, *Visigothic Spain*; King, *Law*; Stroheker, "Spanische Senatoren"; Thompson, "End" and *Visigoths*; and Ziegler, *Church*.

27. See Ziegler, *Church*.

28. See Raby, *Poetry*, pp. 142–153; Rusch, *Latin Fathers*, pp. 198–204; Schanz, *Geschichte*, pp. 623–630; and Wright and Sinclair, *Literature*, pp. 119–121.

29. See *Clavis* no. 1300, p. 291; and Raby, *Poetry*, pp. 152–153.

30. See Bertolini, "Aristocrazia"; Cracco Ruggini, "Nobilitá"; Hodgkin, *Italy*; Momigliano, "Cassiodorus"; Moorhead, *Catholic Episcopate*; Pietri, "Aristocratie"; and Wickham, *Early Medieval Italy*.

31. See Burns, "Ennodius," p. 168, the "settlement of the Ostrogoths . . . scarcely ruffled the life of the Roman aristocracy," and p. 166, "some [aristocrats] withdrew from society altogether . . . the chaos proved too much for some, who returned to the solitude and security of their remote alpine villas." See also Momigliano, "Caduta," pp. 12–14.

32. See Burns, "Theoderic," pp. 99–106, for "Theodoric's attempt to reconcile Gothic experience with Roman norms"; cf. p. 107, "without the smooth and dependable transference of property . . . the world of the late Roman aristocracy would have crumbled into ruins . . ." See also Barnish, "Pigs," p. 164; di Gianlorenzo, "Barbari"; Jones, *LRE*, p. 263; Martino, "*Laus*"; and Thompson, *Romans*, p. 235.

33. "custos libertatis et propagator Romani nominis" (*CIL* 10.6850).

34. See Clover, "Olybrius," p. 173, "The Anicii . . . were considered to be favorable to the barbarians," and p. 196, "even the aristocracy proved to be adaptable under pressure." See also Löwe, *Theodorich*.

35. "instructus enim trifariis linguis" (Cass. *Var.* 5.40.5); see Thompson, *Romans*, p. 231.

36. See Burns, "Ennodius," p. 156, for the "break in the Roman aristocracy"; and Llewellyn, "Clergy," p. 262, for the "impoverished and dispersed" aristocracy.

37. See Barnish, "Transformation," pp. 140–141; and Bury, *LRE*, p. 466.

38. See Clover, "Olybrius," pp. 170, and 185: "the disturbances of the fifth century helped to bring western senators more actively into public life." For Romans in barbarian service, see Sundwall, *Abhandlungen*; and *PLRE II*, passim.

39. See Llewellyn, "Clergy," pp. 245, 257–258, and "Priests and Senators," p. 10.

40. See Barnish, "Transformation," pp. 138–139: the "episcopal role gave the

aristocracy an alternative, though inevitably unsatisfactory one, focus for its traditions."

41. See Llewellyn, "Clergy," p. 245, who also suggests that Theoderic benefited from this polarization.

42. See Barnish, "Transformation," p. 130.

43. Such as Ennodius' friend and relative Astyrius (Ennod. *Epist.* 1.24, cf. 1.12).

44. For Italian writers, see *Clavis,* pp. 243, 249, 251–252, 254; Raby, *Poetry,* pp. 117–127; Rusch, *Latin Fathers,* pp. 185–189; Schanz, *Geschichte,* pp. 586–623, and passim; and Wright and Sinclair, *Literature,* pp. 73–74, 80–97.

45. See Barnish, "Transformation," p. 135, and p. 150 for a comparison with Gaul; see also Stein, "Disparition."

PRIMARY
BIBLIOGRAPHY

Agroec. *De orth.* = Agroecius, *Ars de orthographia:* H. Keil ed., *Grammatici latini* 7 (Leipzig, 1880) 113–125.

Amb. *Epist.* = Ambrose of Milan, *Epistulae:* O. Faller ed., *CSEL* 82 (Vienna, 1968); *PL* 16.913–1342.

Amm. = Ammianus Marcellinus, *Res gestae:* John C. Rolfe ed., *Ammianus Marcellinus* (3 vols.) (Loeb: London, 1963–1972).

Aug. *Epist.* = Aurelius Augustinus, bishop of Hippo Regius, *Epistulae:* A. Goldberger ed., *CSEL* 34, 44, 57–58 (Vienna, 1895–1925); *Epist.** = J. Divjak ed., *Sancti Aureli Augustini opera, Epistolae ex duobus codicibus nuper in lucem prolatae, CSEL* 88 (Vienna, 1981).

Augustan History: see *SHA.*

Aurelius Victor, *Liber de caesaribus:* Fr. Pichlmayr and R. Gruendel eds., *Sextus Aurelius Victor. Liber de caesaribus* (Leipzig: Teubner, 1970).

Aus. *Grat.act., Mos., Par.* = Ausonius, = *Gratiarum actio, Mosella, Parentalia:* Hugh G. White ed., *Ausonius* (2 vols.) (Loeb: London, 1919–1921).

Auspic. *Epist.ad Arbog.* = Auspicius of Toul, *Epistula ad Arbogastem: MGH Epist.* 3.135–37 no.23 = *MGH Poet.lat.* 4.2.614.

Avit. *Carm., Epist.,* and *Serm.* = Alcimus Ecdicius Avitus, *Carmina, Epistulae,* and *Sermones:* R. Peiper ed., *Alcimi Ecdicii Aviti Viennensis episcopi. Opera quae supersunt, MGH AA* 6.2 (Berlin, 1883).

Basil, *Hom.in divit.* = Basil of Caesarea, *Homilia in divitiis: PG* 31.293–296.

Boniface, bishop of Rome, *Epistulae: PL* 20.

Caes. = Caesarius of Arles: G. Morin ed., *Sancti Caesarii arelatensis, Opera varia. Epistulae, concilia, regulae monasticae, opuscula theologica, testamentum, vita ab eius familiaribus conscripta* (Maretioli, 1942) and *Sermones, Corp.chr.lat.* 103–104 (Turnholt, 1953).

Carm.de prov.dei = *Carmen de providentia dei:* see Prosper of Aquitania.

Cass. *Chron.* = Cassiodorus, *Chronica:* T. Mommsen ed., *Cassiodori senatoris, Chronica ad a. DXIX, MGH AA* 11 = *Chronica minora saec. IV. V. VI. VII.* 2 (Berlin, 1894, repr. Munich, 1981) 109–161.

Cass. *Coll.* = Johannes Cassianus, *Conlationes:* E. Pichery ed., *Jean Cassien, Conférences* (3 vols.) *Sources chrétiennes* 42, 54, 64 (Paris, 1955–1959); E. Petschenig ed., *CSEL* 13 (Vienna, 1886).

Cass. *Inst.* = Johannes Cassianus, *De institutis coenobiorum:* J.-C. Guy ed., *Jean Cassien, Institutions cénobitiques, Sources chrétiennes* 109 (Paris, 1965), M. Petschenig ed., *De institutis coenobiorum et de octo principalium vitiorum remidiis, CSEL* 17 (Vienna, 1888).

Celest. *Epist.* = Celestinus, bishop of Rome, *Epistulae: PL* 50.

Chron.gall.452 = *Chronica gallica anno 452:* T. Mommsen ed., *MGH AA* 9 = *Chronica minora saec. IV. V. VI. VII.* 1 (Berlin, 1892, repr. Berlin, 1961) 615–662.

Chron.gall.511 = *Chronica gallica anno 511:* T. Mommsen ed., *MGH AA* 9 = *Chronica minora saec. IV. V. VI. VII.* 1 (Berlin, 1892, repr. Berlin, 1961).

CJ = *Codex justinianus:* P. Krüger ed., *Corpus iuris civilis,* vol.2, *Codex justinianus* (Berlin, 1954).

Claud. = Claudius Claudianus, *Carmina:* T. Birt ed., *MGH AA* 10 (Berlin 1892).

Claud.Mamert. *De stat.anim.* and *Epist.ad Sapaud.* = Claudianus Mamertus, *De statu animae* and *Epistula ad Sapaudum:* A. Engelbrecht ed., *Claudiani Mamerti opera, CSEL* 11 (Vienna, 1885).

Cod.Eur. = *Codex Euricianus:* K. Zeumer ed., *Codicis Euriciani fragmenta, MGH Leges* 1.1 (Hanover/Leipzig, 1902) 3–27.

Conc.Aquil.: M. Zelzer ed., *Sancti Ambrosi opera. Pars X. Epistulae et acta. Tom. III. Epistularum liber decimus. Epistulae extra collectionem. Gesta concili aquileiensis, CSEL* 82 (Vienne, 1982).

Concilia: C. Munier ed., *Concilia Galliae a.314-a.506, Corp.chr.lat.* 148 (Turnholt, 1963); C. de Clercq ed., *Concilia Galliae a.511-a.695, Corp.chr.lat.* 148A (Turnholt, 1963); C. Munier ed., *Concilia Africae a.345-a.525, Corp.chr.lat.* 149 (Turnholt, 1974); J. Sirmond ed., *Concilia antiqua Galliae* vol.1 (Paris, 1629).

Const. *Epist.ad Pat., Epist.ad Cens.,* and *VGerm.* = Constantius of Lyons, *Epistula ad Patientem, Epistula ad Censurium,* and *Vita s. Germani episcopi Autessiodorensis:* R. Borius ed., *Constance de Lyon. Vie de saint Germain d'Auxerre, Sources chrétiennes* 112 (Paris, 1965); W. Levison ed., *MGH SRM* 7 (Hanover and Leipzig, 1920) 225–283.

Const.extrav. = *Constitutiones extravagantes:* see *Lex.Burg.*

C.Th. = *Codex theodosianus:* T. Mommsen, P. M. Meyer, P. Krüger eds., *Theodosiani libri XVI cum constitutionibus sirmondianis et leges novellae ad Theodosianum pertinentes* (2 vols.) (Berlin, 1905).

De sept.ord.eccl. = *De septem ordinibus ecclesiae: PL* 30.148–161.

Dyn. *VMaximi* = Dynamius of Marseilles, *Vita s. Maximi episcopi Reiensis: PL* 80.31–40.

Ennod. *Carm., Epist.,* and *VEpiphanii* = Magnus Felix Ennodius, *Carmina, Epistulae* and *Vita s. Epifani episcopi Ticinensis ecclesiae:* F. Vogel ed., *Magni Felicis Ennodi. Opera, MGH AA* 7 (Berlin, 1885); G. de Hartel ed., *CSEL* 6 (Vienna, 1882); G. M. Cook, *The Life of Saint Epiphanius by Ennodius. A Translation with an Introduction and Commentary* (Washington, 1942).

Ennod. *VAntonii* = Magnus Felix Ennodius, *Vita Antonii monachi Lerinensis:* PL 63.239–246.

Epist.arel. = *Epistulae arelatenses genuinae:* W. Gundlach ed., *MGH Epist.* 3 (Berlin, 1892) 1–83.

Epist.aust. = *Epistulae austrasicae:* W. Gundlach ed., *MGH Epist.* 3 (Berlin, 1892) 110–153.

Epist.imp. = *Epistulae imperatorum:* O. Guenther ed., *Epistulae imperatorum pontificum aliorum inde ab a.CCCLXVII usque ad a. DLIII datae avellana quae dicitur collectio, CSEL* 35.1–2 (Vienna, 1895–1898).

Epist. "Perlata ad nos" = Leo of Rome, *Epist.* 99: *Corp.chr.lat.* 148 (Turnholt, 1963) 107–110, PL 54.966–970.

Epit.de caes.: = *Epitome de caesaribus:* Fr. Pichlmayr and R. Gruendel eds., *Sextus Aurelius Victor. Liber de caesaribus* (Leipzig: Teubner, 1970) 131–176.

Euch. *De laud.erem., Form., Instruc., Epist.ad Salv.* = Eucherius of Lyons, *De laude heremi ad Hilarium Lirinensem presbyterum epistula, Formulae spiritalis intellegentiae, Instructionum ad Salonium, Epistula ad Salvium:* C. Wotke, *CSEL* 31.1 (Vienna, 1894) p.177ff; S. Pricoco ed., *De laude heremi* (Catania, 1964).

Euch. *Epist.ad Valer.* = Eucherius of Lyons, *Epistula paraenetica ad Valerianum cognatum de contemptu mundi et saecularis philosophia:* PL 50.701–726.

Euch. *Pass.acaun.mart.* = Eucherius of Lyons, *Passio acaunensium martyrum:* B. Krusch ed., *MGH SRM* 3 (Hanover, 1896) 20–41.

Eunap. = Eunapius of Sardis, *Fragmenta:* C. Müller ed., *Fragmenta historicorum graecorum* vol. 4 (Paris, 1885).

Eutrop. *Epist.* = Eutropius presbyter, *Epistulae:* PL 30.45–50, 75–104 (= 57.933–958), 188–210, PLS 1.529–556.

Exposit. = *Expositio totius mundi et gentium:* J. Rougé ed., *Sources chrétiennes* 124 (Paris, 1966).

Faust. *De grat., De spir.sanct., Epist.,* and *Serm.* = Faustus of Riez, *De gratia, De spiritu sancto, Epistulae,* and *Sermones:* F. Glorie ed., *Eusebius 'Gallicanus', Collectio homiliarum, Corp.chr.lat.* 101 (Turnholt, 1970); A. Engelbrecht ed., *Fausti Reiensis praeter sermones pseudo-Eusebianos opera, CSEL* 21 (Vienna, 1891); B. Krusch ed., *Fausti aliorumque epistulae ad Ruricium aliosque, MGH AA* 8 (Berlin, 1887), 265–298.

Faust. *Serm.* "In litaniis" = Faustus of Riez, *Sermo "In litaniis":* PLS 3.605–608.

Faust. *VMaximi* = Faustus of Riez, *Sermo de sancto Maximo episcopo et abbate:* F. Glorie ed., *Corp.chr.lat.* 101 (Turnholt, 1970) 401–412; S. Gennaro ed. (Catania, 1966) pp. 131ff.

Flavius Vegetius Renatus, *Epit.rei mil.* = *Epitoma rei militaris:* C. Lang ed. (Leipzig: Teubner, 1869).

Fred. *Chron.* = Fredegarius scholasticus, *Chronicarum libri IV:* B. Krusch ed., *MGH SRM* 2 (Berlin, 1888) 1–193.

Gennad. *Vir.ill.* = Gennadius, presbyter of Marseilles, *De viris inlustribus:* E. C. Richardson ed., *Texte und Untersuchungen zur Geschichte der altchristlichen Literatur* 14 (Leipzig, 1896); PL 58.1059–1120.

Gest.epp.autiss. = *Gesta episcoporum autissiodorensium:* G. Waitz ed., *MGH Scriptores* 13 (Berlin, 1881) 393–400; *PL* 138.

Gildas, *De excid.* = Gildas Sapiens, *Liber querulus de excidio et conquestu Britanniae:* T. Mommsen ed., *MGH AA* 13 (Berlin, 1898) 25–85.

Greg.Tur. *Glor.conf., Glor.mart., Virt.Mart., Virt.Jul.,* and *VPat.* = Georgius Florentius Gregorius of Tours, *Liber in gloria confessorum, Liber in gloria martyrum, De virtutibus sancti Martini episcopi, Liber de passione et virtutibus sancti Juliani martyris,* and *Liber vitae patrum:* B. Krusch ed., *MGH SRM* 1.2 (Hanover, 1885).

Greg.Tur. *HF* = Georgius Florentius Gregorius of Tours, *Historia Francorum (Libri historiarum X):* B. Krusch and W. Levison eds., *MGH SRM* 1.1 (Hanover, 1951).

Hieron.: see Jerome.

Hil.Arel. *Epist.ad Euch.* = Hilary of Arles, *Epistula ad Eucherium Lugdunensem:* C. Wotke ed., *CSEL* 31 (Vienna, 1894) p. 197.

Hil.Arel., *VHonorati* = Hilary of Arles, *Sermo de vita sancti Honorati:* S. Cavallin ed., *Vitae sanctorum Honorati et Hilarii episcoporum arelatensium,* Publications of the New Society of Letters at Lund 40 (Lund, 1952).

Hil. *Epist.* = Hilarus, bishop of Rome, *Epistulae: PL* 50.20–22; Thiel, *Epistulae* 137–155; *MGH Epist.* 3.

Hon. *VHilarii* = Honoratus of Marseilles, *Vita s. Hilarii episcopi Arelatensis:* S. Cavallin ed., *Vitae sanctorum Honorati et Hilarii episcoporum arelatensium,* Publications of the New Society of Letters at Lund 40 (Lund, 1952).

Hyd. *Chron.* = Hydatius Lemicus, *Chronica:* A. Tranoy ed., *Hydace: Chronique, Sources chrétiennes* 218–219 (Paris, 1974); T. Mommsen ed., *Hydatii Lemici, Continuatio chronicorum hieronymianorum ad a. CCCCLXVIII, MGH AA* 11 = *Chronica minora saec. IV. V. VI. VII.* 2 (Berlin, 1894, repr. Munich, 1981)

Innoc. *Epist.* = Innocent, bishop of Rome, *Epistulae: PL* 20.468–503.

Isid. *Etym.* = Isidore of Seville, *Etymologiarum:* W. M. Lindsay ed., *Isidori Hispalensis episcopi. Etymologiarum sive originum libri XX* (2 vols.) (Oxford, 1911).

Isid. *Vir.ill.* = Isidore of Seville, *De viris inlustribus: PL* 83.1081–1106.

Jer. *Chron.* = Hieronymus, *Chronicon:* R. Helm ed., *Die grieschischen christlichen Schriftsteller der ersten Jahrhunderts* 24 = *Eusebius Werke* 7.1–2 (2d ed.) (Berlin, 1956).

Jer. *Epist.* = Hieronymus, *Epistulae:* J. Labourt ed., *Saint Jérome, Lettres* (8 vols.) (Budé: Paris, 1949–1963); I. Hilberg ed., *CSEL* 54–56 (Vienna, 1910–1918).

Jer. *Vir.ill.* = Hieronymus, *De viris inlustribus:* E. C. Richardson ed., *Texte und Untersuchungen zur Geschichte der altchristlichen Literatur* 14.1 (Leipzig, 1896) 1–56.

Joh.Ant. = John of Antioch, *Fragmenta:* C. Müller ed., *Fragmenta historicorum graecorum* vols. 4–5 (Paris, 1885).

Jord. *Get., Rom.* = Jordanes, *De origine actibusque Getarum* and *De summa temporum vel origine actibusque Romanorum:* T. Mommsen ed., *MGH AA* 5.1 (Berlin, 1882).

Julius Severianus, *Praecepta artis rhetoricae:* K. Halm ed., *Rhetores latini minores* (Leipzig, 1863) 355ff.

Jul.Pom. *Vit.cont.* = Julianus Pomerius, *De vita contemplativa: PL* 59.415ff.

Leo *Epist.* = Leo, bishop of Rome, *Epistulae: PL* 54; *MGH Epist.* 3; *Acta conciliorum oecumenicorum* 2.4.

Lex *Burg.* = *Liber constitutionum sive lex Gundobada* and *Constitutiones extravagantes:* Katherine Fischer Drew trans., *The Burgundian Code. Book of Constitutions or Law of Gundobad.* Additional Enactments (Philadelphia, 1949).

LHF = *Liber historiae Francorum:* B. Krusch ed., *MGH SRM* 2 (Hanover, 1888) p.215ff.

Mar.Avit. *Chron.* = Marius Aventicensis, *Chronica:* T. Mommsen ed., *Marii episcopi Aventicensis, Chronica a. CCCCLV-DLXXXI, MGH AA* 11 = *Chronica minora saec. IV. V. VI. VII.* 2 (Berlin, 1894, repr. Munich, 1981) 225–239.

Marcel. *Chron.* = Marcellinus Comes, *Chronicon:* T. Mommsen ed., *Marcellini v.c. comitis, Chronicon ad a. DXVIII, MGH AA* 11 = *Chronica minora saec. IV. V. VI. VII.* 2 (Berlin, 1894, repr. Munich, 1981).

Narratio de imperatoribus domus Valentinianae et Theodosianae: T. Mommsen ed., *MGH AA* 9 = *Chronica minora saec. IV. V. VI. VII.* 1 (Berlin, 1892, repr. Berlin, 1961) 630.

Naz. = Nazarius: See *Pan.lat.*

Not.dig.occ. = *Notitia dignitatum occidentalis:* O. Seeck ed., *Notitia dignitatum* (Berlin, 1876).

Not.Gall. = *Notitia Galliarum:* T. Mommsen ed., *MGH AA* 9 = *Chronica minora saec. IV. V. VI. VII.* 1 (Berlin, 1892, repr. Berlin, 1961) 552–612.

Olymp. = Olympiodorus of Thebes, *Fragmenta:* C. Müller ed., *Fragmenta historicorum graecorum* vol.4 (Paris, 1885) 57–68.

Orient. *Comm.* = Orientius of Auch, *Commonitorium:* R. Ellis ed., *Orientii Carmina, CSEL* 16 (Vienna, 1886) 191–261.

Oros. *Hist.adv.pag.* = Orosius, *Historia adversum paganos:* C. Zangemeister ed., *Pauli Orosii Historiarum adversum paganos libri VII, CSEL* 5 (Vienna, 1882) and Orosius, *Commonitorium de errore Priscillianistarum et Origenistarum:* G. Schepss ed., *CSEL* 18 (Vienna, 1889).

Pan.lat. = *Panegyrici latini:* E. Galletier ed., *Panégyriques latins (I-XII)* (2 vols.) (Budé: Paris, 1949–1955).

Patrick, *Epist.ad Corot.* = Patricius, *Epistula ad milites Corotici:* L. Bieler ed., "Liber epistolarum sancti Patricii episcopi," *Classica et mediaevalia* 11(1950) 91–102.

Paul.Diac. *Hist.Lang.* = Paulus Diaconus, *Historia Langobardorum:* L. Bethmann and G. Waitz eds., *MGH Scriptores rerum Langobardorum* (Berlin, 1878).

Paul.Diac. *Hist.rom.* = Paulus Diaconus, *Historiae romanae:* Hans Droysen ed., *MGH Auctores antiquissimi* (Berlin, 1879).

Paul. *Epig.* = Paulinus of Béziers, *Epigramma:* C. Schenkl ed., *CSEL* 16 (Vienna, 1888) 503–508.

Paul. *VAmbrosii* = Paulinus, deacon of Milan, *Vita s. Ambrosii: PL* 14.27–46.

Paul.Nol. *Carm.* = Meropius Pontius Paulinus, *Carmina:* G. de Hartel ed., *Sancti Pontii Meropii Paulini Nolani carmina, CSEL* 30 (Vienna, 1894).

Paul.Nol. *Epist.* = Meropius Pontius Paulinus, *Epistulae:* G. de Hartel ed., *Sancti Pontii Meropii Paulini Nolani Epistulae, CSEL* 29 (Vienna, 1894).

Paul.Pell. *Euch.* = Paulinus Pellaeus, *Eucharisticos:* C. Moussy ed., *Sources chrétiennes* 209 (Paris, 1974); G. Brandes ed., *Paulini Pellaei Eucharisticos, CSEL* 16 (Vienna, 1888) 263–334.

Paul.Pet. *Epist.ad Perp.* and *VMartini* = Paulinus of Périgueux, *Epistula ad Perpetuum* and *De vita sancti Martini episcopi libri VI:* M. Petschenig ed., *Paulini Petricordiae quae supersunt, CSEL* 16 (Vienna, 1888) 1–190.

Philostorg. *HE* = Philostorgius, *Historia ecclesiastica,* J. Bidez ed., *Die grieschischen christlichen Schriftsteller der ersten Jahrhunderts* 21 (Leipzig, 1913).

Poema coniugis ad uxorem: see Prosper of Aquitania.

Polem.Silv. *Laterc.* = Polemius Silvius, *Laterculus anni CCCCXLIX:* T. Mommsen ed., *MGH AA* 9 = *Chronica minora saec. IV. V. VI. VII.* 1 (Berlin, 1892, repr. Berlin, 1961) 511–559.

Possidius, *Vita Augustini:* H. T. Weiskotten ed., *Sancti Augustini vita scripta a Possidio episcopo* (Princeton, 1919).

Prisc. = Priscus of Panium, *Fragmenta:* F. Bornmann ed., *Prisci Panitae Fragmenta* (Florence, 1970).

Prosp. *Chron.* = Prosper Tiro, *Epitoma chronicon:* T. Mommsen ed., *MGH AA* 9 = *Chronica minora saec. IV. V. VI. VII.* 1 (Berlin, 1892, repr. Berlin, 1961) 341–499.

Prosp. *Contr.coll., Epist.ad Ruf.* = Prosper of Aquitania, *De gratia dei et libero arbitrio contra collatorem* and *Epistula ad Rufinum de gratia et libero arbitrio,* also *Pro Augustino responsiones ad capitula obiectionum Gallorum calumniantium, Carmen de providentia dei* [?], *Epigrammata in obtrectatorem Augustini, Epitaphium Nestorianae et Pelagianae haereseon, De ingratis, Poema coniugis ad uxorem* [?], *De vocatione omnium gentium: PL* 51; Michael P. McHugh, *The Carmen de providentia dei Attributed to Prosper of Aquitaine: A Revised Text with an Introduction, Translation, and Notes* (Washington, 1964).

Querolus: F. Corsaro ed. (Catania, 1964); R. Peiper ed., *Aulularia sive Querolus Theodosiani aevi comoedia Rutilio dedicata* (Leipzig: Teubner, 1875).

Ruric. *Epist.* = Ruricius, *Epistulae:* A. Engelbrecht ed., *Ruricii epistularum libri duo, CSEL* 21 (Vienna, 1891), 349–450; B. Krusch ed., *Ruricii epistulae, MGH AA* 8 (Berlin, 1887), 299–350.

Rutil.Namat. *De red.* = Rutilius Claudius Namatianus, *De reditu suo:* E. Doblhofer ed., *Rutilius Claudius Namatianus. De reditu suo sive Iter Gallicum* (Heidelberg, 1972); J. Vessereau and F. Préchac eds., *Rutilius Namatianus, Sur son retour* (Budé: Paris, 1933).

Sallust, *Bell.jurg.* = Sallust, *Bellum jugurthinum:* J. C. Rolfe ed. (London: Loeb, 1971).

Salv. *Ad eccl., De gub.,* and *Epist.* = Salvian of Marseilles, *De gubernatione dei, Ad ecclesiam sive adversus avaritiam,* and *Epistulae:* G. Lagarrigue ed., *Salvien de Marseille. Oeuvres, Sources chrétiennes* 176, 220 (Paris, 1971–1975); F. Pauly ed., *Salviani presbyteri Massiliensis opera omnia, CSEL* 7 (Vienna, 1883); C.

Halm ed., *Salviani presbyteri Massiliensis libri qui supersunt, MGH AA* 1.1 (Berlin, 1877).

SHA = *Scriptores historiae augustae:* H. Peter ed., *Scriptores historiae augustae* (Leipzig, 1894).

Sid.Apoll. *Carm.* and *Epist.* = Sidonius Apollinaris, *Carmina* and *Epistulae:* A. Loyen ed., *Sidoine Apollinaire: Poemes* (Paris, 1960) and vols. 2–3, *Sidoine Apollinaire: Lettres* (Paris, 1970); W. B. Anderson, *Sidonius Apollinaris: Poems and Letters I-II* (Loeb: London, 1936–1965); P. Mohr ed., *C. Sollius Apollinaris Sidonius* (Teubner: Leipzig, 1895); C. Leutjohann ed., *Gai Sollii Apollinaris Sidonii epistulae et carmina, MGH AA* 8 (Berlin, 1887).

Sirm: see *C.Th.*

Soc. *HE* = Socrates, *Historia ecclesiastica:* R. Hussey ed. (Oxford, 1853); *PG* 67.

Soz. *HE* = Sozomen, *Historia ecclesiastica:* J. Bidez and G. C. Hanson eds., *Die grieschischen christlichen Schriftsteller der ersten Jahrhunderts* 50 (Berlin, 1960); *PG* 67.

Stat.eccl.ant. = *Statuta ecclesiae antiqua:* C. Munier ed., *Corp.chr.lat.* 148 (Turnholt, 1963) 162–188.

Sulp.Sev. *Chron.*, *Dial.*, *Epist.* and *VMart.* = Sulpicius Severus, *Chronicorum libri II, Dialogi, Epistulae* and *Vita s. Martini episcopi Turonensis:* J. Fontaine ed., *Sulpice Sévère, Vie de saint Martin*, vol. 1. *Introduction, texte et traduction* and vols. 2–3, *Commentaire et index, Sources chrétiennes* 133–135 (Paris, 1967–1969); C. Halm ed., *Sulpicius Severus, Libri qui supersunt, CSEL* 1 (Vienna, 1866).

Symm. *Epist.*, *Orat.*, and *Rel.* = Q. Aurelius Symmachus, *Epistulae, Orationes,* and *Relationes:* O. Seeck ed., *Q. Aurelii Symmachi quae supersunt, MGH AA* 6.1 (Berlin, 1883).

Synesius of Cyrene, *On Royalty:* Chr. Lacombarde ed., *Le discours sur la royauté de Synésios de Cyrène à l'empereur Arcadios* (Paris: Belles Lettres, 1951).

Theoph. *Chron.* = Theophanes, *Chronographia:* C. de Boor ed. (Leipzig: Teubner, 1883).

Uran. *Epist.ad Pacat.* = Uranius, *Epistula ad Pacatum:* *PL* 53.858–866.

Valer. *Hom.* and *Epist.ad mon.* = Valerianus of Cimiez, *Homiliae* and *Epistula ad monachos:* *PL* 52.691–758.

Ven.Fort. = Venantius Fortunatus, *Carmina:* F. Leo and B. Krusch eds., *MGH AA* 4 (Berlin, 1881–1885).

Ven. Fort. *VLeobini*, *VSeverini*, and *VGerm.Par.* = Venantius Fortunatus, *Vita s. Leobini:* B. Krusch ed., *MGH AA* 4.2 (Berlin, 1885, repr. Berlin, 1961) 73–82 (spurious); *Vita s. Severini Burdigalensis* and *Vita s. Germani Parisiensis:* W. Levison ed., *MGH SRM* 7 (Berlin, 1920) 219–224, 372–418.

Vict.Aquit. *Curs.pasch.* = Victorius of Aquitania, *Cursus paschalis annorum DXXXII ad Hilarum archidiaconum ecclesiae romanae a. CCCCLVII:* T. Mommsen ed., *MGH AA* 9 = *Chronica minora saec. IV. V. VI. VII.* 1 (Berlin, 1892, repr. Berlin, 1961) 667–735.

Vict.Tonn. *Chron.* = Victor Tonnennensis, *Chronica:* T. Mommsen ed., *Victoris episcopi Tonnennensis, Chronica a. CCCCXLIV-DLXVII, MGH AA* 11 =

Chronica minora saec. IV. V. VI. VII. 2 (Berlin, 1894, repr. Munich, 1981) 163–206.

Vict.Vit. *Hist.persecut.* = Victor Vitensis, *Historia persecutionis africanae provinciae,* M. Petschenig ed., *CSEL* 7 (Vienna, 1881) 1–107.

Vinc. *Comm.* = Vincentius of Lérins, *Commonitorium seu tractatus Peregrini:* R. S. Moxon ed. (Cambridge, 1915); *PL* 50.625–686.

Zos. *Epist.* = Zosimus, bishop of Rome, *Epistulae: MGH Epist.* 3; *CSEL* 35; *PL* 20.

Zos. *Hist.nov.* = Zosimus, *Historia nova:* F. Paschoud ed., *Zosime. Histoire nouvelle* (Paris: Budé, 1971ff).

SAINTS' LIVES

VAlbini = *Vita s. Albini episcopi Catalaunensis: AASS* September III 85–89.

VAmbrosii: see Paulinus, deacon of Milan.

VAniani = *Vita s. Aniani episcopi Aurelianensis:* B. Krusch ed., *MGH SRM* 3 (Hanover, 1896) 108–117.

VAntidii = *Vita s. Antidii episcopi Vesontionensis: AASS* June VI 36–47.

VAntonii: see Magnus Felix Ennodius.

VAuctoris = *Vita s. Auctoris episcopi Mettensis:* L. Pertz ed., *MGH SRM* 2 (Berlin, 1888) 262–263.

VAugustini: see Possidius.

VAvit.Miciac. = *Vita s. Aviti abbatis Miciacensis: AASS* June IV 284–290; and B. Krusch ed., *MGH SRM* 3 (Hanover, 1896) 383–385.

VCaesarii: see Caesarius of Arles.

VCaprasii = *Vita s. Caprasii abbatis Lirinensis: AASS* June I 75–78.

VConsortiae = *Vita s. Consortiae: AASS* June V 214–217.

VDan.Styl. = *Vita Danielis Stylitae: Analecta bollandiana* 32(1913) 121–214.

VDomitiani = *Vita s. Domitiani: AASS* July I 45–50.

VDomnoli = *Vita s. Domnoli episcopi Cenomanensis: AASS* May III 606–612.

VEparchi = *Vita s. Eparchii reclusi Encolismensis:* B. Krusch ed., *MGH SRM* 3 (Berlin, 1896) 553–560.

VEpiphanii: see Magnus Felix Ennodius.

VEptadii = *Vita s. Eptadii presbyteri Cervidunensis:* B. Krusch ed., *MGH SRM* 3 (Berlin, 1896) 186–194.

VEugendi = *Vita sancti Eugendi abbatis:* F. Martine ed., *Vie des pères du Jura,* Sources chrétiennes 142 (Paris, 1968) 364–435.

VEuspicii = *Vita s. Euspicii confessoris: AASS* July V 74–76.

VEutropi = Verus of Orange, *Vita s. Eutropii episcopi Arausicensis:* P. Varin ed., *Vie de saint Eutrope évêque d'Orange, Bulletin de Comité Historique des Monuments Ecrits de l'Histoire de France* 1 (1849) 52–64.

VFelicis = *Vita s. Felicis episcopi Treverensis: AASS* March II 612–622.

VFursei = *Vita s. Fursei abbatis Latiniacensis:* B. Krusch ed., *MGH SRM* 4 (Berlin, 1902) 434–440

VGenovefae = *Vita s. Genovefae virginis Parisiensis:* B. Krusch ed., *MGH SRM* 3 (Berlin, 1896) 215–238.

VGermani: see Constantius of Lyons.

VGerm.Par. = *Vita Germani episcopi Parisiensis:* see Venantius Fortunatus.

VHilarii: see Honoratus of Marseilles.

VHonorati: see Hilary of Arles, *Sermo de vita sancti Honorati.*

VIohannis = *Vita s. Iohannis abbatis Reomaensis:* B. Krusch ed., *MGH SRM* 32 (Hanover, 1896) 505–517.

VIusti = *Vita Iusti episcopi Lugdunensis: AASS* Sept. I 373–374.

VLauteni = *Vita s. Lauteni abbatis: AASS* November I 284–286

VLeobini: see Venantius Fortunatus.

VLupi = *Vita s. Lupi episcopi Tricassinae:* B. Krusch ed., *MGH SRM* 7 (Hanover-Leipzig, 1920) 284–302.

VLupicini = *Vita sancti Lupicini abbatis:* F. Martine ed., *Vie des pères du Jura, Sources chrétiennes* 142 (Paris, 1968) 308–363.

VMarcelli = *Vita s. Marcelli episcopi Deensis:* see F. Dolbeau and G. Kirner in Secondary Bibliography.

VMarcellini = *Vita s. Marcellini episcopi Ebredunensis: AASS* April II 749–752.

VMartini: see Sulpicius Severus.

VMaximi: see Dynamius of Marseilles and Faustus of Riez.

VMaxim.Trev. = Lupus Ferrariensis, *Vita s. Maximini episcopi Treverensis: PL* 119.665ff.

VMelanii = *Vita s. Melanii episcopi Trecensis:* H. Moretius ed., *Analecta bollandiana* 24–25 (1915–1916) 289–292.

VOrientii = *Vita s. Orientii episcopi Ausciensis: AASS* May I 60–65.

VPauli = *Vita Pauli Tricastinensis episcopi: Analecta bollandiana* 11(1892) 374–383.

VPaulini = *Vita s. Paulini episcopi Treverensis: AASS* August VI 676ff.

VRemedii = *Vita sancti Remedii:* B. Krusch ed., *MGH AA* 4.2 (Berlin, 1885; repr. Berlin, 1961) 64–67.

VRomani = *Vita sancti Romani abbatis:* F. Martine ed., *Vie des pères du Jura, Sources chrétiennes* 142 (Paris, 1968) 242–307.

VServatii = *Vita s. Servatii episcopi Tungrensis:* B. Krusch ed., *MGH SRM* 3 (Berlin, 1896) 87–91.

VSeverini = see Venantius Fortunatus.

VSolemnis = *Vita s. Solemnis episcopi Carnotensis:* W. Levison ed., *MGH SRM* 7 (Berlin, 1920) 311–321.

VThuribii = *Vita s. Thuribii episcopi Cenomanensis: AASS* April II 413–417.

VViviani = *Vita s. Viviani episcopi Santonensis:* B. Krusch ed., *MGH SRM* 3 (Hanover, 1896) 92–100.

VWandregesili = *Vita s. Wandregesili: AASS* July V 265ff.

SECONDARY
BIBLIOGRAPHY

Achard, G. "L'emploi de 'boni, boni viri, boni cives' et de leurs formes superlatives dans l'action politique de Cicéron." *Etudes classiques* 41 (1973): 207–221.

Alföldi, Andrew. *A Conflict of Ideas in the Late Roman Empire. The Clash between the Senate and Valentinian I.* Translated by Harold Mattingly. Oxford: Clarendon Press, 1952.

Allard, Paul. "Sidoine Apollinaire sous les règnes d'Avitus et de Majorien." *Revue des questions historiques* 83 (1908): 426–452.

Altheim, Franz. *Geschichte der Hunnen* 5 vols. Berlin: W. de Gruyter, 1959–1962.

Applebaum, Shimon. "The Late Gallo-Roman Rural Pattern in the Light of the Carolingian Cartularies." *Latomus* 23 (1964): 774–787.

Arnheim, M. T. W. *The Senatorial Aristocracy in the Later Roman Empire.* Oxford: Clarendon Press, 1972.

Arnold, Carl Franklin. *Caesarius von Arelate und die gallische Kirche von seiner Zeit.* Leipzig: J. C. Hinrichs, 1894. Reprint. Leipzig: Zentralantiquariat der DDR, 1972.

Arsac, P. "La dignité sénatoriale au Bas-Empire." *Revue historique de droit français et étranger* 47 (1969): 198–243.

Auer, J. "Militia Christi. Zur Geschichte eines christlichen Grundbildes." *Geist und Leben* 32 (1959): 340–350.

Auerbach, Erich. *Literary Language and Its Public in Late Antiquity and the Middle Ages.* Translated by Ralph Manheim. New York: Pantheon Books, 1965.

Aymard, André. "Les ôtages barbares au début de l'empire." *Journal of Roman Studies* 51 (1961): 44–66.

Bach, A. *Deutsche Namenkunde. I: Die deutschen Personennamen.* 2d ed. Heidelberg: C. Winter, 1953.

Bach, E. "Théoderic: Romain ou barbare?" *Byzantion* 25–27 (1935–1937): 413–420.

Bachrach, Bernard S. "The Alans in Gaul." *Traditio* 23 (1967): 476–489.

———. "Another Look at the Barbarian Settlement in Southern Gaul." *Traditio* 25 (1969): 354–358.

———. *A History of the Alans in the West.* Minneapolis: University of Minnesota Press, 1973.

————. "A Note on Alites." *Byzantinische Zeitschrift* 61 (1968): 35.

Badewien, Jan. *Geschichtstheologie und Sozialkritik im Werk Salvians von Marseille.* Göttingen: Vandenhoeck & Ruprecht, 1980.

Baldwin, Barry. "Literature and Society in the Later Roman Empire." In *Literary and Artistic Patronage in Ancient Rome*, edited by Barbara K. Gold. Austin: University of Texas Press, 1982, 67–83.

Balsdon, John P. V. D. "Auctoritas, Dignitas, Otium." *Classical Quarterly* 10 (1960): 43–50.

————. *Romans and Aliens.* Chapel Hill: University of North Carolina Press, 1979.

Bang, Martin. *Die Germanen im römischen Dienst bis zum Regierungsantritt Constantins I.* Berlin: Weidmann, 1906.

Banniard, Michel. "L'aménagement de l'histoire chez Grégoire de Tours: à propos de l'invasion de 451 (H.F. II 5–7)." *Romanobarbarica* 3 (1978): 5–38.

Barbieri, G. *L'Albo Senatorio da Settimio Severo a Carino, 193–282.* Rome: A. Signorelli, 1952.

Bardy, Gustave. "Pélerinages à Rome vers la fin du IVe siècle," *Analecta bollandiana* 67 (1949): 224–235.

Barnes, Timothy D. "Who were the Nobility of the Roman Empire?" *Phoenix* 28 (1974): 444–449.

Barnish, Samuel J. "Taxation, Land and Barbarian Settlement in the Western Empire." *Papers of the British School at Rome* 54 (1986): 170–195.

————. "Transformation and Survival in the Western Senatorial Aristocracy, c. A.D. 400–700." *Papers of the British School at Rome* 56 (1988): 120–155.

Barrett, John C., Andrew P. Fitzpatrick, and Lesley Macinnes, eds. *Barbarians and Romans in North-West Europe: From the Later Republic to Late Antiquity.* Oxford: British Archaeological Reports, 1989.

Battisti, C. "Latini e Germani nella Gallia del Nord nei secoli VII e VIII." *Settimane di Studio del Centro Italiano di Studi sull'Alto Medioevo.* Vol. 5, 445–484. Spoleto, 1958.

Bayless, William N. "The Peace of 439 A.D.: Avitus and the Visigoths." *Ancient World* 1 (1978): 141–143.

Baynes, Norman. "The Decline of Roman Power in Western Europe and Its Modern Explanations." *Byzantine Studies and Other Essays.* London: Athlone Press, 1955, 83–96.

Beck, Henry G. J. *The Pastoral Care of Souls in South-East France during the Sixth Century.* Analecta Gregoriana 51. Rome: Gregorian University, 1950.

Benoit, Fernand. "Des fragments de sarcophage chrétiens ou d'époque chrétienne datés, provenent des Aliscamps." *Bulletin de la Société Nationale des Antiquaires de France* (1938): 171–183.

————. "L'Hilarianum d'Arles et les missions en Bretagne (Ve-VIe siècle)" In le Bras-Gilson, eds., *St. Germain*, 181–189.

Bergmann, Wilhelm. *Studien zu einer kritischen Sichtung der südgallischen Predigtliteratur des 5. und 6. Jahrhunderts.* Leipzig: Dieterich'sche Verlag, 1898. Reprint. Aalen: Scientia Verlag, 1972.

Bertolini, O. "L'aristocrazia senatoria e il senato di Roma come forza politica sotto i regni di Odoacre e di Teodorico." In *Atti del primo Congresso Nazionale di Studi Romani*, 462–475. Vol. 1. Rome, 1929.

Beyerle, F. "Zur Frühgeschichte der westgotischen Gesetzgebung." *Zeitschrift der Savigny-Stiftung fur Rechtsgeschichte, Germanistische Abteilung* 67 (1950): 1–33.

Bianchini, M. "Ancora in tema di unione fra barbari e romani." In *Atti dell'Accademia Romanistica Constantiniana. VII Convegno Internazionale. 16–19Ottobre, 1985. Perugia*, 225–249. Naples: Edizioni scientifiche italiane, 1988.

Blasquez, J. M. "The Rejection and Assimilation of Roman Culture in Hispania during the Fourth and Fifth Centuries." *Classical Folia* 32 (1978): 217–242.

Bleicken, J. "Die Nobilität der römischen Republik." *Gymnasium* 88 (1981): 236–253.

Bloch, M. "Observations sur la conquête de la Gaule romaine par les rois francs." *Revue historique* 154 (1927): 161–178.

Blockley, Roger C. "Constantius the Gaul, Secretary to Attila and Bleda." *Classical Views* 6.3 (1987): 355–357.

———. "Roman-Barbarian Marriages in the Late Empire." *Florilegium* 4 (1982): 63–79.

Bouchard, Constance B. "The Origins of the French Nobility: A Reassessment." *American Historical Review* 86 (1981): 501–532.

Bratton, Timothy L. *Tours: From Roman Civitas to Merovingian Episcopal Center c. 275–650 A.D.* (dissertation: Bryn Mawr, 1979: Ann Arbor, Mich.: University Microfilms, 1980).

Brennan, Brian. "Senators and Social Mobility in Sixth-Century Gaul." *Journal of Medieval History* 11 (1985): 145–161.

Brezzi, Paolo. "Impero romano e regni barbarici nella valutazione degli scrittori Christiani alla fine del mondo antico." *Studi Romani* 7 (1959): 260–270.

———. "Romani e barbari nel giudizio degli scrittori cristiani dei secoli IV-VI." *Settimane di Studio del Centro Italiano di Studi sull'Alto Medioevo*. Vol. 9, 565–593. Spoleto, 1962.

Brown, Peter R. L. "Aspects of the Christianization of the Roman Aristocracy." *Journal of Roman Studies* 51 (1961): 1–11.

———. *The Cult of Saints: Its Rise and Function in Latin Christianity*. Chicago: University of Chicago Press, 1981.

———. "The Patrons of Pelagius: The Roman Aristocracy between East and West." *Journal of Theological Studies* 21 (1970): 56–72.

———. *Religion and Society in the Age of St. Augustine*. New York: Harper and Row, 1972.

———. "The Rise and Function of the Holy Man in Late Antiquity." *Journal of Roman Studies* 61 (1971): 80–101. (Also published in Peter R. L. Brown, *Society and the Holy in Late Antiquity*, 103–152. Berkeley: University of California Press, 1982).

———. *Society and the Holy in Late Antiquity*. Berkeley: University of California Press, 1982.

———. *The World of Late Antiquity*. New York: Harcourt, Brace, Jovanovich, 1974.

Brugière, Marie-Bernadette. *Littérature et droit dans la Gaule du Ve siècle*. Paris: Presses Universitaires de France, 1974.

Brunt, P. A. "*Nobilitas* and *Novitas*." *Journal of Roman Studies* 72 (1982): 1–17.

Buchner, Rudolf. *Die Provence in merowingischer Zeit*. Stuttgart, 1933.

Burns, Thomas S. "The Barbarians and the *Scriptores Historiae Augustae*." *Latomus* 164 (1979): 521–540.

———. "Ennodius and the Ostrogothic Settlement." *Classical Folia* 32 (1978): 153–168.

———. "The Germans and Roman Frontier Policy (ca. A.D. 350–378)." *Arheoloski Vestnik* 32 (1981): 390–404.

———. *History of the Ostrogoths*. Bloomington: University of Indiana Press, 1984.

———. *Ostrogoths: Kingship and Society*. Historia Einzelschriften, vol.36. Wiesbaden: Franz Steiner, 1980.

———. "Theodoric the Great and the Concepts of Power in Late Antiquity." *Acta Classica* (Capetown) 25 (1982): 99–118.

Bury, John B. *History of the Later Roman Empire from the Death of Theodosius I to the Death of Justinian (A.D. 395 to A.D. 565)*. 2d ed. London: MacMillan and Co., 1923.

———. *The Invasion of Europe by the Barbarians*. London: MacMillan and Co., 1928.

Butler, R. M. "Late Roman Town Walls in Gaul." *Archaeological Journal* 116 (1959): 25–50.

Byvanck, A. W. "Les Burgondes dans la Germanie Seconde." *Mnemosyne* 73 (1938–1939): 75–79.

Caló Levi, Annalina. *Barbarians on Roman Imperial Coins and Sculpture*. American Numismatic Society Numismatic Notes and Monographs, no. 123. New York: American Numismatic Society, 1952.

Cameron, Alan. "Rutilius Namatianus, St. Augustine, and the Date of the *De reditu*." *Journal of Roman Studies* 57 (1967): 31–39.

Cameron, Alan, Jacqueline Long, and L. Sherry. *Barbarians and Politics at the Court of Arcadius*. Berkeley: University of California Press, 1990.

Carette, E. *Les assemblées provinciales de la Gaule romaine*. Paris: A. Picard et fils, 1895.

Chadwick, Nora K. "Intellectual Contacts between Britain and Gaul in the Fifth Century." In *Studies in Early British History*, edited by Nora K. Chadwick, 189–263. Cambridge: Cambridge University Press, 1959.

———. *Poetry and Letters in Early Christian Gaul*. London, 1955. Reprint. Hamden, Conn.: Archon Books, 1973.

Chaffin, Christopher. "Civic Values in Maximus of Turin and His Contemporaries." In *Forma Futuri. Studi in Onore di Michele Pellegrino*, 1041–1053. Padua: Bottega d'Erasmo, 1975.

Charanis, Peter. "On the Social Structure of the Later Roman Empire." *Byzantion* 17 (1944–1945): 39–57.

Charaux, Augustus. *Tonantius Ferreolus provinciae Galliae praefectus, Imp. Valentiniano III*. Besançon: Armand Colin, 1876.

Chastagnol, André. "L'évolution de l'ordre sénatorial aux IIIe et IVe siècles de notre ère." *Revue historique* 244 (1970): 305–314.

———. " 'Latus clavus' et 'adlectio': L'accès des hommes nouveaux au sénat romain sous le haut-empire." *Revue historique du droit* 53 (1975): 375–394.

———. "Les modes de recrutement de sénat au IVe siècle après J.-C." *Recherches sur les structures sociales dans l'antiquité classique* (Paris, 1970): 187–206.

———. "La naissance de l'ordo senatorius." *Mélanges de l'Ecole Française de Rome. Moyen âge* 85 (1973): 583–607.

———. "Le repli sur Arles des services administratifs gaulois en l'an 407 de notre ère." *Revue historique* 249 (1973): 34–40.

———. *Le sénat romain sous le règne d'Odoacre. Recherches sur l'épigraphie du Colisée au 5e siècle.* Bonn: Habelt, 1966.

———. "Sidoine Apollinaire et le sénat de Rome." *Acta antiqua* (Budapest) 26 (1978): 57–70.

Chatillon, F. "Dardanus et Theopolis (409–417)." *Bulletin de la Societé d'Etudes Historiques Scientifiques et Littéraires des Hautes-Alpes* 62 (1943): 29–151.

Chauvot, Alain. "Représentations du *Barbaricum* chez les barbares au service de l'Empire au IVe siècle après J.-C." *Ktema. Civilisations de l'Orient, de la Grèce et de Rome antiques* 9 (1984): 145–157.

Christ, Karl. "Römer und Barbaren in der hohen Kaiserzeit." *Saeculum* 10 (1959): 273–288.

Christol, M. "L'origine de quelques familles arlésiennes." *Bulletin de la Société des Antiquaires de France* (1973): 117–118.

Chrysos, Evangelios K. "Die angebliche 'Nobilitierung' des Klerus durch Kaiser Konstantin den Grossen." *Historia* 18 (1969): 119–129.

———. "Gothia Romana. Zur Rechtslage des Föderatenlandes der Westgoten im 4. Jhdt." *Dacoromania* 1 (1973): 52–64.

———. "Legal Concepts and Patterns for the Barbarian's Settlement on Roman Soil." In *Das Reich und die Barbaren*, edited by Evangelios K. Chrysos and Andreas Schwarcz, 13–23. Vienna-Cologne: Böhlau Verlag, 1989.

Chrysos, Evangelios K., and Andreas Schwarcz, eds. *Das Reich und die Barbaren.* Vienna-Cologne: Böhlau Verlag, 1989.

Classen, P. "Kaiserreskript und Königsurkunde. Diplomatische Studien zum römisch-germanischen Kontinuitätsproblem." *Archiv für Diplomatik* 1.2 (1955–1956): 1–115.

Claude, Dietrich. "Zur Ansiedlung barbarischer Föderaten in der ersten Halfte des 5. Jahrhunderts." In *Anerkennung und Integration. Zu den wirtschaftlichen Grundlagen der Völkenwanderungszeit 400–600*, edited by Herwig Wolfram and Andreas Schwarcz, 13–16. Vienna: Österreichische Akademie der Wissenschaft, 1988.

———. "Zur Begründung familiärer Beziehungen zwischen dem Kaiser und barbarischen Herrschern." In *Anerkennung und Integration. Zu den wirtschaftlichen Grundlagen der Völkenwanderungszeit 400–600*, edited by Herwig Wolfram and Andreas Schwarcz, 25–56. Vienna: Österreichische Akademie der Wissenschaft, 1988.

————. "Die Bestellung der Bischöfe im merowingischen Reiche." *Zeitschrift der Savigny-Stiftung fur Rechtsgeschichte, Kanonistische Abteilung* 49 (1963): 1–75.

Cleland, D. J. "Salvian and the Vandals." *Studia patristica* 10 (1970): 270–274.

Cloché, P. "Les élections épiscopales sous les mérovingiens." *Le moyen âge* 26 (1924–1925): 203–254.

Clover, Frank M. "The Family and Early Career of Anicius Olybrius." *Historia* 27 (1978): 169–196.

————. *Flavius Merobaudes. A Translation and Historical Commentary.* Transactions of the American Philosopical Society, n.s. vol. 1.1. Philadelphia, 1971.

————. "The Pseudo-Boniface and the Historia Augusta." *Beiträge zur Historia-Augusta-Forschung* 14 (1980): 73–95.

————. "The Symbiosis of Romans and Vandals in Africa." In *Das Reich und die Barbaren*, edited by Evangelios K. Chrysos and Andreas Schwarcz, 57–73. Vienna-Cologne: Böhlau Verlag, 1989.

Clover, Frank M., and R. Stephen Humphreys, eds. *Tradition and Innovation in Late Antiquity.* Madison: University of Wisconsin Press, 1989.

Colin, Jean. "Sénateurs gaulois à Rome et gouverneurs romains en Gaule au IIIe siècle." *Latomus* 13 (1954): 218–228.

Consolino, Franca Ela. *Ascesi e mondanita nella Gallia tardoantica. Studi sulla figura del vescovo nei secoli IV-VI.* Naples: Associazione di studi tardoantichi, 1979.

Corbett, John H. "The Saint as Patron in the Work of Gregory of Tours." *Journal of Medieval History* 7 (1981): 1–13.

Courcelle, Pierre. *Histoire littéraire des grandes invasions germaniques.* 3rd ed. Paris: Etudes augustiniennes, 1964.

————. *Les lettres grecques en Occident, de Macrobe à Cassiodore.* 2d ed. Paris: E. de Boccard, 1948. (Also published as *Late Latin Writers and their Greek Sources.* Translated by Harry E. Wedeck. Cambridge, Mass.: Harvard University Press, 1969.)

————. "Nouveaux aspects de la culture lérinienne." *Revue des études latines* 46 (1968): 379–409.

————. "Sur quelques textes littéraires relatifs aux grandes invasions." *Revue belge* 13 (1953): 23–37.

————. "Trois diners chez le roi wisigoth d'Aquitaine." *Revue des études anciennes* 49 (1947): 169–177.

Cracco Ruggini, L.P. "Nobilitá romana e potere nell'età de Boezio." In *Atti del congresso internationale di studi Boeziani*, edited by Luca Obertello, 73–96. Rome: Herder, 1981.

Cristiani, Leon. *Lérins et ses fondateurs: Saint Honorat, Saint Hilaire d'Arles, Saint Eucher de Lyon.* S. Wandrille, 1946.

————. *Saint Eucher de Lyon. Du méprise du monde.* Paris: Nouvelles Editions Latines, 1950.

Croidys, P. *Sainte Geneviève et les barbares: la splendeur du christianisme au Ve siècle.* Paris, 1946.

Croke, Brian. "A.D. 476: The Manufacture of a Turning Point." *Chiron* 13 (1983): 81–119.

———. "Arbogast and the Death of Valentinian II." *Historia* 25 (1976): 235–244.

Cunliffe, Barry. *Greeks, Romans, and Barbarians: Spheres of Interaction.* London: Batsford, 1988.

Curtius, Ernst R. *Europäische Literatur und lateinisches Mittelalter.* 6th ed. Bern: Francke, 1967.

Czúth, Béla. "Die Rolle des Volkes zur Zeit der Belagerung des Orleans durch Attila (Juni der Jahre 451) (*Vita s. Aniani,* 3.10)." *Acta historica* (Szeged) 76 (1983): 3–9.

Daly, L. J. "The Mandarin and the Barbarians. The Response of Themistius to the Gothic Challenge." *Historia* 21 (1972): 351–379.

Dauge, Yves Albert. *Le barbare. Recherches sur la conception romaine de la barbarie et de la civilisation.* Collection Latomus 176. Brussels, 1981.

Declareuil, J. "Les curies municipales et le clergé au Bas-Empire." *Revue historique du droit française et étranger* 14 (1935): 26–53.

de Coulanges, Fustel. *Histoire des institutions politiques de l'ancienne France.* 7 vols. Paris: Hachette, 1875. Revised by C. Jullian. Paris: Hachette, 1922–1924. Reprint. Brussels: Culture et Civilisation, 1964.

Dekkers, Eligius, and Aemilius Gaar, eds. *Clavis patrum latinorum, qua in novum corpus christianorum edendum optimas quasque scriptorum recensiones a Tertulliano ad Bedam.* 2d ed. Turnhout: Brepols, 1961.

de Laet, Siegfried J. *De Samenstelling van den romeinschen Senaat gedurende de eerste eeuw van het Principaat (28 voor Chr.-68 no Chr.)* Antwerp: De Sikkei, 1941.

Delaruelle, E. "Toulouse capitale wisigothique et son rempart." *Annales dui Midi* 67 (1955): 205–221.

Delehaye, Hippolyte. *Les passions des martyrs et les genres littéraires.* 2d ed. Brussels: Société des Bollandistes, 1966.

della Corte, Francesco. "Rutilio Namaziano ad *Albingaunum.*" *Romanobarbarica* 5 (1980): 89–103.

Demandt, Alexander. "Das Ende des Altertums in metaphorischer Deutung." *Gymnasium* 87 (1980): 178–204.

———. *Der Fall Roms. Die Auflösung des römischen Reiches im Urteil der Nachwelt.* Munich: C. H. Beck, 1984.

———. "Magister militum." In Pauly-Wissowa-Kroll, *Real-Encyclopädie,* supp. 12 (1970), 553–790.

———. "The Osmosis of Late Roman and Germanic Aristocracies." In *Das Reich und die Barbaren,* edited by Evangelios K. Chrysos and Andreas Schwarcz, 75–87. Vienna-Cologne: Böhlau Verlag, 1989.

———. "Der spätrömische Militäradel." *Chiron* 10 (1980): 609–636.

de Mattei, R. "Sul concetto di barbaro e barbarie nel medio evo." In *Studi di storia e diritto in onore di Enrico Besta,* 483–501. Vol. 4. Milan: Giuffre, 1939.

de Montauzan, Germain. "Saint-Eucher, évêque de Lyon et l'école de Lérins." *Bulletin historique du diocèse de Lyon* 2 (1923): 81–96.

Demougeot, Emilienne. "Attila et les Gaules." *Bulletin de la Societé d'Agriculture, Commerce, Sciences et Arts du Département de la Marne* 73 (1958): 7–42.

———. "Constantin III, l'empereur d'Arles." In *Hommage à André Dupont*, 83–125. Montpellier: Féderation historique du Languedoc mediterranéen et de Roussillon, 1974.

———. "Le *conubium* dans les lois barbares du VIe siècle." *Recueil de memoires et travaux publié par la Societe d'Histoire du Droit et des Institutions des Anciens Pays de Droit Ecrit* 12 (1983): 69–82.

———. *L'Empire romain et les barbares d'occident (IVe-VIIe siècles). Scripta varia.* Paris: Publications de la Sorbonne, 1988.

———. "La Gaule nord-orientale à la veille de la grande invasion germanique de 407." *Revue historique* 236 (1966): 17–46.

———. "L'image officielle du barbare dans l'empire romain d'Auguste à Théodose." *Ktema. Civilisations de l'Orient, de la Grèce et de Rome antiques* 9 (1984): 123–143.

———. "Les invasions germaniques et la rupture des relations entre la Bretagne et la Gaule." *Moyen âge* 68 (1962): 1–50.

———. "Modalités d'établissement des fédéres barbares de Gratien et de Théodose." *Mélanges d'histoire ancienne offerts à William Seston* Paris: E. de Boccard, 1974. 143–160.

———. "A propos des solidi galici du Ve siècle apres J.-C." *Revue historique* 270 (1983): 3–30.

———. "Restrictions à l'expansion du droit de cité dans la seconde moitié du IVe siècle." *Ktema. Civilisations de l'Orient, de la Grèce et de Rome antiques* 6 (1981): 381–393.

———. "La septimanie dans le royaume wisigothique, de la fin du Ve siècle à la fin du VIIe siècle." *Actes du IXe journées d'archéologie mérovingienne. Colloque: Gaule mérovingienne et monde méditerranéen*, 17–39. Montpellier: Musée archéologique de Lattes, 1987.

———. "Sidoine Apollinaire et les Gabales." *Bulletin de la Société des Lettres, Sciences et Arts de la Lozère* 18–19 (1972–1973): 41–63.

———. "La symbolique du lion et du serpent sur les *solidi* des empereurs d'occident de la première moitié du Ve siècle." *Revue numismatique* 28 (1986): 94–118.

Depeyrot, Georges. "Les solidi gaulois de Valentinien III." *Swiss Numismatic Review* 65 (1986): 111–131.

de Wretschko, Alfredus. "De usu breviarii alariciani forensi et scholastico per Hispaniam, Galliam, Italiamque regionesque vicinas." In *Theodosiani libri XVI*, vol. 1, edited by Th. Mommsen and Paulus M. Meyer, cccvii–cccxv. Berlin: Weidmann, 1905.

di Gianlorenzo, U. "I barbari nel senato romano al sesto secolo." *Studi e documenti di storia e diritto* 20 (1899): 127–191.

Dill, Samuel. *Roman Society in the Last Century of the Western Empire.* 2d ed. London: MacMillan and Co., 1921. Reprint. New York: Meridian Books, 1958.

———. *Roman Society in Gaul in the Merovingian Age.* London: MacMillan and Co., 1926. Reprint. New York: Barnes and Noble, 1970.

Dolbeau, François. "La vie en prose de saint Marcel, évêque de Die. Histoire du texte et édition critique." *Francia* 11 (1983): 97–130.

Drew, K.F. "Another Look at the Origins of the Middle Ages. A Reassessment of the Role of the Germanic Kingdoms." *Speculum* 62 (1987): 803–812.

Drinkwater, John F. "Gallic Attitudes to the Roman Empire in the Fourth Century: Continuity or Change?" In *Labor omnibus unus. Gerold Walser zum 70. Geburtstag*, edited by Heinz E. Herzig and R. Frei-Stolba, 136–153. *Historia* Einzelschriften, vol. 60. Wiesbaden: Franz Steiner, 1989.

————. *The Gallic Empire. Separatism and Continuity in the North-Western Provinces of the Roman Empire A.D. 260–274*. Vol. 52, *Historia* Einzelschriften. Stuttgart: F. Steiner, 1987.

————. "Patronage in Roman Gaul and the Problem of the Bagaudae." In *Patronage in Ancient Society*, edited by A. Wallace-Hadrill, 189–203. London: Routledge, 1989.

————. *Roman Gaul: The Three Provinces, 58 B.C.–A.D. 260*. London: Croom Helm, 1983.

Duchesne, Louis. *Fastes épiscopaux de l'ancienne Gaule*. 3 vols. 2d ed. Paris: A. Fontemoing, 1907–1915.

Duckett, Eleanor S. *Latin Writers of the Fifth Century*. New York: H. Holt and Co., 1930. Reprint. New York: Archon Books, 1969.

Durliat, J. "Le salaire de la paix sociale dans les royaumes barbares (Ve-VIe siècles)." In *Anerkennung und Integration. Zu den wirtschaftlichen Grundlagen der Völkenwanderungszeit 400–600*, edited by Herwig Wolfram and Andreas Schwarcz, 21–72. Vienna: Österreichische Akademie der Wissenschaft, 1988.

Duval, Paul-Marie. *La Gaule jusqu'au milieu du Ve siècle*. Paris: Editions A. et J. Picard, 1971.

Ebel, Charles. *Transalpine Gaul: The Emergence of a Roman Province*. Leiden: Brill, 1976.

Elert, W. "Redemptio ab hostibus." *Theologische Literaturzeitung* 72 (1947): 265–270.

Emonds, H. "Geistlicher Kriegsdienst. Der Topos der militia spiritualis in der antiken Philosophie." In *Heilige Uberlieferung. Ausschnitte aus der Geschichte des Mönchtums und des heiligen Kultes. Festschrift I. Herwegen*, 21–50. Münster, 1938.

Engelbrecht, A. "Beiträge zur Kritik und Erklärung der Breife des Apollinaris Sidonius, Faustus und Ruricius." *Zeitschrift für die österreichischen Gymnasien* 41 (1890): 481–497.

Ensslin, Wilhelm. "Auctoritas und potestas." *Historische Jahrbucher* 74 (1954): 661–668.

————. "Zum Heermeisteramt des spätrömischen Reiches. III. Der magister utriusque militiae et patricius des 5. Jahrhunderts." *Klio* 24 (1931): 467–502.

Ewig, Eugen. "Kirche und civitas in der Merowingerzeit." *Settimane di Studio del Centro Italiano di Studi sull' Alto Medievo*, 45–71. Vol. 7. Milan, 1960.

————. *Die Merowinger und das Imperium*. Opladen: Westdeutscher Verlag, 1983.

————. *Spätantiken und fränkisches Gallien. Gesammelte Schriften*. 2 vols. Munich: Artemis Verlag, 1976–1979.

————. *Trier im Merowingerreich. Civitas, Stadt, Bistum.* Trier, 1954. Reprint. Aalen: Scientia, 1973.

Fabre, P. *Saint Paulin de Nole et l'amitié chrétienne.* Paris: E. de Boccard, 1949.

Fagerlie, Joan M. "Contact between Italy and the Baltic in the Fifth and Sixth Centuries A.D." *Congresso internationale di numismatico, Roma, 1961,* 411–442. Vol. 2. Rome, 1965.

Fanizza, Lucia. *Delatori e accusatori. L'iniziativa nei processi di età imperiale.* Rome: Bretschneider, 1988.

Favez, Charles. "La Gaule et les Gallo-Romains lors des invasions du Ve siècle d'après Salvien (quelques aspects du pays, attitude et sort des habit)." *Latomus* 16 (1957): 77–83.

Ferreiro, Alberto. *The Visigoths in Gaul and Spain A.D. 418–711. A Bibliography.* Leiden: Brill, 1988.

Février, Paul-Albert, ed. *Premiers temps chrétiens en Gaule méridionale. Antiquité tardive et haut moyen âge, IIIeme-VIIIeme siècles.* Lyons: Association lyonnaise de sauvetage des sites archéoligiques mediévales, 1988.

Fischer, H. "The Belief in the Continuity of the Roman Empire among the Franks of the Fifth and Sixth Centuries." *Catholic Historical Review* 4 (1924): 536–555.

Fischer, Joseph A. *Die Völkerwanderung im Urteil der zeitgenössischen kirklichen Schriftsteller Galliens unter Einbeziehung des heiligen Augustinus.* Heidelberg: Kemper, 1948.

Fontaine, Jacques. "L'apport du christianisme à la prise de conscience de la 'Patrie gauloise' sous la dynastie Théodosienne." In *La patrie gauloise d'Agrippa au VIeme siècle: actes du colloque, Lyon, 1981,* 183–202. Lyons: Hermes, 1983.

————. "L'ascétisme chrétien dans la littérature gallo-romaine d'Hilaire à Cassien." *Atti de Colloquio sul tema Gallia Romana. 10–11 maggio 1971. Promosso dall'Accademia Nazionale dei Lincei,* 87–115. Rome: L'Accademia, 1973.

————. *Isidore de Séville et la culture classique dans l'Espagne wisigothique.* Paris: Etudes augustiniennes, 1959.

————. "Romanité et hispanité dans la littérature hispano-romaine des IVe et Ve siècles." *Assimilation et resistance á la culture greco-romaine dans le monde ancien,* 301–322. Paris: Les Belles Lettres, 1976.

Förstermann, Ernst. *Altdeutsches Namenbuch.* Bonn, 1900. Reprint. Munich: W. Finks, 1966–1967.

Fowden, G. "The Pagan Holy Man in Late Antique Society." *Journal of Hellenic Studies* 102 (1982): 33–59.

Frend, W. H. C. "Paulinus of Nola and the Last Century of the Western Empire." *Journal of Roman Studies* 59 (1969): 1–11.

Gabba, Emilio, and G. Tibiletti. "Una signora di Treviri sepolta a Pavia." *Athenaeum* 38 (1960): 253–262.

Gagnière, S., and J. Granier. "L'occupation des grottes du IIIe au Ve siècle et les invasions germaniques dans la basse vallée du Rhône." *Provence historique* 13 (1963): 225–239.

Gamillscheg, Ernst. *Romania Germanica. Sprach-und Siedlungsgeschichte der Germanen auf dem Boden des alter Römerreichs: Zu den altesten Berührungen* zwischen Römer und Germanen. Grundriss der Germanischen Philologie III. Berlin-Leipzig: W. de Gruyter, 1934.

Gärtner, Hans Armin. "Rome et les barbares dans la poésie latine au temps d'Augustin: Rutilius Namatianus et Prudence." Ktema. Civilisations de l'Orient, de la Grèce et de Rome antiques 9 (1984): 113–121.

Gassmann, P. Der Episkopat in Gallien im 5. Jahrhundert (dissertation: Bonn, 1977).

Gaudemet, Jean. "Les abus des 'potentates' au Bas Empire." Irish Jurist 1 (1966): 228–235.

———. "Survivances romaines dans le droit de la monarchie franque du Vème au Xème siècle." Tijdschrift voor rechtsgeschiedenis 23 (1955): 149–206.

Geary, Patrick. Before France and Germany. The Creation and Transformation of the Merovingian World. New York: Oxford University Press, 1988.

Gelzer, Matthias. "Die Nobilität der Kaizerzeit." Hermes 63 (1928): 113ff. (Also published in Kleine Schriften, vol. 1, edited by Hermann Strasburger and Christian Meier, 136–153. Wiesbaden: F. Steiner, 1962.)

———. The Roman Nobility. Translated by R. Seager. 2d ed. New York: Barnes and Noble, 1969.

Genicot, Leopold. "The Nobility in Medieval Francia: Continuity, Break, or Evolution." In Lordship and Community, edited by Fredric L. Cheyette, 128–135. New York: Holt, Rinehart and Winston, 1968.

———. Noblesse dans l'occident médiéval. London: Variorum Reprints, 1982.

———. "Recent Research on the Medieval Nobility." In The Medieval Nobility. Studies on the Ruling Classes of France and Germany from the Sixth to the Twelfth Century, edited by Timothy Reuter, 17–35. Amsterdam–New York: North Holland, 1979.

Giardina, Andrea. Aspetti della burocrazia nel basso impero. Rome: Edizioni dell'Ateneo et Bizzarri, 1977.

Gilliard, Frank D. "Senatorial Bishops in the Fourth Century." Harvard Theological Review 77 (1984): 153–175.

———. "Who Were the Senators of Sixth-Century Gaul?" Speculum 54 (1979): 685–697.

Glorie, Fr. "La culture lérinienne (Notes de lecture)." Sacris erudiri 19 (1969–1970): 71–76.

Glover, Terrot R. Life and Letters in the Fourth Century. New York: G. E. Stechert, 1968.

Goetz, Hans-Werner. "Orosius und die Barbaren. Zu den umstrit denen Vorstellungen eines spätantiken Geschichtstheologen." Historia 29 (1980): 356–376.

Goffart, Walter A. Barbarians and Romans (A.D. 418–584): The Techniques of Accommodation. Princeton, N.J.: Princeton University Press, 1983.

———. "Rome, Constantinople, and the Barbarians." American Historical Review 86 (1981): 275–306.

———. "The Theme of 'The Barbarian Invasions' in Late Antiquity and Modern Historiography." In Das Reich und die Barbaren, edited by Evangelios K. Chrysos and Andreas Schwarcz, 87–107. Vienna-Cologne: Böhlau Verlag, 1989.

Grahn-Hoek, Heike. Die frankische Oberschicht im 6. Jahrhundert. Studien zu *ihrer rechtlichen und politischen Stellung.* Vorträge und Forschungen 21. Sigmaringen: Jan Thorbecke, 1976.

Griffe, Elie. "L'épiscopat gaulois de 481 à 561. Le choix des évêques." *Bulletin de littérature écclésiastique* 79 (1978): 285–300.

———. "L'épiscopat gaulois et les royautés barbares de 482 à 507." *Bulletin de littérature écclésiastique* 76 (1975): 261–284.

———. *La Gaule chrétienne à l'époque romaine.* 3 vols. Paris: Letouzy et Ané, 1964–1965.

———. "La pratique religieuse en Gaule au Ve siècle. Saeculares et sancti." *Bulletin de littérature écclésiastique* 63 (1962): 241–267.

———. "Les relations entre évêques au VIe siècle." *Bulletin de littérature écclésiastique* 81 (1980): 55–57.

———. "Les royautés barbares et l'épiscopat de 501 à 571." *Bulletin de littérature écclésiastique* 79 (1978): 267–284.

Grünert, Heinz, ed. *Römer und Germanen in Mitteleuropa.* Berlin: Akademie Verlag, 1975.

Gundlach, Wilhelm. "Der Streit der Bisthümer Arles und Vienne um den Primatus Galliarum." *Neues Archiv der Gesellschaft für ältere deutsche Geschichtskund* 14 (1888): 251–342; 15 (1889): 9–102.

Haarhoff, Theodore J. *Schools of Gaul. A Study of Pagan and Christian Education in the Last Century of the Western Empire.* London: Oxford University Press, 1920.

Hagendahl, Harald. *La correspondance de Ruricius.* Göteborg: Wettergren & Kerber, 1952.

Hamman, A. G. "L'actualité de Salvien de Marseille. Idées sociales et politiques." *Augustinianum* 17 (1977): 381–393.

Hammond, Mason. "Composition of the Senate A.D. 68–235." *Journal of Roman Studies* 47 (1957): 74–81.

Harmand, Louis. *Le patronat sur les collectivités publiques des origines au bas-empire. Un aspect social et politique du monde romain.* Paris: Presses universitaires de France, 1957.

Harries, Jill D. *Bishops, Aristocrats and Their Towns: Some Influences on, and Developments in, the Role of Churchmen from Gaul from Paulinus of Nola to Sidonius Apollinaris* (unpublished dissertation: Oxford, 1981. Cited in *Bulletin of the Institute for Classical Studies* 24 [1977]).

Hatt, J. J. *Histoire de la Gaule romain (120 avant J.-C.– 451 après J.-C.).* Paris: Payot, 1959.

Heinzelmann, Martin. *Bischofsherrschaft in Gallien: Zur Kontinuität römischer Führungsschichten von 4. bis 7. Jahrhundert.* Munich: Artemis Verlag, 1976.

———. "Gallische Prosopographie 260–527." *Francia* 10 (1982): 531–718.

———. "Neue Aspekte der biographischen und hagiographischen Literatur in der lateinischen Welt (1.-6. Jh.)." *Francia* 1 (1973): 27–44.

———. "Prosopographie et recherche de continuité historique: l'exemple des Ve-VIIe siècles." *Mélanges de l'Ecole Française de Rome. Moyen âge* 100 (1988): 227–239.

Held, Wieland. "Die gallische Aristokratie im 4. Jahrhundert hinsichtlich ihrer

Siedlungsstandorte und ihrer zentralen Stellung zur römischen Provinzial-bzw. Zentraladministration." *Klio* 58 (1976): 121–140.

Higounet, Charles. "Les saints mérovingiens d'Aquitaine dans la toponymie." *Etudes mérovingiens* (Paris, 1953): 157–167.

Hill, H. "Nobilitas in the Imperial Period." *Historia* 18 (1969): 230–250.

Hodgkin, T. *Italy and Her Invaders.* 5 vols. Oxford: Clarendon Press, 1880–1889.

———. *Theoderic the Goth: The Barbarian Champion of Civilisation.* 2d ed. New York: G. P. Putnam's Sons, 1923.

Hopkins, K. *Death and Renewal.* Sociological Studies in Roman History, no. 2. Cambridge: Cambridge University Press, 1983.

Hopkins, M. K. "Social Mobility in the Later Roman Empire: The Evidence of Ausonius." *Classical Quarterly* 11 (1961): 239–249.

Irsigler, Franz. "On the Aristocratic Character of Early Frankish Society." In *The Medieval Nobility. Studies on the Ruling Classes of France and Germany from the Sixth to the Twelfth Century*, edited by Timothy Reuter, 106–136. Amsterdam–New York: North Holland, 1979.

Jacques, F. "L'ordine senatoria attraverso la crisi del III secolo." In *Società romana e impero tardoantico*, vol. 1, edited by Andrea Giardina, 80–225. Rome: Laterza, 1986.

James, Edward. "Childéric, Syagrius et la disparition du royaume de Soissons." *Revue archéologique de Picardie* 3–4 (1988): 9–12.

———. *The Origins of France: From Clovis to the Capetians, 500–1000.* New York: St. Martin's Press, 1982.

James, Edward, ed. *Visigothic Spain: New Approaches.* Oxford: Clarendon Press, 1980.

Janson, Tore. *Latin Prose Prefaces. Studies in Literary Conventions.* Studia Latina Stockholmensia, no. 13. Stockholm: Ivar Haegström, 1964.

Jerg, Ernst. *Vir venerabilis. Untersuchungen zur Titulatur der Bischöfe in den ausserkirchlichen Texten der spätantike als Beitrag zur Deutung ihrer öffentlichen Stellung.* Vienna: Herder, 1970.

Joannou, Périclès-Pierre. *La législation impériale et la christianisation de l'empire romain (311–476).* Orientalia Christiana Analecta, no. 192. Rome: Pontifical Institute of Oriental Studies, 1972.

Johne, Klaus-Peter. "Germanen im römischen Dienst." *Das Altertum* 34 (1988): 5–13.

Jones, Arnold H. M. "The Constitutional Position of Odoacer and Theoderic." *Journal of Roman Studies* 52 (1962): 126–130.

———. *The Decline of the Ancient World.* London: Longmans, 1975.

———. *The Later Roman Empire A.D. 284–640. A Social, Economic, and Administrative Survey.* Norman: University of Oklahoma Press, 1964.

Jones, W. R. "The Image of the Barbarian in Medieval Europe." *Comparative Studies in Society and History* 13 (1971): 376–407.

Jullian, Camille. *Histoire de la Gaule.* 8 vols. Paris: Librairie Hachette, 1920–1926.

Kaegi, Walter. *Byzantium and the Decline of Rome.* Princeton, N.J.: Princeton University Press, 1968.

Kahane, Henry, and Renée Kahane. "On the Meanings of *Barbarus*." *Hellenika* 37 (1986): 129–132.

Kaufmann, G. "Rhetorenschulen und Klosterschulen oder heidnische und christliche Kultur in Gallien wahrend des 5. und 6. Jahrhunderts." *Historisches Taschenbuch* 10 (1869): 1–94.

Kellett, Frederick W. *Pope Gregory the Great and His Relations with Gaul.* Cambridge: Cambridge University Press, 1889.

Kidd, Beresford J. *A History of the Church to A.D. 461. Volume III. A.D. 408–461.* Oxford: Clarendon Press, 1922.

King, P. D. *Law and Society in the Visigothic Kingdom.* Cambridge: Cambridge University Press, 1972.

Kirner, G. "Due Vite Inedite di s. Marcello Vescovo di Die." *Studi Storici* 9 (1900): 289–329.

Klauser, Theodor. "Bischofe als staatliche Prokuratoren im dritten Jahrhundert?" *Jahrbuch für Antike und Christentum* 14 (1971): 140–149.

———. *Der Ursprung der bischöflichen Insignien und Ehrenrechte.* Bonn: Scherpe Verlag, 1948.

Klingshirn, William. "Charity and Power: Caesarius of Arles and the Ransoming of Captives in Sub-Roman Gaul." *Journal of Roman Studies* 75 (1985): 183–203.

Koenig, Ingemar. *Gallischen Usurpatoren von Postumus bis Tetricus.* Vestigia, no. 31. Munich: C. H. Beck, 1981.

Krause, Jens-Uwe. "Das spätantike Städtpatronat." *Chiron* 17 (1987): 1–80.

Kuhoff, Wolfgang. *Studien zur zivilen senatorischen Laufbahn im 4. Jahrhundert n.Chr. Amter und Amtsinhaber in Clarissimat und Spectabilität.* Frankfurt: Peter Lang, 1983.

Kurth, Godefroid. "Les sénateurs en Gaule au VIe siècle." In *Etudes franques,* 97–115. Vol. 2. Brussels: A. Dewit, 1919.

Labroue, Emilio. "L'école de Périgueux au Ve siècle. Poètes et rhéteurs." *Atti del Congresso Internazionale di Scienze Storiche* 2 (1905): 161–174.

Labuske, H. "Die Barbaren. Problema in Ideologie und Propaganda der Spätantike." In *Festschrift W. Hartke,* edited by H. Scheel, 99–108. Berlin, 1973.

Ladner, Gerhart B. "Justinian's Theory of Law and the Renewal Ideology of the *Leges barbarorum*." *Proceedings of the American Philosophical Society* 119 (1975): 191–200.

———. "On Roman Attitudes toward Barbarians in Late Antiquity." *Viator* 7 (1976): 1–25.

Lagarrigue, G. "Le Carmen de Providentia Dei. Optimisme religieux et espoir patriotique." In *Hommages à Robert Schilling,* edited by Hubert Zehnacker and Gustave Hentz, 137–145. Paris: Les Belles Lettres, 1983.

———. "L'opinion de Salvien sur les barbares. Interpretations actuelles." *Revue des études latines* 42 (1964): 70–71.

Laistner, Max L. W. *Thought and Letters in Western Europe, A.D. 500 to 900.* London: Methuen, 1931.

Lambrechts, Pierre. *La composition du sénat romain de l'accession au trône d'Hadrien à la mort de Commode (117–192).* Studia historica, no. 108. Antwerp: De Sikkel, 1936.

————. *La composition du sénat romain de Septime Sévère à Dioclétien, 193–284.* Studia historica, no. 53. Budapest: Magyar Nemzeti Muzeum, 1937.

Langgärtner, Georg. *Die Gallienpolitik der Päpste im 5. und 6. Jahrhunderts. Eine Studie über den apostolische Vikariat von Arles.* Bonn: Peter Hanstein Verlag, 1964.

Langlois, P. "Les invasions germaniques du Ve siècle et les lettres latines." *Revue des études anciennes* 70 (1960): 121–128.

Larde, G. *Le tribunal du clerc dans l'empire romain et la Gaule franque.* Moulins, 1920.

Larsen, Jakob A. O. "The Position of Provincial Assemblies in the Government and Society of the Late Roman Empire." *Classical Philology* 29 (1934): 209–220.

Latouche, Robert. *The Birth of the Western Economy: Economic Aspects of the Dark Ages.* Translated by E. M. Wilkinson. 2d ed. London: Methuen, 1967.

————. *Les grandes invasions et la crise de l'occident au Ve siècle.* Paris: Editions Montaigne, 1946.

Lear, Floyd S. "The Public Law of the Visigothic Code." *Speculum* 26 (1951): 1–23.

le Blant, E. "Note sur le rachat des captifs au temps des invasions barbares." *Revue archéologique* 10 (1864): 435–448.

le Bras, Gabriel, and Etienne Gilson, eds. *St. Germain d'Auxerre et son temps.* Auxerre: L'Universelle, 1950.

Lécrivain, Charles. "Un épisode inconnu de l'histoire des Wisigoths." *Annales du midi* 1 (1889): 47–51.

————. "Note sur la vie de saint Orientius, évêque d'Auch." *Annales du midi* 3 (1891): 257–258.

————. *Le sénat romain depuis Dioclétian à Rome et à Constantinople.* Paris: E. Thorin, 1888.

Lepelley, C. "Quot curiales, tot tyranni. L'image du décurion oppresseur au bas-empire." In *Crise et redressement dans les provinces européennes de l'empire (milieu du IIIe—milieu du IVe siècle ap. J.-C.),* edited by Edward Frezouls, 143–156. Strasbourg: AECR, 1983.

Lesne, E. "La contribution des églises et monastères de l'ancienne Gaule au sauvetage des lettres antiques." *Revue d'histoire de l'église de France* 23 (1937): 473–485.

Levillain, L. "La crise des années 507–508 et les rivalités d'influence en Gaule de 508 à 514." *Mélanges offerts à M. Nicolas Iorga,* 537–567. Paris: J. Gamber, 1953.

Levison, Wilhelm. "Zur Geschichte des Frankenkönigs Chlodowech." *Bonner Jahrbucher* 103 (1898): 42–67.

Liebeschuetz, John H. W. G. *Barbarians and Bishops: Army, Church, and State in the Reign of Arcadius and Chrysostom.* Oxford: Clarendon Press, 1990.

Liebs, D. "Amterpatronage in der Spätantike." *Zeitschrift für Rechtsgeschichte* 95 (1978): 158–186.

Llewelyn, Peter A. B. "The Roman Church during the Laurentian Schism: Priests and Senators." *Church History* 45 (1976): 1–11.

Löhken, Henrik. *Ordines dignitatum: Untersuchungen zur formalen Konstitu-ierung der spätantiken Führungsschicht.* Cologne-Vienna: Böhlau Verlag, 1982.

Lot, Ferdinand. *The End of the Ancient World and the Beginning of the Middle Ages.* New York: Harper, 1931.

———. *La Gaule. Les fondements ethniques, sociaux et politiques de la nation française.* Paris: A. Fayard, 1947.

———. *Les invasions germaniques. La pénétration mutuelle du monde barbare et du monde romain.* Paris: Payot, 1945.

———. "Du régime de l'hospitalité." *Revue belge de philologie d'histoire* 7 (1928): 975–1011.

———. "La *Vita Viviani* et la domination wisigothique en Aquitaine." In *Mélanges Paul Fournier,* 467–477. Paris: Recueil Sirey, 1929. Reprint. Aalen: Scientia, 1982.

Lotter, Friedrich. "Zu den Anredeformen und ehrenden Epitheta der Bischöfe in Spätantike und frühem Mittelalter." *Deutsches Archiv für Erforschung des Mittelalters* 27 (1971): 514–517.

Loyen, Andre. "Les débuts du royaume wisigoth de Toulouse." *Revue des études latines* 12 (1934): 406–415.

———. *Recherches historiques sur les panégyriques de Sidoine Apollinaire.* Paris: Champion, 1942.

———. "Résistants et collaborateurs en Gaule à l'époque des grandes invasions." *Bulletin de l'Association G. Budé* 22 (1963): 437–450.

———. "Le rôle de saint Aignan dans la défense d'Orléans." *Comptes rendus de l'Academie des Inscriptions et Belles-Lettres* (1969): 64–74.

———. *Sidoine Apollinaire et l'esprit précieux en Gaule aux derniers jours de l'empire.* Paris: Les Belles Lettres, 1943.

Macbain, Bruce. "Odovacer the Hun?" *Classical Philology* 78 (1983): 323–327.

MacMullen, Ramsay. "Barbarian Enclaves in the Northern Roman Empire." *Antiquité classique* 32 (1963): 552–561.

———. *Corruption and the Decline of Rome.* New Haven: Yale University Press, 1988.

———. *Enemies of the Roman Order. Treason, Unrest, and Alienation in the Empire.* Cambridge, Mass.: Harvard University Press, 1967.

Malcus, Bengt. *Le sénat et l'ordre sénatorial au Bas-Empire: Etudes I* (dissertation: Lund, 1970).

Mandouze, André. *Prosopographie chrétienne du Bas-Empire I. Prosopographie de l'Afrique chrétienne (303–553).* Paris: Editions du Centre National de la Recherche Scientifique, 1982.

Manitius, Max. *Geschichte der lateinischen Literatur des Mittelalters. I. Von Justinian bis zur mitte des zehnten Jahrhunderts.* Munich: C. H. Beck, 1911.

Markey, Thomas L. "Germanic in the Mediterranean: Lombards, Vandals, and Visigoths." In *Tradition and Innovation in Late Antiquity,* edited by Frank M. Clover and Stephen Humphreys, 51–71. Madison: University of Wisconsin Press, 1989.

Markus, Robert A. "Chronicle and Theology: Prosper of Aquitaine." In *The Inheritance of Historiography 350–900,* edited by Christopher J. Holdsworth and

T. P. Wiseman, 31–43. Exeter Studies in History, no. 12. Exeter: University of Exeter, 1986.

Marrou, Henri-Irenée. "L'épitaphe vaticane du consulaire de Vienne Eventius." *Revue des études anciennes* 54 (1952): 326–331.

———. *Histoire de l'éducation dans l'antiquité.* 3d ed. Paris: Editions du Seuil, 1955. Translated by G. Lamb, under the title *A History of Education in Antiquity.* New York: Sheed and Ward, 1956.

———. "Un lieu dit 'Cité de Dieu'." *Augustinus magister* 1 (1954): 101–110.

Martindale, Joan. "The French Aristocracy in the Early Middle Ages: A Reappraisal." *Past and Present* 75 (1977): 5–45.

Martindale, John R. "Prosopography of the Later Roman Empire: *Addenda* and *Corrigenda* to Volume I." *Historia* 23 (1974): 247ff.

———. *The Prosopography of the Later Roman Empire. Volume II. A.D. 395–527.* Cambridge: Cambridge University Press, 1980.

Martino, Paul. "*Gothorum laus est civilitas custodiat* (Cassiod. *Var.* 9,14,18)." *Sileno* 8 (1982): 31–45.

Mathisen, Ralph W. "Avitus, Italy and the East in A.D. 455–456." *Byzantion* 51 (1981): 232–247.

———. *The Ecclesiastical Aristocracy of Fifth-Century Gaul: A Regional Analysis of Family Structure* (dissertation: University of Wisconsin, 1979; Ann Arbor, Mich.: University Microfilms, 1980).

———. *Ecclesiastical Factionalism and Religious Controversy in Fifth-Century Gaul.* Washington: Catholic University Press, 1989.

———. "Emigrants, Exiles, and Survivors: Aristocratic Options in Visigothic Aquitania." *Phoenix* 38 (1984): 159–170.

———. "Episcopal Hierarchy and Tenure in Office: A Method for Establishing Dates of Ordination." *Francia* 17 (1990): 125–140.

———. "Epistolography, Literary Circles, and Family Ties in Late Roman Gaul." *Transactions of the American Philological Association* 111 (1981): 95–109.

———. "The Family of Georgius Florentius Gregorius and the Bishops of Tours." *Medievalia et Humanistica* 12 (1984): 83–95.

———. "Hilarius, Germanus and Lupus: The Aristocratic Background of the Chelidonius Affair." *Phoenix* 33 (1979): 160–169.

———. "The Last Year of Saint Germanus of Auxerre." *Analecta bollandiana* 99 (1981): 151–159.

———. "Patricians as Diplomats in Late Antiquity." *Byzantinische Zeitschrift* 79 (1986): 35–49.

———. "Petronius, Hilarius and Valerianus: Prosopographical Notes on the Conversion of the Roman Aristocracy." *Historia* 30 (1981): 106–112.

———. "PLRE II: Suggested *Addenda* and *Corrigenda.*" *Historia* 31 (1982): 364–386.

———. "Reconstruction of the List of Subscriptions to the Council of Orange (AD 441)." *Annuarium historiae conciliorum* 20 (1988): 1–12.

———. "Resistance and Reconciliation: Majorian and the Gallic Aristocracy after the Fall of Avitus." *Francia* 7 (1979): 597–627.

————. "Sidonius on the Reign of Avitus: A Study in Political Prudence." *Transactions of the American Philological Association* 109 (1979): 165–171.

————. "Some Hagiographical Addenda to *P.L.R.E.*" *Historia* 36 (1987): 448–461.

————. "A Survey of the Significant *Addenda* to *P.L.R.E.*" *Medieval Prosopography* 8 (1987): 5–30.

————. "Ten Office-Holders: A Few *Addenda* and *Corrigenda* to *P.L.R.E.*" *Historia* 35 (1986): 125–127.

————. "The Theme of Literary Decline in Late Roman Gaul." *Classical Philology* 83 (1988): 45–52.

————. "The Third Regnal Year of Eparchius Avitus." *Classical Philology* 80 (1985): 192–196.

————. "Thirty-Three Missing Patricians." *Byzantinische Forschungen* 15 (1990): 87–99.

Matthews, John F. "Gallic Supporters of Theodosius." *Latomus* 30 (1971): 1073–1099.

————. "Hostages, Philosophers, Pilgrims and the Diffusion of Ideas in the Late Roman Mediterranean and Near East." In *Tradition and Innovation in Late Antiquity*, edited by Frank M. Clover and Stephen Humphreys, 29–49. Madison: University of Wisconsin Press, 1989.

————. *Western Aristocracies and Imperial Court A.D. 364–425.* Oxford: Clarendon Press, 1975.

McCormick, Michael. "Clovis at Tours, Byzantine Public Ritual, and the Origins of Medieval Ruler Symbolism." In *Das Reich und die Barbaren*, edited by Evangelios K. Chrysos and Andreas Schwarcz, 155–180. Vienna-Cologne: Böhlau Verlag, 1989.

————. *Eternal Victory: Triumphal Rulership in Late Antiquity, Byzantium, and the Early Medieval West.* Cambridge: Cambridge University Press, 1986.

McGeachy, John A. *Quintus Aurelius Symmachus and the Senatorial Aristocracy of the West* (dissertation: Univ. of Chicago, 1942; Chicago: Univ. of Chicago Libraries, 1942).

McHugh, Michael P. *The Carmen de Providentia Dei, Attributed to Prosper of Aquitaine: A Revised Text with an Introduction.* Washington: Catholic University Press, 1964.

McShane, Philip. *La romanitas et le pape Léon le Grand. L'apport culturel des institutions impériales à la formation des structures ecclésiastiques.* Tournai: Desclée, 1979.

Mitteis, L. "Über dem Ausdruck 'Potentiores' in den Digesten." In *Mélanges Paul Frédéric Girard: Etudes de droit romain*, 225–235. Vol. 2. Paris: A. Rousseau, 1912.

Moebus, G. "Nobilitas. Wesen und Wandlung der führenden Schicht Roms im Spiegel einer Wortprägung." *Neue Jahrbücher für Antike und deutsche Bildung* (Leipzig, 1942): 275–292.

Momigliano, Arnaldo. "La caduta senza rumore di un impero nel 476 D.C." *Rivista storica italiana* 85 (1973): 5–21.

————. "Cassiodorus and the Italian Culture of his Time." *Proceedings of the British Academy* 41 (1955): 207–245.

Moorhead, John A. *The Catholic Episcopate in Ostrogothic Italy.* Liverpool, 1974.
————. "Clovis' Motives for Becoming a Catholic Christian." *Journal of Religious History* 13 (1985): 329–339.
Morin, Germain. "Castor et Polychronius: un épisode peu connu de l'histoire ecclésiastique des Gaules." *Revue bénédictine* 51 (1939): 31–36.
————. *Etudes, textes, découvertes. Contributions à la littérature et à l'histoire des douze premiers siècles.* Vol. 1. Paris, 1913.
Morris, John. *The Age of Arthur. A History of the British Isles from 350 to 650.* New York: Scribner, 1973.
Morrison, Karl. *Tradition and Authority in the Western Church, 300–1140.* Princeton: Princeton University Press, 1969.
Moss, J. R. "The Effects of the Policies of Aetius on the History of the Western Empire." *Historia* 22 (1973): 711–731.
Musset, Lucien. *Les invasions. Les vagues germaniques.* Paris: Presses universitaires de France, 1965.
Myres, J. N. L. "Pelagius and the End of Roman Rule in Britain." *Journal of Roman Studies* 50 (1960): 21–36.
Nagel, Peter. *Die Motivierung der Askese in der alten Kirche und der Ursprung des Mönchtums.* Berlin: Akademie Verlag, 1966.
Nehlsen, H. "Alarich II als Gesetzgeber. Zur Geschichte der 'Lex romana visigothorum.'" In *Studien zu den germanischen Volksrechten: Gedächtnisschrift für Wilhelm Ebel,* edited by Götz Landwehr, 143–203. Frankfurt: Peter Lang, 1982.
Nesselhauf, Herbert. *Die spätrömische Verwaltung der gallisch-germanischen Länder.* Berlin: Verlag der Akademie der Wissenschaften, 1938.
Noethlichs, Karl Leo. *Beamtentum und Dienstvergehen. Zur Staatsverwaltung in der Spätantike.* Wiesbaden: Franz Steiner, 1981.
————. "Zur Einflussnahme des Staates auf die Entwicklung eines christlichen Klerikerstandes, schicht- und berufsspezifische Bestimmung für der Klerus in 4. und 5. Jahrhunderts in den spätantiken Rechtsquellen." *Jahrbuch für Antike und Christentum* 15 (1972): 136–153.
————. "Materialien zum Bischofsbild aus den spätantiken Rechtsquellen." *Jahrbuch für Antike und Christentum* 16 (1973): 28–59.
Nürnberg, Rosemarie. *Askese als sozialer Impuls. Monastisch-asketische Spiritualität als Wurzel und Triebfeder sozialer Ideen und Aktivitäten der Kirche in Südgallien im 5. Jahrhundert.* Bonn: Borengasser, 1988.
Oost, Stewart I. *Galla Placidia Augusta, A Biographical Essay.* Chicago: University of Chicago Press, 1968.
Opelt, I. "Briefe des Salvian von Marseille: zwischen Christen und Barbaren." *Romanobarbarica* 4 (1979): 161–182.
Otto, W. "Die Nobilität der Kaizerzeit." *Hermes* 51 (1916): 73ff.
Overbeck, Mechthild. *Untersuchungen zum afrikanischen Senatsadel in der spätantike.* Frankfurter Althistorische Studien, no. 7. Kallmünz: Lassleben, 1973.
Palanque, Jean-Rémy. "La date du transfert de la préfecture des Gaules de Trèves à Arles." *Revue des études anciennes* 36 (1934): 358–365.

————. "Du nouveau sur la date du transfert de la préfecture des Gaules de Trèves à Arles?" *Provence historique* 23 (1973): 19–38.

Papini, Annunziata Maria. *Ricimero. L'agonia dell' impero romano d'Occidente.* Milan: Gastaldi, 1959.

Paschoud, François. *Roma Aeterna. Etudes sur le patriotisme romain dans l'Occident latin à l'époque des grandes invasions germaniques.* Rome: Institut Suisse, 1967.

————. "Romains et barbares au début du Ve siècle après J.-C.: le témoignage d'Eunape, d'Olympiodore et de Zosime." In *La nozione di 'Romano' tra cittadinanza e universalità,* 357–367. Naples: Edizione scientifiche italiane, 1984.

Paunier, D. "Un refuge du bas-empire au Mont-Musiège (Haute-Savoie)." *Museum helveticum* 35 (1978): 295–306.

Percival, John. *The Roman Villa. An Historical Introduction.* London: Batsford, 1976.

————. "Seigneurial Aspects of the Late Roman Estate Management." *English Historical Review* 84 (1969): 449–473.

Perrenot, Th. "Du mode d'établissement des Burgondes dans l'Est et le Sud-Est de la Gaule." *Mémoires de l'Institut Historique de Provence* 2 (1925): 62–73.

Perroud, Marc. "La Savoie Burgonde (443–534)." *Mémoires et documents publiée par la Société Savoisienne d'histoire et d'archéologie à Chambay* 66 (1929): 263–276.

Peter, Hermann W. G. *Der Brief in der römischen Literatur.* Leipzig, 1901. Reprint. Hildesheim: Olms, 1965.

Pflaum, Hans-Georg. "Une famille arlésienne à la fin du Ier siècle et au IIe siècle." *Bulletin de la Société des Antiquaires de France* (1970): 265–272.

————. *Le Marbre de Thorigny.* Paris: H. Champion, 1948.

Pietri, Luce. "Aristocratie et société cléricale dans l'Italie chrétienne au temps d'Odoacre et de Theoderic." *Mélanges de l'Ecole Française à Rome* 93 (1981): 416–467.

————. "L'ordine senatorio in Gallia del 476 al fine del VI secolo." In *Società romana e impero tardoantico,* edited by Andrea Giardina, 307–323. Vol. 1. Rome: Laterza, 1986.

Piganiol, Andre. *L'Empire chrétien (325-395).* 2d ed. Paris: Presses universitaires de France, 1972.

Prevost, G. A. "Les invasions barbares en Gaule au Ve siècle et la condition des gallo-romains." *Revue des questions historiques* 26 (1879): 131–180.

Pricoco, Salvatore. "Barbari, senso della fine e teologia politica. Su un passo del 'De Contemptu Mundi' di Eucherio di Lione." *Romanobarbarica* 2 (1977): 209–229.

————. *L'isola dei santi. Il cenobio di Lerino e le origini dei monachesimo gallico.* Rome: Edizioni dell'Ateneo et Bizzarri, 1978.

Prinz, Friedrich. "Aristocracy and Christianity in Merovingian Gaul. An Essay." In *Gesellschaft, Kultur, Literatur. Rezeption und Originalität im Wachsen einer europäischen Literatur und Geistigkeit: Beiträge K. Wallach gewidmet,* edited by K. Bosl, 153–165. Stuttgart: Hiersemann, 1975.

————. "Die bischöfliche Stadtherrschaft im Frankenreich vom 5. bis zu 7. Jahrhundert." *Historische Zeitschrift* 217 (1973): 1–35.

————. *Frühes Mönchtum im Frankenreich. Kultur und Gesellschaft in Gallien, den Rheinlanden und Bayern am Beispiel der monastische Entwicklung (4.- 8. Jahrhundert).* Munich-Vienna: Oldenbourg, 1965.

————. *Klerus und Krieg im früheren Mittelalter. Untersuchungen zur Rolle der Kircle beim Aufbau der Königsherrschaft.* Stuttgart: Hiersemann, 1971.

Raby, Frederic J. E. *A History of Secular Latin Poetry in the Middle Ages.* Oxford: Clarendon Press, 1934.

R.-Alfoldi, Maria. "Zum Datum der Aufgabe der Residenz Treviri unter Stilicho." *Jahrbuch für Numismatik* 20 (1970): 241–249.

Randers-Pehrson, Justine Davis. *Barbarians and Romans. The Birth Struggle of Europe, A.D. 400–700.* Norman: University of Oklahoma Press, 1983.

Rattenbury, R. M. "An Ancient Armored Force." *Classical Review* 56 (1942): 113–116.

Reinhold, Meyer. "Usurpation of Status and Status Symbols in the Roman Empire." *Historia* 20 (1971): 275–302.

Rémondon, R. *La crise de l'empire romain de Marc-Aurèle à Anastase.* Paris: Nouvelle Clio, 1964.

Reuter, Timothy, ed. *The Medieval Nobility. Studies on the Ruling Classes of France and Germany from the Sixth to the Twelfth Century.* Amsterdam-New York: North Holland, 1979.

Rey, R. "La tradition gallo-romaine dans la civilisation méridionale jusqu' à l'invasion sarrasine." *Pallas* (1954): 155–175.

Reydellet, M. *La royauté dans la littérature latine de Sidoine Apollinaire à Isidore de Séville.* Bibliothèque des Ecole Françaises d'Athènes et de Rome, no. 243. Rome: Ecole Française, 1981.

Riché, Pierre. *Education et culture dans l'Occident barbare, VIe-VIIIe siécles.* Paris: Editions du Seuil, 1962. Also published as *Education and Culture in the Barbarian West, Sixth through Eighth Centuries.* Translated by J. Contreni. Columbia: University of South Carolina Press, 1976.

————. *Les invasions barbares.* Paris: Presses universitaires de France, 1953.

————. "La survivance des écoles publiques en Gaule au Ve siècle." *Le moyen âge* 63 (1957): 421–436.

Roger, M. *L'enseignement des lettres classiques d'Ausone à Alcuin, introduction à l'histoire des écoles carolingiennes.* Paris: A. Picard et fils, 1905.

Rouche, Michel. *L'Aquitaine des Wisigoths aux Arabes, 418–781: Naissance d'une région.* Paris: Editions de l'Ecole des Hautes Etudes en Sciences Sociales, Editions Touzot, 1979.

Rousseau, Philip. *Ascetics, Authority and the Church in the Age of Jerome and Cassian.* Oxford: Clarendon Press, 1978.

————. "In Search of Sidonius the Bishop." *Historia* 25 (1976): 356–377.

————. "The Spiritual Authority of the Monk-Bishop. Eastern Elements in Some Western Hagiography of the Fourth and Fifth Centuries." *Journal of Theological Studies* 22 (1971): 388–419.

Rusch, William G. *The Later Latin Fathers.* London: Duckworth, 1977.

Rutherford, Hamish. *Sidonius Apollinaris. l'homme politique, l'écrivain, l'évêque. Etude d'une figure gallo-romaine de Ve siècle.* Clermont-Ferrand: J. de Bussac, 1938.

Saddington, D. B. "Roman Attitudes to the *externae gentes* of the North." *Acta classica* 1 (1958): 90–138.

Samson, Ross. "The Merovingian Nobleman's House. Castle or Villa?" *Journal of Medieval Archaeology* 13 (1987): 287–315.

Saunders, J. J. "The Debate on the Fall of Rome." *History* 48–49 (1963): 1–17.

Sawyer, P., ed. *Names, Words and Graves: Early Medieval Settlement.* Leeds: University of Leeds, 1979.

Schanz, Martin. *Geschichte der römischen Litteratur bis zum Gesetzgebungswerk des Kaisers Justinians. Vierter Teil: Die römische Litteratur von Constantin bis zum Gesetzgebungswerk Justinians. Zweite Hälfte: Die Litteratur des fünften und sechsten Jahrhunderts.* Munich: C. H. Beck, 1920.

Schlumberger, Jörg A. "*Potentes* and *potentia* in the Social Thought of Late Antiquity." In *Tradition and Innovation in Late Antiquity,* edited by Frank M. Clover and Stephen Humphreys, 89–104. Madison: University of Wisconsin Press, 1989.

Schmid, Karl. "The Structure of the Nobility in the Earlier Middle Ages." In *The Medieval Nobility. Studies on the Ruling Classes of France and Germany from the Sixth to the Twelfth Century,* edited by Timothy Reuter, 37ff. Amsterdam–New York: North Holland, 1979.

Schmidt, Joel. *Sainte Geneviève et la fin de la Gaule Romaine.* Paris: Perrin, 1990.

Schmidt, Ludwig. "Aus den Anfängen des salfränkischen Königstum." *Klio* 34 (1942): 306–327.

―――. "Das Ende der Römerherrschaft in Gallien (Chlodowech und Syagrius)." *Historisches Jahrbuch* 48 (1928): 611–618.

―――. *Geschichte der deutschen Stämme bis zum Ausgang der Völkerwanderung.* Vol. 1, *Die Ostgermanen.* Vol. 2, *Die Westgermanen.* 1934–1941. Reprint. Munich: C. H. Beck, 1969.

Schmitz, Hermann J. "Die Tendenz der Provinzialsynoden in Gallien seit dem 5. Jahrhundert und die römischen Büssbucher." *Archiv für katholisches Kirchenrecht* 71 (1894): 21–33.

Schreibelreiter, Georg. *Der Bischof in merowingischer Zeit.* Vienna: Böhlau, 1983.

Scott, L. R. "Antibarbarian Sentiments and the 'Barbarian' General in Roman Imperial Service: The Case of Ricimer." In *Proceedings of the VIIth Congress of the International Federation of the Societies of Classical Studies,* edited by Janos Harmatta, 23–33. Vol. 2. Budapest: Akademiai Kiado, 1984.

Seeck, Otto. *Geschichte des Untergangs der antiken Welt,* vol. 6. 1920. Reprint. Stuttgart: J. B. Metzler, 1966.

―――. *Regesten der Kaiser und Päpste für die Jahre 311 bis 476 n. Chr. Vorarbeit zu einer Prosopographie der christlichen Kaiserzeit.* Stuttgart: J. B. Metzler, 1919.

Selb, Walter. "Episcopalis audientia von der Zeit Konstantins bis zur Nov. XXXV

Valentinians III." *Zeitschrift der Savigny-Stiftung für Rechtsgeschichte, Romanistische Abteilung* 84 (1967): 162–217.

Selle-Hosbach, Karin. *Prosopographie merowingischer Amtsträger in der Zeit von 511 bis 613.* Bonn: Reinischen Friedrich-Wilhelms-Universität, 1974.

Shchukin, Mark B. *Rome and the Barbarians in Central and Eastern Europe, 1st Century B.C.–1st Century A.D.* Translated from Russian. Oxford: British Archaeological Reports, 1989.

Silber, Manfred. *The Gallic Royalty of the Merovingians in Its Relationship to the 'Orbis terrarum romanum' during the 5th and 6th Centuries A.D.* Berne: Lang, 1970.

Sinko, Tadeuszn. *Der Romanorum viro bono.* Cracow, 1903. (Also published as *Vir bonus. Podrecznik do nauki jezyka lacinskiego dla III-ej klasy gimnazjow ogolnoksztalcacych.* Hanover: Nakl. Polskiego Zwiazku Wychodzctwa Przymusowego, 1946.)

Sivan, Hagith S. "On *Foederati, Hospitalitas,* and the Settlement of the Goths in A.D. 418." *American Journal of Philology* 108 (1987): 759–772.

———. "Rutilius Namatianus, Constantius III and the Return to Gaul in Light of New Evidence." *Mediaeval Studies* 48 (1986): 522–532.

———. "Sidonius Apollinaris, Theodoric II, and Gothic-Roman Politics from Avitus to Anthemius." *Hermes* 117 (1989): 85–94.

Speigl, Jakob. "Zum Problem der Teilnahme von Laien an den Konzilien im kirchlichen Altertum." *Annuarium historiae conciliorum* 10 (1978): 241–248.

Stein, Ernst. "La disparition du sénat de Rome à la fin du sixième siècle." *Bulletin de l'Academie Belge, Classe des Lettres* 5.25 (1939): 308–327.

———. *Geschichte des spätrömischen Reiches vom römischen zum byzantinischen Staate (284–476 n. Chr.).* Vienna: L. W. Seidel und Sohn, 1928. (Also published as *Histoire du Bas-Empire. Tome premier. De l'état romaine à l'état byzantine [284–476].* Translated by Jean-Rémy Palanque. Paris, 1959. Reprint. Amsterdam: A. M. Hakkert, 1968.)

Stein, S. "Der Romanus in den fränkischen Rechtsquellen." *Mitteillungen der österreichen Institut für Geschichtsforschung* 43 (1929): 1ff.

Sterzl, A. G. *Romanus-Christianus-Barbarus. Die germanische Landnahme im Spiegel der Schriften des Salvian von Massalia und Victor von Vita* (dissertation: Erlangen, 1950).

Stevens, Courtenay E. "Marcus, Gratian, Constantine." *Athenaeum* 35 (1957): 316–347.

———. *Sidonius Apollinaris and His Age.* Oxford: Clarendon Press, 1933.

Stevens, Susan T. "The Circle of Bishop Fulgentius." *Traditio* 38 (1982): 327–341.

Straub, Johannes. "Christliche Geschichtsapologetik in der Krisis des römischen Reiches." *Historia* 1 (1950): 52–81.

Stroheker, Karl F. "Alamannen im römischen Reichsdienst." In *Eranion, Festschrift fur Hildebrecht Hommel,* edited by Jurgen Kroymann, 30–53. Tübingen: M. Niemeyer, 1961.

———. *Eurich, König der Westgoten.* Stuttgart: W. Kohlhammer, 1937.

———. *Germanentum und Spätantike.* Die Bibliothek der alten Welt. Zurich: Artemis Verlag, 1965.

————. "Zur Rolle der Heermeister fränkischer Abstammung im späten vierten Jahrhundert." *Historia* 4 (1955): 314–330.

————. "Die Senatoren bei Gregor von Tours." *Klio* 34 (1942): 293–305.

————. *Der senatorische Adel im spätantiken Gallien.* Tübingen: Alma Mater, 1948. Reprint. Darmstadt: Wissenschaftlichen Buchgesellschaft, 1970.

————. "Spanische Senatoren der spätrömischen und westgotischen Zeit." *Madrider Mitteilungen* 4 (1963): 107–132.

Sundwall, Johannes. *Abhandlungen zur Geschichte des ausgehenden Römertums.* Helsinki: Centraltryckeri och Bokbinderi Aktiebolag, 1919. Reprint. New York: Arno Press, 1975.

————. *Weströmische Studien.* Berlin, 1915.

Täckholm, Ulf. "Aetius and the Battle on the Catalaunian Fields." *Opuscula romana* 7 (1969): 259–276.

Talbert, Richard J. A. *The Senate of Imperial Rome.* Princeton: Princeton University Press, 1984.

Teillet, Suzanne. *Des Goths à la nation gothique. Les origines de l'idée de nation en Occident du Ve au VIIe siècle.* Paris: Les Belles Lettres, 1984.

Thompson, Edward A. "Barbarian Invaders and Roman Collaborators." *Florilegium* 2 (1980): 71–87.

————. "Christianity and the Northern Barbarians." In *The Conflict between Paganism and Christianity in the Fourth Century*, edited by Arnaldo Momigliano, 56–78. Oxford: Clarendon Press, 1963.

————. "The End of Roman Spain." *Nottingham Medieval Studies* 20 (1976): 3–26; 21 (1977): 3–31; 22 (1978): 3–22; 23 (1979): 1–21.

————. *A History of Attila and the Huns.* Oxford: Clarendon Press, 1948.

————. "Peasant Revolts in Late Roman Gaul and Spain." *Past and Present* 2 (1952): 12–22.

————. *Romans and Barbarians. The Decline of the Western Empire.* Madison: University of Wisconsin Press, 1982.

————. *Saint Germanus of Auxerre and the End of Roman Britain.* Woodbridge: Boydell Press, 1984.

————. "The Settlement of the Barbarians in Southern Gaul." *Journal of Roman Studies* 45 (1956): 65–75.

————. "The Visigoths from Fritigern to Euric." *Historia* 12 (1963): 105–126.

————. *The Visigoths in the Time of Ulfila.* Oxford: Clarendon Press, 1966.

Thouvenot, M. "Salvien et la ruine de l'empire romain." *Mélanges de archéologie et d'histoire de l'Ecole Française de Rome* 38 (1928): 145–163.

Turbessi, Giuseppe. *Ascetismo e monachesimo prebenedettino.* Rome: Editrice Studium, 1961.

Twyman, Briggs L. "Aetius and the Aristocracy." *Historia* 19 (1970): 480–503.

Ullmann, Walter. "On the Use of the Term 'Romani' in the Sources of the Earlier Middle Ages." *Texte und Untersuchungen* 64 (1955): 155–163.

van Acker, Lieven. "*Barbarus* und seine Ableitungen im Mittellatein." *Archiv für Kulturgeschichte* 47 (1965): 125–140.

Van Dam, Raymond. *Leadership and Community in Late Antique Gaul.* Berkeley: University of California Press, 1985.

Vassili, Lucio. "Il *comes* Agrippino collaboratore di Ricimero." *Athenaeum* 14 (1936): 175–180.

Vercauteren, F. "Note sur la ruine des villes de la Gaule après quelques auteurs contemporains des invasions germaniques." *Mélanges Bidez*, 955–963. Vol. 2. Brussels: Secretariat de l'Institut, 1934.

Vieillard-Troiekouroff, May. *Les monuments religieux de la Gaule d'après les oeuvres de Grégoire de Tours.* Paris: H. Champion, 1976.

Viscido, Lorenzo. "Sull'uso del termine barbarus nelle 'Variae' di Cassiodoro." *Orpheus* 7 (1986): 338–344.

Vismara, Giulio. *Scritti di storia giuridica. I. Fonti del diritto nei regni germanici. I. Edictum Theoderici.* Milan: Giuffre, 1987.

Vogt, Joseph. "Kulturwelt und Barbaren. Zum Menschheitsbild der spätantiken Gesellschaft." *Abhandlungen der Akademie der Wissenschaften in Mainz* 1 (1967): 1–68.

von Harnack, A. *Militia Christi. Die christliche Religion und der Soldatenstand in den ersten drei Jahrhunderten.* Tübingen: J. C. B. Mohr, 1905. Reprint. Darmstadt: Wissenschaftliche Buchgesellschaft, 1963. (Also published as *Militia Christi. The Christian Religion and the Military in the First Three Centuries.* Translated by David I. Gracie. Philadelphia: Fortress Press, 1981.)

von Müller, Achatz. *Gloria bona fama bonorum. Studien zur sittlichen Bedeutung des Ruhmes in der frühchristlichen und mittelalterlichen Welt.* Husum: Matthiesen Verlag, 1977.

von Petrikovits, H. "Fortifications in the North-Western Roman Empire from the Third to the Fifth Centuries A.D." *Journal of Roman Studies* 61 (1971): 207–213.

Waas, Manfred. *Germanen im römischen Dienst im 4. Jahrhundert n.Chr.* Bonn: Habelt, 1965.

Wallace-Hadrill, John M. "The Bloodfeud of the Franks." *Bulletin of the John Rylands Library* 41 (1959).

———. "Gothia and Romania." *Bulletin of the John Rylands Library* 44 (1961): 219–237.

———. *The Long-Haired Kings, and Other Studies in Frankish History.* New York: Barnes and Noble, 1962.

Walsh, Patrick G. *The Letters of St. Paulinus of Nola.* 2 vols. London: Longmans, Green, 1966.

Weber, Siegrid. "Stadt und Land in des Leges Barbarorum." *Klio* 64 (1982): 189–194.

Wes, Marinus A. *Das Ende des Kaisertums im Westen des römischen Reichs.* s'Gravenhage: Staatsdrukkerij, 1967.

Wickham, Chris. *Early Medieval Italy. Central Power and Local Society, 400–1000.* Totowa, N.J.: Barnes and Noble, 1981.

Wieruszowski, Hélène. "Die Zusammensetzung des gallischen und fränkischen Episkopats bis zum Vertrag von Verdun (843) mit besonderer Berücksichtigung der Nationalität und des Standes." *Bonner Jahrbucher* 127 (1922): 1–83.

Wightman, Edith. *Gallia Belgica.* London: Batsford, 1985.

———. "North-Eastern Gaul in Late Antiquity: The Testimony of Settlement

Patterns in an Age of Transition." *Berichten van de Rijksdienst voor het Oud-heidkundig Bodemonderzoek* 28 (1978): 241–250.

———. "Peasants and Potentates: An Investigation of Social Structure and Land Tenure in Roman Gaul." *American Journal of Ancient History* 3 (1978): 97–128.

———. *Roman Trier and the Treveri*. London: Rupert Hart-Davis, 1970.

Will, Ernst. "Remarques sur la fin de la domination romaine dans le nord de la Gaule." *Revue du nord* 48 (1966): 517–534.

Willems, Pierre G. H. *Le sénat de la république romaine*. 2 vols. Louvain: C. Peeters, 1883–1885. Reprint. New York: Arno Press, 1975.

Wolfram, Herwig. *Geschichte der Goten, von der Angfängen bis zur Mitte des sechsten Jahrhunderts. Entwurf einer historischen Ethnographie.* Munich: C. H. Beck, 1979.

———. *Intitulatio. I. Lateinische Königs- und Furstentitel bis zum Ende des 8. Jahrhunderts.* Graz-Vienna-Cologne: Böhlau Verlag, 1968.

Wolfram, Herwig, and Andreas Schwarcz, eds. *Anerkennung und Integration. Zu den wirtschaftlichen Grundlagen der Völkenwanderungszeit 400–600.* Vienna: Österreichische Akademie der Wissenschaft, 1988.

Wood, Ian N. "Disputes in Late Fifth- and Sixth-Century Gaul: Some Problems." In *The Settlement of Disputes in Early Medieval Europe*, edited by Wendy Davies and Paul Fouracre, 7–22. Cambridge: Cambridge University Press, 1986.

———. "The End of Roman Britain: Continental Evidence and Parallels." In *Gildas: New Approaches*, edited by M. Lapidge and D. Dumville, 1–25. Studies in Celtic History, no. 5. Woodbridge: Boydell Press, 1984.

Woodward, Ernest L. *Christianity and Nationalism in the Later Roman Empire.* London: Longmans, Green, 1916. Reprint. New York: AMS Press, 1990.

Wormald, Patrick. "The Decline of the Western Empire and the Survival of its Aristocracy." *Journal of Roman Studies* 66 (1976): 217–226.

———. " 'Lex scripta' and 'Verbum regis': Legislation and Germanic Kingship from Euric to Cnut." In *Early Medieval Kingship*, edited by P. H. Sawyer and I. N. Wood, 105–138. Leeds: University of Leeds Press, 1977.

Wright, Frederick Adam, and T. A. Sinclair. *A History of Later Latin Literature. From the Middle of the Fourth to the End of the Seventeenth Century.* New York: MacMillan, 1931. Reprint. New York, 1969.

Zecchini, Guiseppe. *Aezio: L'ultima difesa del'occidente romano.* Richerche e documentazione sull'antichita classica, no. 8. Rome: Bretschneider, 1983.

Zeiller, J. "L'apparition du mot *Romania* chez les écrivains latins." *Revue des études latines* 7 (1929): 194–198.

Zeller, Joseph. "Das concilium der Septem Provinciae in Arelate." *Westdeutsche Zeitschrift* 24 (1905): 1–19.

Ziegler, Aloysius K. *Church and State in Visigothic Spain.* Washington: Catholic University Press, 1930.

Zöllner, Erich. *Geschichte der Franken bis zur Mitte des sechsten Jahrhunderts.* Munich: C. H. Beck, 1970.

INDEX

Printed and bound by CPI Group (UK) Ltd, Croydon, CR0 4YY

13/04/2025

14656494-0004